The Basics of Financial Management

Rien Brouwers MSc

Wim Koetzier MSc

Fourth edition

Noordhoff Uitgevers Groningen / Utrecht

© Noordhoff Uitgevers bv

Cover design: G2K (Amsterdam - Groningen)
Cover illustration: iStock

Any comments about this publication or others may be addressed to: Noordhoff
Uitgevers bv, Afdeling Hoger Onderwijs, Antwoordnummer 13, 9700 VB Groningen,
or through 'contact' at www.mijnnoordhoff.nl.

0 / 18

© 2018 Noordhoff Uitgevers bv Groningen/Houten, The Netherlands

ISBN 978-90-01-88921-0
NUR 782

Preface to the Fourth Edition

The Basics of Financial Management offers a complete and accessible introduction to the subject.
It can be used by first-year students in higher economic education programs, but is also suitable as a basic course for non-economic academic programs.

Part 1 of this book offers a fully-fledged introduction to financial management which serves to acquaint students with the behavior and the most important associated underlying economic aspects of companies. Parts 2, 3 and 4 discuss the disciplines of finance, management accounting and financial accounting. These parts can be studied and reviewed in any order.

In the third edition, we opted for a seamless connection between *The Basics of Financial Management* and its Dutch version *Basisboek Bedrijfseconomie*. This fourth edition continues that approach. Both works approach the subject matter from an international perspective, and the English edition also discusses the institutional aspects (such as tax and corporate law) that are important in a Dutch context.

There has also been a number of changes since the previous edition. The current edition includes explanations of new and modern financing concepts, such as *angel investors, crowdfunding, credit unions* and *staple financing*. The terminology used in the discussion of investment projects has been updated to match the current literature on the subject: *cash flows* have been replaced with *free cash flows*. The discussion of financing markets pays more attention to derivatives, and the problems and issues specific to futures have been omitted.
The revised regulations for the publication of annual accounts have been incorporated. The chapter on financial statements has been restructured; more attention is paid to *impairments*. In light of the decline in practical significance of the replacement value system (as used in the Netherlands), the notions of nominalism an substantialism as theoretical concepts are no longer discussed.
Naturally, all interludes, partial annual accounts and statistics have been updated.

The Basics of Financial Management incorporates various test questions and multiple-choice questions. The answers to these questions are provided at the back of the book.
The accompanying *Exercise Book* contains a large number of questions and cases of increasing difficulty. Several of these are fully explained in *Answers and Solution*; remaining answers can be found in the teacher

section of the website: www.basicsfinancialmanagement.noordhoff.nl.
The student section of the website also includes additional assignments,
interactive practice questions, summaries, and online courses covering
terms and concepts.

It has been eleven years since the publication of the first edition of *The Basics of Financial Management*; the enthusiastic appreciation with which later editions have continued to be met by both students and teachers alike has encouraged us to remain focused on continuing to improve on its usefulness and usability.
Remarks or comments from our readers are, as always, very welcome.

The authors

Contents

Introduction

The Basics of Financial Management offers (future) professionals in a non-specific financial position an understanding of finance related issues that will allow them to act as fully-fledged interlocutors of financial specialists. In addition, the book offers basic training to prepare students in a financial-economic education for a more in-depth study of the subjects.

To maximize the usability of the book, a brief explanation on its possible uses is provided here.

The book comprises four parts: 1 *Financial management in business*, 2 *Finance*, 3 *Management accounting* and 4 *Financial accounting*. The first part provides an understanding of some of the basic concepts in business economics. Readers are recommended to start with this part. Armed with new-found or reinforced knowledge, the remaining three parts can be studied independently of one another.
To support students interested in studying one specific topic (for example, because they are enrolled in a problem-based or project-based education program), the introduction incorporates a schedule that shows the mutual relationships between the chapters of the book. This will allow students to verify whether knowledge of information discussed in other chapters is required before starting a new one. The comprehensive table of contents and index can be used to find other subjects quickly.

The presentation of the subject material is based on the principle that students should be able to study the theory independently.
To help with self-study, many clarifying examples have been provided. Students can also assess whether the material is understood with the aid of test questions. The answers to the test questions can be found at the back of the book, and let readers verify their answers and their understanding of the theory. To illustrate the practical relevance of the discussed theory, explanatory texts with photos, newspaper cuttings and fragments of financial statements have been included. Key terminology is emphasized by including it in the margin. Each chapter concludes with a glossary and a series of multiple-choice questions.
The answers to the multiple-choice questions are found at the back of the book.

The theory can be tested with the aid of the assignments in the Exercise Book. The exercises are sorted by degree of complexity. Answers and solutions can be found in *Answers and solutions*, on the website. A number of exercises is discussed in detail there.

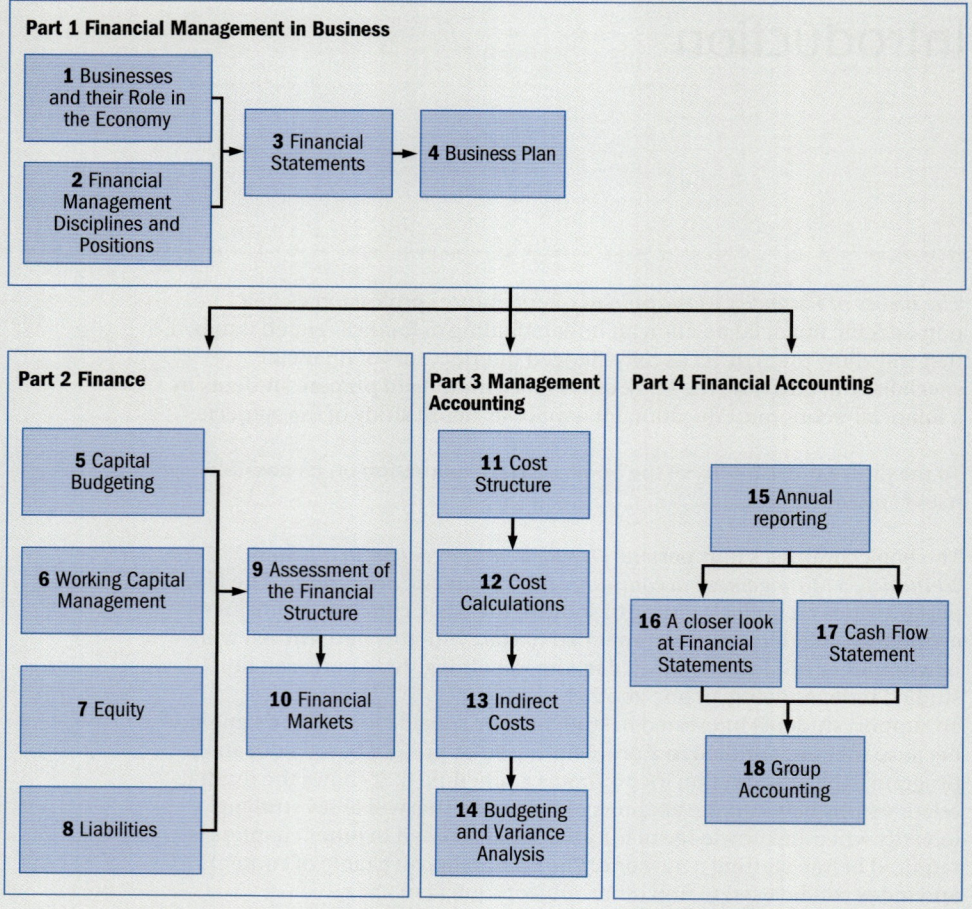

Part 1 Financial Management in Business

1 Businesses and their Role in the Economy

2 Financial Management Disciplines and Positions

3 Financial Statements

4 Business Plan

Part 2 Finance

5 Capital Budgeting

6 Working Capital Management

7 Equity

8 Liabilities

9 Assessment of the Financial Structure

10 Financial Markets

Part 3 Management Accounting

11 Cost Structure

12 Cost Calculations

13 Indirect Costs

14 Budgeting and Variance Analysis

Part 4 Financial Accounting

15 Annual reporting

16 A closer look at Financial Statements

17 Cash Flow Statement

18 Group Accounting

Flexible learning routes

As suggested by the introduction, there are different learning routes for studying the material in this book. The first route follows the sequence of the subjects in the book, dealing first with finance, then management accounting and finally financial accounting. This is the authors' preferred reading order as it matches the consecutive order of the problems that fledgling entrepreneurs are faced with.

The second major route first focuses on the management accounting section, followed by finance and financial accounting.
This is the more traditional sequence used in the field of financial management, with the initial focus on issues concerning cost calculations.

In principle, it is also possible to start with financial accounting after the first introductory part: a rather unusual approach when studying all the topics, though the set-up of the method does allow for it.

PART 1
Financial Management in Business

1

Businesses and their Role in the Economy

A company can be defined as a production organization aiming to make profit; paragraph 1.1 discusses the various elements of this definition. The essential difference between companies and non-profit organizations is described in paragraph 1.2, where it will become clear that financial management techniques are also applicable to non-profit organizations. In paragraph 1.3, business activities are divided into four major types of business: agriculture and mining, manufacturing, trade and services. The choice of activity determines the nature of the resources required by the company. Companies require a legal form to be able to conduct business. The legal form is important for liability of the owner for the company's debts, for its fiscal position and for various other aspects. Paragraph 1.4 discusses these aspects in detail. Paragraph 1.5 covers value added tax, which all entrepreneurs have to deal with. Lastly, paragraph 1.6 discusses different forms of cooperation between companies, varying from completely abandoning autonomy to cooperative forms that leave autonomy largely intact.

1

1.1 Consumers and Manufacturers

People have many needs: housing, food, cars or bicycles for transport, help with filing their tax returns, leisure activities such as a weekend break, etc. All these products and services have to be 'manufactured'. The use of a car requires a car manufacturer; a weekend break may call for a hotel. Prior to the emergence of large-scale bartering, consumers were also automatically manufacturers: they baked their own bread and built their own housing. In developed economies, this is no longer the case.

Production organizations

Production organizations also referred to as businesses, manufacture products and services and sell these to consumers at a certain price. Consumers obtain purchasing power from the income generated by working for these companies.

Economy

The economy deals with questions connected to the ways in which people strive to optimize their 'prosperity': how can the supply of products and services be optimized using minimum resources?

Economics

Economics studies the relationship between consumers and businesses and the mutual interactions between businesses. A distinction can be made between micro and macroeconomics. *Microeconomics* comprises, among other things, the theory behind markets: how does the price mechanism work in a particular market, such as the market for holiday travel? Determining factors include the number of suppliers and customers in a particular market. Markets will be briefly discussed in paragraph 1.6.

Microeconomics

Macroeconomics

Macroeconomics studies economic problems that affect society as a whole, such as inflation and unemployment.

Business economics

Business economics focuses on economic behavior in a production organization. In this context, 'production' should be interpreted broadly: it not only concerns the production of physical goods, but also trade and services. In economic terms, production organizations would not only refer to car manufacturing plants but also to car dealerships or workshops, for example. Paragraph 1.3 discusses the different forms of production. The economic system assigns an important role to production by companies. Companies are production organizations focused on earning income for their owners 'on the market'. They are therefore, production organizations in pursuit of profit. A further discussion of two important elements in the definition of a company is found below.

A company is a production organization

In a production organization, resources are combined and transformed into products during a production process.
A production organization operates between two markets: the supplier market, where resources are obtained; and the retail market, where manufactured goods or services are sold.
Resources may comprise commodities/(raw materials) on the one hand, and machines, buildings and similar things on the other. The latter category is called fixed assets or fixed assets, since – compared to raw materials – these assets remain in (service of) the company for extended periods of time.
Labor, supplied by a company's employees, is of course also a resource.
Figure 1.1 shows the schematic production process.

FIGURE 1.1 Production process

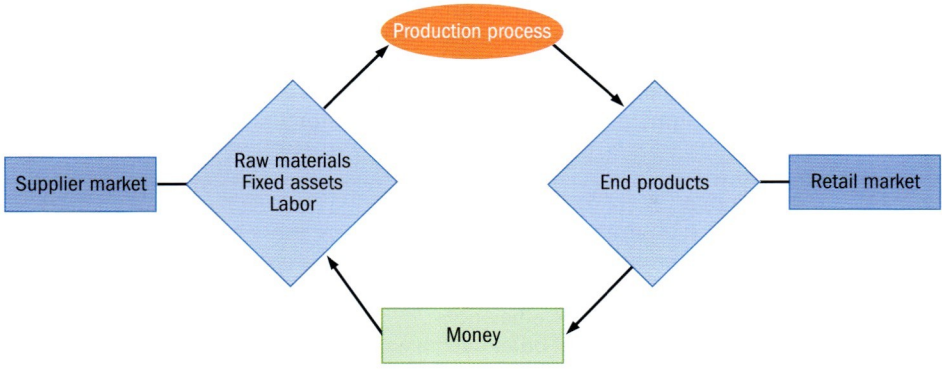

EXAMPLE 1.1

A brewery buys hops and water and converts these into beer through a series of processes. The water and the hops are the raw materials used for the end product: beer. In addition to raw materials, the company needs fixed assets: a building, boilers for brewing, trucks, computers, etc. Of course, employees are an indispensable link in the production chain.

A production organization is therefore a joining of the production factors particularly labor and capital. 'Capital' refers to the raw materials and fixed assets used by a company.   **Capital**

A production organization can have a formal nature, with the rights and obligations of the participants laid down in writing: the empowerment of shareholders, directors and employees are described in the articles of association and in the job descriptions. The term 'production organization' can also be used to describe two students starting a courier service, for example, with the only agreements being that they will take turns in answering the phone and making deliveries.

TEST QUESTION 1.1

The owners and employees are the direct participants in a company. Broadly speaking, there are more participants who have an interest in the company's success.
Name some other participants.

A company seeks to maximize its profit

A company participates in the economic process with the intent to make its owners 'better off'. It strives for 'value creation': the sales of the produced goods and services need to outweigh the price paid for the production factors (labor, raw material, fixed assets) at the supplier market. The owners of the company are the beneficiaries of the surplus in payment: the profit. The objective of maximizing profit is what distinguishes companies from businesses in general. Every business produces goods and/or services. The following paragraph describes those businesses without a profit target.

Efficiency
Effectiveness

1

The level of profit depends on efficiency on the one hand, and effectiveness of the production process on the other. *Efficiency* relates to the cost-effectiveness of the production process and *effectiveness* to the ability to meet target objectives of the production process, or the extent to which end products meet customer requirements. A production process is efficient if a given quantity is produced at minimum costs. It is effective if the end product is appreciated by customers, and customers are willing to pay for it.

EXAMPLE 1.2

The brewery in example 1.1 strives to produce every hundred liters of beer by using labor and fixed assets as efficiently as possible. The company tries to achieve the given quality standards at minimum cost. Cost is therefore a measure for efficiency.

The end product should be of such a nature that it allows the company to acquire a market share. The product's taste, price-quality ratio and positioning through commercials should contribute to this. The effectiveness is determined by the level of success at which the brewery generates sales. In figure 1.2, the roles of efficiency and effectiveness in the production process are shown.

FIGURE 1.2 Efficiency and effectiveness in the production process

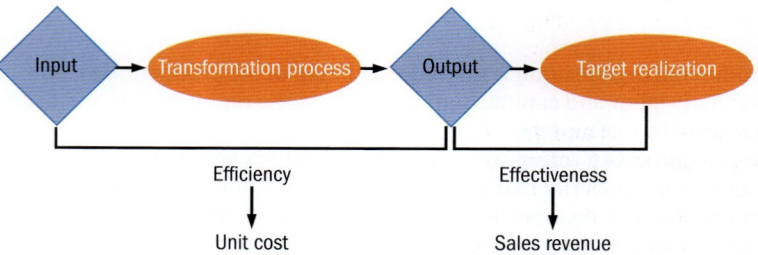

Profit
Sales revenue
Turnover
Costs

It is typical for a company to use profit as a measure for efficiency as well as effectiveness: after all, it is the difference between sales revenue or turnover (measure of effectiveness) and costs (measure of efficiency).

Maximizing profit is a company's priority; the manner in which this profit is acquired is of secondary importance. If a shipping company establishes that the shipping business no longer has profitable prospects, the company will generally not feel any compunctions about switching to a different activity. Although some employees will regret the loss of a rich piece of shipping history, financial considerations will prevail.

Profit is the target; the activities are a means to an end.

The following information should also be kept in mind:

Continuity

- Maximizing profit 'at all cost' is usually not given the highest priority; the continuity of the company is also an important concern. However, profit is necessary to assure continuity; only a profitable company will have the required financial resources to survive independently. Concerning a company's continuity, a long-term perspective towards profit targets is also necessary: making 'a fast buck' by offering inferior products as top quality is a counter-productive strategy in the long run.

- It may sometimes seem as though the major company target is optimizing sales revenue instead of optimizing profit. Corporate managers often appear to feel that bigger is better. Company X may be acquired by company Y without the takeover being based on any well-founded expectations regarding company X's contributions to overall profits.
- Companies generally present their own *mission statement*, outlining their targets without addressing their drive for profit as a prominent factor, instead focusing on environmental issues, job satisfaction for employees, etc. Here are several examples from major companies.

Mission statement

PHILIPS

At Philips, we strive to make the world healthier and more sustainable through innovation. Our goal is to improve the lives of 3 billion people a year by 2025. We will be the best place to work for people who share our passion. Together we will deliver superior value for our customers and shareholders.

AHOLD DELHAIZE

At Ahold Delhaize, our ambition is to bring fresh inspiration every day to customers, communities and colleagues, and to make life a little easier, healthier and more affordable for everyone. We are proud of our companies' long-standing roots in local communities and commitment to the needs of local shoppers.

SHELL

We believe that oil and gas will remain a vital part of the global energy mix for many decades to come. Our role is to ensure that we extract and deliver these energy resources profitably and in environmentally and socially responsible ways. We seek a high standard of performance, maintaining a strong and growing long-term position in the competitive environments in which we operate. We aim to work closely with our customers, our partners and policymakers to advance a more efficient and sustainable use of energy and natural resources.

1.2 Profit and Non-profit Organizations

Companies focus on maximizing profit and are part of the profit sector. This book pays particular attention to that sector. The Netherlands, however, also has many non-profit organizations. A distinction can be made between public and private non-profit enterprises.

- The *public sector* comprises the state, provinces, municipalities and regional water authorities. The government mainly provides *public goods and services* for the general public, such as roads, protection against the sea and general safety. These facilities cannot be provided by private enterprises due to failure of the *market mechanism*: consumers cannot purchase a small piece of sea defense to protect themselves against the tide. Hence, the *budget mechanism* is applied to produce public goods

Public sector

Market mechanism

Budget mechanism

and services: the government imposes compulsory contributions (tax) and provides a budget to finance the production of public goods. There are also general facilities that, in the past, have been offered by the government to influence their availability to a larger public, but in principle could be provided by companies. In recent years, the

Privatizing   government has supported a trend towards *privatizing* these activities: where applicable, the activities are separated from the government and must prove themselves to be viable as part of a market. Examples are public transport, telecommunications, mail delivery and the supplying of energy.

- *Private non-profit businesses* comprise a wide variety of organizations from amateur sports clubs to charitable organizations such as the Red Cross. The latter is also known as a fund-raising institution as it attempts to raise funds to achieve a worthy social objective.

Organizations in the non-profit sector differ from companies in the following aspects:

- The target set by non-profit organizations is to provide certain (socially important) facilities. The activities they perform are connected to their social objectives. Médecins Sans Frontières/Doctors without Borders provides medical activities in developing countries because that is its reason for existence. Changing their activities based on financial reasons is not a consideration. Donors would strongly object if the organization would suddenly switch to other activities. Shareholders of a profit organization such as Unilever would not lose sleep if the production of laundry detergents were to be replaced by other activities with higher profit prospects.
- Non-profit organizations cannot exist by conducting business transactions and are – in contrast to companies – not economically independent. They depend on 'gifts', such as contributions, subsidies, inheritances, etc. To some extent, a non-profit organization can also operate on the market, for example, by selling T-shirts with a logo.
- The assessment of the effectiveness of non-profit enterprises is much more difficult than that of a company. As established earlier for the latter, profit is an indication of both effectiveness and efficiency during production. Obviously, profit cannot be used as a key indicator in the non-profit sector.
  A foundation focusing on victim aid is effective if it succeeds in solving the problems of its clients as much as possible. This type of aid or relief cannot be expressed in money. Effectiveness must be established in another way, for example, by registering waiting times or conducting client satisfaction surveys. Non-profit businesses can monitor their efficiency by calculating their costs. A foundation for victim aid could, for example, calculate the costs of one-hour consultations.

The subjects discussed in this book are mainly applicable to companies, although they are also relevant for non-profit businesses. This applies in particular to the subjects in the section on Management Accounting, as non-profit businesses should also attempt to work as efficiently as possible. In the section on finance, a number of the financial resources discussed, such as shares, only applies to companies. Other subjects are also applicable to non-profit organizations.

Financial reporting, as discussed in the Financial Accounting section, can also be applied to non-profit organizations, although making a profit does not automatically imply that an organization performs well, since profit is not a primary objective in the non-profit sector.

Income statement World Wildlife Fund 2015/2016 (year ended 30 June)

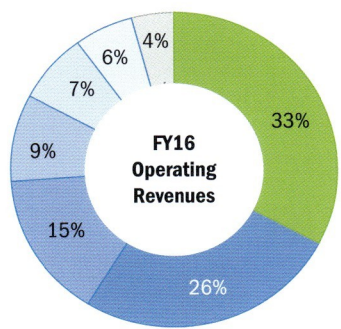

Individuals	$100,355,045	33%
In-kind and other	79,845,124	26%
Government grants	46,365,374	15%
Foundations	26,543,278	9%
Other non-operating contributions	20,493,975	7%
Network	17,934,104	6%
Corporations	13,671,189	4%

Programs	$259,505,203	85%
Fundraising	32,750,779	11%
Finances and administration	12,950,274	4%

Source: http://www.worldwildlife.org

TEST QUESTION 1.2
Were the 2015/2016 results (revenues – expenses) for the WWF positive or negative? Is it possible to conclude, based on the outcome, whether the WWF performed well in 2015/2016?

1.3 Business Activities

In paragraph 1.1, a company was described as a production organization focused on profit. The company aims to generate profit by purchasing resources and converting these into goods or services that are sold at a higher price than the purchase price.
The following classification of companies is based on the nature of the transformation process:
• agriculture and mining
• industry
• trade
• services

Figures 1.3a and 1.3b provide an overview of the four sectors in terms of their stake in the overall European and Dutch economy.

FIGURE 1.3a Number of companies per sector in Europe (2010)

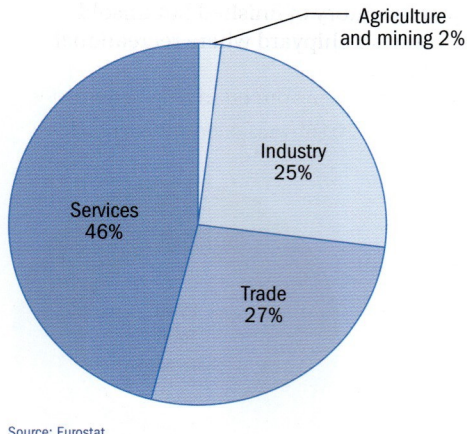

Source: Eurostat

FIGURE 1.3b Number of companies per sector in the Netherlands (2016)

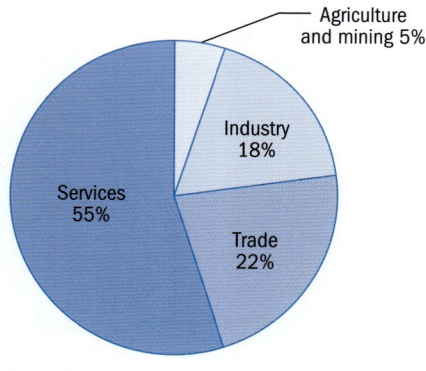

Source: CBS

Agriculture and mining

Companies in the agriculture and mining sector typically use 'nature's bounty'. With a relatively small quantity of raw materials, a large quantity of end product is achieved. To a farmer, the cost of seed is merely a small percentage of the crop revenues. Mining companies involved in extraction of mineable minerals, such as gold or copper, and commodities such as gas or oil, do not use up raw materials at all as they are in the business of producing them. Obviously, fixed assets are still very important: farmland for a farmer, a concession for a mine or the oilfield for an extraction company – and there may also be a lot of equipment required.

Industry

Industrial companies create a physical, tangible product that did not yet exist before its production. There is a distinction between mass and job

Job production   production. In *job production*, production is customized. Each product is tailored to customer requirements and products are made to order: a sale is agreed upon before production starts.

Job production causes no build-up of inventory of finished but unsold products. An example of job production is a shipyard where recreational yachts are built to customer specifications.

In *mass production*, a single type of product is produced in large quantities. **Mass production** Specific customer requirements are not taken into account. There is usually a build-up of inventory. A sugar refinery is an example of mass production. Table 1.1 summarizes the differences between job and mass production.

TABLE 1.1 Differences between job and mass production

Job production	Mass production
Customized product	Standard product
Intended for one particular customer	Intended for the 'market'
Made to order	Made for build-up of inventory

Between the two extremes (mass and job production), there are intermediate production processes that generate a series of identical (half) products *(batch production).*

In a *batch-job production process,* the idea is that every customer gets a particular individual product, but costs are saved by producing the components in larger quantities (and therefore cheaper). If the previously mentioned shipyard produces various types of hulls, masts, cabins and other items in batches, and customers can choose from the available components to create their own dream boat, this is considered batch-job production.

In a *batch-mass production process*, a variety of models of the standard product are produced, and every so often the machines are adjusted to produce a different variant. If a sugar refinery not only produces granular sugar but also occasionally switches to sugar cubes, this is considered batch-mass production.

The importance of the three resources (raw materials, fixed assets and labor) varies, depending on which type of industry a company operates in. For an oil refinery, raw materials and fixed assets are a major part of the costs, whereas labor costs are a prevailing factor for a manufacturer of artisanal wooden kitchens. As automation progresses, the significance of fixed assets for total costs increases.

Trade

Trading companies do not produce new products. There is no transformation process in the technical sense. Trading companies derive their existence from the fact that there is an imbalance between production and consumption. This imbalance can be related to:

1 the scale of production and consumption
2 the composition of production and consumption
3 the moment of production and consumption
4 the location of production and consumption

1

EXAMPLE 1.3
For a Japanese manufacturer of computers, it would be problematic to
sell computers directly to European consumers. Trading companies are
a solution to this problem. A chain of computer stores can import many
computers from Japan (1), add other articles that customers may need
to the product range (2), build up an inventory to allow customers to buy
a computer at any given time (3), and offer its goods closer to where the
consumers live (4).

The transformation process in a trading company relates to transformation
in scale, product range, time and place. For trading companies, a distinction
can be made between the wholesale and retail trade. *Retail trade* is the
Retail trade   final link in the chain; the retail trade supplies directly to the end user: the
consumer.

Wholesale trade   *Wholesale trade* purchases from the manufacturer and redistributes
the purchased goods among the retail trade. The wholesale trade is
characterized by 'business-to-business': both suppliers and customers are
companies. To be able to fulfill an independent function in the economy,
the wholesale trade's strength has to be in delivering the right products at
the right time to the store. This requires important investments in logistics
systems.

The trading costs consist mainly of the purchased merchandise. Apart from
this, of course other fixed assets are also involved (buildings, cars and so
on). Labor costs can also be considerable, particularly in retail trade.

Due to the emergence of online trade, there are major shifts in the trade
industry overall. Retail trade, in particular, is under pressure: wholesale
traders can offer their products directly to customers through internet
stores.

Services

Service companies provide a service to their customers without
manufacturing a new product or redistributing an existing one. This applies
to companies of a varied nature.
Some important categories:
- financial services (banks, insurance companies)
- hospitality industry
- transport
- IT-services (software firms, computer consultancies)
- facility services (security, catering, cleaning)

Typical for the service industry is that no (or hardly any) raw materials are
purchased from suppliers. Fixed assets can be very important for service
companies: consider a hotel located in the center of a major city, or a
shipping company with a fleet of container ships.

Labor costs are nearly always very important since service rendering is a
'people business': consider IT-specialists working for a software company,
or security guards at a security firm.

Due to increasing automation, companies in the service industry are also becoming increasingly less reliant on using staff. One example of this is in the world of banking. By encouraging self-service, in the forms of online banking or the use of ATMs, customers rarely need to visit their bank's offices in person. After all, there's nothing to be done there that one would not be able to do at home. As of 2000, there has been a downward trend in the number of employees in this industry (see figure 1.4).

FIGURE 1.4 The development of employee figures in the banking industry

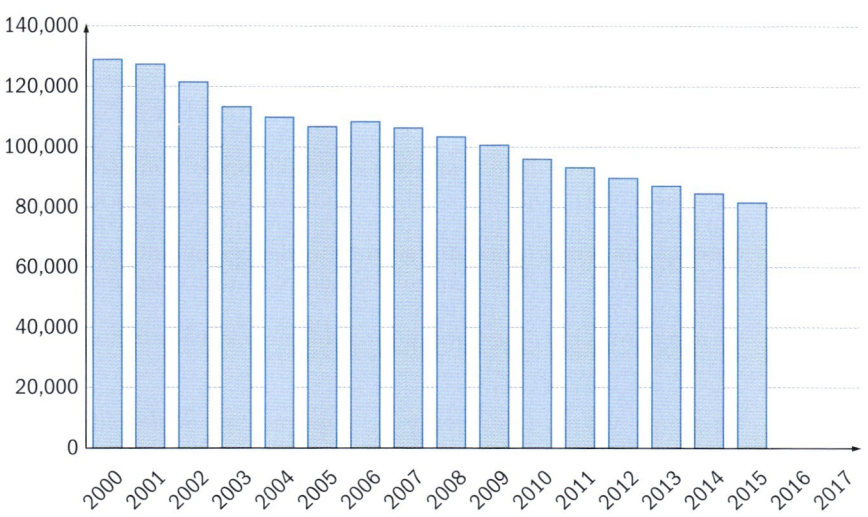

Source: Nederlandse Vereniging van Banken (NVB)

According to figures by the UWV (the Dutch government institution in charge of implementing and administrating employee insurances) between 55,000 to 60,000 jobs were lost across the whole of the Dutch financial industry over the past decade. Banks everywhere are making cutbacks in their staff numbers: from HR, IT and risk management to regional offices, customer care and reception staff.

TEST QUESTION 1.3

The following cost ratios belong to three internationally operating Dutch companies:

	1	2	3
Raw materials	69%	72%	0%
Labor costs	21%	15%	47%
Other costs	10%	13%	53%
Total cost	100%	100%	100%

These three companies are:
• Ahold Delhaize, a supermarket chain
• ING, a bank
• Unilever, a manufacturer of nutrition and healthcare products

Which number relates to which company?

1.4 Legal Forms of Businesses

Every company has a legal form. The choice of legal form determines the nature of legal relationships within the company and legal relationships between the company and the outside world.
Important aspects determined by the legal form are:
• establishing who has ultimate control over a company's decisions
• defining the ways in which a company attracts financial resources
• a company's potential options for ensuring long-term continuation
• the extent to which owners are liable for the debts incurred by the company
• a company's fiscal position
• the extent to which the company is obliged to disclose its financial results

Legal entity

Companies can be divided into two major categories: companies with a *legal entity* and companies without. A company operating as a legal entity is considered an independent party in legal agreements made during business transactions. It may hire staff, conclude a sales agreement and borrow from a bank. Private individuals are, of course, required to conclude such an agreement on behalf of the legal entity.
If a company is not a legal entity, the agreement is made in the name of the owner.

Sole proprietorship

If a company is not a legal entity and is the property of one individual, it is called a sole proprietorship. If there are several owners and the company is not a legal entity, it is called a partnership.
In the US, companies with a legal entity (separate from the owners) are called 'business corporations'. In the Netherlands, there are three types of companies with a legal entity: nv (corporation), bv (limited liability company) and coöperatie (cooperative).
In the US, business corporations can also be non-profit organizations. There are two different types of non-profit organizations: foundations and associations. In the Netherlands, foundations and associations are both legal

entities. An elected board acts on behalf of the organization. These legal entities are not further discussed in this book.

Over the course of the following paragraphs, the properties of the different legal forms are explored.

Sole proprietorship

In a sole proprietorship, the owner is also the management. The owner status is derived from having made the investment of the capital used to run the company. It is possible for an owner to have invested not just his own capital, but to also have taken out a loan. However, this loan does not give the lender (usually a bank) control of the business.

Of course, there may be several persons working in a company with sole proprietorship, although these would then be members of staff employed by the owner.

A sole proprietorship depends entirely on the entrepreneur. If the entrepreneur becomes incapacitated, the company ceases to exist. This implies that the continuity of the company is uncertain in the long run. If the entrepreneur is no longer active in the company, a successor must be found, from among either relatives or outsiders.

As previously mentioned– and discussed in detail in the financing part – a company can be financed with capital invested by the owner or by loans. The first method of financing is using the owner's *equity*; the second method is using *liabilities* or debts. **Equity** **Liabilities**

The size of a sole proprietorship is normally limited, due to the limited availability of equity.

When a company is created, the owner must invest private assets; strengthening the company's financial position can be done by retaining profits. This implies that profits cannot be used for private purposes by the owner but remain in the company.

As it is the entrepreneur in his or her personal capacity and not the company who enters into legal agreements, the entrepreneur is liable for the debts incurred by the company.

EXAMPLE 1.4

A starting entrepreneur has invested her savings in a hairdressing business. She borrows the remaining required capital from the bank. The business fails to attract enough customers. The entrepreneur cannot meet the interest and principal sum repayment obligations to the bank. The styling chairs and further store inventory are sold; however, the proceeds are low. The bank demands the entrepreneur uses her private assets to clear the debt. Under extreme circumstances, this could result in the entrepreneur's car or house being sold.

An entrepreneur pays income tax on the profits made by the sole **Income tax** proprietorship. Most European countries have a progressive income tax system with increasing tax rates for higher incomes above a certain threshold. Entrepreneurs can usually enjoy certain fiscal advantages and reduce their taxable income through deductions or receive reductions on the payable tax.

This is explained in the following example, based on Dutch income tax law.

The Dutch income tax system has three different tax boxes. Income is taxed progressively in box 1, which includes social security (in particular, as a consequence of the General Old Age Insurance Act). Box 2 documents all income derived from substantial shareholding (see companies with share capital) and box 3 holds all income derived from savings and investments. As, in fiscal terms, profit acquired by a sole proprietorship is considered the income of the entrepreneur, profit is taxable in box 1.

BOX 1 Income tax rates (2018)

Tax bracket	Taxable income	Tax percentage
1	Up to €20,142	36.55%
2	From €20,143 up to €33,994	40.85%
3	From €33,995 up to €68,507	40.85%
4	From €68,507 and upwards	51.95%

Entrepreneurial tax deduction

Self-employed tax deduction

Startup tax deduction

SME exemption

Entrepreneurs are entitled to various fiscal advantages. One of the favorable arrangements is the *entrepreneurial tax deduction*, consisting of the self-employed and startup tax deductions, which allows entrepreneurs to deduct an amount from their profit. In 2018, the self-employed tax deduction was €7,280. This amount is increased by the startup tax deduction, an amount of €2,123, for the first year of a new business. For any profit above this amount, 14% (2018) is exempt from taxation – this is known as the SME exemption.

Furthermore, every taxpayer liable for income tax is entitled to a reduction on the amount of tax to be paid. The general tax credit depends on the amount of taxable income, as shown in this table:

General tax credit (2018)

Taxable income		General tax credit
From	Up to	
€0	€20,142	€2,265
€20,142	€68,507	€2,265 – 4.683% × (taxable income – €20,142)
€68,507	–	€0

All persons with income deriving from work activities are entitled to an additional labor tax credit. The labor tax credit is based on taxable income. For the entrepreneur, this is the profit prior to the self-employed deduction and the SME exemption.

Labor tax credit (2018)

Work income		Labor tax credit
From	Up to	
€0	€ 9,468	1.764% × work income
€ 9,468	€ 20,450	€167 + 28.064% × (work income – €9,468)
€ 20,450	€ 33,112	€3,249
€ 33,112	€123,362	€3,249 – 3.6% × (work income – €33,112)
€123,362	-	€0

In addition, there are additional tax credits for people in particular circumstances, for example, single parents, young disabled persons and pensioners. These types of credit fall outside the scope of this book.

Schematically, the calculation of the amount of tax payable by the entrepreneur is:

Incurred profit	
— Entrepreneurial tax deduction	
Profit after entrepreneurial tax deduction	
— Profit exemption	(14% of profit after entrepreneurial tax deduction)
Taxable profit	
× Rate	(according to table)
Taxes	
— Tax credits	
Payable taxes	

TEST QUESTION 1.4
Mr Van Damme has a sole proprietorship in the Netherlands and acquires a profit of €40,000 in 2018.
Van Damme has no other income. Calculate the actual amount of tax he has to pay.

All entrepreneurs have a legal obligation to maintain an administration; these *accounting obligations* allow the tax authorities to inspect the company's tax returns.

Accounting obligations

The owner of the sole proprietorship is not obliged to disclose any financial information, the sole proprietorship has no disclosure requirements.

The partnership
If two or more persons decide to work together in a business without a legal entity, this is called a partnership.
For professionals such as doctors, lawyers, accountants and similar the Netherlands have a special form of partnership: the professional partnership (maatschap). The owners of a partnership will henceforth be referred to as partners. Unless stated otherwise, the information provided also applies to professional partnerships.

The control of the business is held by its joint partners. The advantage of a partnership is that each partner may have his own specific expertise, and mutual consultation can result in better decisions. The downside is that more than one captain on a ship can result in differences of opinion. This will influence the odds for the continuation of the partnership. The loss of a partner is not necessarily fatal for a business, but differences of opinion may lead to a premature ending of the business.
It is possible to acquire extra equity by offering new partners the possibility of buying themselves into the business.
The partnership has a separated capital, which implies that business creditors have priority over individual partner creditors in the event of defaults.

1

Jointly and severally liable

The partners are *jointly and severally liable* for the debts of the partnership. This implies that a creditor can demand payment in full from either partner. The partners in a professional partnership are not jointly liable for the entire debt but are severally liable for an equal share of the debt.

EXAMPLE 1.5

The partnership Smith & Jones trades in antiques and curios. Each partner holds an equal stake in the partnership. The partnership has bought a shipment of antiques for an amount of €50,000. The bill has not yet been paid. Due to a downturn in the economic situation, the sales revenue from this shipment are only €30,000. There are no other assets in the partnership.
The importer is now entitled to demand, for example, the remaining €20,000 from Smith. Smith is left with the problem of claiming half of this amount back from Jones.

The partnership is not acknowledged by the tax authorities. Each partner is assumed to run his own business (for the amount of his profit share). The income tax is based on this profit share. The partners are also entitled to the same fiscal advantages as the owner of the sole proprietorship. The partnership is not obliged to disclose financial information.

Limited partnership

Limited partners

Silent partners

The general partnership is run and owned by the same persons. The *limited partnership* has a partial separation of ownership and control: limited partners, also known as silent partners, can be owners of a business because they invested capital, but they do not control the business. The general partners in a limited partnership are both owners and in control. An advantage of a limited partnership is that it comes with the opportunity to attract extra capital without the risk of disputes among partners. Limited partners are not liable to meet the debts of the business with private assets. Limited partners also pay income tax on their share of the profit. Unlike the general partners, however, they are not entitled to the fiscal advantages granted to sole proprietorships.

Joint-share companies

Limited liability company

Corporation

Limited Company

Public Limited Company

A joint-share (joint-stock) company is a legal entity with limited liability. In the United States, the limited liability company (LLC) and the Corporation (Inc.) are examples of joint-share companies.
In the UK the corresponding names are Limited Company and Public Limited Company. In the Netherlands besloten vennootschap (bv) and naamloze vennootschap (nv). In joint-share companies a legal separation is made between ownership and control.
In the following paragraph, the mutual characteristics of the joint-share companies are discussed, followed by the differences between the two types of joint-share companies.

Shares

Annual general meeting of shareholders

The equity of a joint-share company is divided into *shares*. The annual general meeting of shareholders (AGM) is the highest authority in a joint-share company. All important decisions, such as appointing the board of directors, are made by and during the annual shareholders meeting. The board of directors handles daily management.

One of the differences between an LLC and a corporation, is the involvement in daily business of one (or several) shareholder(s) at an LLC. At LLCs, arising from a sole proprietorship or a partnership, one or more major shareholders (the previous owners of the company) often hold a position on the board of directors, thus being managing director and shareholder.
A corporation is usually created with the purpose of gathering large capital. There will be many shareholders not involved in day-to-day business management; however, larger LLCs can also make a clear separation between ownership and control.
It is possible that there is a third body, in addition to the AGM and the board of directors – the supervisory board (SVB). The SVB supervises the board of directors on behalf of the shareholders.
In many countries, including the Netherlands, the management of companies is subject to certain rules. These rules are known as the Corporate Governance Code. The fundamental principle behind *corporate governance* is that companies should be run properly, and demonstrably so. This refers to the way in which company management takes into account other interests than those of the company, such as the interests of shareholders, employees and society in general. In short, it deals with the nature of good governance, and how to ensure, monitor, and demonstrate this good governance adequately to interested parties.

Corporate governance

Both the LLC and corporation can acquire additional equity if the AGM decides to pass up on dividend payments and retain profit. It is also possible to issue additional shares. Due to the separation between control and ownership, the company's continuity is better guaranteed. The shareholders have limited liability. They cannot be obligated to compensate the company's debts with their private assets. Nor can management be held accountable for a company's debts, unless there has been identifiable mismanagement. In that case, responsible parties can be obligated to apply their private assets.

The taxation of profits of LLCs and corporations is rather complicated, as both the company and the shareholders are taxed. Corporate tax is paid on the profits of both LLCs and corporations. Shareholders pay income tax on their share of the profit.

Corporate tax

Every country applies its own rules concerning corporate tax. The two main systems are the classical tax system and the imputation system. Under the classical tax system, the company pays corporate tax on profit, and the shareholder pays income tax on dividend. As a result, all dividends paid are taxed twice. Under the imputation system, the company pays corporate tax, which is considered to be tax paid on behalf of the shareholder. The shareholder pays income tax on their share of company profit and can deduct the tax that was already paid on their behalf from the amount of income tax they have to pay. The difference between the two systems is illustrated in this simplified example.

- -

EXAMPLE 1.6
An LLC generates €100,000 profit before tax. The entire profit after tax is paid to the shareholders. The corporate tax rate is 20%, the income tax rate is 25%.

Under the classical system, the corporate tax and the income tax are applied independently. The LLC pays 20% × €100,000 = €20,000 in corporate tax. The profit after tax is €80,000. This profit is paid to the shareholders, who pay 25% × €80,000 = €20,000 income tax on this amount. The total amount of tax paid is €40,000.

Under the imputation system, there would also be €20,000 in corporate tax; however, this can be deducted from the income tax of the shareholders. The income tax for the shareholders would amount to 25% × €100,000 = €25,000 over the total profit before tax. As the LLC already paid €20,000, the shareholders would only have to pay the remaining €5,000. The total amount of tax paid is now €25,000.

In the Netherlands, the classical tax system is applied. The corporate tax rate in the Netherlands is given in the following table.

Corporate tax rates (2018)

For the taxable amount	Rate
up to €200,000	20%
above €200,000	25%

Loss offset

Fiscally speaking, it is possible to offset losses incurred in one year by profits from another year in order to lower payable taxes – this is known as the loss offset.

A loss from a particular year can be calculated in either of two ways:

Loss carry back

- The loss is offset by the taxable profit from the previous year. This is known as loss carry back.

Loss carry forward

- The loss is offset by the profits from no more than 9 subsequent years. This is known as loss carry forward.

In principle, losses have to be offset by the profit from the preceding year. Companies are only allowed to carry a loss forward if there is no possibility of offsetting the loss against profit from the preceding year.

The shareholder pays income tax over the distributed profits. In the Netherlands, a distinction is made between shareholders who own at least 5% of the share capital and shareholders who do not.

Substantial business interest holder

A shareholder of the first category, is considered to be a *substantial business interest holder*. They are taxed in box 2 of the income tax (rate for 2017: 22% up to €250,000 and 25% for everything above that amount) on the dividend they receive from the company and for possible profit on share sales. This implies that, on each Euro of profit, at least 37.6% is paid in tax, with the initial 20% in corporate tax on the profit paid by the company, and the remaining 17.6% in income tax (22% of 80%) paid by the shareholder.

The LLC often only has one shareholder, who then becomes the managing director and sole shareholder. The salary of the managing director/shareholder is a cost to the company and deductible for corporate tax.

However, the managing director/shareholder must pay income tax on his salary. The dividend received by the managing dirrector/shareholder is not a cost – it is profit distribution, taxed in box 2.

A shareholder with less than 5% of shares will be taxed in box 3 of the income tax system. This box assumes a revenue in the form of a fictional interest rate returned from capital as that capital increases. Therefore, the actual revenue is not important. The assumed revenue is taxed at 30%. Income up to €30,000 is tax exempt. The next €70,800 is subject to an assumed interest of 2.02%; the next €907,200 after that is subject to an assumed 4.33%; and any excess to an assumed 5.38% (2018 percentages).

EXAMPLE 1.7

Shipping agent Ferry LLC achieves an annual profit of €120,000, of which €80,000 is paid in dividend to its shareholders. The shareholders of the company are J. Talk (with 97 shares) and P. Hasseldorf (with 3 shares). The market value of one share Ferry LLC is €25,000. The LLC pays corporate tax over €120,000, being: 20% of €120,000 = €24,000.
J. Talk is a substantial business interest holder; he has to pay income tax on €77,600 (97% of €80,000). In box 2, this amount is taxed at 25%, being €19,400.
The dividend of P. Hasseldorf is taxed in box 3. The value of his share package is €75,000. The first €30,000 investment is tax exempt. The next €45,000 is subject to an assumed interest of 2.02% × €45,000 = €909, on which he pays 30% × €909 = €272.

The fiscal position of both the company and the shareholders is presented in figure 1.4.

FIGURE 1.5 Fiscal position company and shareholders

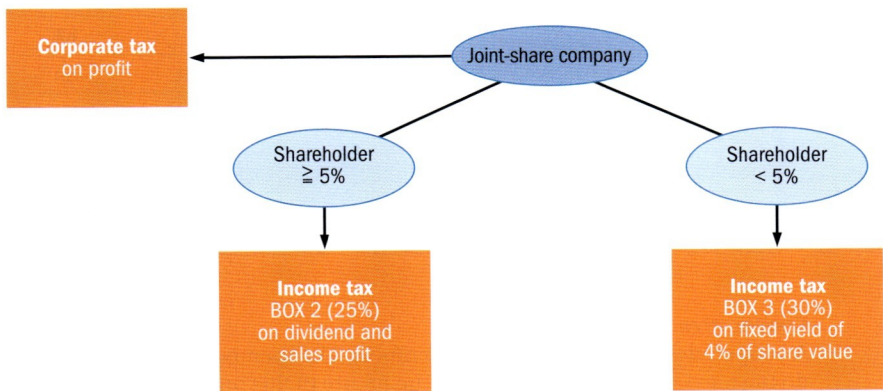

1

In the event of dividend payment, the company must withhold 15% dividend tax and pay it to the tax authorities. This does not increase tax pressure, however, as the shareholder can offset the paid dividend tax against the payable income tax.

Both the LLC and corporation have disclosure requirements. This implies that they have to publish their financial reports by filing them at the office of the Trade Register, where interested parties can consult them. The Chamber of Commerce maintains the Trade Register.
The amount of information that must be disclosed depends on the company size; this will be further discussed in chapter 15.

Differences between LLC and corporation
The three major differences between both forms of joint-share company are:
1 LLC's shares are always *registered shares*. A corporation has the possibility of issuing *bearer shares*, which can easily change legal owners. Stock exchange listed companies are therefore always corporations.
2 An LLC can enter a *blocking clause* into the articles of association, putting restrictions on selling shares. A shareholder intending to sell could, for example, be obligated to offer his shares to the other shareholders first. A corporation cannot restrict the sale of shares.
3 In the Netherlands the creation of a corporation requires an initial minimum capital of €45,000. There is no required minimum capital for setting up an LLC.

Blocking clause

Although regulation varies per country, every country has company forms similar to the LLC and corporation. The following overview gives the names of the legal form that most closely matches the LLC and corporation for each country.

Country	Similar to LLC		Similar to corporation	
Denmark	Anpartsselskab	ApS	Aktieselskab	A/S
France	Société à responsabilité limitée	SARL	Société anonyme	SA
Germany	Gesellschaft mit beschränkter Haftung	GmbH	Aktiengesellschaft	AG
Italy	Societa a responsabilita limitata	Srl	Societa per Azioni	SpA
Japan	Godo kaisha	GK	Kabushiki kaisha	KK
Spain	Sociedad Limitada	SL	Sociedad Anónima	SA
The Netherlands	Besloten vennootschap met beperkte aansprakelijkheid	bv	Naamloze vennootschap	nv
United Kingdom	Limited company	Ltd	Public limited company	PLC
United States	Limited liability company	LLC/Co.Ltd	Corporation or Incorporated	Inc.

Cooperative
A cooperative acts on behalf of its members. The members of a cooperative do business with their cooperative. The nature of this business can vary:
1 In a *production cooperative*, the members are suppliers of raw material for the production process. In a cooperative dairy, the members might

supply milk; in a cooperative sugar refinery, they might supply sugar beets.
2 In a *purchasing cooperative,* members buy their supplies such as seeds, propagating material or fertilizer from the cooperative.
3 A *cooperative bank* lends money to its members.

If insurances are sold to members, the insurer is called a *mutual association* – which strongly resembles a cooperative.

Mutual association

In a cooperative, the members are the highest authority. The management is nominated by the members and is responsible for day-to-day business. In some cases, there is a supervisory board, whose function resembles that of the supervisory board at an LLC or corporation.

TEST QUESTION 1.5
The bond between the members and the cooperative is usually much tighter than that between shareholders and their corporation. What could be the reason for this?

Traditionally speaking, cooperatives were mainly to be found in the agricultural and financial industries. These days, cooperatives may also be found in other industries, with an example being a windmill owner cooperative in the energy industry.

The financing of cooperatives can be difficult. There is no share capital. Retaining profits is a sensitive subject as making profits would imply that the cooperative has set its prices below market prices (when it concerns a production cooperative) or above market prices (when it concerns a purchasing cooperative). To meet requirements for extra capital, it is possible to issue 'member certificates' with the characteristics of long-term loans. The continuity of the cooperative is guaranteed because members cannot suddenly leave the cooperative. Members can also be obliged to deal only with the cooperative.

Like shareholders of an LLC or corporation, members of a cooperative usually have limited liability for the debts of the cooperative. In the Netherlands, there are three legal forms of cooperatives:
1 *Legal liability:* the members are liable for the debts of the cooperative.
2 *Excluded liability*: the members cannot be obliged to pay the cooperative's debts.
3 *Limited liability*: the members are responsible for the cooperative's debts up to a maximum amount per member.

A cooperative's profit is taxed in accordance with the corporate tax system; however, there is a special arrangement that prevents all profit from being taxed. If the members are entrepreneurs, any profit payments will be taxed according the income tax law in box 1.
There are disclosure requirements for the cooperative.

Table 1.2 summarizes the characteristics of the different legal forms.

TABLE 1.2 Overview of consequences of legal forms for companies

Type of company	Legal entity status	Separation control and ownership	Financing with private assets	Continuity	Liability	Fiscal position in the Netherlands	Disclosure requirements
Sole Proprietorship	No	No	Deposit private assets by owner	Stands or falls with the owner	Fully liable	Entrepreneur: income tax Box 1	No
Partnership	No	No	Deposit private assets by partners Acquisition of a partner share	Departure of a partner can be compensated by other partners, possibility of conflicts	Several liability (equal share)	Partners: income tax Box 1	No
Limited partnership	No	Yes	Deposit private assets Acquisition of business share by new general or limited partner	Less possibilities for conflicts because capital can be attracted without adding a leader	General partners: several liability Limited partners: total amount of contribution of private assets	Partners: income tax Box 1 Limited partners: without entrepreneurs benefits	No
LLC	Yes	Yes	New issue of shares to current shareholders (blocking clause)	In principle, independent existence as legal entity but in the event of manager/ shareholder owner strong dependency	Limited to amount of contribution of private assets	LLC: corporate tax main shareholders: income tax Box 2	Yes
Corporation	Yes	Yes	New issue of shares	Independent existence as legal entity	Limited to amount of contribution of private assets	Corporation: corporate tax Shareholders: income tax Box 3	Yes
Cooperative	Yes	Yes	Member certificates	Independent existence as legal entity	Legal, excluded or limited liability	Cooperative: corporate tax (special arrangement) Members: income tax Box 1	Yes

1.5   Value Added Tax

This paragraph discusses value added tax (VAT), which all companies in Europe and in most other countries have to deal with, regardless of its legal form. Value added tax is a tax raised on consumptive expenditures, which means that the end user of a product or service pays the tax.
To achieve this, a tax system on added value has been implemented. Every time a company makes a sale. Value Added Tax is included in the paid price. Every country in the EU applies different rates. The basic rules imposed by the EU are:
- For delivery of products and services, the standard rate should be at least 15%.
- For a limited number of specified products and services, member states can apply one or two reduced rates of at least 5%.

In the Netherlands, the standard rate for value added tax is 21%, and there is a reduced rate of 6% on food and certain services. The applicable rate is added to the selling price of a product or service. The company transfers the tax to its customers by increasing the selling price by the amount of tax due. Tax is due regardless of whether the delivery is to an end consumer or to another company. If the buyer is a company, it is entitled to reclaim the charged VAT. If the buyer is an end consumer, they cannot reclaim the tax. The tax 'sticks' to his purchase.

- -

EXAMPLE 1.8
A manufacturer of household appliances produces air fryers at a cost of €100 each. They sell the air fryers to a wholesaler at €150 each. The wholesaler sells them to a retailer at €170 each, and the retailer resells the article to the end consumer at €200 each.

If the manufacturer sells one air fryer to the wholesaler, they pay 21% of €150 = €31.50 in value added tax. They charge this to the wholesaler, who receives the following bill:

Delivery of 1 air fryer	€ 150
21% VAT	€ 31.50
	€ 181.50

The wholesaler sells the air fryer to the retailer at €170; they pay 21% of €170 = €35.70 in value added tax, and bill the retailer as follows:

Delivery of 1 air fryer	€ 170
21% VAT	€ 35.70
	€ 205.70

The wholesaler pays €35.70 to the tax authorities, but can reclaim the €31.50 in value added tax paid to the manufacturer. As a result, they pay €4.20, which is equal to 21% of the added value of €20 (€170 selling price − €150 purchase price).

The retailer sells the air fryers to the consumer at €200 each. The consumer pays 21% of €200 = €42 in value added tax. The consumer is billed as follows:

Delivery of 1 air fryer	€200
21% VAT	€ 42
	€242

The retailer pays €42 to the tax authorities, but he can reclaim €35.70, which was charged to him. As a result he will pay €6.30, which is equal to 21% of the added value of €30 (€200 selling price – €170 purchase price).

The calculations of the sales process are summarized in the following table.

Tax consequences for the entrepreneurs

		Price incl. VAT	VAT to pay	VAT to receive	Net price	Profit
Manufacturer	Cost	€100			€100	
						€50
	Selling price	€181.50	€31.50		€150	
Wholesaler	Purchase price	€181.50		€31.50	€150	
						€20
	Selling price	€205.70	€35.70		€170	
Retailer	Purchase price	€205.70		€35.70	€170	
						€30
	Selling price	€242	€42		€200	
Consumer	Purchase price	€242			€242	

Based on the table of example 1.8, the following conclusions can be drawn:
- Value added tax is not a cost to the company: the value added tax due is charged to the customer, and the value added tax paid to a supplier is reclaimed from the tax authorities.
- Value added tax is eventually charged to the consumer. In the given example, the consumer will be charged €42, which they cannot reclaim. For consumers, value added tax is a *cost-increasing tax*.

Cost-increasing tax

VAT does not play a role on the income statement (see chapter 3). Both revenues and costs are shown without VAT.
Normally, the tax authorities require that VAT be settled every three months, at which point the balance of payable and claimable value added tax is paid to the tax authorities (or received from those authorities if the claimable VAT is more than the payable VAT).

TEST QUESTION 1.6
Under what circumstances would a company receive the balance of the value added tax from the tax authorities?

Special circumstances for value added tax

- *Exemptions*

Certain products and services are exempt from value added tax. These concern, for example, services rendered by banks and insurances, medical services, education, agricultural supplies and supplies or services concerning real estate.

An exemption has two consequences:

1 The company is not liable for value added tax on the product or service they provide.
2 The company cannot reclaim value added tax they pay to suppliers.

In fact, a company that is exempted from value added tax holds the same position as a private person.

EXAMPLE 1.9

Living LLC rents apartments to private persons. A customer is charged €500 for the rent in April. Living LLC receives a bill of €1,500 plus €315 VAT from a roofing company for roof repairs to one of its apartment buildings.

The company is not liable for value added tax on the rental revenue and therefore cannot charge the value added tax to the tenants.
The amount of €315 which is included in the bill cannot be reclaimed by Living LLC.

- *Export*

Value added tax relates to consumptive expenditures within a particular country. Products sold from the Netherlands to other countries are not subject to value added tax in the Netherlands. These products will be subject for value added tax in the country of destination (if this tax exists in the country concerned). The products will cross the border 'free of tax'; this is achieved by applying a *zero rate*.

Zero rate

EXAMPLE 1.10

Dutch Trading LLC buys wooden furniture from Dutch manufacturers and exports them to the United States. It receives a bill from a Dutch furniture manufacturer for the amount of €10,000 plus €2,100 VAT. An American buyer receives a bill for €15,000.

Dutch Trading LLC can reclaim the €2,100 value added tax it paid. The delivery to the United States is not subject to Dutch value added tax. The United States will have to charge tax on the imported furniture.

A Dutch company that imports products from abroad, is liable for Dutch value added tax. It can reclaim the paid value added tax if the imported products are used for taxable services.

1

1.6 Types of Cooperation between Companies

Companies can cooperate to varying degrees. In doing so, they abandon their independence partly or entirely. What was formerly a competitor has now become a colleague. Three forms of cooperation are discussed in the following paragraphs: mergers and takeovers, franchising and cartels.

Mergers and takeovers

If a company wishes to grow, one option would be to start new activities. However, it is often easier to take over an entire company rather than pursue autonomous growth. Takeovers are normally achieved by one company buying the shares in another company. A merger is a situation in which two equal parties join together.

Takeover

The difference in relationship between the acquirer and acquiree is best explained using terminology from industry and supply chain. A supply chain is the total chain of companies involved in the production of a product or service. It concerns all stages of the combined process that a product follows on its way from producer to consumer. The companies that operate at one level of the supply chain form what is known as an industry.

Supply chain

Figure 1.6 shows two supply chains.

FIGURE 1.6 Supply chains

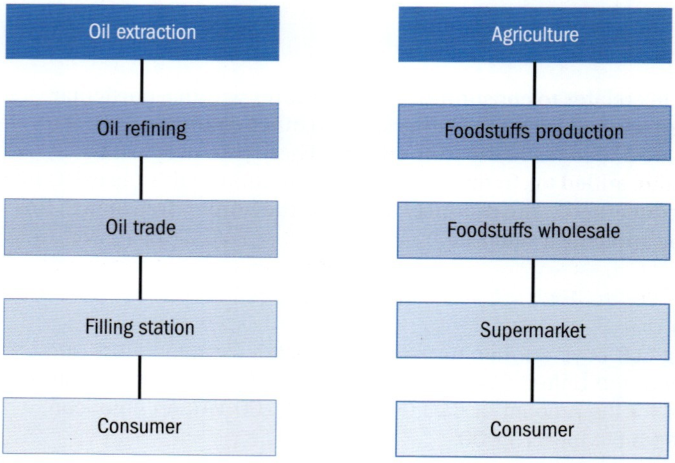

There are distinctly different types of takeovers and mergers, namely:
1 Acquirer and acquiree operate in the same industry. If a chain of gas stations were to take over another chain of gas stations, this could offer advantages in terms of less competition and a reduction in costs, for example, through economies of scale.
2 Acquirer and acquiree operate at consecutive levels of the supply chain; for example, if an oil extraction company were to take over an oil refinery. This is called *vertical integration*. Vertical integration is common practice

Vertical integration

in the oil industry; for example, Royal Dutch Shell controls the entire supply chain both up and downstream.

3 Acquirer and acquiree operate at the same level of different supply chains; for example, if an oil wholesaler were to take over a wholesaler in another industry, for example, food (which can be used to supply stores at gas stations). Such a takeover is an example of *horizontal integration*, widening the assortment.

Horizontal integration

4 Acquirer and acquiree operate at different levels and in different supply chains. In the past, many takeovers were used to create conglomerates: business groups active in various levels of various supply chains. The idea was that it would be an effective way to spread risk. Nowadays, these *conglomerates* are no longer popular, as such a mix of different companies proved to be very difficult to control by a centralized management. In the past few years, a trend towards 'back to core business' has been observed: companies are focusing on their core business and selling off other parts of the company.

Conglomerates

Franchising

The format that is characterized by a single entrepreneur joining a chain and using certain facilities offered by that chain, such as purchasing, marketing and store layout, is known as *franchising*.

For the franchiser, it is important that the entrepreneur is familiar with the local market. The franchisee runs the company as if he were an independent entrepreneur, but profile the business activities as part of a large chain, assisting and managing the entrepreneur. The franchisee pays a fee to the franchiser. Franchising is common practice nowadays, both in retail trade and in services.

Cartels

Cartels are agreements between manufacturers; they are designed to restrict competition. The opportunity to draw up such agreements depends on the market structure in which the companies operate.

In a perfectly *competitive market*, there are many companies offering a standardized product to many customers. This results in harsh competition. The other extreme is a *monopoly*, in which there is only one provider and therefore no competition.

Competitive market

Monopoly

Cartels do not exist under either competitive markets or monopolies.

An *oligopoly* is a market with relatively few providers. Road construction is a good example.

Oligopoly

TEST QUESTION 1.7
Name two other examples of industries that operate in an oligopoly market.

In an oligopoly, companies can easily be persuaded to collude and make price agreements with one another. They could even divide the market between them. This behavior is what gives rise to a cartel situation. Due to the potentially damaging effects for consumers, the European Union has made fighting cartels a top priority. Cartel agreements are illegal under European Competition Law, and the European Commission heavily fines companies found participating in such agreements. As cartel agreements are illegal, they are made secretively, and it is difficult to prove their existence. The Leniency Notice encourages companies to provide inside information on cartel agreements to the European Commission.

1

Whichever participant in a cartel agreement is first to inform the European Commission is then exempt from any fine. In the Netherlands, the Authority for Consumers and Markets (ACM) plays an important role in fighting cartel agreements and imposes heavy fines on companies that enter into (price) agreements.

The issues concerning markets and competitive relations are part of general economics but, of course, have important consequences for business economics.

For fourteen years, Europe's major truck manufacturers made illegal price agreements. Initially struck in the fringes of truck fairs, these agreements were followed up by phone calls once the top level managers returned to the Netherlands, Germany and Italy. The cartel moved to the digital highway following the ubiquitous spread of email and the internet in 2004. In July 2016, the European Commission slapped five manufacturers with a record fine for their role in the cartelization between 1997 and 2011. DAF, Volvo/ Renault, Daimler and Iveco settled their cases, and have been required to pay a combined €2.9 billion for striking illegal price arrangements relating to the introduction of a new exhaust norm, and for delaying the introduction of cleaner engine technology. MAN, the cartel whistleblower, has not been fined. Scania refuses to acknowledge any fault, and is now involved in a separate legal procedure.

Glossary

Business corporation	Company with a legal entity status and usually freely transferable shares, divided capital equity.
Business economics	Discipline in economics that studies economic behavior in companies.
Capital	The production factor consisting of raw material and fixed assets of a company.
Cartel	Companies that collude to limit competition. An agreement between these companies is called a cartel agreement.
Company	Production organization striving for profit.
Cooperative	Association performing business activities on behalf of its members.
Economics	Science that studies human behavior with respect to the striving for wealth, being the optimal provision of goods and services.
Effectiveness	Focus of the production process on the production of goods and services that will be in demand by customers.
Efficiency	Expedience of a production process to produce a certain amount at minimal cost.
Franchising	Formula in which an entrepreneur, on payment of a fee, joins a chain to be able to use certain facilities offered by the chain.
General partner	Partner in a limited partnership who is both manager and partner.
Horizontal integration	A company adds activities from the same level of a different production chain, and therefore different production process, to its business activities.
Industry	The combined companies in one level of a supply chain.
Job production	Production method for producing a product adapted to the specific needs of a customer.

Legal entity	Independent body with its own equity, rights and obligations.
Limited liability company	Company with a legal entity status and freely transferable shares, divided capital equity.
Limited partner	Partner in a limited partnership, owner but not managing the business.
Limited partnership	Cooperation between two or more natural persons in which one or more persons functions as a money supplier.
Mass production	Production method for producing one type of product in large quantities.
Merger	The joining of two previously separate companies into one.
Organization	Cooperation between people and resources, with the aim to achieve a particular objective.
Partnership	Cooperation between two or more natural persons to perform business activities under a joint name.
Production	The creation of goods and services to provide human needs.
Sole proprietorship/ sole trader	Company run by one person, who is manager and owner.
Substantial business interest holder	Taxable person who owns at least a 5% share capital of an LLC or a corporation, will be taxed in box 2 of income tax.
Supply chain	A chain of companies that succeeds one after another in the production process.
Value added tax (VAT)	Tax paid by entrepreneurs on the sale revenues is charged to the buyer. Entrepreneurs can reclaim the tax they paid.
Vertical integration	A company adds a production level of the supply chain to its business activities, previously performed by a different company.

Multiple-choice questions

1.1 Which of the following organizations is *not* a company?
a A CD-store.
b A university medical center.
c A shipping company.
d A tax consultancy.

1.2 Which of the following activities is *not* in the field of efficiency?
a Bundling purchases and dealing with a limited number of suppliers to achieve larger discounts.
b Modifying a product to shorten production process time.
c Sending invoices faster.
d Modifying a product to tailor it to customers' requirements.

1.3 Which of the following statements is correct?
a Changing the nature of their activities is more difficult for companies than for non-profit organizations.
b Non-profit organizations are economically independent because they receive 'free gifts'.
c Offering discounts to regular customers corresponds with the view of striving for maximum profit.
d Companies act according to budget mechanism rather than market mechanism.

1.4 Which of the following statements is *not* correct?
a Assessment of effectiveness is more difficult in companies than in non-profit organizations.
b Non-profit enterprises can also strive to work as efficiently as possible.
c Public goods and services are produced by the government because the market mechanism fails for those goods and services.
d A negative financial result does not necessarily imply that a non-profit organization performs poorly.

1.5 Which of the following statements is *not* correct?
a A service company purchases hardly any raw materials.
b Mass production focuses on production to build up inventory, not to order.
c One of the transformation functions of trading is time.
d For service companies, personnel costs are usually an insignificant part of the total cost.

1.6 A car is produced with two different engine types. What type of production is this?
a Job production.
b Batch-job production.

c Batch-mass production.
d Mass production.

1.7   Which of the following statements is correct?
Statement 1: Wholesale is a 'business-to-business' market.
Statement 2: Wholesalers trading in seasonal products play an important role in bridging the time gap between production and consumption.
a Both statements are correct.
b Statement 1 is correct, statement 2 is wrong.
c Statement 1 is wrong, statement 2 is correct.
d Both statements are wrong.

1.8   Which of the following legal forms has *no* financial disclosure requirements?
a Partnership.
b Corporation.
c Limited Liability Company.
d Cooperative.

1.9   Which of the following statements is correct?
Statement 1: Increasing the number of partners in a partnership offers creditors more options for debt recovery if the partnership should fail to pay its debts.
Statement 2: A limited partner holds a more favorable position than a general partner when it concerns liability.
a Both statements are correct.
b Statement 1 is correct, statement 2 is wrong.
c Statement 1 is wrong, statement 2 is correct.
d Both statements are wrong.

1.10   The limited partnership ABC has two general partners and one limited partner. General partner A has invested €100,000, partner B €50,000 and limited partner C €450,000. The partnership has a total debt of €1 million. For which amount is partner A liable?
a €100,000
b €500,000
c €550,000
d €1,000,000

1.11   A retailer buys 1,000 radios in one quarter, at €20 each. He sells 700 radios in the Netherlands at €30 each and exports 300 radios to Belgium at €40 each. All prices exclude VAT. The value added tax rate is 21%.
How much value added tax will the retailer have to pay to the tax authorities for that quarter?
a €210
b €1,470
c €2,730
d €4,410

1.12   What does a supply chain comprise?
a A number of companies performing the same production process.
b A number of companies following one after another in the production process from raw material to end product.

c All companies operating in a particular industry.
d Competing companies that produce the same product.

1.13   A wholesaler takes over a retailer. What is this called?
a Conglomerate.
b Vertical integration.
c Horizontal integration.
d Merger.

1.14   For what purpose do companies form a cartel?
a To share the risk of setting up a new company.
b To buy out competitors through takeover.
c To be stronger in their mutual negotiations with the unions.
d To limit mutual competition.

1.15   In which market(s) can cartels easily occur?
a Monopoly.
b Oligopoly.
c Perfectly competitive market.
d All named markets.

2

Financial Management Disciplines and Positions

Paragraph 2.1 briefly explains the three financial management disciplines: financing, management accounting and financial accounting. Over the following chapters, these disciplines will be discussed in greater detail. The interaction of these disciplines with other disciplines, such as bookkeeping and law, is the subject of paragraph 2.2. Paragraph 2.3 discusses three typical positions in financial management: the treasurer, the controller and the accountant.

2.1 Financial Management Disciplines

It is common practice to divide financial management into *finance* and *accounting*.
Accounting can be divided into management accounting and financial accounting. These three disciplines are briefly discussed below. A more elaborate discussion follows in the respective chapters on these subjects.

Corporate finance

The discipline of corporate finance entails more than its name implies. Corporate finance is not only about how to finance company resources, it also determines which would be the best investments and best resources in which to invest (capital budgeting). Therefore, it not only concerns issues of finance, but also investment politics. The following is a closer look at the issues typical for both aspects of the discipline.

Investments

Paragraph 1.3 discussed how types of activities determine the nature of the resources in which a company should invest. Industrial companies make large-scale investments in production installations, whereas this is not a point of interest for companies in the service industry. The build-up of inventories is relatively important to trading companies.
A company invests in resources to be able to create added value through the transformation process. The added value of the goods or services that are manufactured using the resources needs to be higher than the investment. When considering an intended investment, there are often several alternative options, which means that certain selection criteria must be used to determine the best option for the company.

EXAMPLE 2.1
An international transport company is investigating whether the increased demand for its services can best be met by ordering new trucks with trailers, or by building a loading terminal near the railroad, which would allow container transport by rail.

To help make a decision, investment consequences need to be expressed in terms of money as much as possible. An estimate of the extra sales revenue derived from the investment is made and compared to ongoing operating costs during the project. The costs made to acquire finances for the project are also included. There are different methods for comparing this data.

Of course, there are also non-financial factors that can influence the investment decision. In example 2.1, the environmental aspect could be considered important. From a financial management perspective, however, the role of environmental policy in the total costs would only be considered if it had immediate financial consequences for the company. One example of the impact of the environmental aspect would be environmental tax imposed on polluting activities.

Example 2.1 concerns a separate investment decision. However, companies continually make investments that are derived from the transformation process more or less automatically.

EXAMPLE 2.2

As is customary in the industry, a wholesaler in fresh food has offered a term of payment of one month to its retailers. As a result, there is a month's difference between the moment of sales and the moment of cash inflow. The time in-between is an 'investment' by the wholesaler in the claim on his customers.

As every investment has financial costs, this type of 'obliged' investment should be restricted to a minimum. Offering a discount for cash payment could be a profitable option.

Finance

Once a decision has been made on the investments, adequate methods of financing must be explored. As costs precede benefits, the time between an investment and cash inflow must be bridged.

It is not always necessary to 'buy' an investment. Resources can often be rented or leased without requiring a large starting capital. In this situation, the financing for the investment is arranged at once.

The legal form of a company also determines its financing possibilities, as discussed in paragraph 1.4. This applies, in particular, to a company's own equity, which is capital made available by the owners to the company. The equity of a sole proprietorship is limited by the owner's own financial means. A large corporation can acquire many millions in equity through issue of shares.

Accounting

The accounting discipline focuses on providing the company with mainly financial information. Depending on the target group of this information, a distinction is made between management accounting and financial accounting.

Management accounting relates to information provided to internal management. The purpose of management accounting is to support management in the decision-making process.

Management accounting

EXAMPLE 2.3

An insurance company is faced with the question of whether it is necessary to maintain an in-company printing service. It may be cheaper to outsource printing work.

Management accounting can prove useful here as it can provide an overview of the costs of the in-company printing service in comparison to the costs of outsourcing the work.

Cost accounting is an important aspect of this discipline. A company's activities determine its cost structure, as briefly discussed in paragraph 1.3. For the financial control of the company, it is important to set up a planning and control system. This allows for the analysis of financial data, which can be used to measure company performance and, if applicable, used as a motivation for intervention. The set-up and maintenance of such a budgeting system is an important part of management accounting.

Financial accounting

Financial accounting is the external financial reporting system, with information provided by company management to external stakeholders. These stakeholders include shareholders, employees, creditors (for example, banks) and the government (tax authorities).

The name 'financial accounting' may lead to misunderstanding considering that management accounting also chiefly concerns financial information. Financial accounting is focused on the disclosure of the annual accounts. The most important of these accounts are the financial statements, comprising the balance sheet and the income statement – which are discussed in chapter 3.

Financial accounting just like management accounting has a *decision-supporting purpose*, but it fulfills this purpose to accommodate third parties. For example, banks can use the information to assess a company's credit request. Furthermore, there is an *accountability purpose:* the owners of the company (for example, the shareholders) use the financial information (in particular, profit figures) to assess management performance during the previous year.

Due to the differences in target groups, there are certain discrepancies between management accounting and financial accounting. Management accounting has a decision-supporting purpose and, by its nature, is future-oriented. Financial accounting has an important accountability purpose and is mainly focused on the past. This is explained further in example 2.4.

EXAMPLE 2.4

A software company negotiates a contract for €5 million to supply customized software to a major client. If the system is not operational by 1 January, €0.3 million will be deducted from the price as a fine.

The software company has already invested €4.5 million in this project. The company needs to decide whether to hire external programmers – at high cost – and achieve the deadline of 1 January, *or* to continue the project using only its own staff, which will result in the system not being operational on 1 January.

For management accounting, the invested amount of €4.5 million is not relevant. The question of whether to hire external programmers is not affected by this investment, because those costs will not be reversed by any decision. For financial accounting, however, the invested amount is important – it is one of the factors that determine the profit (or loss) on this project.

Management will be held accountable for the result to the shareholders.

Regulations

A second important difference between both types of accounting is applicability of regulations. Company management decides how the management accounting system is set up and which information it has to provide. Management can act according to its own views in determining the management accounting system. Financial accounting, however, is subject to legal requirements. Companies with a legal entity are obligated to disclose certain financial information by law. The legal form of a company is a determining factor in this matter. Financial accounting, therefore, also has a legal aspect.

Management might feel tempted to provide 'colored' information to the outside world: for example, by publishing higher profits than actual profits. This phenomenon is called *creative accounting*. As for internal reporting, there is little point in fooling oneself and creative accounting does not, in principle, occur in internal reports.

Creative accounting

EXAMPLE 2.5

A paper producer has had a worse year than usual. Company management will need to make some tough decisions (for example, to divest in certain activities). Thus, it is important that they understand the company's financial position correctly – no matter if that information is good or bad. For external purposes, management may be interested in hiding bad results by manipulating financial information. Their reasons could be to help secure profit-related bonuses, but also to avoid problems with the bank, which could withdraw credit facilities.

TEST QUESTION 2.1

Although, in principle, creative accounting does not occur in management accounting, there are situations in which it does conceivably occur. Provide an example of such a situation.

Furthermore, the decision-making focus of management accounting often results in very detailed information, which should be available to management without delay. Financial accounting focuses on accountability after the facts, which implies aggregated information and less urgency.

The differences between management accounting and financial accounting are summarized in table 2.1.

TABLE 2.1 Differences between management accounting and financial accounting

	Management accounting	**Financial accounting**
Target group	Management	Other stakeholders
Objective	Decision-supporting	Accountability
Focus on	Future	Past
Regulations	No	Yes
Inclination to creative accounting	No	Yes
Nature of information	Detailed	Aggregated
Priority	High	Low

2.2 Relationships to Other Disciplines

The business economic disciplines – finance, management accounting and financial accounting – depend on other disciplines if they are to properly fulfill their tasks.
The most important related disciplines are discussed here.

Bookkeeping

Information requires accounting data. This data is obtained from the company's bookkeeping department. Basic accounting data, such as sales revenue over a particular period or salaries paid during that period, are processed further and analyzed for further use in management accounting and financial accounting.

Ledger accounts

The backbone of the bookkeeping process is the system of ledger accounts, in which changes in the company's assets, debts, revenue and costs occurred during that period, are registered. For example, the ledger account *Company buildings* is used to register investments in business premises and depreciation in value over time, and the ledger account *Interest* is used to register costs deriving from debts. A general ledger can comprise dozens of ledger accounts.
The bookkeeping process should be set up in such way as to provide the required data in a simple and organized manner.

Company law

Paragraph 2.1 addressed the fact that financial accounting and external reporting are subject to legal requirements. Legislation regulates what types of companies are obliged to disclose which financial information in which financial statements, which information has to be made available and according to which accounting principles. Furthermore, regardless of whether a company has a disclosure obligation, all companies are obligated to maintain a bookkeeping system.
Paragraph 1.4 discussed the possible legal forms for businesses. There, company law also has its influence, in particular, with respect to financing.

Tax law

Profit generated by a company is subject to taxation. The income tax system is applicable to sole proprietorship and partnerships. Joint-share companies are liable for corporate tax. The taxable profit of a company is calculated according to the principles of financial accounting.

Organizational behavior

One of the focal interests of management accounting is the internal supervision and control of the company. To that end, management accounting requires not only a proper information system, but also an effective and efficient organization structure.
Both the budgeting process and the cost accounting system are influenced by the choice of organizational structure.

EXAMPLE 2.6
A major telecommunications concern could set up a division structure based on one of the following criteria:
Divided into product groups: Division Mobile   Division Land line
Divided into geographical areas: Division Benelux   Division Germany   Division France
Divided into customer groups: Division Business   Division Private

----

Marketing
A company's commercial marketing policy is also crucial for its success. Marketing efforts need to generate cash inflow. Although this is a more general business economics issue, *marketing* is often considered a separate discipline.   **Marketing**
In this book, marketing policy is not further discussed – but one should never forget that, without a commercial attitude, there will be no business.

The relationship between the different disciplines is shown in figure 2.1.

FIGURE 2.1 Relations between disciplines

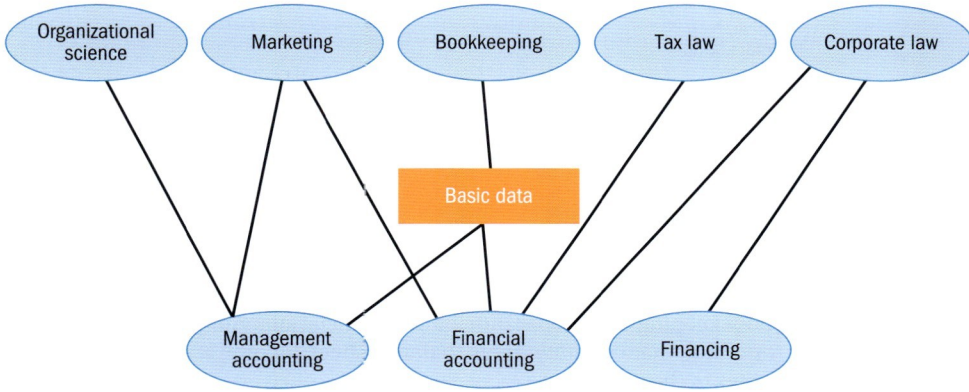

2.3 Positions in Financial Management

In business life in general, as well as in governmental and private non-profit organizations, there are many positions with a financial management perspective.
Of course, the organization chart will depend on the size of the organization. In small organizations, it is possible for a single person to be responsible for the finances and perform all tasks of a financial nature: making financial arrangements with the bank, supervising the administration, monitoring the budgeting cycle, etc. In such cases, the individual concerned is an allrounder, familiar with all aspects of financial management.

In a larger organization, a certain level of specialization occurs, based on disciplines. This gives rise to positions such as:
- Bookkeeper: focuses on registration of sales and purchases, salary payments, depreciation, etc.
- Internal auditor: reviews the bookkeeping system, inspects whether ledger entries are accurate representations of daily business.
- Controller: manages the overall financial control of the organization; is responsible for the set-up of a cost accounting system, the budgeting, financial back up of investment plans and compiling the financial statements.
- Treasurer: supervises an optimal cash management for the company; arranges the necessary financing and invests (temporary) excess cash.

Table 2.2 demonstrates the characteristics of the positions for each discipline (the greater the number of stars, the more relevant the discipline is for the position).

TABLE 2.2 Positions and disciplines

	Bookkeeping	Finance	Management accounting	Financial accounting
Bookkeeper	***			
Internal auditor	**			**
Controller	**		***	*
Treasurer		***		

These positions can all occur in an organization, but it is also possible to outsource certain financial management activities. Accounting firms specialize in taking over financial management activities, such as:
- bookkeeping and preparation of the financial statements
- auditing financial statements (balance sheet, income statement and notes to the accounts)
- providing advice on cost accounting system, investments, financing, etc.
- providing organizational advice
- handling of the organization's tax liabilities

The title of 'accountant' is legally protected in most countries. In the Netherlands, there are two types of accountants: the certified accountant (certified public accountant or CPA in the US, and the authorized public accountant (AAPA), who services the SMA.

External accountant

With respect to the auditing of financial statements, there is often a legal obligation to outsource. Companies operating as a legal entity and with a certain minimum size (see chapter 15) are obligated to involve an external accountant in the audit of the financial statements. The accountant issues an audit report that declares whether the financial statements provide an accurate account of the financial position of the company.

THE BIG FOUR

For years, the world of accounting firms has been dominated by a group of four companies. At an annual $36.8 billion revenue, Deloitte (in full: Deloitte Touche Tohmatsu) is the largest in the world, and employed approximately 244,400 persons towards end of 2016. Second is PricewaterhouseCoopers (PWC), whose revenue is $35.9 billion, followed by Ernst&Young (E&Y) at $29.6 billion and Klynveld Peat Marwick Goerdeler (KPMG) at $25.4 billion. Following several years of decline on the heels of the credit crisis, 2016 was the first year to see a growth in the total revenue in the industry. Compared to the situation prior to 2010, the combined loss in revenue suffered by the accountancy firms still comes to 5%.

Apart from the previously described financial management positions, there are several other positions in which financial management, alongside other disciplines, can play an important role. Portfolio managers at a bank, for example, need knowledge of both financing and accounting as they have to assess the financial statements of companies submitting credit requests. Employees with a marketing position also need basic financial management knowledge.

TEST QUESTION 2.2
Why would someone in a marketing position need to have a grasp of financial management?

Glossary

Accounting	Business economic discipline focused on providing of (mainly financial) information of a company.
Bookkeeper	Employee who processes the administration of transactions with financial consequences for the company.
Controller	Employee responsible for the financial control of the organization, in particular the budgeting process and investment selection.
Creative accounting	Using optimistic estimates for the financial statements, to make the company look better.
External accountant	Audits the financial statements provided by the company.
Finance	Business economic discipline focused on which assets could be best invested in and how to finance assets.
Financial accounting	External reporting; disclosure of (mainly financial) information by company management to stakeholders.
Internal auditor	Employee who audits the bookkeeping system.
Management accounting	Focused on providing information to management with the purpose of decision-making.
Treasurer	Employee responsible for the optimal cash flow in the company, in particular for attracting financial resources.

Multiple-choice questions

2.1 To which business economic discipline do investment decisions belong?
  a Finance.
  b Management accounting.
  c Financial accounting.
  d Bookkeeping.

2.2 In which of the following situations is an investment automatically the result of requirements in the production process?
  a Investment in a new computer system.
  b Leasing trucks.
  c Sale on credit.
  d Purchase of a business building.

2.3 Which of the following concepts is *not* part of management accounting?
  a Cost accounting.
  b Set-up of a budgeting system.
  c Disclosure of financial figures.
  d Decision on whether or not to outsource.

2.4 Which of the following statements is correct?
  a The legal form of a business is not important in financial accounting.
  b In financial accounting, a company's management could resort to creative accounting.
  c Financial accounting only has an accountability function.
  d Financial accounting concerns mainly future-oriented information.

2.5 Which statement is correct?
  a Organizational behavior influences the discipline of finance.
  b The function of management accounting is to provide basic data to the bookkeeping department.
  c Corporate law influences the discipline of finance.
  d Marketing is part of the discipline of management accounting.

2.6 Which discipline is tax law mainly related to?
  a Finance.
  b Management accounting.
  c Financial accounting.
  d Organizational behavior.

2.7   Who is responsible for setting up a budgeting system in a company?
a   The bookkeeper.
b   The internal auditor.
c   The external auditor.
d   The controller.

2.8   Who is responsible for supervising the bookkeeping system in a company?
a   The bookkeeper.
b   The internal auditor.
c   The external auditor.
d   The controller.

2.9   Who is responsible for the accuracy of financial statements in the annual report?
a   The bookkeeper.
b   The internal auditor.
c   The external auditor.
d   The controller.

2.10   Which of the following statements is correct?
a   All companies with a legal entity status are obligated to involve an external accountant to audit the financial statements.
b   In the Netherlands, the occupational group of accountants consists of certified accountants.
c   In the Netherlands, the authorized accountant works mainly for large companies.
d   Tax advice is part of the work of accountancy firms.

3

Financial Statements

3.1   **Investment and Financing**
3.2   **Balance Sheet and Income Statement**
3.3   **Profit versus Cash Flow**

A company has to invest in resources. These investments have to be financed, using one or more of several potential financial resources. An initial distinction can be made between equity and liabilities.
Paragraph 3.1 describes this concept. Paragraph 3.2 discusses two statements documenting a company's financial position: the balance sheet, which describes the status of the resources and their financing at a particular moment; and the income statement, which describes the sales revenues and costs (and therefore also profit) during a particular period.
Paragraph 3.3 discusses the essential difference between profit as a result of sales revenues and cost on the one hand and the transactions (= changes) in financial resources as the balance of cash inflows and outflows on the other. Three important related topics are covered: depreciation, provisions and direct equity transactions.

3.1 Investment and Financing

Running a company requires resources. The resources needed depend on the company's activities. An auto manufacturer needs buildings, production lines, inventory, etc.

A tax consultant can suffice with a workspace, telephone and computer. Paragraph 1.3 discussed the influence of the company's activities on the need for resources. These resources are known as 'assets' in financial terms. There is a distinction between fixed and current assets.

Fixed assets

Fixed assets can serve a business over a long period of time (longer than one year). Buildings have an economic life of many years, vehicles usually last five to ten years. In theory, some assets have an unlimited life; for example, the business terrain.

Current assets

Current assets are present in a business for any period shorter than a year. The time between purchase and usage of inventory is usually a few months or less. Current assets also include accounts receivable, from customers who have received deliveries but who have not yet paid.

These assets have to be financed somehow; there is time between the moment of purchasing resources and – due to deployment in the business process of an asset – the moment of cash inflow as a result of sales of produced goods or services. For fixed assets, capital is required for several years; for current assets, this is less than a year.

Financing can be done by using either equity or liabilities.

Equity

Equity is capital made available by the owner(s) of the company. It concerns, for example, the savings of the starting entrepreneur, or deposits by shareholders to acquire new shares in an LLC or corporation (see paragraph 1.4).

Equity made available by the owners is linked to the right of control of the company. One characteristic of equity is its availability for an unlimited period of time – which does not imply that equity cannot be refunded. There is no prior agreement about the moment of repayment. The reward for providing equity is the profit generated by the company for the benefit of its owners. The owners determine whether they actually want to receive a share of that profit or retain the earnings (thus building up a reserve), in which case additional equity is available.Considering that the size of profit depends on all kinds of uncertainties related to running a business, equity is

Risk-bearing capital

also called *risk-bearing capital*.

Liabilities

Liabilities are capital made available by creditors. Accordingly, it is not linked to formal control of the business. Liabilities are always temporary financial resources in the sense that prior agreements on repayment are made. Usually, a fixed interest rate is paid on credit, independent of the company's profits. This is why liabilities are considered *risk-avoiding capital*. Of course,

Risk-avoiding capital

providing credit is never without risk as a company may not (be able to) meet its interest or principal sum repayments. In the event of bankruptcy, creditors will receive a refund of (part of) their money before equity providers are considered.

TEST QUESTION 3.1

Credit does not give a lender formal control of the business; and yet, banks do sometimes have a voice in the company's policy. Explain the reason for this.

In table 3.1 the differences between equity and liabilities is shown.

TABLE 3.1 Differences between equity and liabilities

	Equity	Liabilities
Provided by	Owners	Creditors
Duration of availability	Indefinite period	Temporary
Compensation	Depends on profit	Usually fixed
By nature	Risk-bearing	Risk-avoiding

3.2 Balance Sheet and Income Statement

At all times, it is possible to capture, in a sort of snapshot, a comparison between the value of resources a company invested in (assets) and the financial resources used to finance these assets (liabilities). This snapshot is called the balance sheet. It is usually presented in a T-format, with the left side (the *debit side*) listing all investments and the right side (the *credit side*) listing the financial resources.

Balance sheet

EXAMPLE 3.1
On 1 January 2018, La Paz started a small rental business, offering a classic Cadillac cabriolet as a rental vehicle for weddings and other occasions. The purchase price of the car was €30,000. It was financed with La Paz' €20,000 savings plus a remainder borrowed from the bank at 7% interest per year, to be repaid in five equal annual installments. Interest and principal sum repayments take place annually, on 30 December.

On 1 January 2018, the balance sheet is as follows:

Balance sheet 1 January 2018 (in Euros)

Fixed assets		Equity	20,000
Car	30,000	Liabilities	
		Bank loan	10,000
	30,000		30,000

The car has been registered on the balance sheet under 'fixed assets' to indicate it is intended to be able to serve the business for several years.

As every Euro invested on one side has to be financed by a Euro on the other, the balance sheet is, by definition, in balance.

A company's equity is equal to the difference between the value of its assets and its debts. In a new business, equity can also be established by taking into account the capital invested by the owner(s). After a business has been up and running for some time, the equity should (hopefully) increase as a result of profits made.

In everyday speech, the term 'balance' is sometimes used to describe the traditional set of scales used to determine the weight of the object in one of the scales by placing weights in the other scale until the two are balanced out. In the world of business economics, the balance sheet consists of a figurative set of scales which weighs assets on the one hand against capital used to fund those assets on the other. The equity is what brings balance to those scales since the equity amounts to the difference in the monetary value of the assets placed in the one scale and the value of the debts in the other.

TEST QUESTION 3.2
Is it possible for a company's equity to be negative?

Profit can be determined by assessing the increase in equity over a certain period. To this end, two balance sheets have to be drafted: one at the beginning of a period and one at the end.

EXAMPLE 3.1 CONTINUED

Over the course of 2018, La Paz generates €30,000 from the car rental;
he has already received €28,000 by 31 December 2018. From rentals on
28 and 29 December €2,000 is still utstanding. Rent for his office and the
garage for storing the Cadillac amounts to €500 per month. Rent over each
month is paid on the tenth of every next month. Over the course of 2018,
La Paz paid a total of €10,000 for gasoline, maintenance, tax and insurances.
At its purchase La Paz estimated that the Cadillac – if regularly maintained –
would last ten years, after which both the bodywork and engine would be so
worn out that the car would be fit for the scrap yard.
For all cash payments and receipts, La Paz has taken a current account at
the bank.

3

The balance sheet on 31 December 2018 is:

Balance sheet 31 December 2018 (in Euros)

Fixed assets		*Equity*	30,300
Car	27,000	*Liabilities*	
Current assets		Bank loan	8,000
Accounts receivable	2,000	Rent payable	500
Current account	9,800		
	38,800		38,800

A closer look at the entries on the balance sheet:

Car
The car has an economic life of ten years for the company.
The value of the car will be gradually reduced over the course of those ten
years, from €30,000 to zero. The annual value reduction of the car (€3,000)
is a depreciation cost, which is deducted from the profit. On 31 December   **Depreciation**
2018, the book value of the car is €30,000 – €3,000 = €27,000.

Accounts receivable
On 31 December, La Paz's customers still owe him €2,000 in total. This
claim is documented on the balance sheet under accounts receivable.

Current account
The balance on the current account is the result of following transactions:

Cash inflows from rentals	€ 28,000
Cash outflows from rent of office and garage 11 × €500	– € 5,500
Cash outflows from other company costs	– € 10,000
Cash outflows from interest on loan	– € 700
Cash outflows from repayment of loan	– € 2,000
	€ 9,800

Bank loan
The annual repayments amount to €10,000/5 = €2,000; on 31 December
2018, the remaining debt is €8,000. On 31 December 2018, paid interest
amounts to 7% × €10,000 = €700.

Rent payable
On 31 December, an amount of €500 in rent is still due for the month of
December.

Equity
This is a remaining entry on the balance sheet.
Profit made by the company equals the increase of equity over a year:

Equity 31 December 2018:	€ 30,300
Equity 1 January 2018:	– € 20,000
	€ 10,300

3

Income statement

Profit can be further analyzed by taking a closer look at sales revenue and costs over the period concerned. Such a comparison of sales revenue and costs is called an *income statement*.

Revenues

The *revenues* (turnover) of a particular period do not necessarily have to coincide with the cash inflows (receivables). Revenue is assigned to the period during which a company delivers and invoices goods or services to its customers, regardless of whether the delivery of these goods or services results in payment during that period.

Costs

Similarly, *costs* incurred during a period are not automatically equal to the cash outflows (expenses) during that period. The most illustrative example is depreciation: the cash outflow for a fixed asset occurs at the time it is purchased and the cost is booked during the economic life of the asset, which results in the asset gradually losing its value.
Repayments of debts are not included on the income statement, as they do not change equity; the decrease in cash for repayments of debts (debit side) is equal to the decrease in debts themselves (credit side).

EXAMPLE 3.1 CONTINUED
For La Paz, the income statement over 2018 is:

Income statement 2018 (in Euros)

Sales revenue		30,000
Depreciation car	3,000	
Garage rent	6,000	
Interest on loan	700	
Other operating costs	10,000 +	
Total costs		19,700 –
Profit		10,300

Here is a closer look at the entries of the income statement:

Revenue
The sales revenue is the rent from the car. In 2018, the sales revenue of the car rental was €30,000. Of that amount, €2,000 had not been received by 31 December 2018. There is a clear difference between sales revenue and cash inflows. The sales revenue over 2018 was €30,000; followed by cash inflows of €28,000 in 2018 and €2,000 in 2019.

Depreciation of the car
Depreciation allocated to the year 2018 is €3,000.

Garage rental costs
Although €5,500 was spent on rental costs in 2018, the statement recognizes costs of €6,000 – this is due to the fact that the cause for the unpaid amount of €500 in rent is found in 2018, and constitutes the rental costs for the garage in December.

Interest costs on loan and other operating costs
There is no difference between costs in 2018 and cash-outflows in 2018.

3.3 Profit versus Cash Flow

As established in paragraph 3.2, period profit (sales revenue minus costs) should not be confused with cash flow during that period (cash inflows minus cash outflows). This is illustrated further in example 3.1.

EXAMPLE 3.1 CONTINUED
The table shows an overview of sales revenue/costs and cash inflows/outflows and their contribution to profit or changes in cash. Relevant changes to the balance sheet entries are also shown.

Differences between sales revenues/costs and cash inflows/outflows (in Euros)

	Profit	Cash flow	Difference	To balance sheet
Rental	30,000	28,000	2,000	Accounts receivable
Car	- 3,000		3,000	Car
Garage rent	- 6,000	- 5,500	500	Payable rent
Interest on loan	- 700	- 700		
Repayment of loan		- 2,000	2,000	Bank loan
Other expenses	- 10,000	- 10,000		
	10,300	9,800		

There are three items that create a difference between cash flow and profit:
• depreciation
• provisions
• direct equity transactions

These items are discussed in the following paragraphs.

Depreciation
Fixed assets exist in the service of a company for a number of years. To provide a correct representation of a company's financial position, an investment should not be considered an *immediate* cost on the income statement for the entire amount, but should be *spread* over the economic life of the asset.
In order to determine annual depreciation, an estimate of the potential economic life and the value after that period should be made.
Next, a depreciation method should be selected. There are a number of depreciation methods.

Straight-line depreciation

Accelerated depreciation

Sum-of-the-years-digits method

Declining balance method

The easiest method is *straight-line depreciation*: the asset is depreciated by the same amount every year.

Accelerated depreciation can be used if the asset performs better during its first years than its later years. Accelerated depreciation results in higher depreciation during the first years when compared to later years. There are two methods for applying accelerated depreciation:
- *Sum-of-the-years-digits method*: annual depreciation is calculated using a decreasing weighting factor, being the years of economic life remaining.
- *Declining balance method*: annual depreciation is calculated by a fixed percentage of the book value of the asset on the balance sheet. The book value is the asset's value after having deducted the depreciation over previous years. The percentage is usually twice what would be used in straight-line depreciation.

Annual depreciation can also depend on the (expected) use of the asset. The methods are explained further in example 3.2.

EXAMPLE 3.2

Biscuit maker Famous Biscuits buys a packaging machine for its products. The purchase price is €400,000. The estimated economic lifespan of the asset is five years, after which it is expected to be sold for €40,000.

The total amount of depreciation costs is €400,000 − €40,000 = €360,000. This should be spread over the five years of economic life of the asset.

Straight-line depreciation

Annual depreciation is the same every year: €360,000/5 = €72,000.

Sum-of-the-years-digits method

This method uses a weighting factor for each year of the economic lifespan of the asset; here, five years. Year 1 is given weighting factor 5; each subsequent year is given a weighting factor one lower.
Annual depreciation is as follows:

Years	Weighting factor	Annual depreciation	
1	5	5/15 × €360,000 =	€ 120,000
2	4	4/15 × €360,000 =	€ 96,000
3	3	3/15 × €360,000 =	€ 72,000
4	2	2/15 × €360,000 =	€ 48,000
5	1	1/15 × €360,000 =	€ 24,000
	15		€ 360,000

Declining balance method

When applying straight-line depreciation, annual depreciation is €72,000. Given as a percentage of the purchase price, this is €72,000 / €400,000 × 100% = 18%. Using a double percentage for depreciation of the book value results in 2 × 18% = 36%.

Annual depreciation will be as follows (rounded off to whole figures in Euros):

		€	
	Purchase price	€	400,000
Year 1	Depreciation 36% of €400,000 =	€	144,000
	Book value end year 1	€	256,000
Year 2	Depreciation 36% of €256,000=	€	92,160
	Book value end year 2	€	163,840
Year 3	Depreciation 36% of €163,840 =	€	58,983
	Book value end year 3	€	104,857
Year 4	Depreciation 36% of €104,857 =	€	37,749
	Book value end year 4	€	67,108
Year 5	Depreciation 36% of €67,108 =	€	24,159
	Book value end year 5	€	42,949

Applying the (double) declining balance method as described, the remaining value is not equal to the estimated economic remaining value.

Based on use
This depreciation method does not determine annual depreciation in advance. Instead, it depends on the usage of the asset over the estimated economic life; here, five years. Assuming that the machine produces the following annual amounts of packaging, then the corresponding depreciation amounts are:

Year	Produced packaging	Annual depreciation		
1	300,000	300,000 / 1,600,000 × €360,000 =	€	67,500
2	440,000	440,000 / 1,600,000 × €360,000 =	€	99,000
3	320,000	320,000 / 1,600,000 × €360,000 =	€	72,000
4	300,000	300,000 / 1,600,000 × €360,000 =	€	67,500
5	240,000	240,000 / 1,600,000 × €360,000 =	€	54,000
	1,600,000		€	360,000

Figure 3.1 shows the progress of the different depreciation methods.

FIGURE 3.1 Progress of depreciation

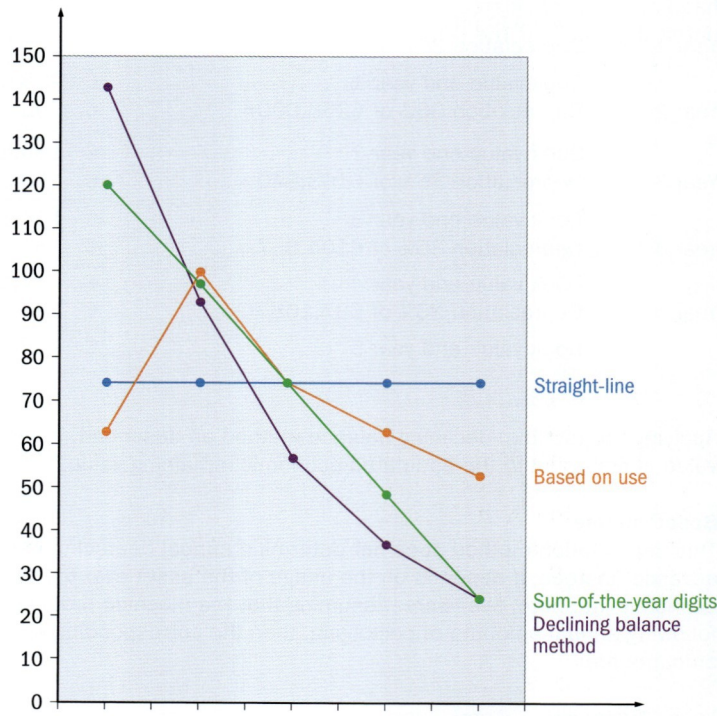

Provisions

Provisions

Provisions have to be recognized in the event of future obligations as a consequence of business activities in the past year. By creating provisions, costs are recognized on the income statement before any actual payment takes place. This is explained in example 3.3

EXAMPLE 3.3

Restaurant The Old Oak began its activities in early 2018, with an equity of €200,000. On 31 December 2018, the following preliminary balance sheet was made:

Balance sheet 31 December 2018 (in Euros)

Building	520,000	Equity	256,000
Equipment	45,000	Debts	336,000
Inventory	4,000		
Cash	23,000		
	592,000		592,000

However, when drawing up the balance sheet, an ongoing court case with respect to an earlier dismissal of a former member of the waiting staff had not been considered. If the dismissal should be ruled as having been unfair, it could cost The Old Oak up to €20,000.

If, on the date the balance sheet is drawn up, the restaurant is estimated to be likely to lose the case, a provision of €20,000 would be made on the credit side of the balance. On 31 December, equity would not be €256,000, but €236,000. Period profit would not be €56,000, but €36,000. An extra cost of €20,000 would be recognized on the income statement.

If it should turn out that, in 2019, the former employee is indeed entitled to the €20,000 payment, this payment would not result in costs: the reduction in cash is equal to the reduction of the provision, so the equity does not change.

Since provisions are based on estimates, they are a subjective element in profit calculations – aptly captured by the expression 'cash is fact, profit is opinion'. Cash flows cannot be manipulated; profits, however, can be adjusted up or down by overly optimistic or pessimistic estimates of provisions. In external reporting (disclosure of financial statements) there may be a tendency to paint an overly rosy picture of a company's financial position. This is an example of *creative accounting*. Provisions are **Creative accounting** particularly suitable for this type of tinkering.

TEST QUESTION 3.3
Provide three reasons why management might resort to creative accounting.

Direct equity transactions
As previously mentioned, period profit is equal to the increase in equity over that period. However, this need not always be the case. If an owner deposits money into, or withdraws money from, a company, these *owner* **Owner deposits** *deposits* and *owner withdrawals* have no influence on profit, because their **Owner** origin is not related to business activities. **withdrawals** This is explained in example 3.4.

EXAMPLE 3.4
On 1 January 2018, Hatty Vanderkamp drew up the balance sheet for her advertising company StellarBoost:

Balance sheet 1 January 2018 (in Euros)

Equipment	24,000	Equity	20,000
Accounts receivable	2,000	Bank loan	10,000
Cash and cash equivalents	4,000		
	30,000		30,000

Over the course of 2018, the following events took place:
- A total amount of €60,000 was invoiced for work carried out, and €59,000 was received from customers.

- A total of €30,000 was paid, covering rent, interest and other costs; this entire amount was related to costs over 2018.
- €2,500 was repaid on the existing bank loan.
- Depreciation of the office equipment was 40% of the book value.
- In February, Hatty deposited €15,000 she won in a lottery as additional equity.
- Every month, Hatty withdraws €2,000 from the business to cover her cost of living.

On 31 December 2018, the balance sheet is:

Balance sheet 31 December 2018 (in Euros)

Equipment[1]	14,400	Equity	31,400
Accounts receivable[2]	3,000	Bank loan[4]	7,500
Cash and cash equivalents[3]	21,500		
	38,900		38,900

[1] €24,000 – 40% × €24,000
[2] €2,000 + €60,000 – €59,000
[3] €4,000 + €59,000 – €30,000 – €2,500 + €15,000 – €24,000
[4] €10,000 – €2,500

Equity increase over 2018 is:

Equity 31/12	€ 31,400
Equity 1/1	€ 20,000
	€ 11,400

Equity increase is not equal to profit. There is an owner deposit of €15,000 on the one hand, and owner withdrawals of 12 × €2,000 = €24,000 on the other. Neither fact should influence the profit.

Profit can be calculated as follows:

Increase equity		€ 11,400
Owner deposit	– € 15,000	
Owner withdrawals	+ € 24,000	
		€ 9,000
		€ 20,400

The income statement over 2018 is:

Income statement over 2018 (in Euros)

Sales revenue		60,000
Depreciation	9,600	
Other costs	30,000	
		– 39,600
Profit		20,400

The owner's private deposits and withdrawals are not documented on the income statement, as they are not the result of business activities but of an equity transaction between the company equity and the owner's private capital.

Similarly, deposits made by the shareholders of a joint-share company in the event of issuing new shares do not affect the profit, nor does paying dividend affect the costs.

3

Glossary

Accelerated depreciation	Depreciation method which applies higher depreciation in the first years than in the last.
Assets	The resources in which a company invests.
Balance sheet	Overview of values of all assets in which a company has invested on one side, and the financial resources used to finance these assets on the other.
Creative accounting	Using optimistic estimates for the financial statements to make the company's financial position appear stronger.
Equity	Capital provided by owner(s) for an unlimited period of time; return depends on the profit.
Income statement	Overview of sales revenue and costs over a period.
Liabilities	Financial resources provided by creditors for a limited period of time. Return is usually fixed.
Liabilities and equity	Financial resources of a company, comprising debt(s) and/or equity.
Provisions	Balance entry representing possible future obligations derived from business activities over the past year.
Straight-line depreciation	Depreciation method which reduces book value by the same amount for every year of an asset's economic lifespan.

Multiple-choice questions

3.1   Which of the following statements is *not* correct?
a Share capital is a type of equity.
b Providing credit holds greater risk than providing equity.
c Liabilities are temporary capital.
d In the event of bankruptcy, creditors receive repayment before providers of equity.

3.2   A starting entrepreneur buys a delivery van and pays €10,000 in cash. He buys inventory at a wholesaler for €5,000; he has to pay for the goods within a month. The bank grants him a loan of €3,000. He finances the remainder using his private capital.
Calculate the value of the balance sheet total and the equity at the start of the company's activities.
a The balance sheet total is €10,000; equity is €7,000.
b The balance sheet total is €15,000; equity is €7,000.
c The balance sheet total is €10,000; equity is €8,000.
d The balance sheet total is €15,000; equity is €8,000.

3.3   In 2018, a company purchases a machine with an estimated economic life of five years. Which of the following statements is correct?
a 2018 sees both cash outflows and costs, but the amounts are different.
b 2018 sees both cash outflows and costs, and the amounts are the same.
c 2018 sees only cash outflow(s).
d 2018 sees only costs.

3.4   Which of the following events that take place in December 2018 are *not* a cost in 2018?
a Payment of salaries over December 2018.
b Recognizing a provision for a pending lawsuit, started in 2018.
c Payment of the interest over 2019 of a bank loan.
d Payment of the rent over the last quarter of 2018.

3.5   Which of the following statements is *not* correct?
a An owner's withdrawal reduces profit.
b Mortgage payments are not a cost.
c A company's equity is the difference between the value of the assets and of the liabilities.
d Creative accounting is possible by using optimistic estimates when drawing up the financial statements.

3.6   On 1 January 2018, a company was still due to receive €25,000 from customers. Over 2018, the company generated €150,000 in sales revenue. That year, the company received €165,000 from sales.
What was the amount of the balance entry 'Accounts receivable' on 31 December 2018?
a €10,000
b €25,000
c €40,000
d €150,000

3.7   On 1 January 2018, the balance of a company is:

Balance sheet on 1 January 2018 (in Euros)			
Building	200,000	Equity	155,000
Inventory	50,000	5% loan	100,000
Bank	5,000		
	255,000		255,000

The building has a remaining economic lifespan of 20 years and the other fixed assets have a remaining lifespan of two years. The residual value of the building and the other assets is zero. The annual repayment of the loan is €20,000, paid on 31 December; interest over the year is paid on the same date. The company generates €300,000 sales revenue in 2018; at the end of the year, €290,000 of that amount has been received. The remaining amount is to be received in 2019. Operating costs over 2018 were €180,000.
Calculate the profit over 2018.
a €60,000
b €70,000
c €75,000
d €80,000

3.8   Refer to question 3.7. Calculate the balance sheet total on 31 December 2018.
a €305,000
b €310,000
c €315,000
d €335,000

3.9   On 1 January 2018, the equity of an LLC is €1.5 million; on 31 December 2018, the equity is €4 million. In 2018, €250,000 in dividend was paid to the shareholders. By issuing new shares, the company acquired an additional €1 million in 2018.
Calculate the profit over 2018.
a €250,000
b €1,750,000
c €2,500,000
d €3,250,000

3.10   A company has purchased a delivery van costing €30,000; it is expected to have an economic lifespan of 5 years and a residual value of €6,000. Calculate the depreciation in the third year when applying straight-line depreciation.

    a   €3,500
    b   €4,800
    c   €6,400
    d   None of the above.

3.11   A company has purchased a delivery van costing €30,000; it is expected to have an economic lifespan of 5 years and a residual value of €6,000. Calculate the depreciation in the third year when applying 30% depreciation of the book value.

    a   €3,500
    b   €4,800
    c   €6,400
    d   None of the above.

3.12   A company has purchased a delivery van costing €30,000; it is expected to have an economic lifespan of 5 years and a residual value of €6,000. Calculate the depreciation in the third year when applying the sum-of-the-years-digits method.

    a   €3,500
    b   €4,800
    c   €6,400
    d   None of the above.

3.13   A company has purchased a computer system for €10,000; it is expected to have an economic lifespan of 4 years and no residual value.
The company has to decide between two depreciation methods: straight-line or sum-of-the-years digits.
Which of the following statements is correct?

    a   Depreciation according to the straight-line method is €500 lower in the third year than that based on the sum-of-the-years digits method.
    b   Depreciation according to the straight-line method is €500 higher in the third year than that based on the sum-of-the-years digits method.
    c   The book value of the computer according to the straight-line method is €1,000 lower at the end of the third year than the book value based on sum-of-the-year digits.
    d   The book value of the computer according to the straight-line method is €1,000 higher at the end of the third year than the book value based on sum-of-the-years digits.

3.14   Which depreciation method can have higher depreciation in later years and lower depreciation in the earlier years?

    a   Straight-line.
    b   Sum-of-the-years digits.
    c   Fixed percentage of the book value.
    d   Depreciation based on use.

3.15   A dissatisfied customer brought a lawsuit against a company in 2017, demanding compensation for damages for a total of €20,000. The claim seems realistic. Towards late 2018, the court orders payment of €15,000. In 2019, the money is transferred to the customer. What influence do these events have on the profits of 2017, 2018 and 2019?

a In 2017 and 2018, there are no consequences for profit; in 2019, profit is reduced by €15,000.

b In 2017, there are no consequences for profit; in 2018, profit is reduced by €15,000; in 2019, there are no consequences for profit.

c In 2017, profit is reduced by €20,000; in 2018, there are no consequences for profit; in 2019, profit is increased by €5,000.

d In 2017, profit is reduced by €20,000; in 2018, profit is increased by €5,000; in 2019, there are no consequences for profit.

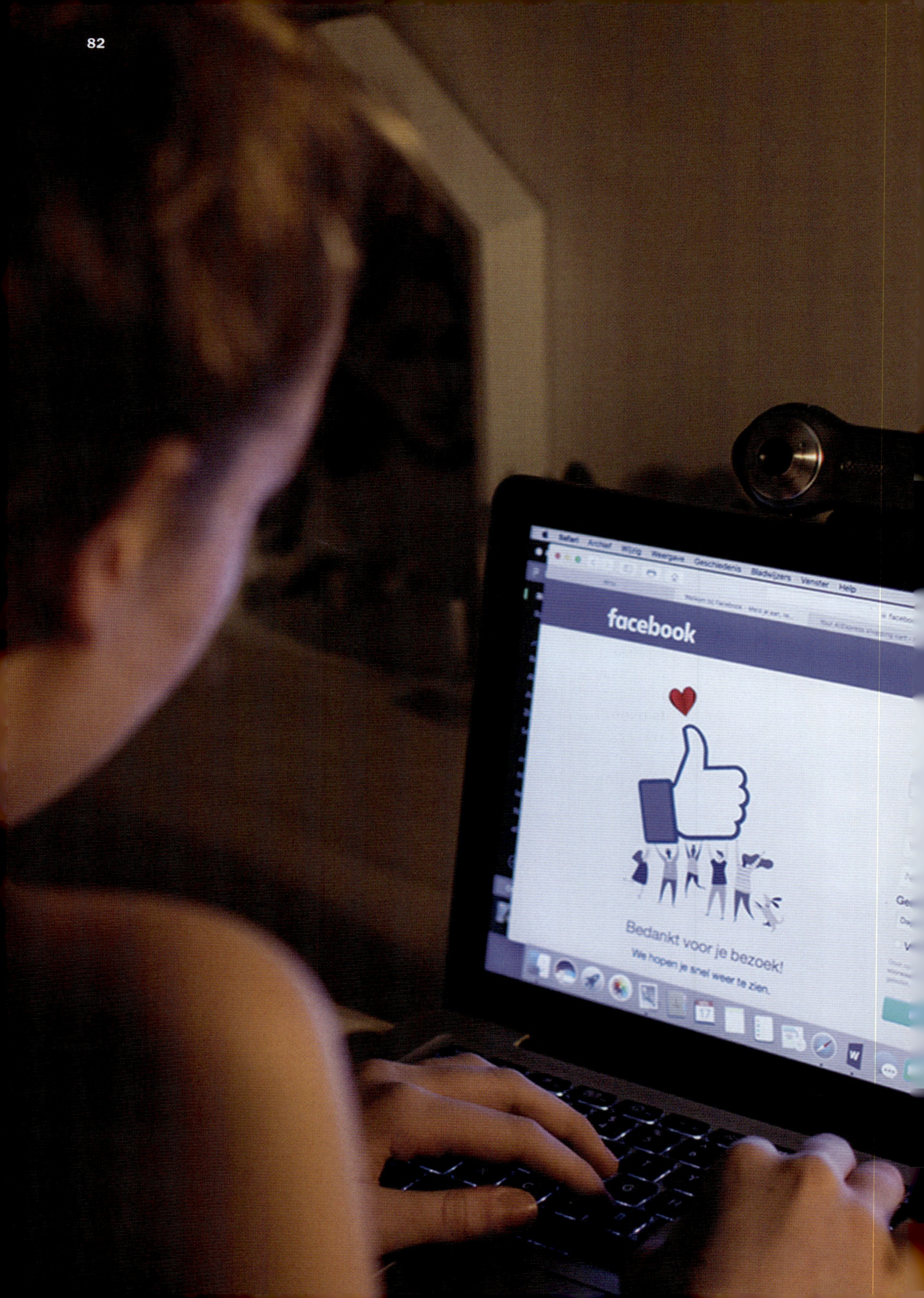
Safari
Archief
Wijzig
Weergave
Geschiedenis
Bladwijzers
Venster
Help
facebook
Bedankt voor je bezoek!
We hopen je snel weer te zien.

4

Business Plan

A good business plan is the key to a successful company. Before the
business plan is discussed comprehensively in later paragraphs, paragraph
4.1 first offers some facts and figures on startup entrepreneurs in Europe
and the Netherlands. Paragraph 4.2 discusses the purposes of the business
plan, illustrating its usefulness to the entrepreneur – particularly as a tool to
help convince financiers to invest in a company. Paragraph 4.3 enters into
the different parts of the business plan, such as company objectives and the
legal, commercial and financial focal points.

4.1 Startup Businesses in Europe and the Netherlands: Facts and Figures

The European Union gathers economic data from all member states and publishes these in the online Eurostat database. Eurostat also includes information on companies. The European Union has over 26 million active companies, 1.5 million of which operate in the Netherlands. Based on their numbers of employees, most companies are small.

56% of all European companies are sole proprietorships; in the Netherlands, this figure is 75%. Approximately 95% of companies have fewer than 10 employees. Of the companies in the Netherlands and in Europe, 99% belong in *small and medium enterprises* (SME) category; this concerns companies with a maximum of 250 employees.

Every year, more people take the plunge and start a new business. Figure 4.1 shows the number of startup companies as a percentage of the number of existing companies per European region.

FIGURE 4.1 Annual growth in European companies: start-up companies as a percentage of the total (2014)

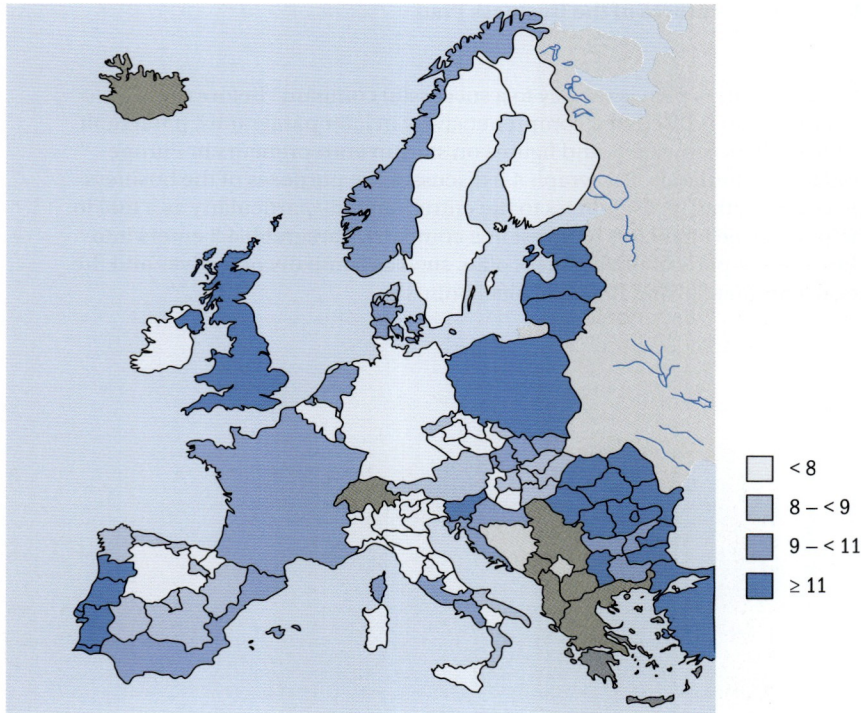

	< 8
	8 – < 9
	9 – < 11
	≥ 11

Source: Eurostat

In the Netherlands, the majority of new startups are own-account workers. In 2016, nearly 167,000 new companies were founded in the Netherlands. The majority of all startups are active in the service industry.

The 'mortality' rate among startup companies is high. After one year, 16-18% of starters has already given up on their business. After three years, that percentage increases to 25-30%; after five years, the figure is nearly 50%. This does mean, however, that Dutch startup companies are among the best performing startup companies in Europe (see figure 4.2).

FIGURE 4.2 Percentage of start-ups still in business after five years

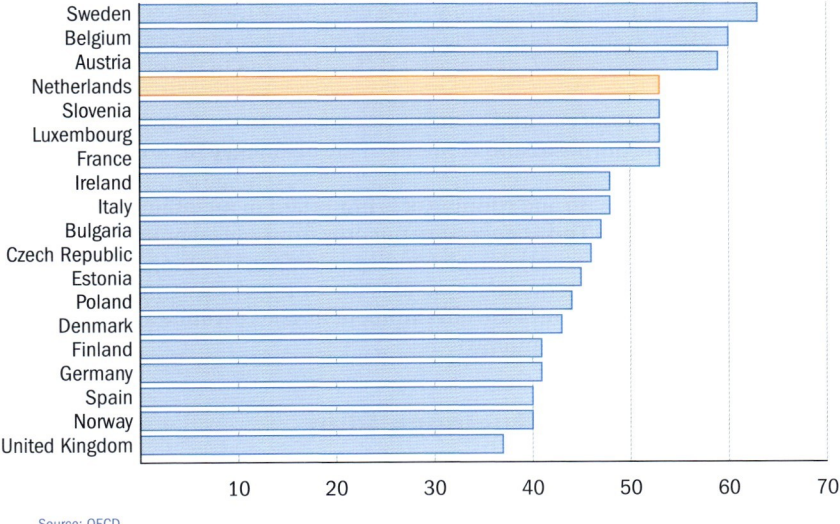

Source: OECD

One of the causes of the high percentage of failure is lack of preparation. Starters ought to be sensible and carefully assess which activities and which customer groups they want to target.
Subsequently, they should analyze whether enough customers can be acquired to achieve a profitable exploitation.

In 2004, Mark Zuckerberg and four fellow students at Harvard University founded Facebook. Facebook was born from one of Zuckerberg's earlier software programs: Facemash. Facemash showed two pictures of fellow students at a time (which were illegally obtained from the university's database). This allowed visitors of the site to choose which of the two students shown was the 'hottest' of the two. Later,

after having nearly been expelled from the university by the board, Zuckerberg founded Facebook. In 2012, Facebook welcomed its one-billionth user. Zuckerberg's estimated worth is approximately $56 billion as per 2017.

Zuckerberg is convinced that being able to translate your passion into a business is the hallmark of good entrepreneurship.

These aspects are all covered in the business plan. In the following paragraphs, the purposes and contents of the business plan are discussed in greater detail.

Once a company is up and running, it is important to maintain a proper accounting system. This is necessary not only from a legal point of view (for example, for tax purposes), but also indispensable for keeping a company 'under control'. The accounting system is the compass that guides a company because it shows the development in sales revenue and costs per period (for example, per month).

4.2 Purposes of the Business Plan

Writing a business plan is important for a starting entrepreneur, as well as for other stakeholders – in particular, potential investors.

First of all, drawing up a business plan encourages a starting entrepreneur to reflect on whether his ideas are realistic or mere pipe-dreams. The activities a company wishes to develop should be explained in the business plan, as well as whether these activities add something that is not offered by products or services already provided by other companies. Secondly, a good business plan also provides a starting entrepreneur with an overview of all the steps required before his business can begin. Required permits, choice of legal form, investments needed and many other aspects must be addressed in the business plan.

Starters usually have insufficient means to make the necessary investments. They will often have to rely on others to close the financial gap. Those others will, naturally, only be prepared to invest in the company if they are sufficiently confident about its success. By means of a business plan, financiers can be convinced they are dealing with a serious, realistic starting entrepreneur.

Financiers can provide equity or issue credit. Where equity is concerned, a starting entrepreneur can opt for the legal form of limited partnership or limited liability company. In a limited partnership, there are silent partners who invest money but do not interfere with the daily management of the company. In a limited liability company, the starting entrepreneur can be director and shareholder and attract other shareholders to invest. *Venture*

Venture capital companies

capital companies participate in starting companies; when those companies reach 'maturity', the venture capital companies dispose of its shares. In this context, the investment is considered *venture capital*, because there are relatively large risks in financing starting companies.

Venture capital

A relatively new associated phenomenon is that of the so-called angel investor. An angel investor (sometimes known as a business angel) is usually a former entrepreneur who has made some money through the sale of a previously self-started company. Angel investors tend to invest in (pre)startups and entrepreneurs during the early growth stages of those companies. These investments often come in the form of a loan or a share investment, and generally amount to anywhere between €50,000 and €250,000 Euros. In addition to money, angel investors offer their knowledge and expertise, and the use of their personal networks. Angel investors make their presence feel known in day-to-day activities, particularly during the early stages of their investment. They offer support from the perspective of their entrepreneurial experience. Once the company they have invested in becomes more sure-footed, the angel investors gradually begin to withdraw from general proceedings.

Angel investor

Issuing credit carries less risk than investing in equity because, normally, fixed interest is paid on credit – and, in case of bankruptcy, creditors are the first to be refunded. Only after the creditors have received their money back are the equity providers paid for their investment. It is clear that financing of starting entrepreneurs in particular carries high risk.

Credit can be issued by means of a loan. Banks are financial institutions, specializing in lending money.

Since starting companies have no track record, banks are often hesitant to finance them. European governments have implemented regulations, allowing banks to partly forego the risk of losing out on the repayment of a loan. If a loan is a *government guaranteed loan*, companies that fail to repay the loan result in the government compensating the bank.

Government guaranteed loan

Startup companies are often financed with a *subordinated loan*: loans of which the interest and principal sum repayments are only made after all other obligations towards creditors have been fulfilled. These loans bear a risk level somewhere between equity and other liabilities. To make the financing of starting enterprises more attractive, special tax facilities for subordinated loans are in place. Similar to providers of equity, creditors use the business plan as a means of risk assessment.

Subordinated loan

4.3 Key Features of the Business Plan

Every business plan is unique. A number of items that should always be included in the business plan is featured below.

The qualifications of the entrepreneur
This part describes the starting entrepreneur's background, education and work experience. It also describes the motivation for setting up and running the business; for example, by answering the following questions:
- Why do I want to become an entrepreneur?
- What do I wish to achieve with my business?
- Which particular skills do I have to become an entrepreneur?
- How will I develop myself as an entrepreneur?

Business idea
A description of the entrepreneur's intended activities, methods of performing those activities, and the intended customers. Overall, the business idea should demonstrate the feasibility of the entrepreneur's plan. It should answer the following questions:
- What type of company do I intend start and when?
- What needs or desires will my company fulfill?
- How will I make my business successful?
- What are the expected risks and advantages?

EXAMPLE 4.1
After earning a degree in hospitality management, Francine Monk worked in the hospitality industry for various companies for ten years. She now wants to start her own business.
Francine intends to open a coffee corner at the refurbished station square in her hometown. She believes the busy location offers a good opportunity to tempt hasty travelers with a good cup of coffee (on the go).

Market and marketing mix
This part should always pay attention to the following points:
- the intended focal business activities
- differences between the business and its competitors (its *unique selling points*)
- results of any market research

Unique selling points

EXAMPLE 4.1 CONTINUED
Francine Monk wants to focus her coffee corner *Cappa* on offering a varied assortment of first grade coffee products. She has targeted two groups of customers in particular: rail travelers with half an hour to spare and personnel from nearby offices looking for a good cup of quality coffee and a bite to eat in a pleasant environment. The intended opening times are 10.00 till 18.00 daily, with the exception of Saturdays and Sundays.
Although there are other catering establishments in the area, *Cappa* would be the only coffee corner. Its contemporary chrome interior design is unique and will have more appeal to the targeted public than the 'old Dutch' style of Francine's competitors.
Francine has asked a marketing student to conduct a brief survey concerning the expected demand. He came up with the following estimates: an average of 120 customers a day; an average spend of €5 per customer. The expected sales revenue per year is approximately €150,000.

The marketing mix is a combination of variables that determine the attractiveness of a company for its customers. These variables are also known as the *four Ps* that need to be addressed by the company:
- Product: the assortment of products (which, in the broader sense, includes both goods and services) naturally determines the success of a company. The extent to which products meet customer requirements is crucial.

Marketing mix

Four Ps

- Price: the price mainly determines sales. Of course, it is not always easy to determine the trade-off between a reduction in price and an increase in sales.
- Promotion: the various methods used to market a product – advertising activities in all their shapes and forms.
- Place: not only the actual place where the product is sold but also which distribution channels to use.

In literature, a fifth P for *personnel* is sometimes added to this list. Employees can make or break a company. In the service industry in particular, the quality of staff is critical to a company's success.

EXAMPLE 4.1 CONTINUED

Cappa's marketing mix comprises trendy, high quality coffee products with matching price tags. There will be an introductory campaign with adverts. Following this campaign, word of mouth will be the most important factor. The location of the coffee corner is attractive for both passersby and regular customers. The targeted group is one with customers to whom price is less important. Francine intends to act as host as often as possible, which will lead her to swiftly become a familiar face to her customers. She already has her intended assistant in mind.

4

Legal aspects
In the section on legal aspects, the choice of legal form should be addressed first. The selected legal form has important consequences for such things as owner liability, fiscal position and possible obligations with respect to the disclosure of the financial statements.
A starting entrepreneur normally chooses between sole proprietorship and limited liability company. These legal forms are discussed in paragraph 1.4. From a liability point of view, the LLC offers a major advantage over the sole proprietorship: the owner of a sole proprietorship is responsible for the company's debts, in principle, the shareholders of an LLC are not. Note, however, that, in the event of 'malpractice', personal liability is still a possibility.
The LLC can also offer fiscal advantages, particularly if an important part of profit is retained within the company. The income tax rate (which applies to profit withdrawn from the company), is higher than the corporate tax (which applies to profit of the LLC).

EXAMPLE 4.1 CONTINUED

Initially, Francine decides to run her business as a sole proprietorship. Considering the profit expectations, she does not expect to be in the running for any of the fiscal advantages that an LLC would offer.
Although the owner of a sole proprietorship is liable for all debts and the shareholder of an LLC is not, financiers such as banks will, in practice, insist that the director of an LLC commits to liability as a condition of the loan. For Francine, the lower VAT rate applies because she sells food and non-alcoholic beverages.

Additionally, the business plan contains a list with required permits and certificates. The extent to which permits or certificates are required depends on the type of industry: no permits are required to start a software business, but the same cannot be said for a business in the hospitality industry.

EXAMPLE 4.1 CONTINUED
Francine incorporates the following list into her business plan:
• Liquor license: as she will not be serving liquor, she will not require a liquor license.
• Food handler's certificate: Francine holds this certificate.
• Zoning plan: the location Francine intends to rent is designated for the hospitality industry.
• Open terrace permit: Francine has applied for one.

Organization

Own-account worker

A company's organizational structure depends on its size. Many starting entrepreneurs are an *own-account worker*; the division of tasks and authorities will not be an issue. In larger companies, these aspects must be organized unambiguously. The nature of activities also plays a part. An advertising agency with 'creative professionals' working independently has room for a less fixed structure than an industrial organization.

EXAMPLE 4.1 CONTINUED
Cappa's organization is very transparent. All essential tasks are performed by Francine. She will train her employee to be able to take over purchasing activities if necessary. An authorized accountant consultant will provide the necessary administrative support.

Finance

Investment plan

Financing plan

The first step is to provide an overview with all the required investments in resources (the *investment plan*) and the manner in which the starting entrepreneur wishes to finance these investments (the *financing plan*). There may sometimes be a financing gap, meaning that the initial capital provided by the starting entrepreneur and the available external credits are not sufficient to finance the planned investments.
Using the business plan for support, the entrepreneur will need to persuade financiers.
Investment plan and financing plan together are actually the forecast opening balance of the business.
The next step is to draw up the forecast income statement for the first year, with a prognosis of the profit for the coming years. The starting point should be the sales estimate, incorporated in the marketing part of the business plan.
Cash flow, forecast cash inflows and outflows are also included.
Lastly, the prognosis of the balance sheet at the end of the first year is drawn up. This is based, in part, on the data derived from the income statement and cash flow.

EXAMPLE 4.1 CONTINUED

Francine Monk has included the following reports in her business plan:

Investment plan (in Euros)

Rent paid in advance	50,000
Coffee machine	15,000
Tables	4,000
Other fixed assets	6,000
Coffee inventory	1,000
Cash and cash equivalents	2,000
Total investments	78,000

TEST QUESTION 4.1

Why did Francine include the entry 'Rent paid in advance' in her investment plan?

EXAMPLE 4.1 CONTINUED

Financing plan (in Euros)

Required capital		78,000
Available:		
Savings	30,000	
Loan supplier	10,000	
		40,000
Still to be financed		38,000

Opening balance sheet at start of first business year (in Euros)

Fixed assets		Equity	30,000
Coffee machine	15,000		
Furniture	4,000	Liabilities	
Other fixed assets	6,000	Loan supplier	10,000
Current assets		Financing gap	38,000
Coffee inventory	1,000		
Rent paid in advance	50,000		
Cash and cash equivalents	2,000		
	78,000		78,000

Francine assumes that there will be a bank prepared to close the financing gap with a ten-year loan.

4

In 2016, the number of establishments serving beverages and drinks (bars, coffee bars, discos and similar) in the Netherlands came to well over 11,600. Of these, around 650 were coffee bars. Traditional cafés are encountered increasingly less frequently whereas the number of coffee bars is on the rise. Consumers tend to keep opting for more surprising concepts which focus on the experience or a particular unique feature.

Purchasing drinks comes to an average (percentage of revenue) of 25–30%; staff comes at 30%, rent and depreciation at 15–20%, other costs at 5%, and financing costs at 5–10%. This leaves an average of 10–20% of revenue as profits for the owner-operator, which of course includes his compensation for any activities performed in the line of business.

EXAMPLE 4.1 CONTINUED

Based on key industrial figures, Francine has estimated her expected costs. She has arrived at the following forecast income statement and cash flow budget:

Forecast income statement for the first business year (in Euros)

Sales revenue		150,000
Cost of goods sold	25,000	
Rent	50,000	
Personnel costs	20,000	
Depreciation	5,000	
Other costs	15,000	
Interest on bank loan (still to be acquired)	2,500	
		117,500
Profit		32,500

Francine intends to retain a profit of €7,500; the remaining money is to be used for living expenses.

Cash flow for the first business year (in Euros)

Opening balance cash and cash equivalents		2,000
Cash inflows from sales:		150,000 +
Cash outflows:		
Purchasing of coffee etc.	25,000	
Rent following year	52,000	
Personnel	20,000	
Other expenses	15,000	
Repayment loan supplier	2,000	
Repayment bank loan (to be acquired)	3,800	
Interest on bank loan (to be acquired)	2,500	
Owner withdrawal by Francine	25,000	
		145,300 –
Estimated balance cash and cash equivalent at the end of the first year		6,700

4

TEST QUESTION 4.2
Why is the repayment of the loan included in the cash flow but not on the forecast income statement?

EXAMPLE 4.1 CONTINUED

Forecast balance sheet at the end of the first year (in Euros)

Fixed assets		*Equity*		37,500
Coffee machine	12,000			
Furniture	3,000	*Liabilities*		
Other fixed assets	5,000	Loan supplier		8,000
Current assets		Bank loan (to be acquired)		34,200
Coffee inventory	1,000			
Rent paid in advance	52,000			
Cash and cash equivalents	6,700			
	79,700			79,700

Reconciliation of equity increase and profit

Expected equity end of the first year	€ 37,500
Initial equity	€ 30,000
Forecast equity increase	€ 7,500
Forecast owner withdrawals	€ 25,000
Forecast profit first year	€ 32,500

Glossary

Angel investor	Former entrepreneur who invests in a company and supports an entrepreneur from a business perspective.
Business plan	Plan in which a starting entrepreneur describes the marketing, legal, organizational and financial aspects of his business.
Financing gap	The difference between the required investment capital and the acquired financing.
Financing plan	The manner in which a starting entrepreneur intends to finance his initial investments.
Government guaranteed loan	Credit provided by banks, with the government carrying the risk of having to compensate in case of default.
Investment plan	Overview of the required investments at the start of the business.
Marketing mix	Combination of factors that determines the attraction of a company to a customer. Consists of the four Ps: product, price, promotion, place (sometimes supplemented with personnel).
Own-account worker	Sole proprietor without personnel, an entrepreneur running his own business without other staff.
SME	Small and medium enterprises, with maximum of 250 employees.
Subordinated loan	Loan on which interest and principal sum repayments are only paid after all other obligations to creditors are settled.
Venture capital	Capital invested in a starting business, with high risk as a main characteristic.
Venture capital company	Company whose purpose is to provide venture capital to starting companies.

Multiple-choice questions

4.1   Which of the following statements is *not* correct?
a The majority of companies in Europe are small and medium enterprises.
b Most starting entrepreneurs start an industrial company.
c A business plan is, among other uses, to convince financiers to invest money in the company.
d A good accounting system is one of the factors that determines whether a company will survive.

4.2   Which of the following statements is *not* correct?
a Companies often start as a corporation.
b A starting entrepreneur can acquire extra capital by taking a 'silent partner'.
c A venture capital company provides venture capital to starting entrepreneurs.
d One of the problems of financing a starting company is that there is no track record to prove a successful operating business.

4.3   What is the type of loan in which interest and principal sum repayments are only paid after all other obligations towards creditors have been met?
a Risk-avoiding loan.
b Government guaranteed loan.
c Bank loan.
d Subordinated loan.

4.4   Which of the following factors is *not* one of the four Ps?
a Promotion.
b Place.
c Product.
d Planning.

4.5   An LLC is fiscally advantageous compared to a sole proprietorship if ...
a ... there is much profit, which remains in the company.
b ... there is little profit, which remains in the company.
c ... there is much profit, which is paid to the owner(s).
d ... there is little profit, which is paid to the owner(s).

4.6   Which financial overview includes both the investment plan and the financing plan?
a The forecast opening balance sheet.
b The forecast end of year balance sheet.
c The forecast income statement.
d The forecast cash flow.

4

4.7   For a starting company, an investment of €20,000 fixed assets and €40,000 in inventory are required. The supplier of the inventory has promised to grant two months' credit. The rent of the business premises (€30,000) must be paid at the start, in advance. The starting entrepreneur has €25,000 in savings to invest in his business.
Calculate the financing gap.
a €0
b €25,000
c €50,000
d €90,000

4.8   In the financial part of the business plan, prognoses on the income statement and cash flow are included. Which of the following entries is part of the forecast income statement but not of the cash flow?
a Depreciation.
b Paid interest.
c Salaries and wages.
d Repayment of a loan.

4.9   A starting company foresees important investments during its first year; it also expects the primary customer base to be government institutions who will pay only after three months.
Which statement is correct?
a Profit will probably be higher than cash flow.
b Profit will probably be lower than cash flow.
c Profit will probably be equal to cash flow.
d Nothing can be said about the relationship between profit and cash flow.

4.10   In the business plan of a sole proprietorship, which relationship is there between the profit on the forecast income statement and equity on the forecast balance sheet?
a Equity opening balance – equity closing balance + owner withdrawals – owner deposits = Profit.
b Equity opening balance – equity closing balance – owner withdrawals + owner deposits = Profit.
c Equity closing balance – equity opening balance + owner withdrawals – owner deposits = Profit.
d Equity closing balance – equity opening balance – owner withdrawals + owner deposits = Profit.

PART 2
Finance

DUTCH FINTECH INFOGRAPHIC 4.0

Payments

Personal Finance & Planning

Insurance

Risk & Compliance

Consumer Lending

Asset Management

DLT & Cryptocurrencies

Bank Platform Software

Administration

Identity & Security

Data & Analytics

Alternative Finance

HOLLAND FINTECH

5

Capital Budgeting

This chapter examines the issue of investments, usually referred to as capital budgeting, and discusses the considerations that play a role in drawing up and analyzing investment plans.

Paragraph 5.1 highlights the characteristics of investment projects and describes how to determine free cash flows based on an example. This is followed by a discussion of the assessment of investment projects. In paragraph 5.2, this is based on a well-known criterion: profitability – carried out based on a comparison of consecutive free cash flows in paragraph 5.3. Paragraph 5.4 discusses the criteria that explicitly deal with the time value of money: the net present value and the internal rate of return. The concept of time value of money is explained, based on several interest calculations. Lastly, paragraph 5.5 focusses on leasing as an alternative to purchasing fixed assets.

5.1 Capital Budgeting and Free Cash Flow

Capital budgeting

Capital budgeting is defined as analyzing alternative investment options and selecting the options to be implemented. Investing means tying up capital in the form of assets (capital goods). Investments are generally linked to expensive fixed assets, such as buildings and machines, but any form of tying-up of financial resources is considered an investment, even if it concerns current assets. Purchasing of raw material, creating accounts receivable and even maintaining cash: these are all investments. Capital budgeting, therefore, focuses on the size and composition of the assets in which the company's capital is invested. It is recognized on the debit side of the balance sheet.

If new investment plans are drawn up, their feasibility and profitability must be verified. At that point, financing the plans is not yet relevant. The first priority regarding the decision on whether investments should actually be made is to assess their possible contribution to the business objectives. Business continuity and profit objectives should be particular points of consideration. Only after the decision to execute the plans has been made should the method of financing be investigated.

The term capital budgeting clearly indicates what investing is about: the budgeting of capital assets.

Replacement investments

Expansion investments

There is a distinction between two types of investments, both of which should maintain or increase the vitality of the company. *Replacement investments* preserve production capacity, whereas *expansion investments* increase production capacity.

TEST QUESTION 5.1

Explain the connection between replacement and expansion investments on the one hand and business objectives on the other.

On average, financial service companies invest 15% of their annual turnover in fintech. Fintech is a combination of the words 'financial' and 'technology'. The term fintech is relatively new, but the underlying changes are happening ever since the introduction of computers in financial servicing. Nowadays, it represents the application of technology to accommodate new, modern ways for providing financial services, by newcomers, but also by established parties. Fintech covers a variety of novel concepts from payment apps, crowdfunding, transaction architecture construction, digital accountanting and risk management to digital mortgage lenders and bitcoin traders. Traditional banks and insurance companies are definitely starting to feel fintech startups breathing down their collective necks. Global investments in fintech startups amount to approximately $40 billion. For a large part, these investments drive new technological possibilities such as cloud computing, artificial intelligence, big data and blockchain technology, which are used for core financial service processes, such as payment and trade systems as well as digital access and identification.

According to Holland Fintech, fintech is nota about a specifiek business, but it represents the changes in the financial value chain, driven by technology, new rules and regulations, and changing customer behavior. It offers a healthy competitive playing field and lots of cooperation options, such as APIs. Holland Fintech focuses on the playing field, the knowledge and the required contacts to optimally use the available solutions. The infographic shows how involved fintech companies have become in nearly all aspects of Dutch financial service providing.

The biggest paradigm shift are the increased possibilities for smaller companies (like startups) to have a global impact using technology, as a competitor of established players, but most of all as a supplier or partner. Early 2017, 65% of Dutch financial institutions had struck partnerships with fintech companies. This causes an increase of players in the financial vlaue chain and a decrease in player size.

If a company wishes to invest, purchasing only one fixed asset will not suffice. An investment also results in an increase in other assets. Investing in a machine is useless if other resources (raw materials, lubricating oil, etc.) that are necessary to make the machine work are not purchased. Assessing whether a particular investment will be useful means also considering all additional investments.

An *investment project* is the sum of all related investments in fixed and current assets. This chapter therefore refers to 'investment projects' instead of 'investments in fixed assets'.   **Investment project**

If an investment project is to be executed, it results in a series of cash outflows necessary for the purchase and replacement of assets. A major number of cash outflows occurs at the start of a project because the fixed assets and supplies need to be purchased first.

An investment project only makes sense if there are sufficiently high cash inflows to cover cash outflows. Assessment of a project should be focused on the expectations for or *free cash flows*, during the project. *Free cash flow*   **Free cash flow** is the difference between cash inflows generated by sales and cash outflows related to purchasing and using resources in a particular period.

5

In other words, free cash flow is the amount freely available to the providers of equity and of interest-bearing liabilities. Freely available means that the company has met all of its obligations to other stakeholders (e.g. suppliers, employees) and that all investments required to implement company strategy have also been completed.

The theory differentiates between the concepts of *free cash flow* and *cash flow* to distinguish between the cash flow from an investment project (*free cash flow*) and general cash flow. A company's general cash flow over a certain period is comprised of the difference between all cash inslows and cash outflows over that period, including the cash inflows and cash outflows related to financing, such as receiving a principal loan sum, repaying a loan, or paying interests or dividends. As previously indicated, financing is not an aspect that is considered when assessing investment projects – nor, therefore, are the associated incomes or expenses. The free cash flows of an investment project therefore only deal with the incomes and expenses related to operational activities.

Assessment of potential investment projects is therefore focused on the size of the free cash flows instead of on profits (sales revenue minus costs). Contrary to cash flow, profit is not an unambiguous concept, as mentioned in chapter 3: 'cash is a fact, profit is an opinion'. Another reason is that, for determining profit, the moment of actually receiving or making a payment is of little or no relevance. Generally speaking, cash flows are preferably received as soon as possible. A certain amount of money *now* is worth more than the same amount of money in the future. Those who have the choice between receiving €1,000 now or in one year, choose to receive the money now, and can put it in a deposit account or invest it in shares. The revenue received during that year is an indication of the difference in value between two equal amounts received at different moments in time. This phenomenon is known as *time value of money*. The economic term for missing out on this revenue due to an amount being received later is *opportunity costs*.

Time value of money

Opportunity costs

Weighted average cost of capital

The time preference of a company is usually expressed by the *weighted average cost of capital*. This is the average cost against which a company can attract capital. The cost of capital comprises a compensation either to equity providers or to creditors. If the profitability (based on free cash flow measurements) of an investment is equal to the weighted average cost of capital, the investment generates the cash flow that exactly meets the requirements of the capital providers (interest and dividend).

To determine whether an investment project should be executed, a company should analyze free cash flows.
In business economics, it is more common to measure success by profits made during a period. *Period profit* is calculated by the difference between sales revenue and costs of that period.

Period profit

There is, however, a definite link between free cash flow and period profit. This is discussed in detail in chapter 3. The main difference between the profit and free cash flow over a period is in costs that do not result in cash outflows: *depreciation* on fixed assets.

Depreciation

Depreciation should therefore be added to profit after tax to calculate free cash flow.
A special situation occurs at the start and end of an investment project. At the start, certain assets required to execute the project will need to be purchased. Purchasing the fixed and current assets creates cash outflows while there

are no sales or costs. This results in a negative free cash flow for the amount invested in fixed and current assets. At the end of the project, assets purchased for the project will no longer be needed. The invested capital tied up in these assets becomes available once more – in particular, the residual value of the fixed assets. This is called *disinvestment*. Disinvestments create **Disinvestment** extra cash inflow during the last year of the investment project. Figure 5.1 provides a visual illustration of this process.

FIGURE 5.1 Free cash flows in an investment project

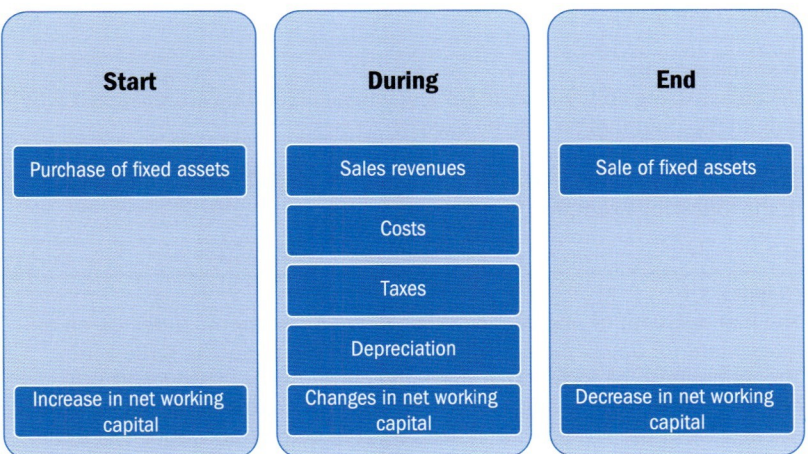

As previously mentioned, at the time of assessing an investment project, the financing method will not yet have been determined. It is therefore unknown what the interest and principal sum repayments will be, how much dividend will need to be paid, etc. When calculating free cash flows, these aspects have therefore not been considered.

When assessing an investment project, however, this information should be considered explicitly. Free cash flow must be at least sufficient to meet all obligations to capital providers. After all, when calculating free cash flow, no considerations were made with respect to the compensation that needs to be paid for making capital available. Free cash flows must be sufficient to pay dividend and interest payments to equity providers or creditors.

TEST QUESTION 5.2
Why are financing transactions and their consequences not considered in the free cash flow calculations?

The extent of the free cash flow over a certain period can be derived from the profit over that period. Generally speaking, the relationship between free cash flow and period profit can be described as follows:

Free cash flow = period profit after tax + depreciations – investments + disinvestments

5

Marginal tax rate

In this calculation the period profit after tax is, in fact, equal to the period profit before the deduction of interest and taxes (EBIT: earnings before interest and taxes) minus taxes. This is because interest payments are not a matter of consideration for these purposes. The amount of taxes is calculated based on the company's marginal tax rate: the tax rate paid on additional project profit in addition to profit incurred from existing activities. If, during one or more years of the execution of an investment project, a loss is incurred before the deduction of interest or taxes, a negative tax amount is assigned to that period. This is done because the loss incurred by the project has a negative effect on the company's overall profit, leading to a lower taxable amount of profit. The lower tax amount is then assigned to the project cash inflow.

TEST QUESTION 5.3
When assessing an investment project when calculating annual taxes, why should the marginal tax rate be used?

The calculation of the free cash flow using the period profit is demonstrated in the following example.

- -

EXAMPLE 5.1
The management of engineering office E-con Germany must decide on an investment for a new project. The duration of the project is three years. The amounts to be invested in fixed and current assets are €400,000 and €100,000 respectively: in total €500,000. Annual depreciation is set at 25% of the investment in fixed assets, being €100,000. The total residual value of all current and fixed assets in three years is estimated at €200,000. Turnover is expected to amount to €800,000 during the first year. In the second and third years, turnover is estimated at €1,000,000. Operating costs (excluding depreciation) will be 50% of sales turnover. Operating costs are paid in the year that they are made. E-con's marginal corporate tax rate is 25%.

Before the annual free cash flow can be determined, period profit after tax for each year are calculated first. This is done by calculating the sales revenue and subtracting all costs and corporate tax (all amounts are × €1,000).

	Year 1		Year 2		Year 3	
Sales revenue		800		1,000		1,000
Operating costs	400		500		500	
Depreciation	100		100		100	
Total cost		500		600		600
Profit before tax		300		400		400
Corporate tax		75		100		100
Profit after tax		225		300		300

With these results, annual free cash flows can be calculated.
For completeness, the original investment will also be mentioned (year 0).
Cash inflows are mentioned as positive and cash outflows as negative
amounts (all amounts are × €1,000).

	Year 0	Year 1	Year 2	Year 3
Profit after corporate tax		+225	+300	+300
+ Depreciation		+100	+100	+100
– Investments	–500			
+ Disinvestments				+200
Free cash flow	–500	+325	+400	+600

Since corporate tax payments reduce cash inflows, the free cash flows are
not calculated by taking the straightforward difference between cash inflows
and outflows but by first calculating profit before tax. This is necessary in
order to calculate the amount of corporate tax due.
Although annual depreciation is not a cash outflow, it influences the
amount of free cash flows due to corporate tax. If, for example, it were
possible to use higher depreciation during the first year, the resulting free
cash flow would be higher in the first year.

TEST QUESTION 5.4
Calculate the free cash flow in year 1 in example 5.1, assuming a
depreciation during the first year of €150,000.

The following paragraphs discuss capital budgeting assessment criteria,
the extent to which these criteria take into account the time value of money
and profitability, and the ratio which relates profits or free cash flows to the
invested amount.
If a company has the choice between various investment projects, it is
necessary to make an assessment of the different projects and also to
express a preference for one or more alternatives.
The assessment criteria have to be considered as the selection measures;
therefore, the suitability of the various criteria as selection measures is also
discussed.

5.2 Assessment Based on Period Profit

The first assessment criterion relates to the traditional assessment method
based on profitability. Generally, *profitability* is the relationship between   **Profitability**
profit (income) and the capital that generated this profit:

$$\text{Profitability} = \frac{\text{Profit}}{\text{Average invested capital}}$$

Every year of its duration, an investment project generates profit (or loss)
with the invested capital. Calculating annual profitability is easy, but the
figure will differ each year. In order to calculate the profitability of an entire

project, the average of each annual profit should be related to the average invested capital for the duration of the project.

The average annual profit is calculated by adding annual profits and dividing the outcome by the duration of the project in years.

The average invested capital is calculated by adding the initial invested capital to the residual value at the end of the project and dividing the sum by two.

Accounting rate of return

The calculated profitability of an investment project is known as ARR *accounting rate of return*.

The following example explains the calculation of the accounting rate of return to compare two projects. The same example is used in later paragraphs that discuss other assessment criteria.

EXAMPLE 5.2

A party and catering company intends to expand. It has the choice of two investment projects. Based on an analysis of both projects, the following data have been calculated (amounts in Euros):

	Project A	Project B
Duration in year(s)	3 years	4 years
Investment	500,000	300,000
Annual depreciation	100,000	50,000
Residual value	200,000	100,000
Free cash flow year 1	150,000	100,000
Free cash flow year 2	200,000	100,000
Free cash flow year 3	400,000	100,000
Free cash flow year 4		200,000

The free cash flow during the final year of the project includes the residual value of the investment. To simplify matters, it is assumed that all free cash flows are received at the end of the relevant year.
The calculation of the accounting rate of return is as follows:

Period profit is not given in the example, only annual free cash flow. In the previous paragraph, free cash flow was derived from period profit; the opposite is also possible. Period profit is calculated by deducting depreciation from free cash flow. In the final year, disinvestments (= residual values) also have to be deducted.

For project A, this results in:
Period profit after tax year 1 = €150,000 – €100,000 = €50,000
Period profit after tax year 2 = €200,000 – €100,000 = €100,000
Period profit after tax year 3 = €400,000 – €100,000 – €200,000 = €100,000

Total profit over the entire duration of the project is €50,000 + €100,000 + €100,000 = €250,000. Average annual profit is therefore:

$$\frac{€250,000}{3} = €83,333$$

For project B:
Period profit after tax year 1 = €100,000 – €50,000 = €50,000
Period profit after tax year 2 = €100,000 – €50,000 = €50,000
Period profit after tax year 3 = €100,000 – €50,000 = €50,000
Period profit after tax year 4 = €200,000 – €50,000 – €100,000 = €50,000.
Since the profit amounts to €50,000 every year, this means the average annual profit for project B must also be €50,000.

The average invested capital in project A is:

$$\frac{€500,000 + €200,000}{2} = €350,000$$

and for project B:

$$\frac{€300,000 + €100,000}{2} = €200,000$$

The accounting rate of return is calculated by dividing the average annual profit by the average invested capital.
Project A:

$$ARR_A = \frac{€83,333}{€350,000} = 0.238\,(23.8\%)$$

Project B:

$$ARR_B = \frac{€50,000}{€200,000} = 0.25\,(25\%)$$

If the decision were to be based on the accounting rate of return, project B scores higher than project A and would therefore be preferable.

Compared to free cash flow calculations, period profits only give a shift of amounts in time.
In a free cash flow calculation, the initial investment is assigned to the start of the project; in period profit calculation, the investment is distributed over the duration of the entire project through annual depreciation. If all free project cash flows including the investment are added up, the result equals the sum of all period profits. This is because the investment is exactly equal to the sum of all depreciation and the residual value. For project A in the example, the sum of all free cash flows is:

– €500,000 + €150,000 + €200,000 + €400,000 = €250,000

which is equal to the sum of all profits. Average annual project profit can therefore also be calculated by dividing the sum of all free cash flows, including the original investment, by the duration of the project. In an investment project, the accounting rate of return based on profits is therefore equal to the average profitability based on the free cash flows.

TEST QUESTION 5.5
Why is the sum of all free cash flows always equal to the sum of all period profits of an investment project?

A project is executable if the calculated accounting rate of return is sufficient (larger than the weighted average cost of capital).

Since the criterion of average accounting rate of return is based on the average period profit, the distribution of the profits (and thus the distribution of the free cash flows) over time is not relevant. This is an important objection against the use of the accounting rate of return as a criterion: it ignores time value of money. It is based on average profit. The distribution of free cash flows over the duration of the project is not used as a consideration. If the free cash flow sequence in project A were exactly the opposite (first year = €400,000, second year = €200,000, third year = €150,000), the average annual profit and therefore the accounting rate of return would still be the same.

5.3 Assessment Based on Free Cash Flows

The calculation of the accounting rate of return in the previous paragraph is based on profit and not on cash flows. Although accounting rate of return as a criterion measures profitability, it does not consider time value of money. This paragraph discusses how investment projects can be assessed based on free cash flows, taking into consideration the moment of cash inflow. This is done by determining the payback period of an investment project. The original cash outflows related to the investments must be compensated by annual free cash flows during the project, eventually resulting in a positive figure.
The difference between cash inflows and cash outflows progresses more or less as shown in figure 5.2.

FIGURE 5.2 Progression of cumulative free cash flow for an investment project

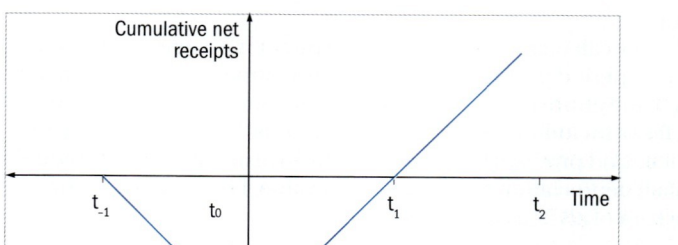

At the start phase of a project $(t_{-1} - t_0)$, cash outflows for the purchase of the required resources take place, resulting in a negative balance equal to the invested amount I_0 at time t_0. During the project $(t_0 - t_2)$, cash inflows supersede cash outflows. This is called 'earning back the original investment'. The period until the point in time when the difference between cash inflows and cash outflows $(t_0 - t_1)$ becomes nil is the 'payback period'. Upon completion of the project, there is a positive difference.

One important factor when considering an investment is sustainability. Lego bricks are made using oil. Lego has scheduled a one-step transition to sustainable bricks for 2030. This requires a €130 million investment. Lego sells over 70 billion bricks per year, meaning a turnover of €1.9 billion. Lego's Chinese competitor, Banbao, is scheduled to market bio-based bricks in 2017. Banbao produces its bricks for the European market at Banbao Europe, in Ter Aar, the Netherlands. 10 million bricks are produced in Ter Aar every year; only a small portion of the total production by Banbao's Chinese facilities, which amounts to 2.5 billion bricks annually. Banbao's change to bio-based bricks took an investment of €2.5 million, a fraction of Lego's investment.

Payback period

The *payback period* is the period between the point in time of the original investment and the point in time when this amount is fully returned to the company by way of the free cash flows.

5

EXAMPLE 5.2 CONTINUED

For project A, the investment is €500,000. After one year, a free cash flow of €150,000 is received. This is less than the original investment.
After two years, the free cash flow of the first year plus the free cash flow of the second year is received: €150,000 + €200,000 = €350,000 cash inflow.
After two years, the investment has not yet been paid back. After three years, when the free cash flow of the third year is also received, the sum of the free cash flows (€150,000 + €200,000 + €400,000 = €750,000) is higher than the investment. Therefore, the payback period of project A is three years.
The payback period of project B is also three years. After three years, the sum of the free cash flows (€100,000 + €100,000 + €100,000 = €300,000) is exactly equal to the investment.

The payback periods of both projects are equal, so it is not possible to base a decision between the two projects on this criterion: the payback period cannot provide an answer to the question of whether either or both of these projects are suitable investments.
After all, nothing is said about the profitability of a project. Free cash flows after the payback period are completely ignored.

In the previous calculation, it was assumed that free cash flows were received at the end of each year. If the calculation assumes that free cash flows are instead received gradually throughout the year, the payback period of project A would be less than three years. At the end of year 3, €750,000 would be received, which would still be more than the investment of €500,000. The payback period for project B would still be three years, because at the end of the third year the sum of all free cash flows would be exactly the same as the invested amount. Under these circumstances, the payback period of project A would be shorter than that of project B, meaning project A would be preferable.

TEST QUESTION 5.6
Calculate the payback period of project A, assuming that free cash flows are gradually received throughout the year.

The payback period method only takes the time value of money into limited consideration as the focus is on earning back the investment as soon as possible. The criterion of the payback period is mainly based on liquidity rather than profitability.
It should be clear that the payback period should not be valued too highly in terms of its usefulness as an assessment criterion. The advantage of this method is in its simplicity.

5.4 Assessment Based on Free Cash Flows, Considering Time Value of Money

One of the characteristics of investment projects is their extended duration. This aspect raises a particular problem. The moment at which required assets are purchased and that at which cash inflows deriving from sales manufactured with those assets are received, can be far apart. This makes it difficult to compare cash inflows and cash outflows.

Financial arithmetic

To compare the different moments in time with one another, some simple basic principles derived from *financial arithmetic (time value of money calculations)* can be used. These principles are concerned with interest calculations.

Financial arithmetic

There is a distinction between simple and compound interest. In *simple interest*, the interest is always calculated on the original amount. There is no interest calculated on the interest itself.

Simple interest

EXAMPLE 5.3
An amount of €10,000 is borrowed at 6% simple interest per year for two years. After two years, the following amount has to be paid:
€10,000 + 2 × 6% of €10,000 = €10,000 + 2 × €600 = €11,200.
Total interest paid is therefore €1,200.

Under *compound interest*, the interest is calculated on the original amount as well as on the interest already due, which is a continuously increasing amount. The interest also bears interest.

Compound interest

EXAMPLE 5.4
An amount of €10,000 is borrowed at 6% compound interest per year for two years. After one year, the amount receivable is:
€10,000 + 6% of €10,000 = €10,600 and after two years €10,600 + 6% of €10,600 = €11,236.
The total interest is €1,236. This is €36 more than it would have been under simple interest. The €36 is the interest on interest, 6% of the €600 which was due after one year.

TEST QUESTION 5.7
Which type of interest does a bank pay on a savings account: simple or compound interest?

The amount of €11,236 in example 5.4 is called the *future value* of the starting capital of €10,000 after two years.
If a number of (equal) amounts is invested over a period of time, their future value can also be calculated.

Future value

EXAMPLE 5.5

Someone deposits €1,000 into a savings account at the beginning of the year for four years, and receives 2% compound interest per year.

These amounts can be shown in a timeline:

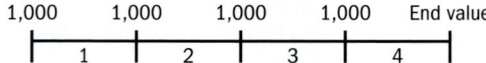

The future value is equal to the sum of the future values of the separate amounts:

$$
\begin{aligned}
\text{Future value} &= €1{,}000 \times 1.02^4 + €1{,}000 \times 1.02^3 + \\
&\quad €1{,}000 \times 1.02^2 + €1{,}000 \times 1.02 \\
&= €1{,}000 \times (1.02^4 + 1.02^3 + 1.02^2 + 1.02) \\
&= €1{,}000 \times 4.20404 \\
&= €4{,}204.04
\end{aligned}
$$

Present value

The opposite of the future value is the *present value*. The present value is the current value of amounts due in the future.

EXAMPLE 5.6

Someone deposits money into a savings account with the goal of receiving a capital of €50,000 in five years. The bank pays 2% compound interest per year. The sum that needs to be paid now, i.e. present value of €50,000, amounts to:

$$
\frac{€50{,}000}{1.02^5} = €45{,}286.54
$$

The interest rate used to calculate a present value is called the discount rate. Here, discount is used to signify the opposite of compound.
The present value of a series of payments is, of course, equal to the sum of the present values of the separate amounts.

EXAMPLE 5.7

Someone is entitled to receive an annual payment from 2018 up to (and including) 2021, at the end of each year. The parties involved agree to replace annual payment by a one-off payment on 1 January 2018, based on the present value of the amounts at a compound interest rate of 8% per year.

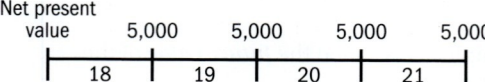

The lump sum payment is:

$$= \frac{€5,000}{1.08} + \frac{€5,000}{1.08^2} + \frac{€5,000}{1.08^3} + \frac{€5,000}{1.08^4}$$

$$= €5,000 \times \left(\frac{1}{1.08} + \frac{1}{1.08^2} + \frac{1}{1.08^3} + \frac{1}{1.08^4} \right)$$

$$= €5,000 \times 3.312127 = €16,560.64$$

Assessment criteria that take time value of money into consideration can be found among the discounted cash flow methods. These methods use the compound interest calculations shown previously. Two methods are discussed: the net present value method and the internal rate of return method.

Net present value method
The *net present value method* calculates the net present value of expected free cash flows at the start of the project, including the original investment, using the weighted average cost of capital as discount rate.

Net present value method

EXAMPLE 5.2 CONTINUED
Assuming a weighted average cost of capital of 8%, the net present value of these projects can be calculated (amounts × €1,000):

$$\text{NPV}_A = -500 + \frac{150}{1.08} + \frac{200}{1.08^2} + \frac{400}{1.08^3} = 127.890 \ (€127,890)$$

$$\text{NPV}_B = -300 + \frac{100}{1.08} + \frac{100}{1.08^2} + \frac{100}{1.08^3} + \frac{200}{1.08^4} = 104.716 \ (€104,716)$$

In principle, a project is executable if its net present value is positive because then the profitability is higher than the weighted average cost of capital. This means that the project's free cash flows are large enough to accommodate the payments (in the forms of distribution of profit and interest) desired by the capital providers.
The net present value method can also be used as a project selection criterion. The net present value of project A is higher than that of project B. This makes project A preferable.

Internal rate of return
The *internal rate of return method* measures the profitability of an investment project by determining the discount rate at which the present value of the expected free cash flows is equal to the investment.

Internal rate of return method

EXAMPLE 5.2 CONTINUED

The internal rate of return for project A in the example is determined either as: (amounts × €1,000)

$$\frac{150}{(1 + i)} + \frac{200}{(1 + i)^2} + \frac{400}{(1 + i)^3} = 500$$

or as

$$\frac{150}{(1 + i)} + \frac{200}{(1 + i)^2} + \frac{400}{(1 + i)^3} - 500 = 0$$

The correct value for i can be determined by *trial and error*.
For example, if the value on the left side is calculated for i = 0.20:

$$\frac{150}{1.20} + \frac{200}{1.20^2} + \frac{400}{1.20^3} - 500 = -4.630$$

Since the result is a negative, the present value of the three free cash flows in years 1 through 3 is smaller than the investment. The discount rate is too great. By using a lower value for i, the present value of the free cash flows increases.

Figure 5.3 displays the net present value of the free cash flows (including the investment amount) in the equation for i values from 0 to 0.25.

FIGURE 5.3 Net present value as a function of discount rate

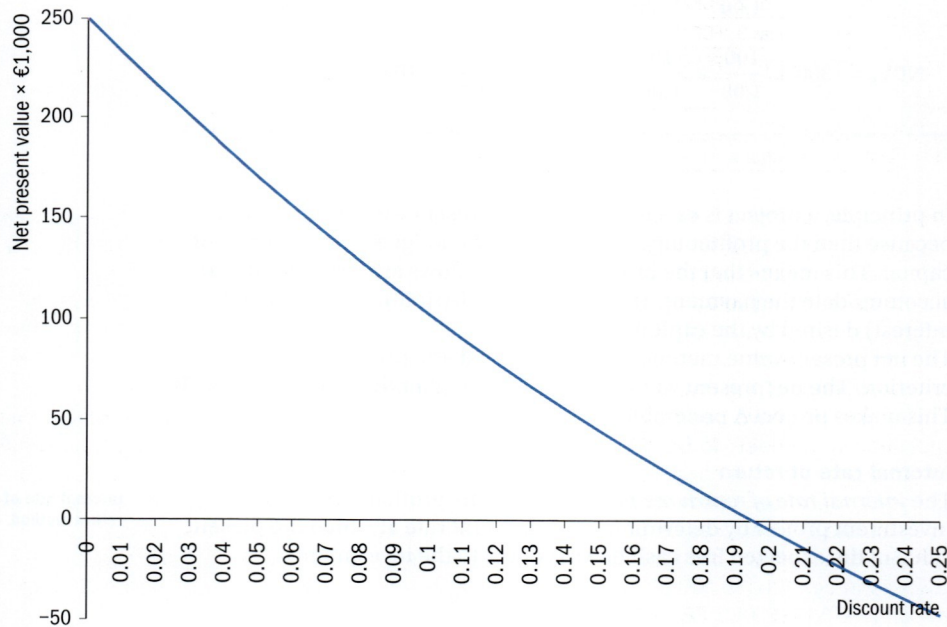

The graph demonstrates that the value of i_A is approximately 0.195 for a net present value of 0.

The internal rate of return for project B can be calculated similarly:

$$\frac{100}{(1 + i)} + \frac{100}{(1 + i)^2} + \frac{100}{(1 + i)^3} + \frac{200}{(1 + i)^4} - 300 = 0$$

The value for $i_B = 0.211$.

- -

Generally speaking, a project is executable if its internal rate of return is higher than the company's average weighted cost of capital.

The internal rate of return can also be used as a selection criterion to decide between projects. The internal rate of return of project B is higher than that of project A; this makes project B more attractive than project A.

TEST QUESTION 5.8
Verify the internal rate of return of both projects via calculation.

- -

	A	B	C	D	E
1			**Project A**		**Project B**
2	Duration in year(s)		3 years		4 years
3	Discount rate		8%		8%
4	Investment (I_0)		– 500,000		–300,000
5	Free cash flow year 1 (FCF1)		150,000		100,000
6	Free cash flow year 2 (FCF2)		200,000		100,000
7	Free cash flow year 3 (FCF3)		400,000		100,000
8	Free cash flow year 4 (FCF4)				200,000
9					
10	Net present value		127,890		104,716
11	Internal rate of return		19.5%		21.1%

With the aid of modern spreadsheet programs, performing financial calculations has become much simpler. There is built-in functionality for calculating the net present value and the internal rate of return for an investment project.

The basic data of the investment projects in example 5.2 have been copied into the indicated worksheet. To be able to use built-in functions, the free cash flows have to be in the correct order by row or column.

To calculate the net present value, Microsoft Excel uses the NPV function. The formula in cell C10 is NPV(C3;C5:C7)+C4, in cell E10 NPV(E3;E5:E8)+E4. The internal rate of return is calculated in Excel using the IRR(values, guess) function. The formula in cell C11 is IRR(C4:C7;0.2), in cell E11 it is IRR(E4:E8;0.2).

Using a spreadsheet program saves a great deal of time and effort. This is particularly useful when performing a sensitivity analysis based on several scenarios (as discussed below).

Although both the internal rate of return method and net present value method take the concepts of profitability and time value of money into consideration, it should be clear that the usefulness of these methods as a selection criterion is limited. The conclusions derived from applying these methods to example 5.2 contradict each other.

With respect to the usefulness of these methods as a selection criterion, the following should be noted:

The net present value method does not measure the profitability of a project. There is no relationship to the amount of the investment.

Although project A has the highest net present value, it also requires a much higher investment. Furthermore, the net present value method does not consider the difference in duration between alternative investment projects.

This means that projects with a longer duration have an advantage.

When applying the internal rate of return method, the free cash flows received before the end of the project duration are assumed to be intended to be invested elsewhere for the rest of the duration, making a return that equals the internal rate of return of the project. This is doubtful, particularly for projects with a high internal rate of return such as that in example 5.2.

The characteristics of the assessment criteria discussed are summarized in table 5.1.

TABLE 5.1 Characteristics of the assessment criteria

	Accounting rate of return	Payback period	Net present value	Internal rate of return
Measures profitability	Yes	No	No	Yes
Takes time value of money in consideration	No	Limited	Yes	Yes
Suitable for assessment of project acceptance	Yes, at ARR > WACC*	No	Yes, at NPV > 0	Yes, at IRR > WACC*
Suitable for selection between alternative projects	Yes	Limited, based on liquidity	Yes	Yes

* WACC: Weighted Cost of Capital

The influence of uncertainty

A typical feature of the assessment of investment projects is that it involves future values. Since the values are not known in advance, the use of estimates is a given. The results of these estimates should always be treated with necessary caution. In practice, sales may be much lower than forecast or costs may be much higher. This results in lower free cash flows and possibly lower values for the payback period, accounting rate of return, net present value and internal rate of return.

A method for dealing with this uncertainty about future values is working with several scenarios. The first estimate of the sales could be considered the expected value. Apart from the expected scenario, a pessimistic or optimistic scenario could also be drawn up, with sales and thus profits and free cash flows amounting to lower or higher figures.

The analysis of the effect of a change in sales on profit and free cash flows is known as a *sensitivity analysis*.

EXAMPLE 5.2 CONTINUED
In a pessimistic scenario, future annual free cash flows of project A and B
are 20% lower than expected. Annual cash flows are:

	Project A	**Project B**
Investment	500,000	300,000
Free cash flow year 1	120,000	80,000
Free cash flow year 2	160,000	80,000
Free cash flow year 3	320,000	80,000
Free cash flow year 4		160,000

At a weighted average cost of capital of 8%, the net present value of the
projects is (amounts × €1,000):

$$\text{NPV}_A = -500 + \frac{120}{1.08} + \frac{160}{1.08^2} + \frac{320}{1.08^3} = 2.312 \ (\text{€2,312})$$

$$\text{NPV}_B = -300 + \frac{80}{1.08} + \frac{80}{1.08^2} + \frac{80}{1.08^3} + \frac{160}{1.08^4} = 23.773 \ (\text{€23,773})$$

With lower free cash flows, the net present value of project A lowers faster
than that of project B. A careful decision-maker would therefore prefer
project B, based on these calculations.

Another method of considering uncertainty when assessing an investment
project, is increasing the discount rate with a risk premium. This would   **Risk premium**
mean that, when calculating the net present value, free cash flows would be
calculated at a higher discount rate that would reduce the net present value.

5.5 Leasing

The purchasing of fixed assets for execution of investment projects nearly
always involves large capital, which has to be invested for a long period of
time.
Such a large sum of money is not always available, nor will companies in a
number of situations want to borrow such sums or even have the possibility
of doing so. In this event, hiring fixed assets can be an alternative to buying.
This is called *leasing* of fixed assets.   **Leasing**
Two types of leases exist: financial lease and operational lease.

A *financial lease* is a long-term rental agreement that cannot be canceled.   **Financial lease**
Often a purchasing option is included in the contract, allowing the lessee to
buy the fixed asset, for example, by providing an extra payment.
In a financial lease, the risk is entirely for the lessee (the user of the asset).
They have 'economic ownership' and carry the same risks as if they had
bought the asset, such as technical and economic obsolescence. The leased
asset is on the debit side of the balance sheet. The payment obligations of
the lease contract are on the credit side of the balance sheet.

Operational lease

An *operational lease* is a rental agreement that can be canceled at short notice, with maintenance costs for the lessor (the leasing agency). Operational leasing is interesting for fixed assets that are sensitive to economic obsolescence.
In operational leasing, the risk is with the leasing company. The object is therefore not mentioned on the balance sheet of the lessee.

An advantage of operational lease when compared to purchasing fixed assets financed by means of a loan is that it does not affect the company's financial structure, and so the possibilities for obtaining new loans remain intact. A company's capacity to loan is maintained by leasing.
However, it should be noted that leasing leads to regular (monthly) obligations. Potential creditors do take these payment obligations into consideration. It should also be noted that, although cash outflows for the investment can be avoided by leasing, investements in additional (current) asssets still require additional funding.

Table 5.2 lists the differences between financial and operational lease.

TABLE 5.2 Financial and operational lease

	Financial lease	Operational lease
Nature of the agreement	Financing	Rent
Duration	Equal to economic life	Shorter than economic life
Economic property	Lessee	Lessor
Legal property	Lessor	Lessor
Activate on the balance sheet	Lessee	Lessor

A lease can be described as an investment project, just like the purchase of fixed assets.

EXAMPLE 5.8
A company wishes to execute a new investment project in which the required fixed assets are not purchased but acquired through an operational lease. The duration of the project is three years. Annual lease payments are €200,000. The investments in current assets are €100,000. This amount will become available again at the end of the project.

Sales revenue is for the first year are expected to amount to €800,000. In the second and third year, sales revenue is expected to amount to €1 million. The operating costs will be 50% of sales revenue. Marginal corporate tax rate is 25%. The weighted average cost of capital for the company is 8%.

All cash inflows and cash outflows are assumed to take place at the end of the relevant year. The investment in current assets is made at the end of the previous year.

First, the annual profit after tax for this investment project is calculated (all amounts are in × €1,000).

	Year 1		Year 2		Year 3	
Sales revenue		800		1,000		1,000
Operating costs	400		500		500	
Lease payments	200		200		200	
Total cost		600		700		700
Profit before tax		200		300		300
Corporate tax		50		75		75
Profit after tax		150		225		225

Next, the annual free cash flows are calculated (in × €1,000).

	Year 0	Year 1	Year 2	Year 3
Profit after tax		150	225	225
Depreciation		0	0	0
Investments	−100			
Disinvestments				100
Free cash flow	−100	150	225	325

The payback period of this project is one year. The net present value is:

$$-100 + \frac{150}{1.08} + \frac{225}{1.08^2} + \frac{325}{1.08^3} = 489.786 \,(\text{€}489{,}786)$$

TEST QUESTION 5.9
Calculate the accounting rate of return for the investment project in example 5.8 and give an explanation for the result.

Glossary

5

Average book rate of return	The ratio between the average annual profit and the average invested capital in a project.
Compound interest	Interest is calculated on the original amount as well as on the interest.
Expansion investments	Investments that aim to increase the production capacity.
Financial lease	Long-term rental agreement that cannot be canceled.
Free cash flow	The difference between gross cash inflows from sales and cash outflows related to the purchase and use of resources.
Future value	The value of capital at a future moment.
Internal rate of return	The discount rate at which the present value of the expected free cash flows is equal to the investment.
Investment project	The total present investment in related fixed and current assets.
Lease	Rental agreement for fixed assets.
Net present value	The total value of all free cash flows (including the original investment).
Operational lease	Rental agreement in which the lessor is responsible for maintenance etc.
Payback period	The period from the moment of the original investment until the moment the initial investment is recovered through the free cash inflows of the project.
Present value	The current value of capital available in the future.
Replacement investments	Investments that aim to preserve the production capacity.
Simple interest	Interest is calculated on the original amount.

Time value of money	Concept stating that money available at the present is worth more than the same amount in the future.
To invest	To tie-up capital in assets.
Weighted average cost of capital	The average cost at which a company can attract capital.

5

Multiple-choice questions

5.1 What are the characteristics of an investment project?
 a The total investment made in the project.
 b The fixed and current assets in which are invested.
 c The cash inflows and cash outflows during the project.
 d The duration of the payback period.

5.2 The following data are collected for one of the years in which an investment project is executed:
 Sales revenue €500,000.
 Operating costs (excluding depreciation) €300,000.
 Depreciation €100,000.
 During this year, no investments or disinvestments in current or fixed assets will be made. The marginal corporate tax rate is 25%.
 Calculate this year's free cash flow.
 a €100,000
 b €175,000
 c €180,000
 d €200,000

5.3 A project requires an investment of €5 million at the beginning of the first year and another €2.5 million at the beginning of the second year.
 The residual value at the end of the five-year project is €1 million.
 From the first to the fifth year, the free cash flows (excluding investments and disinvestments) amount to the following (in sequence): €2.5 million, €2.5 million, €1.5 million, €1.5 million and €0.5 million.
 Calculate the payback period for this project.
 a Two years.
 b Three years.
 c Four years.
 d Five years.

5.4 A company has a choice of project A or B. The free cash flows of both are received and paid at the end of the year.
 These free cash flows are as follows:

	t_0	t_1	t_2	t_3
A	−1,000	800	300	100
B	−500	400	100	0

The standard for payback periods is set at two years. Which project will be selected based on the payback period?

a Project A.
b Project B.
c Neither, because neither of the projects is attractive.
d Neither, an additional criterion is required.

5.5 A capital of €25,000 is deposited in a savings account for a period of four years at 6% compound interest per year.
What is the future value after four years?

a €31,632.98
b €31,561.92
c €31,000
d €29,246.46

5.6 Which deposited amount in a savings account is required to receive €15,000 in four years, if the compound interest rate is 5%?

a €12,328.91
b €12,340.54
c €12,500
d €12,957.56

5.7 The net present value of an investment project is equal to zero. What does this mean for the internal rate of return of the project?

a The internal rate of return is higher than the weighted average cost of capital.
b The internal rate of return is equal to the weighted average cost of capital.
c The internal rate of return is lower than the weighted average cost of capital.
d The internal rate of return cannot be calculated.

Questions 5.8 through 5.10 concern the following investment project, for which the following annual free cash flows are given:

Year 0 –120
Year 1 40
Year 2 40
Year 3 40
Year 4 40

All amounts are paid or received at the end of the year.
The investments have no residual value at the end of the project.
The weighted average cost of capital is 7.5% per year.

5.8 What is the accounting rate of return of this project?

a 8.33%
b 16.67%
c 33.33%
d 66.67%

5.9 What is the internal rate of return of this project?

a 10.2%
b 11.4%
c 12.6%
d 13.8%

5.10   What is the net present value of this project?
   a 11.43
   b 13.97
   c 16.25
   d 19.71

5.11   Company management is particularly focused on the liquidity of the
   company when selecting an investment project. Which selection criterion
   will they use to make a choice between the different projects?
   a Payback period.
   b Accounting rate of return.
   c Net present value.
   d Internal rate of return.

5.12   If, during the assessment of an investment project, one needs to take into
   account the uncertainty regarding sales and costs of the project, which of
   the following approaches is not suitable?
   a Using the payback period as a selection criterion, because the investment is
   paid back as soon as possible.
   b Increasing the weighted average cost of capital with a risk premium when
   calculating the net present value.
   c Increasing the required internal rate of return of a project with a risk
   premium.
   d Performing a sensitivity analysis of the net present value of the project for
   the deviations in sales and costs based on several scenarios.

5.13   Which of the following selection criteria are most suited to make a choice
   between different investment projects?
   a The payback period.
   b The net present value.
   c The internal rate of return.
   d Neither of the above criteria.

5.14   Which of the following statements is *not* correct?
   a In financial leasing, the economic property is with the lessee.
   b In operational leasing, the legal property is with the lessor.
   c In financial leasing, the lessee will mention the leasing obligations on the
   balance sheet.
   d The duration of an operational lease contract is equal to the economic life of
   the leased asset.

5.15   A company wishes to execute a project but still has to make a choice
   between leasing or purchasing the fixed assets. Which effect will leasing
   have?
   a The payback period of the project will be shorter.
   b The accounting rate of return will be lower.
   c The net present value will be lower.
   d The internal rate of return will be lower.

6

Working Capital Management

6.1	**The Cash Flow Cycle**
6.2	**Inventory Management**
6.3	**Credit Management**
6.4	**Cash Management**

The focus of chapter 5 was on investments in fixed assets.
It discussed the inability of fixed assets to produce anything on their own.
Additional investments in current assets are necessary in order to be able
to work with fixed assets. Hence the alternative name for current assets:
working capital.
Paragraph 6.1 discusses how the execution of the production and sales
process inevitably results in investments in working capital, and hence
creates capital requirements. Although investments in current assets are
necessary, it is, of course, also important for a company to control the need
for financial resources to finance these assets, thus realising an efficient use
of the current assets.
In paragraphs 6.2, 6.3 and 6.4, all aspects related to inventory, accounts
receivable and cash management are discussed.

6

6.1 The Cash Flow Cycle

Working capital

The previous chapter argued that investments in current assets are necessary in order to be able to work with fixed assets. Current assets are therefore also called *working capital*. Investments in current assets also create a requirement for financial resources. It is therefore essential to limit these investments. Before getting into the individual components of working capital in the following paragraphs, it is relevant to know more about how the amount of working capital needed and the resulting financing requirements are influenced by the execution of the production and sales process. This is shown with the aid of the cash flow cycle.

Cash flow cycle

The *cash flow cycle* is the transformation process that is related to the production and sales process from the moment of purchasing raw materials up to the moment of the delivery of an end product to the customer, as shown in figure 6.1.

FIGURE 6.1 The cash flow cycle for a production company

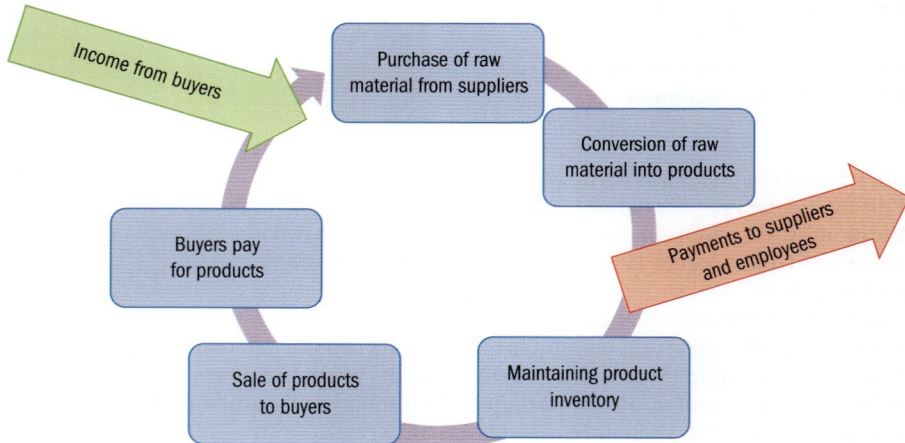

The previous description is based on a company that is a production organization. The cash flow cycle also applies to the trade business and, to a lesser extent, to the service business, where the process consists of fewer steps. In a trade company, the purchased products are not processed but sold in the same condition.

Not every investment in current assets results in an explicit financing requirement. The purchase of goods on credit, for example, results in an increase of inventory and, at the same time, an equal increase of the balance sheet entry 'Creditors'. The financing is, as it were, automatic. Only when the payment period has expired will the purchased goods have to be paid for and separate financing, for example, through a bank loan, be required. The credit can be repaid when the goods are sold to a customer, after they pay.

EXAMPLE 6.1

Wholesale business Eureco buys 100 products for a total amount of €10,000. Eureco uses the full net term of 30 days granted by the supplier. The products are in storage for 40 days and then sold for a total amount of €15,000. The customer pays the bill after 50 days.

The transactions that are part of this process are explained step by step, with the changes in the relevant balance sheet items indicated in each step.

The purchased goods are recognized on the balance sheet for the amount of €10,000. At the same time, the trade credit is recognized at the credit side of the balance sheet as 'Accounts payable' by the same amount.

Balance sheet (in Euros)

Inventory	+10,000	Accounts payable	+10,000

After 30 days, the creditor is paid. The balance sheet entry 'Accounts payable' is reduced by €10,000 and the line of credit is increased by the same amount.

Balance sheet (in Euros)

		Accounts payable	–10,000
		Bank credit	+10,000

The sales of the goods lead to changes on the balance sheet but not to changes in the required line of credit. The balance sheet entry 'Inventory' of €10,000 is replaced by the entry 'Accounts receivable' of €15,000 on the debit side. The difference is recognized as gross profit on the credit side of the balance sheet.

Balance sheet (in Euros)

Inventory	–10,000	Gross profit	+5,000
Accounts receivable	+15,000		

The line of credit is paid when the payment from the customer is received, 90 days after the start of the process.

Balance sheet (in Euros)

Inventory	–15,000	Gross profit	–10,000
Accounts receivable	+5,000		

The wholesale business therefore needs an additional credit of €10,000 from the bank for 60 days.

This process is shown schematically in figure 6.2.

FIGURE 6.2 The cash flow cycle

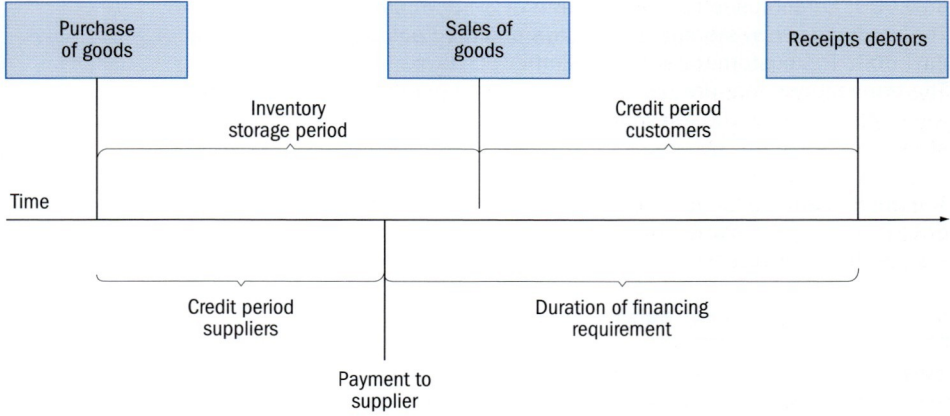

Figure 6.2 shows how long additional funding is needed to finance the working capital. This additional funding leads to extra costs. The objective of working capital management should therefore be to reduce the investment in working capital. This should not negatively affect the progress of the production and sales process, for example, by not being able to sell due to insufficient inventory.

EXAMPLE 6.1 CONTINUED

Wholesale business Eureco purchases 100 products at the beginning of each month. As a result, the process described in example 6.1 is repeated each month. After 30 days, every purchase of 100 products results in an increased credit from the bank for a period of 60 days (two months). After repayment of the credit line using the proceeds from the sales, a new credit is required to finance the next purchase. A continuous line of credit is therefore needed to finance the inventory build-up of two consecutive purchases.

Throughout the year, the average bank credit will be 2 × €10,000 = €20,000.

TEST QUESTION 6.1

How much is the average bank credit in example 6.1 if the actual credit period for accounts receivable is reduced by 15 days?

6.2 Inventory Management

The presence of inventory not only results in an investment but also additional costs. This applies to both the inventory of raw materials, semi-finished products, end products in a production company and the inventory of goods in a trade business. Keeping an inventory creates

Carrying costs *carrying costs*, such as warehouse costs, financing costs and, in some cases, also the costs of decay and aging. Something has to balance these costs, otherwise the costs associated with having an inventory could best be prevented by not having any inventory.

The most important advantage is the *decoupling function* with respect to the different phases in the production process. By maintaining intermediate inventory for the supply, transit and dispatch of goods, stagnation in the production chain can be avoided. Additional advantages are the economies of scale resulting from buying large quantities of raw materials or products, and the saving on transport costs. A cost-benefit analysis can determine whether the advantages of additional supplies outweigh the costs. Inventories can also be the result of purchasing in large quantities, speculating on future price increases.

Decoupling function

6

Both creating and maintaining an inventory results in costs, for example, for a trade company. A trade business buys products, stores them and sells them again. The purchase order generates *ordering costs*. Buyers will have to search the market, request bids, fill out forms and inspect delivered supplies. The ordering costs are generated for every new order and are barely influenced by the size of the order. It is therefore more advantageous to place as few orders as possible. Fewer orders results in larger orders, consecutively leading to build-up of inventory. The greater the inventory, the higher the carrying costs. Carrying costs and ordering costs develop in opposite directions, resulting in optimization issues. The order size with the lowest total ordering and carrying costs is considered to be the *economic order quantity*.

Inventory costs

Ordering costs

Carrying costs

Economic order quantity

- -

EXAMPLE 6.2

Wholesaler Borsumij imports sports shoes and supplies to sports stores. The demand for a particular type of shoe is 75,000 sets (a set is a box with a pair of shoes) per year. The sales are spread evenly throughout the year. The carrying costs are €3 per pair per year. Every purchase order involves an amount of €500 in ordering costs.
The total of the carrying and ordering costs is determined for different order sizes.

One possibility would be to split the annual order amount of 75,000 sets into four orders of 18,750 sets and place the orders at the beginning of each quarter.
Considering regular sales, the inventory reduces gradually from 18,750 at the beginning of each quarter to 0 at the end. The average inventory is therefore 18,750/2 = 9,375 sets. This is shown visually in figure 6.3.

Carrying costs are now 9,375 × €3 = €28,125 per year.
Ordering costs are 4 × €500 = €2,000.
Total inventory costs in this situation will be €28,125 + €2,000 = €30,125.

The annual sales volume could also be purchased in smaller, more frequent orders every week, every two weeks or every month. The related costs are shown in the following table.

FIGURE 6.3 Inventory cycle and average inventory

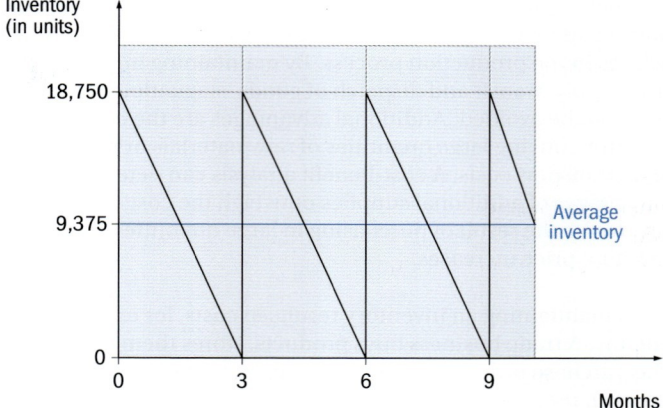

	One order every			
	Week	**Fortnight**	**Month**	**Quarter**
Number of orders	50	25	12	4
Order quantity	1,500	3,000	6,250	18,750
Average inventory	750	1,500	3,125	9,375
Carrying costs per year	€2,250	€4,500	€9,375	€28,125
Ordering costs per year	€25,000	€12,500	€6,000	€2,000
Inventory costs per year	€27,250	€17,000	€15,375	€30,125

The overview shows the lowest inventory costs at an order quantity of 6,250 sets. However, it is not certain that this is the optimal order size since only a few possibilities were calculated. The cost development for each order size is given in figure 6.4.

FIGURE 6.4 Inventory costs as a function of order quantity

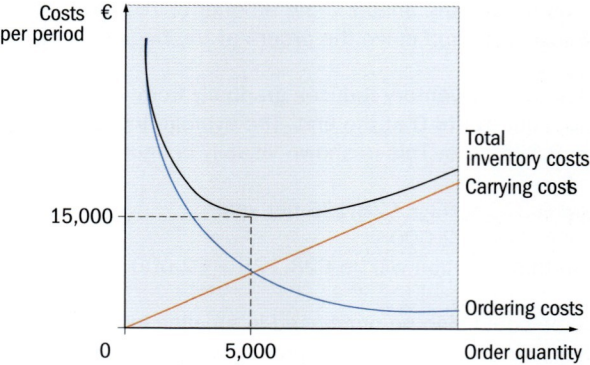

In figure 6.4, the total annual inventory costs are at their lowest at an order quantity of 5,000 sets. This, therefore, is the optimal order size.

We can calculate economic order quantity directly with a formula, better
known as the Wilson Formula:

Wilson Formula

$$Q^* = \sqrt{\frac{2 \times D \times F}{c}}$$

where
Q* = Optimal order quantity
D = Total demand per period
F = Fixed ordering costs per order
c = Carrying costs per unit per period

6

EXAMPLE 6.2 CONTINUED
The economic order quantity calculated by using the Wilson Formula:

$$Q^* = \sqrt{\frac{2 \times 75{,}000 \times 500}{3}} = \sqrt{25\,\text{million}} = 5{,}000$$

The previous example was only concerned with the order quantity, not with
the moment at which the order should be placed. However, the *lead time*
should also be taken into consideration. A new order must be placed before
the inventory runs out, otherwise the inventory will be depleted which will
prevent deliveries from taking place for some time. The inventory level at
which a new order must be placed, is called the *reorder point*.
The reorder point can be calculated as follows:

Lead time

Reorder point

Reorder point = Sales volume per day × Order lead time

EXAMPLE 6.2 CONTINUED
Processed orders take five days to be delivered.
Annual sales volume for sports shoes is 75,000 sets. Based on 250
working days, daily sales volume is 75,000 / 250 = 300 sets.
The economic order quantity is 5,000 sets. The delivery of an order
requires five working days.
Five working days before the inventory is depleted, a new order must be
placed.
The reorder point is therefore:
Reorder point = Sales volume per day × 5 = 300 × 5 = 1,500 sets

---

TEST QUESTION 6.2
What is the influence of the length of the lead time of an order on the
economic order quantity?

Uncertainty

In practice, sales volume fluctuates from day to day. Sales are higher one day and lower again the next. Nor is the lead time of an order ever exactly the same. In other words: there is *uncertainty*.

This uncertainty influences the reorder point. The possibility of higher than average sales, as well as the possibility of longer lead times, should both be considered.

EXAMPLE 6.2 CONTINUED

Annual sales volume of 75,000 corresponds with an average daily sales volume of 75,000/250 = 300 sets. However, daily sales volume is higher than 300 sets on one day and lower on another. Suppose the following: Daily sales volume varies between the lowest level of 250 sets and the highest of 350 sets. The lead time of an order of 5,000 sets is on average five working days, but could also be six. If it is essential that the inventory does not become depleted, the highest daily sales and the longest lead time should be considered.

The reorder point would be:

Maximum daily sales volume × Maximum order lead time = 350 × 6 = 2,100 sets

---

The example shows that the reorder point becomes higher due to the influence of uncertainty.

The difference between a reorder point *with* uncertainty and a reorder point *without* uncertainty is called the *safety inventory*.

Safety inventory

If, during the order lead time, sales volume is equal to average sales volume and the lead time is also an average, then the total inventory at the time of delivery of the order is equal to the safety inventory. The safety inventory then remains. The purpose of the safety inventory is only to accommodate higher than average sales volume during the lead time of a new order. This is illustrated graphically in figure 6.5.

FIGURE 6.5 Inventory cycle and uncertainty

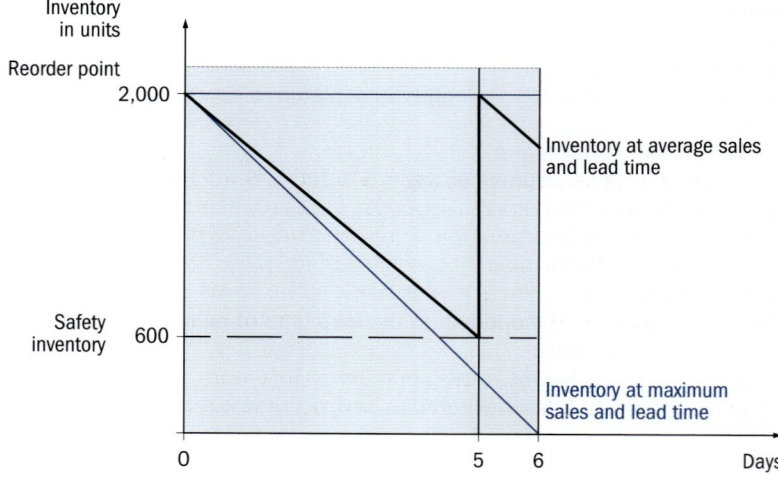

On average, the safety inventory is permanently present.
The increase in carrying costs per period due to the presence of a safety inventory is:

> Increase in carrying costs = Safety inventory × carrying costs per unit

TEST QUESTION 6.3
Do ordering costs increase due to the presence of a safety inventory?

Although the inventory problems described so far have been limited to a trade business, a production business also deals with similar issues for both raw materials and end products.
For inventories and orders of raw material, the problem is completely parallel to that of a trade business. For batch production of end products, the same principles apply.
Instead of ordering costs, the term *set-up costs* is used when discussing production companies. These are the costs that must be made to set up the machines to produce a new batch of products. Instead of the lead time of an order, the *manufacturing time* is used for a new batch and the optimal order quantity becomes the *optimal batch size*.

Set-up costs
Manufacturing time

Optimal batch size

EXAMPLE 6.3
Princess, a manufacturer of household appliances, produces various products, including a particular type of coffee maker. The demand for this appliance is 500 items per year. Daily sales volume varies between 0 and 5 coffee makers per day.
The carrying costs per end product are €10 per year. Every production order involves set-up costs of €100 for adjusting the machines.

The calculation of the optimal batch size of end products is as follows:

$$Q^* = \sqrt{\frac{2 \times 500 \times 100}{10}} = 100 \text{ units}$$

For a batch manufacturing time of two days, the production of a new series must be started at an inventory level of:

Maximum daily sales volume × 2 = 5 × 2 = 10 coffee makers.

The Wilson Formula is only valid under a number of assumptions. For one thing, it is assumed that the inventory gradually depletes, that the purchasing costs are fixed and that the order is received in one delivery. This implies that the formula is based on a rather theoretical situation that does not often occur in practice. Nevertheless, the formula can be used to obtain an estimate of the optimal order size in a number of cases.

In modern logistics, however, this approach to inventory management based on cost analysis is considered to have become outmoded.

Logistics

Maintaining an inventory of a large number of ready-made products is not something that can accommodate the demand for custom-made products. Modern logistics strive to eliminate inventories, giving rise to clever concepts based on advanced cooperation in the supply chain: from the original extractor of the raw material to the supplier of the end product to the customer. The most far-reaching of these concepts is the *just-in-time* principle of delivery (JIT): the goods are only delivered at the moment they are needed for the next step in the production process. This requires a profound level of cooperation between supplier and buyer. In the automobile industry, this concept is very advanced. But it is found in supermarkets as well: the supplied goods are stacked on the shelves immediately, without first being stored in a warehouse behind the store.

Just-in-time

Inventory turnover ratio

The extent to which a company succeeds in inventory management is expressed by the *inventory turnover ratio*. For a trade business, the calculation is as follows:

$$\text{Inventory turn over ratio} = \frac{\text{Cost of goods sold}}{\text{Average inventory}}$$

The inventory turnover ratio indicates how often the average inventory present in the business is sold per year. A low rate indicates that the goods remain in the warehouse for a long period of time. A value of 1, for example, indicates that the goods remain in the inventory exactly one year on average. A high value indicates a short inventory period. If the just-in-time principle is applied, the turnover ratio is very high.

- -

EXAMPLE 6.4

In its 2016 financial statement, the Dutch Jumbo Group (the holding company whose assets include the Dutch Jumbo chain of supermarkets) recorded the following data:

Cost of goods sold	4,581,341 (× €1,000)
Inventory on 31 December 2016	145,255 (× €1,000)
Inventory on 1 January 2016	145,139 (× €1,000)

Average inventory in 2016 was (145,255 + 145,139)/2 = 145,197 (× €1,000).

Average inventory turnover ratio in 2016 was 4,581,341/145,197 = 31.6.

- -

TEST QUESTION 6.4

On average, how long do products remain on their shelves at Jumbo group stores?

The Dutch Albert Heijn chain of supermarkets is applying a concept they call 'Today-For-Tomorrow'; an example of modern-day inventory management. In a time of growing product assortments, Albert Heijn was faced with a problem. The chain has opted to keep its supermarket shelf and storage space as empty as possible, and in order to create space for new products. This has led to the introduction of Today-For-Tomorrow, a revolutionary distribution concept which entails that stores are supplied not two or three times per week, but every day, using two trucks: one for fresh produce and one for dry goods. Thanks to those rapid resupplies, Albert Heijn is able to quickly anticipate and respond to the demand.

The impact of the Today-For-Tomorrow concept is being felt by suppliers as well. Many of them have been made responsible for maintaining the inventory in Albert Heijn's distribution centers. They are informed of store orders and inventory levels in distribution centers, and allowed to schedule their own resupplies. This concept has led to lower inventory levels in Albert Heijn's distribution centers, as well as to 75% less transport movements. Directly coordinating production from suppliers with distribution based on customer demand makes it possible for Albert Heijn to supply the goods JIT; the delivery of products in the smallest amounts, just when products are needed.

6.3   Credit Management

Accounts receivable are created when a company provides *trade credit*. The buyer does not pay for the products or services straight away. The company has a claim on its customer which is recognized on the balance sheet as *accounts receivable*.

Trade credit

Accounts receivable

Granting trade credit increases the company's capital requirement.
It also brings extra costs: administration costs and costs of collecting. These are important disadvantages.
However, companies still sell on credit on a large scale. On the one hand, this can be explained by competition considerations. Other companies sell on credit, therefore customers expect it. In business-to-business transactions, cash payments hardly ever occur.

On the other hand, rendering trade credit appeals to customers. 'Buy now, pay later' can persuade potential customers who would not be buying if cash payment was required.

Payment terms
Net term

If a company is to grant trade credit to its customers, *payment terms* must be established. A *net term* or *payment term* must be determined. This is the number of days after the item is purchased when the payment is due in full.

Considering that late repayments are unfavorable for the company with respect to the time value of money (see paragraph 5.4), the company will try to persuade some of its customers to pay sooner by offering a discount for early payment. This *cash discount* can be deducted from the invoice amount in the event of payment within the stipulated number of days: the *discount term*.

Cash discount
Discount term

In practice, however, customers all too often miss the agreed net term. Some payments are late, others are not made at all, at which point the customer is said to be in *default of payment*.

Default of payment

EXAMPLE 6.5

Borsumy applies the following payment terms for deliveries to the retail trade: payment within one and a half months of invoice date; for payment within ten days of invoice date a 2% discount can be deducted (2/10 net 45).
Annual revenue of Borsumy amount to €12 million, of which 75% is on credit. Sales are spread evenly throughout the year. 5% of sales on credit are never received. On average, accounts receivable remain unpaid for two months, after which they are either collected or booked as irrecoverable.

Annual sales on credit amount to 75% of €12 million = €9 million. Based on the granted net term of one month and a half, Borsumy could expect an average balance on the accounts receivable of:

$$\frac{1.5}{12} \times €9,000,000 = €1,125,000$$

The actual average balance on the accounts receivable is actually:

$$\frac{2}{12} \times €9,000,000 = €1,500,000$$

25% of the total sales is paid within the discount period. Annual discount for payment within the discount period is:

$$2\% \times 25\% \times €12,000,000 = €60,000$$

5% of the total sales on credit (€9 million) is uncollectable. Annual loss due to uncollectable payments is:

$$5\% \times €9,000,000 = €450,000$$

Credit management

By means of *credit management*, a company takes appropriate action to control the accounts receivable and limit the number of uncollectable payments.

Good credit management starts before sales and delivery by a *creditworthiness assessment* of the customer. The purpose of the creditworthiness assessment is to ascertain whether the customer will pay the amount due. The following sources can be used to gather information:

Creditworthiness assessment

- personal visits to the customer
- sales representatives
- financial statements of the customer
- credit reporting agencies such as Dun & Bradstreet and Graydon

When a new customer presents himself, a rapid response is required. You will need to take a number of business decisions. Will you accept the customer? Can and will you offer the customer a trade credit? Under what terms and conditions? Reliable information about business relations is an essential factor in making the right choices. D&B offers support during each phase of the "Credit Management Cycle":

1. Calculate risks and opportunities for all new prospects.
2. Assess new relations for creditworthiness, and adjust terms and conditions to match.
3. Properly monitor customers in order to identify any arising risks at an early stage.
4. Base collections and reminders on insolvency risk.

Assess and monitor your own business partners for their creditworthiness online using D&B company information. For entrepreneurs who need to take many credit-related decisions, the implementation of an automated acceptance process is an excellent option. Acceptance process automation can be based on D&B's existing benchmarks, or tailored to your specific needs.

Source: Dun & Bradstreet Nederland (translated)

Credit limit

The result of a creditworthiness assessment is the decision whether or not to offer the customer to buy on credit. It is also possible to set a credit limit. The *credit limit* is the maximum credit a customer is granted during a period.

Credit monitoring

Effective *credit monitoring* is essential. If a net term is exceeded, an immediate response should follow. It is wise to contact large-scale customers by telephone before the due date of the invoice. These measures are part of a collection policy. The *collection policy* concerns all measures applied to speed up or guarantee repayment.

Collection policy

6

If a customer has still not paid after several reminders, the involvement of a collection agency all the way up to legal proceedings can be considered. When taking recovery measures, it should never be forgotten that the debtor is also a customer. If the customer does not pay due to complaints about the delivery, these complaints should be dealt with immediately before a reminder is sent.

Factoring

It is clear that good credit management takes time, money and effort. Furthermore, the financing of accounts receivable requires capital. By making use of factoring, a company can outsource its credit management. In *factoring*, a company transfers its approved receivables to a factoring company. The factoring company takes over the administration and collection of the accounts receivable. The company receives the payments from the factoring company. Payment of the receibables by the factoring company is possible through several constructions. The factoring company can immediately pay for the receivables, making them a form of credit. The factoring company pays an advance to the company. This advance has a financing function. The factoring company can also pay at the end of the credit period or when payment from the customer is received.

An additional advantage of factoring can be to have the factoring company take over the risk of uncollectable debts. In such an event, the factoring company is obligated to pay the receivable to the company regardless of whether it receives payment from the customer.
Of course, factoring companies charge costs for their services.

TEST QUESTION 6.5
What effect does factoring have on total company capital?

Average days of sales outstanding

As with inventory management, credit management can be measured with the aid of a ratio. In this respect, it is common practice to calculate the *average days of sales outstanding*.

$$\text{Average days of sales outstanding} = \frac{\text{Average accounts receivable}}{\text{Sales on credit}} \times 365\,\text{days}$$

The average days of sales outstanding indicates how long it takes on average for the receivables to be paid by customers, or: the speed with which customers pay.

EXAMPLE 6.6

The financial statements of Philips over 2016 provide the following information (amounts × €1 million):

Revenue in 2016	24,516
Accounts receivable on 31 December 2016	5,327
Accounts receivable on 1 January 2016	4,982

The average sum of accounts receivable in 2016 was:

$$\frac{5,327 + 4,982}{2} = 5,154.5 \ (\times \ €1 \ \text{mln})$$

The average days of sales outstanding was: $\dfrac{5,154.5}{24,516} \times 365$ days $= 77$ days

---

6.4 Cash Management

Cash and cash equivalents are maintained by a company in order to be able to process payments – a clear indication of their importance. If a company does not have enough cash or cash equivalents, it cannot fulfill its payment obligations. In a worst-case scenario, this could lead to bankruptcy. Maintaining cash and cash equivalents is therefore a necessity, although it has its disadvantages. Firstly, it creates a capital requirement that needs financing. Secondly, investment in cash and cash equivalents hardly generates any income. Cash generates no income at all, and a positive bank balance gives very low or no interest at all. Cash management should be focused on maintaining sufficient cash and cash equivalents – but definitely not more than required.

Cash management

Generally speaking, there are three motives for maintaining cash and cash equivalents:
1 The *transaction motive* means that sufficient cash and cash equivalents are kept to allow payments that guarantee the continuity of the production process. It concerns the payment of salaries and the purchasing of raw material, the purchasing of fixed assets, tax payments, interest payments, repayments of loans, etc.

Transaction motive

2 The *precautionary motive* means that additional cash and cash equivalents are kept, due to uncertainty concerning the size and time of cash payments and receipts. This avoids problems in the event of an unforeseen expenditure.

Precautionary motive

3 The *speculative motive* means that additional cash and cash equivalents are kept to benefit from price changes of production factors.

Speculative motive

In spite of these three motives, it should be noted that a company can get by with maintaining a very low level of cash and cash equivalents as long as there are alternative ways to acquire cash and cash equivalents at short notice.

A substantial amount of companies has a line of credit with their bank. A *line of credit* means that a company can freely dispose of credit up to a given

Line of credit

maximum (the credit limit). If there is a sudden requirement for cash, the company can use this credit resource which, of course, is subject to interest. A second buffer can be created by temporarily investing available resources in securities (such as shares and bonds). These can also be sold at short notice if a company requires cash. This temporary investment also has the advantage that proceeds can derive from it by means of dividend, interest payments or increased market value.

6

Cash flow forecast

To avoid payment difficulties, a good planning of cash inflows and outflows in the form of a cash flow forecast, is required. The *cash flow forecast* is an overview of the expected cash inflows and outflows during a particular period. As discussed in chapter 4, it is an essential part of the business plan.

Cash flow planning

In cash flow planning, an important distinction is made between very short and longer terms. An exact estimate of cash inflows and outflows can be made for the short term. Longer term cash inflows and outflows, however, are a little more difficult to predict. Companies aiming for good *cash flow planning* draw up two different plans: a cash flow forecast per day for the next week or two and a cash flow forecast per month for the next six months up to a year.
Using a cash flow forecast, the expected balance of cash and cash equivalents can be deduced and potential shortages can be identified early, allowing for precautions to be taken.

EXAMPLE 6.7
A company needs a cash flow forecast for the period from January through April.
The following information is available:
- On the balance sheet of 31 December, the following balance sheet entries occur:
    - inventory of merchandise with a purchase cost of €90,000
    - accounts receivable for the amount of €100,000, with half to be received in January and half in February
    - accounts payable for an amount of €35,000, to be paid in January
    - €10,000 positive bank balance
- Suppliers allow one month of credit, customers receive two months.
- The company wants to have an inventory of merchandise with a purchase cost of €70,000 on 30 April.
- The necessary purchases are spread evenly over the months from January through April.
- The monthly cash outflows due to operating costs are €6,000 plus 10% of sales revenue in that month.
- Depreciation of fixed assets is €3,000 per month.
- In March, a payment of €15,000 should be made for purchasing equipment.
- Projected sales revenue for the months January through April are €40,000, €80,000, €70,000 and €50,000, respectively.
- The gross margin is 30% of sales revenue (therefore, the purchase cost of goods sold is 70%).

In order to draw up the cash flow forecast, the monthly purchase cost must be determined first. The purchase cost of the total revenue for the

months January through April are 70% × (€40,000 + €80,000 + €70,000 + €50,000) = €168,000.
Since the inventory during the planned period is allowed to be reduced by €90,000 − €70,000 = €20,000, goods to the value of €168,000 − €20,000 = €148,000 must be purchased.
The monthly purchases are therefore ¼ × €148,000 = €37,000.

The cash flow forecast (in Euros) is:

	January	February	March	April
Cash inflows:				
Accounts receivable	50,000	50,000	40,000	80,000
Cash Outflows:				
Purchases	35,000	37,000	37,000	37,000
Operating costs	10,000	14,000	13,000	11,000
Equipment	–	–	15,000	–
Total	45,000	51,000	65,000	48,000
Net cash inflows	5,000	– 1,000	– 25,000	32,000
Start bank account	10,000	15,000	14,000	– 11,000
End bank account	15,000	14,000	– 11,000	21,000

The cash flow forecast shows a shortage of cash (deficit) of €11,000 at the end of March. Company management can now take prudent precautions to prevent this shortage, for example, by organizing a line of credit.

TEST QUESTION 6.6
Why is depreciation of fixed assets not recorded on the cash flow forecast?

Glossary

Average days sales outstanding	The average period until an invoice is paid.
Carrying costs	Costs of storage, financing and risks connected to maintaining inventory.
Cash flow cycle	The transformation process related to the production and sales process from the moment of purchasing raw materials up to the moment of delivery of an end product to the customer.
Cash flow forecast	Overview of all expected cash inflows and cash outflows for the coming period.
Collection policy	All measures applied to speed up or guarantee outstanding payments.
Default of payment	Non-payment, partial payment or overdue payment of receivables.
Economic order quantity	The number of products to be ordered to arrive at the lowest inventory.
Factoring	Taking over the administration and collection of a company's accounts receivable by a factoring company.
Inventory turnover ratio	The ratio between the cost of goods sold and the average level of the inventory.
Line of credit	Credit provided by a bank, allowing a company to overdraw on its current account up to a maximum amount (credit limit).
Net term	Period during which a receivable must be repaid.
Ordering costs	Costs that are the result of placing an order.
Reorder point	Inventory level at which a new order needs to be placed.

Safety inventory	Inventory maintained in connection with the uncertainty of sales and lead time.
Trade credit	Credit provided by the supplier to the customer if there is no payment on delivery.
Working capital	Current assets.

6

Multiple-choice questions

6.1   What is the effect of the decision to sell goods on credit if sales do not increase?
 a   The investments in current assets increase.
 b   The line of credit that finances the current assets increases.
 c   The composition of the current assets changes, but not its size.
 d   The line of credit which finances the current assets is reduced.

6.2   Which of the following statements is correct if a company makes no use of trade credit for purchasing goods?
 a   The length of time the additional financing is required.
 b   The capital requirements for current assets increases.
 c   The average amount of the current liabilities increases.
 d   The average amount of the inventories on the balance sheet is reduced.

6.3   Which of the following measures results in a shorter period of additional financing requirement as a result of the cash flow cycle?
 a   Agreeing to a higher credit limit with the bank.
 b   Buying fewer products per order.
 c   Paying suppliers' invoices later.
 d   Reducing the gross profit margin of the products to be sold.

6.4   What is working capital management focused on?
 a   Minimizing inventory.
 b   Minimizing accounts receivable.
 c   Minimizing cash and cash equivalents.
 d   Minimizing working capital as a whole.

6.5   What is the result of using optimal order quantity?
 a   Minimal carrying costs.
 b   Minimal ordering costs.
 c   Both minimal carrying costs and minimal ordering costs.
 d   Minimal sum of carrying and ordering costs.

6.6   What is the effect of using larger order quantity?
 a   More orders per year and a lower average inventory.
 b   More orders per year and a higher average inventory.
 c   Fewer orders per year and a lower average inventory.
 d   Fewer orders per year and a higher average inventory.

6.7   Which statement is correct?
 a   Carrying costs increase when order quantity increases.
 b   Ordering costs are inversely proportional to order quantity.
 c   Both statements are correct.
 d   Neither statement is correct.

6.8 What does the optimal order quantity depend on?
a Sales volume, variable carrying costs and fixed ordering costs.
b Sales volume, fixed carrying costs and variable ordering costs.
c Reorder point, variable carrying costs and fixed ordering costs.
d Reorder point, fixed carrying costs and variable ordering costs.

6.9 A trade company sells a product with an annual sales volume of 10,000 items.
Daily sales vary between 0 and 60 items. Carrying costs are €20 per year per item. An order involves €60 of ordering costs. The lead time of an order is 10 days. Which of the following statements is correct?
a The optimal order quantity of this product is 19 items.
b The optimal order quantity of this product is 245 items.
c The reorder point at which inventory will never be depleted.
d The safety inventory at which inventory will never be depleted is 100 items.

6.10 Which measure is *not* part of credit management?
a Creditworthiness assessment of potential buyers.
b Granting discounts for cash payments.
c Determining a credit limit for a buyer.
d Sending reminders when net terms expire.

6.11 A company generates annual sales revenue of €1,050,000 spread evenly over the year. 80% of sales are on credit. The net term is two months. 10% of accounts receivable is uncollectable. A 2% discount is offered for cash payments. Which statement is correct?
a Balance of accounts receivable is €140,000.
b Annual loss due to uncollectable receivables is €105,000.
c Monthly sales on credit are €70,000.
d Annual discount for cash payment is €21,000.

6.12 What does a high average payment period for accounts receivable indicate?
a Slow payment of current liabilities to the company's creditors.
b A very active collection policy of the company with regard to accounts receivable.
c Slow payment by the company's customers of accounts receivable.
d Quick payment by the company's customers of accounts receivable.

6.13 Which of the following is *not* an advantage of factoring in general?
a Improvement of default of payment.
b Reduction of the risk of default of payment.
c Simplification of the accounts receivable administration.
d Reduction of collection issues.

6.14 Which of the following statements is *not* correct?
a The cash flow forecast contains inventory balance sheet items.
b An investment in securities reduces liquidity issues.
c A line of credit is a flexible capital resource and very useful for cash flow planning.
d Cash and cash equivalents should be kept to a minimum from a profitability point of view.

6.15 What drives the cash and cash equivalents requirement derived from the cash flow forecast?
   a Transaction motive.
   b Precautionary motive.
   c Speculative motive.

6

WY ondergheschreven van weghen de Camere der Compaignie tot Enckhuysen, bekennen by desen hebben vanden E. *Pieter Herman* ~~Soode~~ de somme van *twaelf gul- dens Suyders* ———————————— nde dat voor reste van *drie hondert en vyf* ter mede de voornoemde *Pieter Hermans En.* de voorsz. Compaignie gheregistreert staet te herideren opt nde voorsz. Camere folio 2 5 4. Synde hier mede de *hondert vyftich guldens* — daer mede d *Pieter Hermans* inde voorsz. Compaigr e Thien-Iarighe Rekeninghe participeert, ten vollen opgheb elt: Ende voorts gheannulleert ende te niete ghedaen alle ver de betalinghen opde ghemelde partye ghedaen, voor de ctum den *9 September anno 1606*

7
Equity

A company's equity is provided by its owners.
The nature of equity and its registration on the balance sheet depend on the legal form of the business. Paragraph 7.1 discusses the equity of the sole proprietorship and partnerships. Paragraph 7.2 covers the equity of the joint-share companies, which consists of share capital and reserves. Paragraph 7.3 deals with share value, and paragraph 7.4 with the different types of reserves. The concluding paragraph 7.5 addresses the issue of raising capital through the issuing of new shares.

7.1 Equity in Companies with a Non-legal Entity Status

For companies with non-legal entity status (sole proprietorships and partnerships) equity is equal to the capital contributed by the owner(s). Equity can increase if profits are generated, or if additional private deposits are made by the owner(s). In the event of loss or withdrawal of capital by the owners, the company's equity is reduced.

Sole proprietorship

On the balance sheet of a *sole proprietorship*, equity is shown as a single amount. Equity consists of:

    the original capital contributed by the owner
+   private capital contributions (additional private contributions made by the owner)
+   profits
–   private withdrawals (made by the owner)
–   losses

The owner of a sole proprietorship does not receive a salary. If an owner allocates a pro forma salary, this cannot be deducted from the profit as cost. Private withdrawals are not considered costs. The owner of a sole proprietorship pays income tax on the entire profit, not only on the part that they withdraw from the company by means of private withdrawals – as discussed in paragraph 1.4.

Partnership

In a *partnership*, the amount of capital to be contributed by each partner is established at the set-up of the partnership. The capital contributed by each partner is registered on the balance sheet. It is possible for the agreed amount not to be paid into the company immediately. In such an event, part of the equity must still be settled.

EXAMPLE 7.1

Farnell and Lockhart decide to set up a partnership on 1 January 2018. Both agree to contribute €30,000 in capital. Farnell is not able to contribute this amount by 1 January 2018 and makes a deposit of €20,000. Apart from the equity, they negotiate a bank loan of €50,000 to finance the required assets.

The balance sheet of the partnership at the time of set-up is:

Balance sheet on 1 January 2018 (× €1,000)

Assets	100	Equity Farnell	30	
		Still to be paid	10	
		Paid		20
		Equity Lockhart		30
		Bank loan		50
	100			100

As with a sole proprietorship, the equity of each owner in a partnership can also increase or decrease by private contributions or withdrawals. Profit can be left in the company and increase its equity. A loss reduces equity. After set-up, resulting equity changes from this are not recognized on the balance sheet entries as part of the partners' equity but in a separate entry labelled 'Private'.

EXAMPLE 7.1 CONTINUED

By the end of the first year after set-up, company assets have increased by €20,000. Farnell has deposited €10,000, which makes his contributed equity €30,000 in total. Lockhart has decided to leave €15,000 of his share of the first year's profit in the company. €10,000 has been repaid on the bank loan. Trade credit received from suppliers is €5,000.

The balance sheet of the partnership a year after its set-up is:

Balance sheet on 1 January 2019 (× €1,000)

Assets	120	Equity Farnell	30
		Equity Lockhart	30
		Private Lockhart	15
		Bank loan	40
		Accounts payable	5
	120		120

TEST QUESTION 7.1
What is the equity of the partnership according to the aforementioned balance sheet?

The partners each pay income tax on their share of the profit in the partnership. The procedure in a partnership strongly resembles that in a sole proprietorship; the differences being that equity is registered for each partner individually, and that the equity of a sole proprietorship has only one balance sheet entry.

TEST QUESTION 7.2
Why is equity of a sole proprietorship not registered in two separate balance sheet entries?

In a *limited partnership*, equity is registered in the same manner as in a partnership. The equity of each partner is also recognized separately on the balance sheet.

Limited partnership

7.2 Equity in Companies with a Legal Entity Status

The equity of a joint-share company comprises share capital and reserves. By issuing shares, the company raises capital to use as equity. The buyers of the shares, also called shareholders, are the owners of the company.

Share capital

Authorized share capital

Issued share capital

Paid-up share capital

The total amount of shares that can be issued is laid down in a company's articles of association. This amount is called the *authorized share capital*. The authorized share capital indicates the maximum total par value of the shares. The actual number of shares issued is usually lower than the maximum allowed. It is possible for part of the payments for the issued share capital to be outstanding. In most countries, there is a minimum requirement for a corporation's paid-up share capital. In the Netherlands, the minimum capital requirement for a corporation is €45,000. For a limited liability company, there is usually no minimum requirement, as is the case in the Netherlands. Consecutively, the paid-up share capital of an LLC can be €0.01. The paid-up share capital is recognized on the published balance sheet.

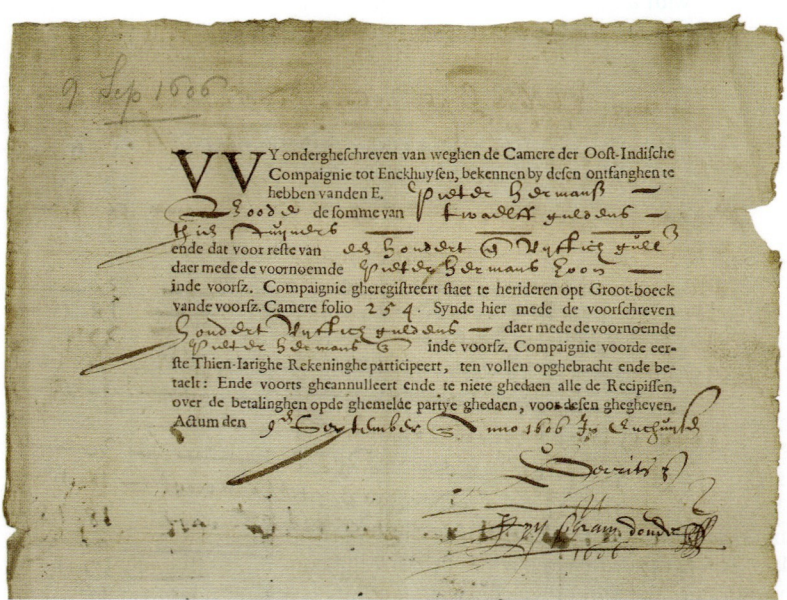

In 2010, Ruben Schalk, history student at Utrecht University, discovered the oldest company share ever found. During research for his thesis in the Westfrisian Archives in Hoorn, the Netherlands, Schalk came across a document dated 9 September 1606, issued by the Enkhuizen Chamber of the VOC. The VOC (Dutch East India Company) was the world's largest trading company during the 17th and 18th centuries. It was the world's first company to issue freely tradable shares. The VOC's open tender ran till 1 September 1602. On 9 September 1606, Pieter Harmensz paid the final term of his 150-guilder investment. As proof of payment Pieter Harmensz received this share, making it a kind of receipt. Trade in VOC shares began virtually immediately after the tender closed, thus kick-starting the formation of the Amsterdam Exchange, the oldest stock exchange in the world.

In principle, any profit earned is for the shareholders. They can, however, choose to retain part of the profit in the company. This part is added to the reserves. A company's articles of association often lay down clauses concerning profit distribution.

The profit distribution is proposed by the board of directors and determined during the general shareholders meeting upon the closing of the financial year. Profit distribution received by the shareholders is called *dividend*. The calculation of dividend is based on the paid-up share capital. It is possible to pay *interim dividend* during the financial year, by way of an advance.

Profit distribution

Dividend

Interim dividend

7

EXAMPLE 7.2
The issued share capital of a corporation is €20 million, consisting of 10 million shares with a par value of €2 each. Of this capital, €2 million still has to be paid.
In the corporation's articles of association, the following is determined with respect to profit distribution:
The shareholders receive 5% primary dividend. Of the remaining profit, 40% is retained and 60% is paid to the shareholders.
Profit after tax for the past financial year was €2.5 million.

The distribution of profit is:
Profit after tax: €2,500,000
5% primary dividend: 5% × €18,000,000 =   − €   900,000

Surplus profit   €1,600,000
Retaining of earnings: 40% × €1,600,000 =   − €   640,000

Secondary dividend   €   960,000

The shareholders therefore receive €900,000 + €960,000 = €1,860,000 in dividend.

Dividend as a percentage of the paid-up share capital is:

$$\text{Dividend percentage} = \frac{€1,860,000}{€18,000,000} \times 100\% = 10.3\%$$

For each fully paid-up share with a par value of €2, the shareholder receives a dividend of: 10.3% of €2 = €0.206.

For a company, the most important function of shares is their financing function. The paid-up share capital is used to finance the company's activities.
For shareholders, shares have two important functions.
Firstly, shares give the holder a *controlling interest* in the company. This is particularly important in smaller businesses. Secondly, shareholders are entitled to a share of the profit if the company pays a dividend.

Controlling interest

Common shares
Ordinary shares

Apart from the previously described shares, also referred to as *common shares* or *ordinary shares*, there are shares with particular characteristics: preferred shares.

Preferred shares

Preferred shares are shares which bestow certain privileges on their holders. These privileges can concern both functions of shares: controlling interest or profit distribution.

Priority shares

Priority shares give the shareholder additional rights with respect to controlling interest.

Preference shares

Preference shares give the holder privileges with respect to profit distribution. These shares are often subject to a fixed dividend percentage, laid down in the articles of association. In the event of cumulative preference shares, dividend payments are passed on to profitable years following those years in which a dividend has been omitted due to insufficient or no profit. In this way, shareholders are guaranteed a fixed dividend payment although, during bad years, they will have to wait a little longer. In the event of liquidation of the company, preference shares can also have privileges.

TEST QUESTION 7.3
For what purpose are priority and preference shares offered?

The equity of a company can be increased by offering shares that have not yet been issued. Existing or new shareholders buy these shares and the attracted capital is added to the equity. Retention of profit also increases the equity of a company.

7.3 Share Value

Par value

In the previous paragraph, the *par value* of shares was mentioned. In determining the value of a share, the par value is irrelevant. The par value is the amount for which a share is registered on the balance sheet. This share value is only important at the time of initial issue as shareholders are obligated to pay at least the par value at that moment or at a later time.

To determine the actual value of a share, two theoretical approaches can be applied. The share value is derived from the value of the company.

Net asset value

The *net asset value* of a company is calculated as the difference between its assets and liabilities; it is therefore equal to the equity. The net asset value is also determined by the accounting policies that the company applies. In part 4, *financial accounting*, this is discussed further. The net asset value is a reflection of the book value of all assets in the company.

Capitalized earnings value

The *capitalized earnings value* of a company is calculated by the present value of expected future profits of the company. This value reflects, as it were, the profit potential of the company.
If a company succeeds in exploiting its assets very profitably, the capitalized earnings value is higher than the net asset value. If the net asset value is higher, the company is performing poorly.

The net asset value and the capitalized earnings value per share are calculated by dividing the value of the company by the number of issued shares.

EXAMPLE 7.3

For a corporation, the following simplified balance sheet is given:

Balance sheet (in Euros)

Various assets	1,800,000	Share capital	500,000
		Reserves	1,000,000
		Liabilities	300,000
	1,800,000		1,800,000

The following is also given:
- The par value of shares is €1.
- The forecast annual profits are €120,000.
- Profits are fully distributed.
- The market interest rate is 6%.

The net asset value of the company is calculated as follows:

Assets − liabilities = €1,800,000 − €300,000 = €1,500,000

The net asset value per share is: $\dfrac{€1,500,000}{500,000} = €3$

The capitalized earnings value of the company is equal to the present value of the forecast profits:

$$\frac{€120,000}{1.06} + \frac{€120,000}{1.06^2} + \frac{€120,000}{1.06^3} + \dots$$

The result is found by calculating how much can be earned annually using €120,000, based on an interest rate of 6%.

0.06 × company's capitalized earnings value = €120,000

Company's capitalized earnings value = $\dfrac{€120,000}{0.06} = €2,000,000$

The capitalized earnings value per share is equal to $\dfrac{€2,000,000}{500,000} = €4$

Apart from the two mentioned theoretical values, shares listed on the stock exchange also have a *market value*. **Market value**
The market value is based on the demand and supply of the underlying share on the stock exchange. The market value of a share is, of course, influenced by its net asset value and capitalized earnings value; but it also depends on external factors such as economic and political developments.

The major advantage of being listed on the stock exchange is the increased tradability of a share. Motives for companies to become listed on the stock exchange can be:
- *Collection motive*: the original shareholders can partly or entirely release the capital invested in the company by selling shares and use the proceeds for other purposes.

- *Financing motive*: the need for additional equity in the future can be covered more easily by increasing the issued share capital.
- *Management motive*: the distance between the ownership and management widens, and shareholders have less influence on the day-to-day business.
- *PR-motive*: stock exchange listing increases brand awareness of the company.
- *Prestige motive*: stock exchange listing significantly increases the prestige of a company, making it a real player in the business world.

A stock exchange listing brings obligations with respect to disclosure of information, which is required for rating the market value on the stock exchange. From a competitive point of view, this could be unfavorable.

TEST QUESTION 7.4
For each of the discussed values of shares, indicate on what it is based and what its importance is.

7.4 Reserves

The equity of a joint-share company consists of share capital and reserves. Reserves can be created in various ways: through retention of profit, a public offering of shares for a higher price than par value and by revaluation of assets.

The shareholders of a joint-share company are entitled to the net profit after payment of interest and corporate tax. The annual general meeting decides on the profit allocation. Part of the profit can be paid to the shareholders as dividend.

Dividend paid to the shareholders is not a deductible cost with respect to corporate tax; however, profit payments to directors and members of the supervisory board are deductible, although the amount of the payment usually depends on the amount of the profit. Such a profit payment is **Bonus** called a *bonus*. In contrast to dividend payments, a bonus is deductible as (remuneration) costs for corporate tax.

Part of the profit can also be retained in the company. The retained profit is **Retained** added to the equity as *retained earnings*. When comparing the increase in **earnings** equity from retaining earnings to the increase from attracting capital by an additional issue of shares, the following advantages present themselves:

- Financing using additional share capital is more expensive than financing using retained profits as shareholders demand a dividend payment.
- There are no issuing costs or administrative burdens involved in profit retention.
- In profit retention, equity growth is gradual, unlike the large sums resulting from public offerings.
- In profit retention, there is no dilution of profit per share; therefore, the market value of the shares is not reduced.

By retaining part of the profit in highly profitable years, a reasonable dividend can still be paid during less profitable years using the reserves, **Dividend** known as a policy of *dividend equalization*. The shareholders are made **equalization** more confident about a solid future dividend policy, which is beneficial to share value. Due to the presence of retained earnings, a higher amount of dividend can be paid than the profit of the year concerned would allow. It should be noted, however, that the par value of the share capital cannot be affected by dividend payments. If no dividend is paid in a particular year, this is called *passing over dividend.*

A reserve can also be created by an additional issue of shares if the price paid per share is higher than the par value. The difference between the offering price and the par value is called the *share premium.* Due to a new issue of shares, the issued share capital is increased by the par value of the new shares.

However, the share premium is also part of the equity of an joint-share company. This amount is added to the reserves, in particular to the *share premium.*

Share premium

The share premium may be reduced if the company decides to issue *bonus shares.* These are shares offered free to existing shareholders and charged to the share premium. This is called the bonus share issue. The issuing of bonus shares is comparable to a share issue at €0. The total equity of the company remains equal, but its composition structure. The par value of the issued share capital increases and the reserves are decreased by an equal amount. This is called *recapitalization.* The result of recapitalization is that the market value of the shares becomes lower, which makes shares cheaper to buy on the stock exchange. Investors are not inclined to buy very 'expensive' shares. By reducing market value, interest in a share can be revived – eventually increasing the possible chances of success for a future additional share issue.

Bonus shares

Recapitalization

A similar effect can be achieved by a *share split.* Here, the par value per share is lowered, while the total issued share capital and the share premium remain equal. In exchange for the original shares, the shareholders receive a larger number of shares at a lower par value and, of course, a lower market value as well. This results in neither financial gain nor loss.

Share split

Shares paid to the shareholder instead of cash dividends leads to an increase in issued share capital. The dividend in shares is called *share dividend.* Paying share dividends has the advantage that the cash and cash equivalents are not used for dividend payments. If a company decides to pay share dividend, a certain amount of *cash dividend* is required because the company needs to pay dividend tax. The tax authorities only accept cash payment. Dividend tax therefore has to be paid entirely from cash dividends.

Share dividend

Cash dividend

- -

EXAMPLE 7.4
A company pays out a part of annual profit in the form of share dividend for the amount of €850,000. The dividend tax rate is 15%. To be able to pay the dividend tax, the company also pays out a cash dividend, which has to be at least equal to the dividend tax due. The required cash dividend can be calculated as follows:

Cash dividend = 15% × (share dividend + cash dividend)
Cash dividend = 0.15 × share dividend + 0.15 × cash dividend
0.85 × Cash dividend = 0.15 × share dividend

$$\text{Cash dividend} = \frac{15}{85} \times €850,000 = €150,000$$

The dividend payout leads to the following entries on the balance sheet:

Balance sheet (in Euros)

| Cash and cash equivalents | −150,000 | Share capital | +850,000 |
| | | Profit | −1,000,000 |

An increase in equity can also occur due to increased value of assets – if the company applies the policy of current cost valuation for its assets (see chapter 16). In this event, a revaluation of assets occurs, thereby increasing the book value. The increase in asset value is shown in the increase in equity, in particular, the increase in the *revaluation reserve*. Legally, the revaluation reserve cannot be paid out to shareholders.

Revaluation reserve

The figures of the previously mentioned reserves are listed on a company's published balance sheet. These are known as the *open reserves*. However, it is possible for a company to hold reserves that are not shown on the published balance sheet.

Open reserves

There is a *hidden reserve* or *secret reserve* if its value cannot be established – which is the case if, for example, the book value of the assets on the balance sheet is too low. By holding hidden reserves, a company hides information on the size of its total assets and the way the assets are financed. This allows them to hide future losses from the public eye.

Hidden reserve
Secret reserve

7.5 Issue of Shares

If a corporation needs to substantially increase its equity, it can do so by effecting an increase in its issued share capital. If the shares of a corporation are listed on the stock exchange, a *public offering* is possible, allowing any interested investor to participate.

Public offering

If the company is not (yet) listed, smaller corporatons have the possibility of effecting a *private placement*: the shares are directly sold to existing shareholders, private investors or to a venture capital company. A venture capital company specializes in providing risk-bearing capital to companies. In a public offering, a company uses the services of one or more banks, which will act as a go-between for the company and the investors.

Private placement

If a bank only acts as a subscription office on behalf of the company, this is called *guichet issue*. The company then bears the risk of an issue failure.

Guichet issue

If a bank takes this risk and guarantees the proceeds of the issue, it is called an *underwritten issue*. An underwritten issue is never made by one single bank but by a *syndicate* or *consortium* of banks bearing the risk together.

Underwritten issue

For interested investors, information is issued by the company in a *prospectus*. The prospectus contains information with respect to the corporation's situation, its financial statements, a copy of the articles of association and the issue price. The determination of the *issue price* is a complicated matter. If the issue price is too high, there will be few buyers and the issue will fail. If the issue price is too low, any reasonable increase in capital will require more new shares to be issued, which creates diluted future profits per share. The issue price should, in any case, be lower than the market value, otherwise it would be more interesting to buy shares on the stock exchange than to participate in the issue.

Prospectus

Issue price

TEST QUESTION 7.5

For a corporation, what is the difference between an investor purchasing shares on the stock exchange and buying new issue shares?

In the event of a *public issue*, subscription is open to every interested candidate. By increasing the number of issued shares for a price below market value, the market value of the share falls; as a result, existing shareholders are disadvantaged by the new issue.
Furthermore, on the arrival of new shareholders, individual shareholder controlling interest of the company is reduced.
To reduce this disadvantage, it is possible to choose a *rights issue*. The *rights issue* grants shareholders the privilege to subscribe with priority. This preferential right is also called a *subscription right*. Because the number of newly issued shares is usually smaller than the existing number of shares, several rights are needed to buy one new share. The number of rights per share is equal to the number of existing shares, prior to the issue, divided by the number of newly issued shares. If an existing shareholder has no intention of subscribing to a particular share issue, he can sell his rights on the stock exchange.

Public issue

Rights issue

Subscription right

TEST QUESTION 7.6

What is financially more advantageous for a corporation: issuing shares *with* a subscription right or *without* a subscription right?

An investor without shares first has to buy these rights on the stock exchange. Only then can he buy any newly issued shares. To acquire a share, the investor must first buy rights and then pay the issue price. The theoretical value of a subscription right can be calculated as follows:

$$\text{Share value after issue} = \text{Number of rights per share} \times \text{Right value} + \text{Issue price}$$

$$\text{Value of a right} = \frac{\text{Share value after issue} - \text{Issue price}}{\text{Number of rights per share}}$$

With the aid of the first comparison, the expectations of the investor with respect to level of the market value of the share after issue can be determined. Based on the market value of the rights, a forecast share market value after issue can be calculated.

- -

EXAMPLE 7.5

At a certain moment, the issued share capital of Prospect Inc. amounts to €120 million, divided across 120 million shares with a par value of €1 each. The market value of these shares is €25. In view of an expansion of activities, the management of Prospect Inc. wishes to attract additional capital of €600 million by a new issue of shares. The issue price is set at €20 per new share. The market value of the share is expected to drop to €22 due to the new issue. The existing shareholders are offered a preferential right to subscribe to the new issue.

The number of shares issued is:

$$\frac{€600,000,000}{€20} = 30,000,000$$

The number of rights required to buy a new share is:

$$\frac{120,000,000}{30,000,000} = 4$$

The theoretical value of the right is calculated as follows:

$$\text{Value of a right} = \frac{(€22 - €20)}{4} = €0.50$$

The total proceeds of the issue (€600 million) results in an increased issued share capital of:

30,000,000 × €1 = €30,000,000

and an increase in share premium of:

30,000,000 × (€20 − €1) = €570,000,000

TEST QUESTION 7.7
What is more financially advantageous for an investor who holds shares of a PLC prior to the rights issue: selling their rights or subscribing to the issue?

Mittal Steel Company issued approximately 1.26 billion new shares in 2016; a figure corresponding to €2.77 billion, thereby constituting a substantial expansion on the existing 1.8 billion shares before the issue. Shares in Mittal before the issues were at €4.09 – meaning the company's value on the share market came to €9.7 prior to the issue. Following the issue, however, ArcelorMittal's total market capitalization came to €12.5 billion.

Investors holding shares after investment hours on 14 March received one claim for each share. For every 10 shares redeemed, they were then given the opportunity to apply for seven new ArcelorMittal shares at an extra payment of €2.20 per new share.

The value of the subscription right represents the difference between the share price and the application price of €2.20 per share. At a price of €4.09 for ArcelorMittal shares, for example, the value of the claim would be: $(7/10) \times (€4.09 - €2.20) = €1.323$.

Glossary

Bonus	Profit distribution to directors and members of the supervisory board.
Bonus shares	Shares issued to shareholders free of charge, charged to the reserves.
Capitalized earnings value	The present value of the forecast future profit of a company.
Dividend	Profit share paid to shareholders as a remuneration for capital provided to the company.
Dividend equalization	The objective of a PLC to pay an equal annual dividend per share each year.
Equity	Capital provided by the owners of a company.
Hidden reserve	Reserve whose existence, but not its value, can be deduced from the balance sheet.
Net asset value	The difference between a company's total assets and debts.
Par value/face value	The minimum amount that has to be paid for a share.
Reserves	Part of the equity of a PLC/LLC above the issued share capital.
Recapitalization	Changing the composition of the equity of a PLC, increasing the issued share capital, charged to the reserves.
Retained earnings	Reserve created by profit retention.
Revaluation reserve	Reserve created by value increase of assets.
Rights issue	Share issue giving existing shareholders priority to subscribe first to the issue.
Shares	Units into which the authorized share capital of a company (PLC or LLC) is divided.
Share dividend	Dividend payment in shares.
Share premium	The amount that is paid on top of the par value at a new issue of shares.

Share premium reserve	Reserve created by the issue of shares at a price above the par value.
Subscription right	Preferential right to subscribe to a new issue, granted to existing shareholders at the time of a new issue.
Venture capital	Risk-bearing capital obtained by private share issue.

7

Multiple-choice questions

7.1 The equity of a sole proprietorship is €50,000 on 1 January. Over the year, the owner pays himself a salary of €3,000 a month, which they spend entirely on living costs. The fiscal profit that year is €50,000. The owner pays €10,000 in income tax. What is the equity of the sole proprietorship at the end of that year?

    a €40,000
    b €54,000
    c €64,000
    d €90,000

7.2 Which components does the equity of a partnership consist of?
    a The issued share capital and the reserves.
    b The capital provided by the partners.
    c The capital provided by the partners at the initial founding of the company.
    d The capital provided by the partners at the initial founding of the company, minus private withdrawals.

7.3 Which of the following calculations results in the net asset value of a company?
    a The sum of the share capital and the share premium.
    b The total of all assets minus the liabilities.
    c The balance sheet total minus all reserves.
    d The balance sheet total minus the sum of the liabilities and all reserves.

7.4 Profit distribution according to a corporation's articles of association is as follows:
the shareholders receive 4% primary dividend. Of the surplus profit (= the profit after deduction of the preferred dividend) 50% is added to the retained earnings and the other 50% is paid to the shareholders. Furthermore, the following information is available on the corporation:
- 10,000 shares are issued with a par value of €100.
- Profit after tax is €160,000.

What is the dividend as a percentage of the issued share capital?
    a 4%
    b 8%
    c 10%
    d 16%

7.5   The simplified balance sheet of a company is as follows:

Balance sheet (amounts × €1,000)

Various assets	2,000	Share capital	1,200
		Liabilities	800
	2,000		2,000

The market interest rate is 8%. The company has an annual profit of €64,000 after tax.
Which of the following statements is correct?
a The net asset value of the company is higher than the capitalized earnings value.
b The net asset value of the company is equal to the capitalized earnings value.
c The net asset value of the company is lower than the capitalized earnings value.

7.6   A corporation pays 4%-share dividend. Which of the following statements is correct?
a The authorized share capital increases by 4%.
b The company's equity increases by 4%.
c The market value of the share will reduce by 4%.
d The par value of the issued share capital increases by 4%.

7.7   A corporation issues bonus shares. Which of the following effects occurs as a result?
a The net asset value of the company and the net asset value per share decreases.
b The net asset value per share increases and the net asset value of the company remains equal.
c The net asset value of both the company and the share remain equal.
d The net asset value per share decreases but the net asset value of the company remains equal.

7.8   What does venture capital comprise?
a The paid-up share capital of a corporation.
b Equity acquired by the sale of capital goods.
c Share capital acquired by private share issue.
d The retained profits of a corporation.

7.9   What is a subscription right?
a A remuneration paid by a company when issuing shares.
b A privilege in subscribing to an issuing of shares.
c A remuneration paid by new shareholders to a company when new shares are issued.
d The issue price of new shares minus the par value, divided by the ratio between the existing and new shares.

7.10   What is a rights issue?
a An issue of shares that is preferred to other forms of issue in fiscal terms.
b An issue that allows conversion.
c An issue giving the existing shareholders subscription rights.
d An issue allowing the holder of a subscription right to express his preference for an issue of shares or an issue of convertible bonds.

8
Liabilities

In order to make money available, a company offers to pay a lender a form of remuneration known as interest. Paragraph 8.1 offers a detailed review of the factors that determine the size of interest payments. Paragraphs 8.2 and 8.3 discuss the different types of long-term liabilities. Long-term liabilities concern money that has been made available to the company for a period longer than one year. First, the most important credit source for companies is discussed: bank loans. This is followed by discussion of a form of credit only available to large companies: bonds. Paragraph 8.4 covers the most frequent forms of short-term credit. Over the past years, and as a result of the banking crisis, new financing tools have rapidly become more important. Examples include crowdfunding, the credit union and staple financing. These new forms of financing are discussed in paragraph 8.5. Provisions are dealt with separately in paragraph 8.6. Although provisions do not cause immediate obligations for a company, they are classified as liabilities.

8.1 Liability Costs

The liabilities of a company comprise debts and provisions. Provisions are discussed in greater detail in paragraph 8.6. Debts occur as the result of a transaction between a company and its lender.

Debts have an expiry date; therefore, liabilities are only present in the company for a limited time. A lender asks for remuneration for making capital available. This capital – in contrast to the remuneration of equity providers – is usually not related to the profit of the company.

Interest

Remuneration is usually paid in the form of interest. The level of interest to be paid depends on a number of factors:

- the market interest rate
- the term to maturity of the loan
- the risk for the lender
- the ranking of the lender(s)
- the tradability of the debt

The following paragraphs discuss these factors in detail.

Market interest rate and term to maturity of the loan

Determining the *market interest rate* requires the market to be divided into a money market and a capital market. The money market interest rate applies to short-term interest and the capital market interest rate to interest over longer terms (for loans with a duration of more than two years).

Short-term interest rate

The benchmark for the *short-term interest rate* is Euribor. Euribor is the abbreviation of Euro Interbank Offered Rate. This is the rate at which European banks provide each other with short-term loans. Euribor is determined daily for durations of one week up to one year and is used as a basis for a large number of financial products, among which are short-term credits. Remarkably, Euribor has been in the negative since early 2016 (see figure 8.1).

FIGURE 8.1   1-month Euribor from 1 January 1999 through 26 April 2017

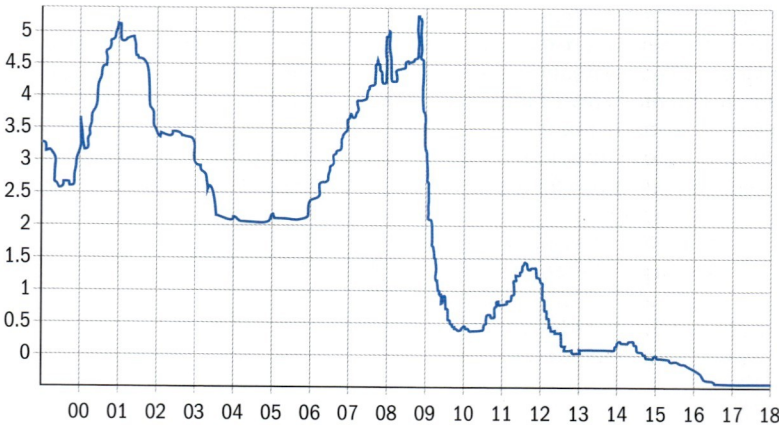

Source: www.actuelerentestanden.nl (translated)

Government bonds are used as a benchmark for the *long-term interest rate*. **Long-term** **interest rate** Considering the low risk of a country not meeting its interest payments and repayments of government bonds, this rate is often used as a basic rate. Other loans, whose risk is higher, incur a risk premium, the premium increasing proportionally with the default probability.
Furthermore, normally the longer the term to maturity of the loan, the higher the interest rate.

FIGURE 8.2 Most recent 10-year state loan from 2 January 1990 through 25 April 2017

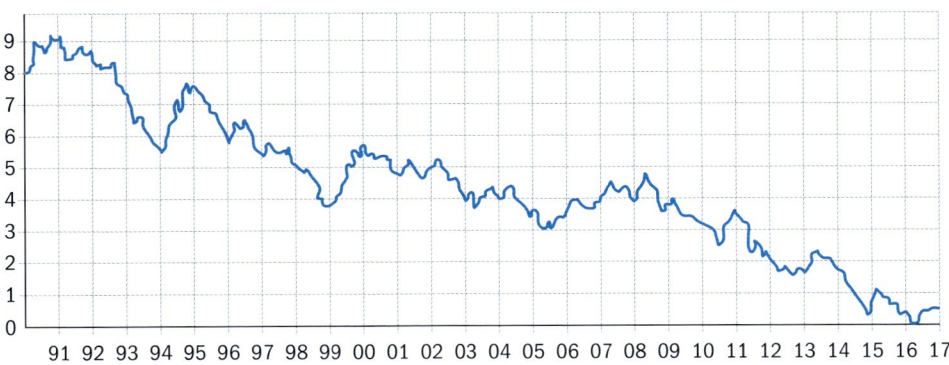

Source: www.actuelerentestanden.nl (translated)

Risk

In addition to the basic market interest rate, a premium is applied. This premium depends on the risk of the company not meeting its obligations. One of the factors determining risk is the amount of equity present in the company.

Default probability is measured by the *creditworthiness* of a company. The **Creditworthiness** creditworthiness of large companies is continuously measured by agencies such as Standard & Poor's and Moody's, which express creditworthiness through a credit rating. The certainty that a borrower will fulfill the obligations increases if the credit rating is higher.

For smaller companies, such ratings are not available. Lenders must make their own estimate of creditworthiness, for which they can make use of the services of information agencies.

These agencies gather information on both companies and private persons. Internationally operating agencies are FICO (Fair Isaac Corporation), Dun & Bradstreet, Graydon and Experian. The best known creditworthiness-assessment organization for individuals in the Netherlands is the Bureau of Credit Registration (BKR – Bureau Krediet Registratie) in Tiel. It registers all loans with official credit lenders (such as banks), documenting the principal of the loan and whether repayments were made in time.

Many people do not yet realize that signing up for a cell phone plan with a 'free' cell phone earns them a mention in the files of the BKR. Ever since new Dutch telecom legislation came into effect on 1 January 2017, holders of a phone plan with a 'free' phone have been registered as entering into a loan for this phone. The monthly credit fee is generally included in the monthly fee. Starting 1 May 2017, these loans have been registered at the BKR. The BKR's new registration related legislation applies to new phones included in a phone plan made after 1 May 2017, and only concerns loan with a principal higher than €250. There is an exception, however: cell phone plans purchased using a down payment that lowers the principal of the loan to below €250 are not registered by the BKR.

Ranking

Credit providers are creditors of a company; equity providers are the owners of a company.

Creditors always have priority over equity providers in the event of insolvency problems, bankruptcy or liquidation. Creditors therefore bear less risk. The more equity a company has, the larger the buffer to meet its obligations to creditors. As an alternative to equity, a company can also enter into a subordinated debt. In the event of bankruptcy, the providers of subordinated debt only receive interest and principal sum repayment after all other financial obligations have been met. If a company goes into bankruptcy, the providers of a subordinated debt are the last creditors to receive their money, although they are still paid before capital providers. In exchange for the subordination, equity providers demand a higher interest rate than usual.

Subordinated debt

Liable capital

Subordinated debt, together with equity, forms a company's *liable capital*. In the event of bankruptcy, liable capital serves as a buffer to meet creditor obligations.

Senior debt holder

The opposite of a subordinated debt holder, is the senior debt holder. The senior debt holder is paid before all other creditors. Examples of senior debt holders are tax authorities and mortgage lenders.

Tradability

There is a final factor that influences the risk for the lender, which is the *tradability* of a debt. If it is possible to sell a debt, lenders are not required to wait for their money until the due date of the loan.

A practical example is the case of bonds, issued by large companies or organizations and tradable on the stock exchange. Bondholders are lenders to a company, but they can sell the bonds on the stock exchange at any moment they wish.

Tradability

8.2 Bank Loans

Banks are the most important source of credit to companies. Total outstanding credit loans from banks to companies in the Netherlands come to approximately €285 billion, €130 billion of which has been lent to SMEs. Of that €130 billion, over €14 billion consists of loans smaller than €250,000. Banks have large sums of money at their disposal, attracted from savers and pension funds. Therefore, this money is the property of third parties, not the banks themselves. It is used for loans on demand. Banks act as an intermediary between capital suppliers and demanders of capital.

8

Following a request for a bank loan, an *acceptance procedure* is effected. Bankers assess the request, based on the following criteria:

Acceptance procedure

a   the borrower
b   the marketing plan
c   the investment plan
d   the financial substantiation
e   the company's buffer

Ad a The borrower
This aspect is particularly important for smaller companies, for which the owner or director-shareholder is a crucial factor in the company's performance. It is difficult for a banker to assess an applicant's entrepreneurial qualities and morality, as these are subjective and determined by, for example, the manner in which a borrower presents himself and whether his application is well substantiated. Morality is tested by internal inquiry based on whether the company had previous business with the bank. A bank can also gather information from external agencies.

Ad b The marketing plan
The marketing plan consists of the well-known 4 to 5Ps (see paragraph 4.3) and risks. From the banker's perspective, all marketing risks should be transparent.

Ad c The investment plan
The investment plan is derived from the marketing plan. This plan indicates the intended investments and how these are to be financed.

Ad d The financial substantiation
The marketing and investment plan is used as the basis for a financial substantiation. Together, these form the business plan (see chapter 4). This plan is the basis for the application.

Ad e   The company's buffer
In case plans do not succeed, the banker will require securities or equity to compensate for temporary or structural losses. The strongest form of security is obtained if credit is covered by a mortgage on real property, which means the bank can sell the company's real property if the interest payments or repayments of the principal sum are not met. The security of a mortgage can only be issued by a notary. A lien can be made on movable property (such as machines, cars, inventory) and accounts receivable. This lien is non-possessory as the assets remain with the company. A non-possessory lien offers less security to the bank than a mortgage because the asset concerned may very well have disappeared by the time the bank wants to confiscate it.

The elements of a loan application largely correspond with the parts of a business plan, as discussed in chapter 4. Starting entrepreneurs also have to provide a business plan when applying for a loan. Existing companies can draw up a business plan using the same format, describing their expectations for the coming years.

Private placement

Term loan

A bank loan is a form of *private placement* on a loan agreement (*term loan*). In a term loan, if one or more lenders provide the company or organization with temporary long-term credit. The company and the money provider(s) are in direct contact allowing negotiations on the loan conditions.

Mortgage loan

A very common type of bank loan is the *mortgage loan*. The borrower hands over security by means of a claim on real estate. If the borrower fails to meet their obligations, which are part of the financial commitment with respect to interest and principal sum repayments, the lender is entitled to use the proceeds of the sale of the real estate to clear the debt.

8.3 Bonds

Bonds

A bond loan is a loan issued by an organization (company, governmental institution), divided into a large number of individual debt securities in round figures. These individual debt securities are called *bonds*. Frequently occurring par values of bonds are €1,000 and €5,000. By issuing a bond loan, an organization attracts long-term financial resources. Unlike share issues, bonds are not strictly reserved to corporations. Companies with other legal forms and governmental institutions (state, municipality) can issue bonds.

Coupon interest rate

Term to maturity

Bonds are usually to bearer and marketable. A fixed interest (*coupon interest rate*) is paid and bonds have a fixed duration (*term to maturity*) which is usually longer than five years and shorter than twenty years.
In addition to its par value (face value, principal value), which will be repaid at the maturity date, a bond also has a market value. Bonds can be traded on the stock exchange. The listing of a bond on the exchange is presented in percentages of its nominal value. The market value of a bond is mainly determined by the market interest rate. If the coupon interest rate is higher than the market interest rate, the bond is quoted above its par value (*at a premium*) (market value > 100%). If the coupon interest rate is lower than the market interest rate, the opposite applies: the bond is quoted below its par value (*at a discount*).

Due to the low price per bond, a large number of people or institutions can provide capital to the company by purchasing one or more bonds. As bonds are easily tradable and have a fairly stable market value, this form of investment is attractive for people who do not wish to take large risks.

In principle, the *repayment* of a bond loan can be arranged in two ways. The first option is for all bonds to be repaid simultaneously at the maturity date. The bondholders receive the par value of the bonds in cash. The disadvantage of this method is that it requires the company (or other institution) to have a large amount of cash available on hand.

Repayment

This disadvantage is less with the second option, gradual repayment in parts: a certain part of the bond is redeemed during a previously determined period at regular points in time. When applied to bond loans, 10% of the bonds could, for example, be redeemed over a period of ten years, with payments at a pre-determined redemption date. This is called random redemption. All outstanding bonds have an equal chance to be drawn.

Random redemption

8

TEST QUESTION 8.1
What differences can be noted when comparing an investment in bonds to an investment in shares?

In order to issue a bond loan successfully, a company must offer its investors certainty that the interest and redemption obligations will be fulfilled throughout the entire term to maturity of the loan. That is why companies sometimes issue mortgage bonds: the company's real estate is used as collateral. In the event of a bankruptcy, the rights of the mortgage bondholders are met by the proceeds of the sale of the property concerned (as much as possible). As the bond loan is generally issued to a large number of investors, there is little to no contact between moneylenders and borrower. To overcome this lack of contact, a *trustee* (either administrative or trust office) is assigned.

Mortgage bonds

Trustee

This trustee acts on behalf of the bondholders if the company fails to meet its payment obligations. In the event of a mortgage bond loan, the assignment of a trustee is legally required.

Mortgage bonds are an example of bonds with special features. There are also other forms of special bonds, described below:

A *subordinated bond* is a bond whose bondholders, in the event of bankruptcy, receive principal redemption only after all financial obligations to other creditors have been fulfilled.

Subordinated bond

Zero bonds are bonds with no interest payments during the term to maturity, but with a repayment at the end of the term that is higher than the issue price of the bond. The issue price is the cash value paid to the bondholders of the redemption and the interest paid at the end of the term. The final amount paid to the bondholders, therefore, includes all interest payments.

Zero bonds

Discount bonds

Discount bonds are bonds with a low coupon rate whose repayment at the end of the term is higher than the issue amount. The final amount includes an extra interest payment.

For zero and discount bonds, market value increases during the term to maturity up to the final redemption amount.
Investors who wish to benefit from the revenue of their investment early will need to sell their bonds.
For companies, the most important advantage of zero or discount bonds is that there are little to no expenses for interest and redemption payments before the end of the term. A disadvantage is that early repayments are virtually impossible, since they would involve the full repayment of the par value, which would make the cost of capital very high.

8

EXAMPLE 8.1
A company starts an investment project with a length of ten years. The project is not expected to be profitable during the first years, but estimated to be able to render high profits at the end of the term. For the financing of this project, a zero bond loan is issued.
The par value of the bonds, to be paid as a redemption after ten years, amounts to €1,000.
The compensation to the bond holders (the yield) is set at 9%.
The issue price of these zero bonds can be calculated as follows:

$$\frac{€1,000}{1.09^{10}} = €422.41$$

The issue rate of these zero bonds is therefore established at 42.241%.

Bonds are sometimes also used for financing very high risk-bearing activities, such as takeovers of other companies. In such cases, the bonds have a very high coupon interest rate to attract investors in spite of the high risk. This type of bonds is also called *junk bonds*. Principal sum repayment and interest are paid using the proceeds of the acquired company, either from the cash flow or from the sale of parts of the company.

Junk bonds

Convertible bonds

Convertible bonds give the holders the right to exchange the bonds for shares at upfront conditions during a certain period (the conversion period). Convertible bonds can be attractive for both companies and bondholders. Companies can attract temporary capital by issuing convertible bonds, which can later be changed into equity. The bondholders is the company's creditor, with the option to become a shareholder.

TEST QUESTION 8.2
For each of the bond types mentioned, indicate what motive an investor could have for buying.

In a profitable company, an investor can exchange their convertible bonds for shares and benefit from the higher dividend payments and increasing market value. In a less successful company, bonds still offer a fixed interest payment and redemption at par value.

This means the investor will likely pay a higher amount for convertible bonds in comparison with ordinary bonds. The market value of a convertible bond is higher than that of a ordinary bond with the same interest payment and the same term to maturity. The difference between these market values is called the *premium over bond value.*

At the issue of a convertible bond, the conversion price is determined. The *conversion price* is the price that holders of a convertible bond pay for exchanging a bond for shares.

Conversion price

If the conversion right is exercised, a holder of a convertible bond pays the conversion price by handing in the convertible bonds. In order to determine the number of shares to be received, the par value of the bonds handed in is divided by the conversion price. If this does not result in a rounded off figure, the remaining part of the share is paid out based on the actual market value of the share.

The *conversion value* is the share value of the convertible bond, or the proceeds from the bond when converted into shares.

Conversion value

EXAMPLE 8.2

The terms of a convertible bond loan include the following information: From 1 January 2020 through 31 December 2022, the conversion of convertible bonds into shares is possible at the conversion price of €9 per share with a par value of €1. The par value of a convertible bond is €1,000.

An investor who holds three convertible bonds on 1 July 2021 wishes to convert his bonds. The market value of the share is €12. In exchange for the three convertible bonds, the investor is entitled to

$3 \times \dfrac{€1,000}{€9} = 333^{1}/_{3}$ shares. Of course, only whole shares can be issued.

The investor receives 333 shares and a cash amount equal to $\dfrac{1}{3}$ of the market value of the share: $\dfrac{1}{3} \times €12 = €4$.

The conversion value of three bonds then becomes: $333\dfrac{1}{3} \times €12 = €4,000$

And for one bond: $\dfrac{€4,000}{3} = €1,333.33$.

A variation on the convertible bond is the *reverse convertible*: it is not the investor who determines whether to convert into shares, but the company. For this reason, the interest paid is higher than that of a normal convertible bond.

Reverse convertible

Medium term notes resemble bonds. These are tradable debt securities to bearer with high par value and a term to maturity of two to five years.

Medium term notes

In a medium-term-note-program, the total debt is divided into separately marketable debt securities.

A company agrees a maximum amount to be raised with a bank that organizes the issue. Depending on the company's requirements and market conditions, attempts are made to issue debt securities. The total amount of the program is not issued at once but in parts.

For the issuing company, the flexibility to adapt to market developments with respect to issue date and term to maturity is an advantage. Furthermore, the issuing costs of medium-term-note-programs are much lower than those of a bond loan because they need only a concise memorandum instead of an elaborate prospectus. Due to the high par value, the market for medium term notes is limited. Only institutional investors managing a large capital are able to participate in a medium-term-note-program.

Table 8.1 summarizes the characteristics of the forms of long-term liabilities discussed.

TABLE 8.1 Characteristics of forms of long-term liabilities

	Bank loan	Bond loan	Medium term notes
Lender	One financial institution	Institutional investors, individuals and companies	Institutional investors
Issue date	Contract date	Issue date	Flexible, in parts
Repayment	Usually in installments	At once or in parts by draw	In parts
Terms of loan	Determined in mutual agreement	Determined by lender (issuing institution)	Determined by lender (issuing institution)

8.4 Current Liabilities

Paragraph 8.3 highlighted several types of long-term liabilities. The current paragraph covers current liabilities. These are obligations to be fulfilled by the company within one year.

Possible types of current liabilities are:
- *bank credit,* usually issued in the form of a line of credit
- *trade credit,* issued for the purchase of goods
- *buyer credit*, an advance payment made by the customer
- *near banking*, a form of mutual credit issuing between companies
- *cash loan*, a form of credit only available to large companies that borrow large sums for short periods
- *commercial paper*, marketable debt securities of companies, in large rounded figures
- *annuals*, such as salaries, tax to be paid, etc.
- *other short-term credits*

The most common forms of current liabilities are discussed in the following paragraphs.

Bank credit
Banks are institutions that are particularly suited to issue short-term credits since they have access to short-term resources entrusted to them in the

form of savings deposits or term deposits. Term deposits are deposits with a fixed term; the lender cannot withdraw freely during the term.
Considering that not all deposits tend to be demanded at once, a bank can make use of these deposits, for example, partly by lending the money for a longer term. Another part of the deposits can be loaned for a short term.
Shorter term loans are usually given the form of a *line of credit*.
A company is given a *credit limit*. This is the maximum amount by which a company may overdraw on its current account (overdraft).
A company pays an interest fee on the line of credit. There are different interest payment options:

- The company pays interest on the maximum amount of credit, independent of the actual amount of credit used.
- The company pays interest on the actual amount of credit used.
- The company pays interest on the actual amount of credit used and a (lower) fine on unused credit.

Line of credit

The interest rate charged for a credit line is higher than for a regular, fixed loan.
A company can repay the line of credit with temporary excess cash.
For a company, the advantage of this type of credit is that it can easily finance (strongly) fluctuating capital requirements.

TEST QUESTION 8.3
Why is a line of credit very suitable in financing a strongly fluctuating capital requirement?

Trade credit
A company receives trade credit if it receives goods (or services) without immediately having to pay for them. Trade credit, therefore, is a source of capital for the purchaser of goods.
A buyer who is offered trade credit recognizes this item on the credit side of the balance sheet under 'Accounts payable'. A supplier documents trade credit granted on the debit side of the balance sheet under 'Accounts receivable'.
The use of trade credit is also said to be a form of *commodity financing*, as the capital is not made available in cash but in the form of supplied goods.
The supplier sets the terms of the trade credit. They determine the period by which the received goods must be paid for. This period is either called the *net term* or the *payment term*.
In the event of early payment, a discount on the invoice amount is often granted. In this case, the *discount rate* and the *discount period* should be established. When setting the payment terms, industry standards are usually upheld.

Commodity financing

Net term
Payment term

Discount rate
Discount period

When receiving trade credit, the capital requirements from inventory build-up can be financed entirely or partially. Additional financing is required if the goods remain in storage for longer than the payment period, i.e.: if the storage period of the goods is longer than the net term. If the storage period of the goods is shorter than the net term, it is even possible to finance other assets with the received trade credit. For small companies, trade credit is an important aid in meeting capital requirements. There are hardly any other means of financing. Large companies have more options to attract capital. Whether a company decides to use trade credit depends on the costs of the various financing methods. For example, the costs of trade credit or bank credit need to be considered.

If a discount can be deducted for payment within a number of days of the invoice date, the costs of the trade credit can be calculated as shown in example 8.3.

EXAMPLE 8.3

A supplier's terms of payment are as follows:
- payment within 30 days of invoice date
- a 1% discount for payment within ten days of invoice date.

The net term is 30 days, the discount period is 10 days and the discount rate is 1%.
For a buyer who buys goods for a total invoice amount of €100, there are now two options:
1 The buyer pays (100% − 1%) of the invoice amount after ten days, being €99.
2 The buyer pays 100% of the invoice amount after 30 days, being €100.

Payment before the end of the discount or net term is not prudent. This only increases the costs, as will be discussed later.

If the buyer does not pay within ten days, they forfeit a discount of 1% of the invoice amount. The forfeited discount can be considered costs of trade credit. The buyer can use the unpaid amount of €99 for twenty days longer. The amount of €100 that must be paid after 30 days, comprises a €99 repayment and a €1 cost of the trade credit.

The costs of using the trade credit in percentages are:

$$\frac{€1}{€99} \times 100\% = 1.0101\%$$

The buyer receives 20 days of credit. Therefore, the annual costs are:

$$\frac{365}{20} \times 1.0101\% = 18.43\%$$

If the buyer decides not to make use of the discount, it would be unwise to repay the seller before the end of the net term, due to higher costs. If, for example, the buyer pays the invoice amount on the eleventh day following the invoice date, annual costs would be:

$$\frac{365}{1} \times 1.0101\% = 368.67\%$$

If the buyer does decide to make use of the offered trade credit, it is advised to use the entire credit term.

TEST QUESTION 8.4

What are the consequences for the required capital in a company when choosing for either trade credit or bank credit?

Buyer credit

Buyer credit is provided by the buyer to the supplier if payment takes place before the delivery of the goods or services.

From an efficiency point of view, and to reduce the risk of default of payment, it is common practice to demand advance payment in certain branches of the service industry and in production companies. For example, it is only be possible to see a movie in a cinema after having bought a ticket. In such an event, the advance payment contributes to the supplier's capital requirements hardly if at all. As there is barely any difference between the moment of payment and delivery, there is no real debt relationship between supplier and buyer.

If buyer credit is given for goods to be supplied, it can indeed have an important contribution to the financing of the supplier's capital requirement. This applies to large projects in particular. For example, it is common practice to pay part of the purchase price of a house that is still under construction. In general, (partial) payment is requested if the product concerned has high costs and long production and delivery times: for example, a house or a ship. The supplier does not want to run the risk of a buyer no longer wanting his product once it has been built and then refusing to pay. The supplier is also confronted with high costs during the production process and will therefore have built up high capital requirements which disappear entirely on delivery. By demanding payment from the buyer, capital requirements can be financed with buyer credit, preventing, for example, a requirement for expensive bank credit. The buyer will be prepared to provide buyer credit to be assured of the delivery of the goods.

The provided buyer credit is recognized on the debit side of the buyer's balance sheet, under 'prepaid amounts' or 'goods receivable'. The supplier documents buyer credit on the credit side of his balance sheet, under 'prepayments received' or 'goods to be delivered'.

TEST QUESTION 8.5
Is it possible to calculate the costs of buyer credit in the same manner as the costs of trade credit?

Commercial paper

Short-term marketable debt securities issued by companies to bearer are indicated by the term 'commercial paper'. By means of issuing a commercial-paper-program, a company can attract a large amount of short-term liabilities. Issuing a commercial-paper-program is done in the same way as issuing medium term notes. The period of these debt securities can vary from a few weeks to a maximum of two years. The minimum par value of commercial paper is €1 million. As the commercial paper is tradable, investors are satisfied with a slightly lower interest rate than what would be paid for short-term bank credit. This makes this form of credit attractive for companies.

Banks will also attract short-term credit by issuing marketable debt securities. In this case, they are not called commercial paper but *certificates of deposits*.

Certificates of deposits

8.5 New Financing Forms

The way in which companies finance their capital requirement has changed dramatically over the past years. SMEs in particular have traditionally always relied on bank credit; but as a result of the credit crisis, banks are required to be more careful in how, and to whom, they lend money. Therefore, companies are finding it harder to meet the terms and conditions set by banks. This has caused an increased interest in alternative forms of financing. Several of those financing forms are discussed in this paragraph, specifically: crowdfunding, credit unions, Qredits, investment funds, NPEX and staple financing.

Crowdfunding

The literal definition of crowdfunding is 'investments by the masses'. Crowdfunding is a relatively new form of financing which lets multiple parties invest in the same product or company simultaneously. Originating in the USA at the start of the century, it now (2017) encompasses $2.1 billion per year. In principle, the crowdfunding process takes place without any involvement or contributions from financial intermediaries. There is direct contact between the investors and the entrepreneurs. The term 'crowdfunding' derives from 'crowdsourcing', which involves contacting multiple parties online and requesting their involvement or input. In the case of crowdfunding, this input consists of investments. The underlying idea behind crowdfunding is that many investors together can accomplish more than they would be able to accomplish alone. Although each individual investor may only (be able to) invest a small amount of money – for example, in a startup company – the combined financial contributions of the investors can amount to the total starting capital the company requires.

Until now, crowdfunding has mainly been used on projects that focus on more than return on investment for the investors. It is, for example, possible to pre-fund the construction of a new (pilot) product using a group of crowdfunding investors.

Entrepreneurs interested in using crowdfunding turn to a crowdfunding platform. In the Netherlands, for example, there are currently over 40 platforms specialized in crowdfunding – and that number keeps growing still. The platform sets up the contracts and ensures that the investors who pledge an investment fulfill their payment(s).

On average, roughly 100 people invest money in a financing request, and companies receive €90,000 from crowdfunding. Legally speaking, the maximum allowed crowdfunded amount is €2.5 million.

There are several distinct possible forms of financing within the concept of crowdfunding:
- Loan: the company returns the loans in the form of interest and principal repayment. The credit term and the interest rate are set in advance. The exact terms and conditions of each loan differ per crowdfunding platform.
- Convertible loan: the company offers the investors the possibility of converting their loan into shares. The date of issue and the conditions are set in advance.
- Shares: the investors become co-owners of the company.

Crowdfunding

A total of €170 million was invested in crowdfunding projects in the Netherlands in 2016; approximately 80% of that was in companies. Around 3,300 companies have been financed using crowdfunding up to 2017, with total investments amounting to €300 million.

WakaWaka is one of the Netherlands' leading social enterprises. Established in 2011, WakaWaka has been focusing on providing people across the world with artificial light using innovative solar-powered lamps.

WakaWaka is more than just an enterprise; it also involves its crowd in the company proceedings. It employs a network of people surrounding the company. WakaWaka took part in no less than nine crowdfunding campaigns between 2011 and 2015. Those campaigns were used as a source of capital enabling growth for the company, and as a way of building on the crowd (the so-called Agents of Light) who have become involved in carrying out WakaWaka's mission over the years. In November 2016, exactly five years following the launch of their first product through crowdfunding, WakaWaka revisited its crowd – successfully. The total amount at the end of the campaign came to €1.1 million, accumulated by eight hundred Agents of Light.

Credit union

A credit unionis a collaborative group (cooperative) of companies within a certain region or industry, focused on mutually lending out and obtaining credit. The founders of the credit union manage the funds of the credit-lending companies within the union, and lend funds to companies within the union requesting financial support. The concept of credit union has been known and used for several years worldwide.
Most credit unions focus on a certain region or industry. In the Netherlands, the number of credit unions is growing rapidly. Approximately €3.5 million in credit was lent to approximately 50 SMEs in 2017.

Credit union

In 2017, the Brabant Credit Union was the first union to be allowed to offer credit that is 50% guaranteed by the Dutch state. This means there is less risk for the lender, allowing the credit union to offer lower interest rates as a result. Credit unions serve to bridge the gap between entrepreneurs with credit needs on the one hand, and entrepreneurs with limited investment opportunities for their available capital on the other. A credit union allows entrepreneurs to make both their resources and their knowledge available to others. This combination of capital, knowledge and expertise aims to contribute to the entrepreneurial climate in a company's own industry or region.

A characteristic feature of a credit union is that entrepreneurs offer credit to others without a bank acting as an intermediary. The advantages of a credit union are said to be:

- lack of a profit motive
- adaptability
- knowledge of the region and/or industry
- the ability to accurately assess risks and opportunities
- the direct involvement of credit union member entrepreneurs and their networks

Credit unions can be set up according to one of two models. There is no difference for the entrepreneur receiving credit, only for the entrepreneur investing in the credit union.

Risk sharing model

1. The risk sharing model
This involves credit being provided from a central treasury which houses resources from all investing entrepreneurs. These investors contribute capital using member certificates. The contributions cannot be withdrawn by the lenders. New credit union legislation, effective per 2016, states that bonds and deposits may also be used to this end. The credit union evaluates all credit requests and provides the credit. This spreads the risk between all members of the credit union. The credit union makes arrangements to mitigate loans that are not repaid. This limits the risk to the money lenders, but also limits return on investment.

Community funding model

2. The community funding model
The credit union assesses the credit request and, upon approval, presents it to the member investment platform. Investing entrepreneurs who are part of the credit union can sign up for investments they wish to take part in. Entrepreneurs are financed by more than one investor, usually between 5 and 25. In this case, credit does not move through a centralized treasury. The risk is shared exclusively between entrepreneurs investing in particular credit requestors. This means that no funds are attracted by the credit union as an entity. This model comes with higher risks for the money lenders since there are no central mitigating mechanisms to deal with unpaid loans; however, allows higher return on investment.

Qredits
Qredits is a private non-profit organization offering micro-credit up to €50,000, and SME-loans up to €250,000 to startups or existing companies in the Netherlands, to be used to set up new or expand on existing companies. Per 1 June 2016, Qredits has also been lending working capital up to €25,000. One condition for receiving an SME-loan is that the request for credit must first have been denied by a bank. Qredits also offers credit requestors a form of guidance in the form of volunteer coaches. Since its founding in 2009, Qredits has been lending credit to well over 9,500 entrepreneurs, to a total of €190 million as of the first quarter of 2017. Qredits, in turn, borrows its funds from major Dutch banks and the European investment bank.

Investment funds
In recent years, several new investment funds have been started, focusing specifically on SMEs.
The Dutch MKB Impulsfonds (SME Impulse Fund) is a financing institution for SME-entrepreneurs looking for a business loan between €250,000 and €1 million. Institutional investors provide the capital used by the MKB Impulsfonds to lend to healthy SMEs with ambitions for growth. The MKB Impulsfonds was started on 1 December 2014; in its first two years, it offered loans to a total of €48 million to 82 enterprises.

The Nederlandse Investeringsinstelling (Dutch Investment Institution, NLII) is a cooperation of insurance companies and pension funds focusing on improving the investment opportunities in the Dutch economy. NLII tries to remove investment obstacles from profitable financing possibilities which, due to their limited scope or insufficiently transparent risks or returns, are less suitable for institutional investors. To that end, NLII has founded two funds that combine financing by institutional investors with bank loans: the Bedrijfsleningenfonds (Company Loans Fund) and the Achtergestelde Leningenfonds (Subordinate Loans Fund).

The Bedrijfsleningenfonds (BLF) was established in September 2015. The BLF takes part in loans that a bank is willing but unable to offer to companies, for example, because it has too many outstanding finances in the company or industry in which that company operates. By assuming part of the financing, the fund makes it possible to increase the total amount offered to the company. The fund can add between €5 and €25 million to a loan. The bank provides a loan for at least an equal amount at equal terms and conditions. As of 2017, the fund has provided €195 million in loans to Dutch SMEs. The funds originate from institutional investors.

The Achtergestelde Leningenfonds (ALF) was established in June 2016. It offers subordinate loans to SMEs which, based on state of their balance sheets, are only partially if at all eligible for a bank loan without a subordinate loan. The fund is financed by institutional investors and provides subordinate loans of at least €150,000 and at most €5 million. For any amount provided as a subordinate loan, the bank provides an equal amount in regular bank loans.

NPEX
NPEX is a relatively new stock exchange, aimed specifically at SMEs. SMEs are not allowed on the major stock exchanges. The NPEX has been filling this gap since 2009. A listing on the NPEX allows SMEs to obtain funds by issuing shares or bonds. Amounts issued are between €1 million to €10-15 million. Most NPEX listings are concerned with (subordinate) bonds, but there are also several companies with listed shares.
Investors looking for a return are thus provided with the possibility of investing in companies or entrepreneurs to whom they previously had no access.
NPEX is an investment company licensed by the Dutch Autoriteit Financiële Markten (Financial Market Authority). NPEX is under continuous supervision by the AFM and De Nederlandse Bank (the Dutch central bank).

Staple financing

Whereas entrepreneurs previously obtained their financing from either banks or investors, nowadays it is possible to make use of multiple combined sources of finance. Staple financing is cutting up the required capital into segments that are each borrowed from different financing agents. It is a trend that has been around for several years, and that is steadily growing stronger.

The advantage of 'stapling' financing resources is that it allows for a higher total sum to be collected. Another advantage of combing financing resources is that it prevents entrepreneurs from having to depend on a single agent or agency. In addition, banks are often more willing to (partially) fund an investment if there are others, e.g. professional investors or crowdfunding participants, who have previously demonstrated their faith in the enterprise.

Entrepreneurs can choose from a variety of financing resources to staple – think of leasing, factoring, subsidizing, mortgaging, subordinate loaning, or making use of micro credits, credit on account, revolving credit, credit unions, angel investors or venture capital. In practice, of course, these sources are not all used together. Frequently found combinations include:

- factoring supplemented with a line of credit financing the growth of an enterprise
- an angel investor in combination with a subsidy helping a startup to develop their technology
- an angel investor and a crowdfunding campaign helping a startup to win its first customers
- a bank and an investment fund helping a company to expand

A disadvantage of staple financing is that it requires an understanding of the different sources of financing used. Each of these forms of financing has its own characteristics, e.g. various monetary resources each have their own terms to maturity. Moreover, capital providers each have their own method to assess a business plan, and apply their own terms and conditions.

An additional challenge to the entrepreneur is ensuring that the funds coming in from different sources are all available in time to help realize the intended goals.

8.6 Provisions

Provisions are a special category of liabilities. A provision is a future obligation, linked to the company's operations in the current period, of which the exact amount and/or time at which it is to occur is not yet known. Provisions differ from liabilities in a sense that a debt holds a legally perfect obligation of payment and a provision does not. In the case of a debt, the exact amounts and times of payment are known in advance. The exact amount of a provision is unknown; it is even possible that the (full) amount does not have to be paid at all.

A provision's size is the best possible estimate of the amount required to fulfill the obligation concerned. This amount is deducted from the profit.

EXAMPLE 8.4

In 2017, a dissatisfied customer began a lawsuit against a company. In 2018, the judge rules in favor of the customer. The judge determines that the amount of damages has to be established by an independent expert. In 2019, the compensation is set at €80,000.

In 2017, it was not clear to the company whether damages would need to be paid and if so, how much. The company needed to make a provision of the estimated amount (for example, €100,000).
In 2018, the company is aware that it will have to settle. The exact amount, however, is still not known.
In 2019, the company has an actual debt at the moment that the amount of the compensation is determined. The payable amount is set at €80,000. This results in €20,000 added to the profit again.
Summarized, the following balance changes (in Euros) will occur:

2017	Provision	+100,000
	Profit	−100,000
2018	No changes	
2019	Provision	− 100,000
	Debt	+ 80,000
	Profit	+ 20,000

The obligations deriving from provisions are not limited to expected payments to others, but can also be related to expected losses.
A manufacturer of household appliances can, for example, create a provision to cover future repair costs of broken appliances during their warranty period.

From a financing point of view, it should be noted that provisions are not a capital resource. Provisions are deducted from profit. Equity is replaced by liabilities.

TEST QUESTION 8.6
What is the characterizing difference between provisions and reserves?

Glossary

Bank loan	A loan issued by a bank to a company.
Bond	Debt security of a company as part of a loan, usually to bearer and freely tradable.
Buyer credit	Credit provided by the buyer to the supplier, when payment takes place before the delivery of the goods or services.
Certificates of deposits	Tradable debt securities to bearer with a short term to maturity, issued by banks.
Commercial paper	Tradable debt securities to bearer with a short term to maturity, issued by companies.
Commodity financing	Capital transfer where the capital is not made available in cash but in the form of supplied goods.
Conversion price	The issue price of shares, that holders of a convertible bond pay when they exercise their right to the exchange the bond for shares.
Convertible bond	Bond whose holder is entitled to exchange the bond for shares, against previously determined conditions, during a certain period.
Credit term	Term by which credit must be repaid.
Credit union	A cooperative of companies within a certain region or industry, focused on mutually lending out and obtaining credit
Crowdfunding	Financing method which involves companies, foundations or private individuals using a crowdfunding platform to pitch their ideas, thereby hoping to attract the funds required to realize the plans they put forth.
Discount bond	Bond which has a low coupon rate during the term of the bond and a higher repayment at the end of the term than the issue amount.
Junk bonds	Bond with a high coupon rate, used to finance company takeovers.

Liabilities	Capital creditors have made available to the company.
Line of credit	Credit provided by a bank, allowing a company to overdraw on its current account up to a maximum amount (credit limit).
Medium term notes	Tradable debt securities to bearer with a term to maturity of at least two years.
Mortgage loan	Loan in which the borrower hands over security by means of a claim on real estate.
Primary capital	Capital which, in the event of bankruptcy, serves as a buffer to meet obligations to creditors.
Provision	Future obligation, linked to a company's operations in the current period, whose exact amount and/or time of occurrence is currently unknown.
Staple financing	Combining different financing forms in order to accommodate a capital requirement.
Subordinated liabilities	Capital whose providers only receive interest and (part of) the principal amount after all financial obligations to all other creditors have been met.
Trade credit	Credit provided by a supplier if a buyer receives goods without immediately having to pay for them.
Term loan	Long-term financial loan whose terms are laid down in a mutual agreement between the lender and the borrower.
Zero bond	Bond with no interest payments during the term, but whose repayment at the end of the term is higher than the issue amount of the bond.

8

Multiple-choice questions

8.1   What is the advantage of a term loan over a bond loan?
a A term loan is more easily tradable.
b A term loan is considered a long-term liability.
c The interest on a term loan is entirely deductible for tax relief.
d A term loan is negotiated with one or a few persons.

8.2   When is the purchasing of a company's own issued bonds (for example, at 7%) advantageous for the company?
a If the interest on the capital market has decreased.
b If the interest on the capital market has increased.
c If early redemption is not possible.
d It is never advantageous.

8.3   Which type of bond gives a bondholder more certainty with respect to interest payments and principal sum repayment?
a A subordinated bond.
b A convertible bond.
c A mortgage bond.
d A zero bond.

8.4   What is the characteristic of discount bonds in comparison with ordinary bonds?
a Tax free interest.
b Higher annual interest rate.
c Higher repayment value.
d Interest payment in the form of shares.

8.5   The par value of a zero bond, with a term maturity of five years, is €1,000. The yield interest rate is set at 12%. What is the issue price of the zero bond (rounded to two decimal places)?
a 32.20%
b 46.32%
c 56.74%
d 68.06%

8.6   What are the consequences of the conversion of convertible bonds into shares for a company's balance sheet?
a Both equity and liabilities increase.
b Both equity and liabilities decrease.
c Equity decreases and liabilities increase.
d Equity increases and liabilities decrease.

8.7   The terms of a convertible bond loan include the following:
From 1 January 2019 through 1 January 2022 trading in convertible bonds for shares is possible at a conversion price of €17.50 per share with a par value of €0.50. The par value of a convertible bond is €1,000.

On 1 January 2019, an investor holds ten convertible bonds and wishes to convert them because the market value of the share is €22. The market value of the convertible bond is 130% on 1 January 2019.
Which of the following statements is correct?
a In exchange for 10 convertible bonds, the investor receives 454 shares and €12 in cash.
b The conversion value of a bond is €1,257.14.
c The premium above conversion value is €4.50 on 1 January.
d None of the above statements is correct.

8.8   What is the advantage of a medium-term-note-program when compared to a bond loan?
a The bank assists in the issue and bears the risk.
b The issuing costs are lower.
c The interest rate is lower.
d More investors can subscribe to the issue.

8.9   Which type of capital is *not* part of current liabilities?
a Dividend to be paid.
b Buyer credit received.
c Prepaid amounts.
d Commercial paper.

8.10   The payment terms of a supplier are as follows: for payment within the discount period of half a month, a 2% discount on the invoice amount is granted; the permitted credit period is two months.
What is the cost of trade credit (rounded to one decimal place):
a 12.0%
b 12.2%
c 16.0%
d 16.3%

8.11   Which form of short-term liability is applicable if a buyer receives credit from his supplier?
a Buyer credit.
b Trade credit.
c Near banking.

8.12   What is the effect on a company's capital requirement if the company grants buyer credit to its supplier(s)?
a The capital requirement is reduced.
b The capital requirement remains equal.
c The capital requirement is increased.

8.13   What advantage does the issue of commercial paper have when compared to a line of credit?
a   The interest payments are deductible for tax relief.
b   It is possible to repay the entire debt in parts.
c   It has a lower interest rate.
d   Commercial paper has a short term to maturity.

8.14   Statement 1: A provision is a retention of profit with the purpose of financing future replacement investments.
Statement 2: Term loans are granted particularly by institutional investors and not tradable at the stock exchange.
Which statement is correct?
a   Both statements are correct.
b   Statement 1 is correct, statement 2 is wrong.
c   Statement 1 is wrong, statement 2 is correct.
d   Both statements are wrong.

8.15   Which of the following is not a provision?
a   The warranty provision of an auto dealer.
b   The provision for unrecoverable receivables of a wholesaler.
c   The provision for major maintenance costs of a housing cooperative.
d   The dividend provision of an IT business.

9

Assessment of the Financial Structure

9.1   **Ratio Analyses**
9.2   **Profitability Ratios**
9.3   **Solvency Ratios**
9.4   **Liquidity Ratios**

The financial structure of a company is determined by the amount and composition of the investments in capital goods and the way in which the related capital requirement is financed. It can be assessed based on a number of aspects. The starting point for the assessment of the financial structure by external analysts is the published financial statements. Based on certain items on the balance sheet and on the income statement, a number of ratios can be calculated, each of which has significance for a particular aspect of the financial structure.
In paragraph 9.1, the possibilities and objections of such an analysis are discussed. Paragraphs 9.2 through 9.4 discuss the ratios which relate to the aspects of profitability, solvency and liquidity, respectively.

9.1 Ratio Analyses

In the world of business, one is frequently confronted with the need to make a judgement on a company's financial structure. Potential investors need to determine whether it is worth buying shares in a particular company; a bank needs to assess whether to grant a loan and a supplier needs to know whether a buyer is capable of actually paying for the goods delivered.

If an outsider needs to assess the financial structure of a company, they have to rely on the annual report published by the company concerned. The annual report will be discussed at length in part 4.

The most important parts of the annual report are the financial statements, comprising the balance sheet, income statement and notes to the accounts. The published figures relate to the last completed financial year and the previous financial year. By linking different entries of the balance sheet and the income statement, it is possible to gain more insight into the financial health of a company.

Ratio analysis This analysis, based on calculating ratios, is called *ratio analysis*. The calculated ratios are divided as follows:
- profitability ratios
- solvency ratios
- liquidity ratios

There is a number of objections to an assessment of the financial structure based on ratios:
- Generally speaking, there are no established standards to which the values of the different ratios should adhere. Therefore, a single calculation of ratios is hardly a basis for a well-considered conclusion. The rules of thumb that are sometimes applied do by no means always prove to be adequate in practice.
- The figures on the balance sheet provide information at a single *moment*. Certain financial obligations that arise immediately after the balance sheet date, such as salary payments, are not visible on the balance sheet.
- The balance sheet can provide a flattering picture of the financial structure in the event of window dressing. *Window dressing* refers to all activities prior to drawing up the balance sheet whose purpose is to create a more favorable financial structure on the balance sheet date. Company management could, for example, decide to quickly pay some short-term debts just prior to drawing up the financial accounts – thus improving the financial structure.

Historical analysis

Comparative business analysis

Despite these objections, ratio analyses can still be useful. By calculating the ratios of a company at consecutive moments, an insight into the development of the financial structure can be gained. Improvement or deterioration can be indicated without having to pass absolute judgment. This is known as a *historical analysis*. It is also possible to compare the ratios of a company to those of other, preferably similar, companies, for example, within the same industry. This is called a *comparative business analysis*.

9.2 Profitability Ratios

Profitability is an important condition for guaranteeing the continuity of a company. Profit can be related to sales revenue. This ratio is called the *gross profit margin*.

$$\text{Gross profit margin} = \frac{\text{Operating income}}{\text{Sales revenue}}$$

The *operating income* consists of the profit before the deduction of interest expenses and tax (*EBIT: earnings before interest and tax*).

The gross profit margin indicates the difference between the selling price and the costs of goods sold. This can be used to derive to what extent the company is resilient to price falls or cost increases.

Profitability is in general the ratio between earnings (profit) and the capital that generates these earnings.   **Profitability**

Profitability is an important measure for a company's long-term management strategy. In order to assess a company's profitability, the return on investment of the company's total capital must be determined. The financing method of the assets is not relevant here. To support a company's continuity, the long-term operating result should be sufficient to allow for the required dividend and interest payments to investors. The profitability of the total investment is calculated on the basis of the operating income.

The profitability of a company's total invested capital, the *Return on assets* (ROA), is calculated as follows: **Return on assets**

$$\text{ROA} = \frac{\text{EBIT}}{\text{Average total assets}} \times 100\%$$

To equity providers (the owners), the operating result is not significant as interest payments on liabilities and tax on profit must still be deducted. Therefore the relevant profit for equity providers is net income. Net income consists of profit after deduction of interest costs and tax.

Return on equity, (ROE) the calculation of the profitability of equity after tax, is: **Return on equity**

$$\text{ROE} = \frac{\text{Net income}}{\text{Average equity}} \times 100\%$$

Note: The calculation of the ROE is based on the average equity. Generally speaking, this would be identified as the ROAE. Nevertheless, the term ROE is far more commonly used and is therefore the term that is used in the formula.

The profitability of equity can also be calculated before tax (ROE_{bt}):

$$\text{ROE}_{bt} = \frac{\text{Operating profit after interest before tax}}{\text{Average invested equity}} \times 100\%$$

For creditors, the profitability of the capital invested in a company is equal to the agreed interest rate.

Average cost of debt

The company considers the interest paid costs. The *average cost of debt* can therefore be regarded as the average return on capital provided by creditors.

$$\text{Average cost of debt} = \frac{\text{Interest}}{\text{Average debt}} \times 100\%$$

EXAMPLE 9.1

The simplified balance sheet of Hansen LLC on 1 January and 31 December 2017 is as follows:

Balance sheet (× €1,000)

	1/1	31/12		1/1	31/12
Assets	10,000	12,000	Share capital	4,000	4,000
			Liabilities	6,000	7,000
			Profit before tax	–	1,000
	10,000	12,000		10,000	12,000

In 2017, interest costs were €400,000.
The profit before tax is distributed as follows:
- Corporate tax   €200,000
- Dividend   €200,000
- Retained earnings   €600,000

The corporate tax and dividend to be paid are part of the liabilities; the retained earnings are part of equity.
Thus the result is:

$$\text{Average total assets} = \frac{€10,000,000 + €12,000,000}{2} = €11,000,000$$

$$\text{Average equity} = \frac{4,000,000 + (€4,000,000 + €600,000)}{2}$$

$$= €\,4,300,000$$

$$\text{Average debt} = \frac{€6,000,000 + (€7,000,000 + €200,000 + €200,000)}{2}$$

$$= €\,6,700,000$$

The profitability ratios are calculated as follows:

$$\text{ROA} = \frac{€400,000 + €1,000,000}{€11,000,000} \times 100\% = 12.73\%$$

$$\text{ROE} = \frac{€800,000}{€4,300,000} \times 100\% = 18.6\%$$

$$\text{ROE}_{bt} = \frac{€1,000,000}{€4,300,000} \times 100\% = 23.26\%$$

$$\text{ACD} = \frac{€400,000}{€6,700,000} \times 100\% = 5.97\%$$

In example 9.1, the average cost of debt is smaller than the ROA: the use of €1 in liabilities costs the company 5.97% in interest payments, and the proceeds for the company are 12.73%. This is an example of a loan being used to generate profit. These proceeds benefit the profitability of equity. This is known as *financial leverage* or the *financial leverage of the financial structure.*

Financial leverage

The debt-to-equity ratio (D/E) is called the *leverage ratio* or gearing ratio. It determines the extent to which equity providers benefit from the return on liabilities.

Leverage ratio
Gearing ratio

In example 9.1, the average invested debt is €6,700,000; therefore, the extra profit on the use of debt for the equity providers is:

$$€6,700,000 \times (0.1273 - 0.0597) = €452,920.$$

The proceeds benefit the profitability of the shareholders' equity.
The average equity is €4,300,000. For each €1 in equity, the extra profit is:

$$\frac{€452,920}{€4,300,000} = 0.1053$$

This profit is equal to the difference between the ROE_{bt} and ROA (0.2326 – 0.1273).

The link between the ROE, ROA and ACD can be represented as follows:

$$\text{ROE}_{bt} = \text{ROA} + (\text{ROA} - \text{ACD}) \times \frac{\text{debt}}{\text{equity}}$$

The financial leverage effect is expressed in this formula by:

$$(\text{ROA} - \text{ACD}) \times \frac{\text{debt}}{\text{equity}}$$

which is added to the ROA to calculate the ROE before tax.

For the profitability of the shareholders' equity after tax, this becomes:

$$\text{ROE}_{at} = (1 - f) \times \text{ROE}_{bt}$$

$$\text{ROE}_{at} = (1 - f) \times \left[\text{ROA} + (\text{ROA} - \text{ACD}) \times \frac{\text{debt}}{\text{equity}} \right]$$

where f = tax rate

In figure 9.1, the financial leverage effect is demonstrated visually.

FIGURE 9.1 The financial leverage effect

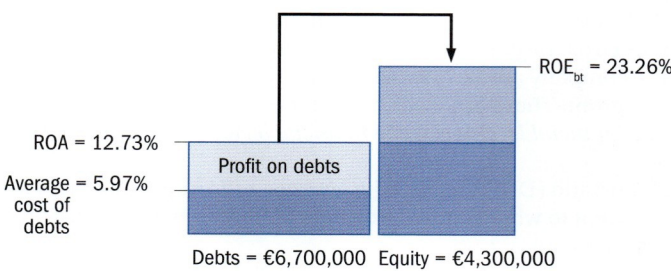

As shown, the profitability of equity in example 9.1 is influenced favorably by financing part of the company's assets with debts. This would seem to indicate that it is in the interest of equity providers to use the leverage effect to a maximum, by financing using liabilities as much as possible. Against this line of reasoning, a number of objections can be made, as is explained in the following paragraphs.

The first objection is that operating income is not known in advance. Profit could be much lower than expected. The obligations to the creditors must always be met, regardless of the amount of profit. If the return on assets were to fall below the average cost of debt, there would be a loss on the use of liabilities. The profitability of equity would then decrease as a result of meeting interest payments.
The uncertainty with respect to the profitability of the total equity is called the *operating risk* or business risk.

Operating risk

A second objection is that a decrease in the ROA is passed on to the ROE after having been magnified by the leverage ratio. This implies that the risk for equity providers is larger than the already mentioned operating risk. The additional risk for equity providers is called the financial risk.

Financial risk

The *financial risk* creates additional uncertainty with respect to the profitability of equity. The following link exists between the financial risk and the operating risk:

Financial risk = Operating risk × Leverage ratio

A final objection could be that the greater the amount in liabilities used for financing, the greater the creditor's risk. Creditors will demand a higher interest rate. As a result, liability costs increase, causing an even further increase in the risk that the ROA will be lower than the average cost of debt.

- -

EXAMPLE 9.2
Greenewold Corporation has an average total invested capital of €4,000,000, consisting of an average equity of €2,500,000 and €1,500,000 in liabilities. On these liabilities, 6% interest is paid (6% of

€2,500,000 = €90,000). The profit before tax for the coming year cannot be exactly predicted, but forecasts put it at no lower than €50,000 and no higher than €250,000.

In a worst-case scenario, this results in:

$$\text{ROA} = \frac{€50,000 + €90,000}{€4,000,000} \times 100\% = 3.5\%$$

$$\text{ROE}_{bt} = \frac{€50,000}{€2,500,000} \times 100\% = 2\%$$

In a best-case scenario, this results in:

$$\text{ROA} = \frac{€250,000 + €90,000}{€4,000,000} \times 100\% = 8.5\%$$

$$\text{ROE}_{bt} = \frac{€250,000}{€2,500,000} \times 100\% = 10\%$$

The possible spread of the ROA amounts to 8.5% − 3.5% = 5%.
The possible spread of the ROE$_{bt}$ amounts to 10% − 2% = 8%.

The possible spread of the ROE$_{bt}$ is therefore 3% higher than that of the ROA.
The spread of the ROA (5%) is the operating risk. The additional spread of the ROE$_{bt}$ (3%) is the financial risk.
The financial risk can be calculated by multiplying the business risk by the leverage ratio (D/E):

$$5\% \times \frac{€1,500,000}{€2,500,000} = 3\%$$

TEST QUESTION 9.1
Explain how and why the profitability of the company's equity can be influenced by the market interest rate.

A tool for further analysis of the profitability of the total invested capital is the *Dupont Chart*. The Dupont Chart splits the profitability of the total invested capital, based on important items on the balance sheet and income statement, in such a manner that the consequences for the profitability of a change in one or more of these items becomes visible. The Dupont Chart uses the following link between the ROA and the gross profit margin:

Dupont Chart

ROA = Total assets turnover ratio × gross profit margin

The *total assets turnover ratio* shows the relationship between sales revenue and total invested capital.

Total assets turnover ratio

FIGURE 9.2 Dupont Chart

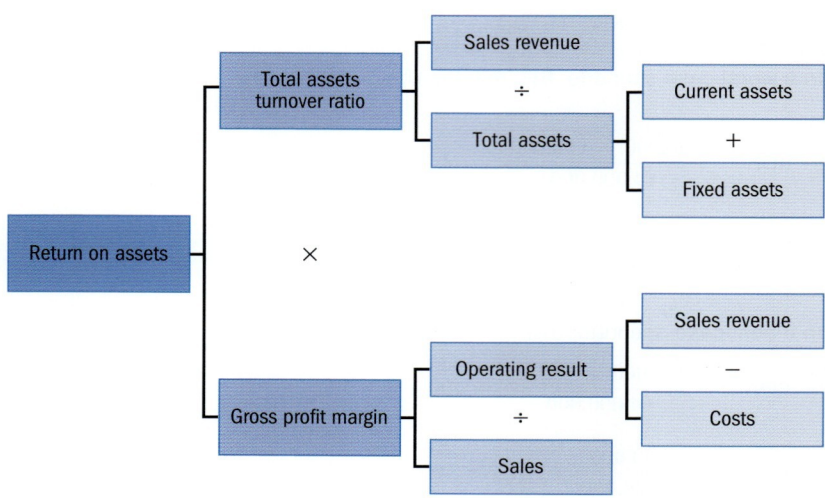

9

American chemical company E.I. du Pont de Nemours & Co was the first to present the relation between a number of ratios in the form of a schedule. The model that was used had been developed by F. Donaldson Brown, an engineer for the treasury department. Following DuPont's purchase of a large number of shares in General Motors at the beginning of the twentieth century, Brown was tasked with bringing order to the financial information of the automobile company. To that end, Brown developed the model that would come to be known as the Dupont Chart. It demonstrates the correlation between a number of items on the income statement and balance sheet and provides an insight into the makeup of the profit.

EXAMPLE 9.3

The trading company BBK Corporation Inc. has published the following simplified financial statements over the financial year 2017:

Balance sheet on 31 December 2016 and 2017 (× €1,000)

	2016	2017		2016	2017
Fixed assets	3,000	3,100	Equity	3,000	3,200
Inventories	1,900	2,500	Long-term liabilities	2,200	2,500
Accounts receivable	1,500	1,400	Current liabilities	1,800	2,300
Cash and cash equivalents	600	1,000			
	7,000	8,000		7,000	8,000

Income statement over 2017 (× €1,000)

Sales revenue		5,000
Costs of goods sold	3,000	
Personnel expenses	500	
Depreciation	600	
Other operating expenses	300	
		4,400
Operating result		600
Interest paid		200
Profit before tax		400

Completing the Dupont Chart to determine the ROA provides the following result for this company:

FIGURE 9.3 Dupont Chart to determine the return on total assets

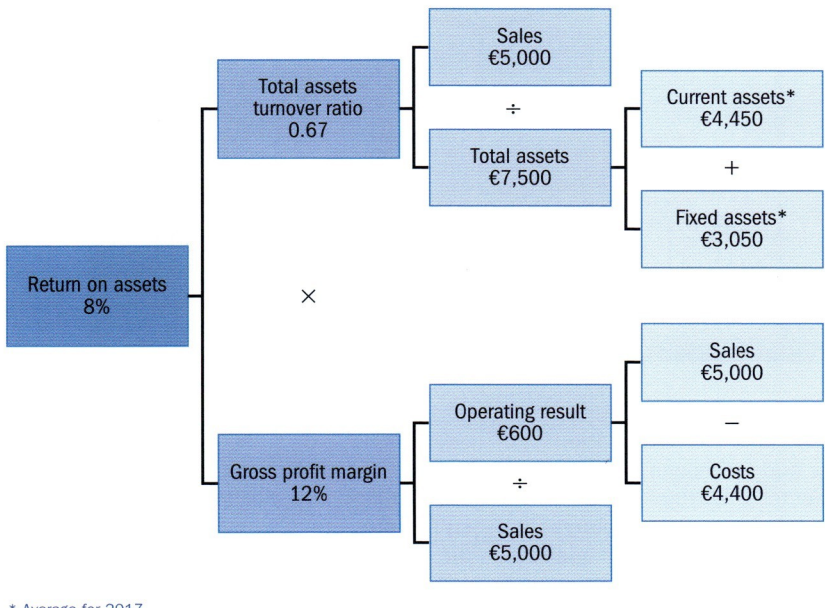

* Average for 2017

9.3 Solvency Ratios

Solvency

Liquidation value

Debt ratio

Solvency is the extent to which a company can meet its financial obligations towards its creditors in the event of bankruptcy; in such an event, the proceeds of sales of all assets should cover the amount of debts, with the equity acting as a buffer because the proceeds of the assets (the liquidation value) of a company going bankrupt is usually lower than their book value. The remaining money (if any) is paid to equity providers.

Since the liquidation value of the assets is not known, the assessment of the solvency is based on the book value as mentioned on the balance sheet out of necessity.

Solvency is usually measured by the ratio of equity/total assets or, in other words, 'which part of the total assets is financed with equity' – but of course the liabilities can also be used as a basis.

The *debt ratio* (DR) indicates which part of the total capital requirement is financed with liabilities.

$$\text{Debt ratio} = \frac{\text{Liabilities}}{\text{Total assets}}$$

The solvency and debt ratio give an impression of the size of the buffer available to the creditors.

Dutch construction company Heijmans suffered severe losses in 2016 as the result of losses and provisions on a number of problem projects. Their total setback: €90 million. This lowered the company's solvency (the ratio of equity to total assets) from 26% to 16% within a year's time. By using the proceeds from the sale of foreign daughter companies, completing the problem projects and setting new financing agreements, Heijmans hopes to prevent having to attract new equity. Increasing equity is not part of the current agreement with the banks. Financers contributing to Heijmans have, however, demanded sufficient security. Should the need arise, the banks have a claim on many of the company's assets, such as land positions and revenues from disinvestments. Heijmans' solvency is expected to increase to 20% over 2017, following the cash inflow from the disinvestment.

Linked to solvency is a company's financial resilience.
Financial resilience is a company's capacity to keep continuing its activities
during unfavorable times. A ratio linked to financial resilience is the *interest
coverage ratio*, which can be calculated as follows:

**Financial
resilience**

**Interest coverage
ratio**

$$\text{Interest coverage ratio} = \frac{\text{Operating profit}}{\text{Interest}}$$

$$= \frac{\text{Earnings before interest and tax (EBIT)}}{\text{Interest}}$$

The interest coverage ratio indicates the extent to which the operating
result is able to fall without jeopardizing interest payments to creditors. For
a value smaller than 1, the achieved profit is insufficiently high to pay the
interest, and the company will need to draw on its equity.

The financing of activities should not be in danger in a period of
disappointing results. Thus, it is necessary for the financial structure to
be flexible instead of rigid. The financial structure should, under both
favorable and unfavorable conditions, be able to adapt to changing
circumstances. This ability is referred to as elasticity. The *elasticity* of the
capital structure indicates to what extent the composition of the available
capital can be adjusted to match a changing capital requirement.

Elasticity

TEST QUESTION 9.2
How is a company's solvency influenced by striving for capital structure
elasticity?

9.4 Liquidity Ratios

The *liquidity* of a company indicates to what extent it can meet its short-
term financial obligations. To assess liquidity, some knowledge of forecast
cash inflow and cash outflow is required. The assessment of liquidity in this
respect is called a dynamic liquidity analysis.
The *dynamic liquidity* indicates whether, during a certain period, the
incoming cash flow exceeds the outgoing cash flow. This is established by
drawing up a cash flow forecast during the preceding period.
The *cash flow forecast* comprises an overview of forecast cash inflows and
outflows for a coming period. If a company, considering both actually
available and cash infow, has sufficient cash to meet all cash outflows, the
company has sufficient liquidity. If this is not the case, additional cash
resources need to be found, for example, by negotiating a loan. The cash
flow forecast was discussed in paragraph 6.4.

Liquidity

Dynamic liquidity

**Cash flow
forecast**

The assessment of the liquidity and the cash flow forecast require internal
data. For an outsider, this information is usually not available since it is
not published. This means outside analysts will need to rely on published
financial data, in particular, the balance sheet, out of necessity. As the
data concerned covers a particular situation at a particular moment,
the resulting analysis is called a static liquidity analysis. In general, the
reliability of this method is lower than the previously mentioned method.

Static liquidity *Static liquidity* indicates whether, considering the amount and composition
of current assets, a company can meet its short-term financial obligations.
The analysis of static liquidity is carried out at a particular moment, based
on the published balance sheet. In the balance sheet, the assets are divided
according to their turnover period (with a distinction between fixed and
current assets), and the available capital is divided into equity and long-
term and current liabilities. The following model should be applied:

Balance sheet on …

Fixed assets	Equity
Current assets	Long-term liabilities
	Current liabilities

For the static liquidity analysis, current assets and current liabilities
are important. However, this analysis relies on more than knowledge of
amounts; it also requires knowledge of asset composition. Not all current
assets have an equal liquidity. In general, inventory is less easily turned into
cash than accounts receivable. The previously discussed inventory turnover
ratio and the average days sales outstanding are good indicators of the
liquidity of these balance sheet entries (see chapter 6).

TEST QUESTION 9.3
Is a company's liquidity analyzed best using the cash flow forecast *or* using
the balance sheet?

There are several concepts and ratios that play an important part in the
static liquidity analysis.
Net working capital refers to current assets that are financed using long-
term capital: equity and long-term liabilities. The net working capital
indicates by what amount the current assets, also known as gross working
capital, exceed current liabilities.
The net working capital is calculated as follows:

Net working capital = Current assets − current liabilities

Since the balance sheet, by definition, is in balance, net working capital can
also be calculated in another way, namely by determining the difference
of the remaining credit items (equity and long-term liabilities) and the
remaining debit items (fixed assets). Therefore:

Net working capital = Equity + long-term liabilities − fixed assets

If the net working capital is positive, it indicates that the company can free
sufficient current assets to meet its short-term obligations. The company's
liquidity position is therefore sufficient.
The calculation of net working capital renders an absolute value. Whether
this value is high or low, also depends on the size of current liabilities. A
value of, for example, €1 million in net working capital is high for current
liabilities of €100,000 and low for current liabilities of €100 million.
To obtain a better picture, it can be helpful to calculate a relative value (or
ratio). The ratios that can be calculated to assess liquidity are the current
ratio and the acid test ratio (quick ratio).

The *current ratio* indicates the relationship between current assets and current liabilities.   **Current ratio**

$$\text{Current ratio} = \frac{\text{Current assets}}{\text{Current liabilities}}$$

There is a close relationship between the current ratio and the net working capital, considering that both use the same balance sheet items (current assets and current liabilities).

In general, inventory has a lower liquidity than accounts receivable or cash and cash equivalents. The *acid test ratio* is a liquidity ratio that does not take   **Acid test ratio** inventory into consideration.
The acid test ratio is calculated as follows:

$$\text{Acid test ratio} = \frac{(\text{Current assets} - \text{Inventory})}{\text{Current liabilities}}$$

or

$$\text{Acid test ratio} = \frac{(\text{Accounts receivable} + \text{Cash and cash equivalents})}{\text{Current liabilities}}$$

9

- -

EXAMPLE 9.4
The following simplified balance sheet is provided for a company:

Balance sheet on 31 December 2017

Premises	30	Share capital	20
Machines	25	Reserves	30
Inventories	15	Mortgage loan	20
Accounts receivable	10	Accounts payable	10
Cash and cash equivalents	20	Short-term bank loan	20
	100		100

The aforementioned ratios are calculated at:

Net working capital = Current assets – current liabilities
                         = (15 + 10 + 20) – (10 + 20) = 15

or

Net working capital = Equity + long-term liabilities – fixed assets
                         = (20 + 30) + 20 – (30 + 25) = 15

Current ratio   = Current assets / current liabilities
                         = (15 + 10 + 20) / (10 + 20) = 45 / 30 = 1.5
Acid test ratio   = (Current assets – inventories) / current liabilities
                         = (45 – 15) / 30 = 1

or

Acid test ratio = (Accounts receivable + cash and cash equivalents) / current liabilities = (10 + 20) / 30 = 1

Company management may window dressing to make the liquidity look better than it actually is. By paying the accounts payable to creditors using cash and cash equivalents just prior to drawing up the balance sheet, the resulting calculation of the current ratio comes to:

Current ratio   =   Current assets / current liabilities
                  =   (15 + 10 + 10) / 20
                  =   35 / 20 = 1.75

The increased value of the current ratio indicates a better liquidity position. However, this is merely due to the early payment of suppliers; it is nothing more than keeping up appearances.

TEST QUESTION 9.4
What is the effect on the current ratio of the payment of accounts receivable with cash and cash equivalents if current liabilities exceed the value of current assets?

Glossary

Acid test ratio	Ratio between the current assets, excluding the inventories and the current liabilities.
Current ratio	Ratio between total current assets and current liabilities.
Debt ratio	Ratio between liabilities and total assets.
Elasticity	The extent to which the capital structure can be adjusted to match a changing capital requirement.
Financial resilience	A company's capacity to continue its activities under unfavorable circumstances.
Financial risk	The extra uncertainty with respect to the return on equity due to capital structure.
Gross profit margin	Ratio between operating income and sales revenue.
Interest coverage ratio	Ratio between the operating income and the interest on liabilities.
Liquidity	The extent to which a company can meet its short-term financial obligations.
Net working capital	The part of the current assets financed with long-term capital.
Operating risk	The uncertainty with respect to the operating result.
Profitability	Ratio between the profit and the capital investments used to generate this profit.
Return on assets	The profitability of a company's total invested capital.
Return on equity	The profitability of a company's equity.

9

Solvency	The extent to which a company can meet its financial obligations to creditors in the event of bankruptcy.
Total assets turnover ratio	Ratio between sales revenue and the total assets.
Window dressing	Activities effected before drawing up the balance sheet, whose purpose is to make the financial structure appear better than it is in reality.

9

Multiple-choice questions

9.1 Which of the following statements is *not* correct?
a A company uses window dressing to make its financial structure appear better.
b A historical analysis provides information on the development of the financial structure of a company.
c By comparing the calculated value of the ratios with absolute standards, a statement on the financial health of a company can be made.
d In comparative business analyses, the ratios of different companies are compared.

9.2 What is the most accurate description of financial leverage?
a Increasing total assets turnover ratio.
b Financing with liabilities to increase the profitability of equity.
c Financing with bonds to increase the profitability of preferred shares.
d Financing with a long-term debt to increase the profitability of equity.

9.3 When does financial leverage effect occur?
a Liabilities = 0.
b Liabilities = equity.
c ROA = average cost of debt.
d ROA = ROE (before tax).

9.4 In a particular year, an LLC has an average equity of €500,000 and €300,000 in liabilities. The average interest on the liabilities is 8%. The profit after tax in that year is €40,000. The corporate tax rate is 20%. Calculate the leverage ratio in this case.
a 0.375
b 0.6
c 0.625
d 1.667

9.5 Refer to question 9.4.
Calculate the ROE (after tax) for the LLC.
a 4%
b 6%
c 8%
d 10%

9.6   What is the ROA at an average equity of €5 million, average liabilities of
€3 million at an average interest of 8%, profit after tax of €640,000 and a
corporate tax rate of 20%?
   a   9%
   b   11%
   c   13%
   d   18%

9.7   For a certain company, the invested equity is greater than the invested
liabilities.
Which of the following statements is correct?
   a   The operating risk is greater than the financial risk.
   b   The leverage ratio is greater than 1.
   c   The ROE is influenced favorably by financial leverage.
   d   The debt ratio is greater than 0.5.

9.8   What happens to the ROA if a corporation issues new shares by public
offering and uses the proceeds for the repayment of long-term liabilities?
   a   The ROA decreases.
   b   The ROA remains equal.
   c   The ROA increases.

9.9   Which of below items is related to the financial resilience of a company?
   a   The interest coverage ratio.
   b   The current ratio.
   c   The debt ratio.
   d   The net working capital.

9.10   What happens to the solvency of a company if it invests cash in fixed assets?
   a   The solvency worsens.
   b   The solvency remains the same.
   c   The solvency improves.

9.11   What happens to the solvency of a company if a line of credit is repaid with
money from a new term loan?
   a   The solvency improves.
   b   The solvency remains the same.
   c   The solvency worsens.

9.12   Which of the following items is related to a dynamic liquidity analysis?
   a   The cash flow forecast.
   b   The current ratio.
   c   The acid test ratio.
   d   The net working capital.

9.13   What happens to the net working capital of a company if the trade credit of
one of its suppliers is paid with cash?
   a   The net working capital reduces.
   b   The net working capital remains the same.
   c   The net working capital increases.

9.14   Which of the following statements is correct, if the current ratio of a company is lower than 1?

   a   The fixed assets are partly financed with current liabilities.
   b   The current assets are smaller than the fixed assets.
   c   The current liabilities are smaller than the current assets.
   d   The net working capital is positive.

9.15   What happens to the liquidity of a company if a line of credit is repaid with money from a new term loan?

   a   The liquidity reduces.
   b   The liquidity remains equal.
   c   The liquidity increases.

9

BEURSPLEIN 5

10
Financial Markets

10

In the previous chapters, the focus has mainly been on the company's role on the demand side of the financial markets. In this chapter, the supply side is the focal point. The supply and demand side coincide on the financial markets.
Naturally, the financial markets are only briefly looked at in this chapter. Only those aspects relevant to the financing of companies are discussed. Paragraph 10.1 deals with the most frequently traded securities: shares, options and bonds. Subsequently, paragraph 10.2 presents a more detailed look at options, while paragraph 10.3 discusses the ratios an investor can use to select between various alternative investment options.

10.1 Investments in Securities

Financial markets are where the demand for and the supply of capital meet. Parties on the demand side include companies, but also governments. Companies with a capital requirement need extra capital to finance their assets. To fulfill this need, a company must be in contact with those who offer capital.

Sometimes this is done directly, for example, by negotiating a loan with a bank or by privately issuing shares. In other cases, the organized market, or **Stock exchange** stock exchange, is used. The *stock exchange* facilitates contact between the demand and supply sides of the financial markets, for example, in the act of a public offering of shares or bonds – but it also organizes the tradability of these securities after their issue.

In principle, every country has its own stock exchange for companies located in that country. Due to globalization, large companies in particular trade worldwide and have their shares quoted on several stock exchanges. Due to mergers, stock exchanges also operate across borders.

The Amsterdam stock exchange AEX is part of the pan-European Euronext exchange, with branch exchanges in Belgium, France, the Netherlands, Portugal and the UK.

The Euronext exchanges use a *single orderbook*: companies listed on more than one exchange have the same market value on each exchange.

In Amsterdam, 25 equity funds that generate the majority of sales together form the AEX; funds 26 through 50 form the AMX. These indexes are important parameters for the stock exchange climate in the Netherlands.

In order to give smaller companies – *small caps* – easier access to the stock exchange, the **Alternext** was created. This is a pan-European stock exchange, with lower access requirements than the Euronext. Besides listing shares, the Euronext also offers a market for bonds, options and futures

There are various parties that can act as capital suppliers on the financial markets:

Banks
Issuing credit is one of the most important tasks of a bank.Money deposited at a bank by means of current account balances, savings, fixed term deposits, etc. is issued by banks as loans to, amongst others, companies.

Institutional investors
Institutional investors are financial organizations that control a large capital and invest this for short or long term, with the purpose of creating profit by means of increases in value dividends or interests. Social funds, pension funds and insurance companies are typical institutional investors.

Private investors
Private persons may prefer investing to saving if they are prepared to take the extra risk of investing.

Companies
Companies with (temporary) excess cash can also make these resources profitable by investing or lending to other companies. The temporary investment of excess resources in shares is not the same as a long-term participation in another company. The former is part of cash management and is intended to generate additional profit with cash resources that are not required for other purposes. Participations in other companies (associates) have the purpose of engaging in a long-term relationship with other companies and possibly gain control.
The mutual granting of credit between companies is also called *near banking*.

Near banking

All parties mentioned can either make capital available to companies privately, or provide capital by purchasing securities at the stock exchange. The most frequently traded securities are company issued shares and company, institution or government issued bonds. Trade in derivatives also exists – derived in this case meaning that the value is based on another product. This other product is known as the underlying value. A characteristic of derivatives is that (compared to shares or bonds) limited investments may yield solid profits – or losses, of course. The best known derivatives are options, futures and turbos (also known as speeders or sprinters).

Derivatives

Options offer the holder the right to buy or sell a specific property, at a fixed price on or up to a fixed date. Equity options bestow the right of buying or selling shares. The market value of an option depends in part on the market value of the underlying share and the price that must be paid when exercising the option. Options are discussed in greater detail in paragraph 10.2.

Options

A *future* is a binding contract to buy or sell a specific property, on a stated future date at a specified price. Futures resemble options, but instead of the right to trade a particular property, it is an obligation.

Future

A turbo offers its holder the opportunity to buy or sell an underlying value, with the majority being financed by a bank. The investor invests in the underlying value the turbo relates to, but pays for only part of the requisite amount.

Turbo

Options, futures and turbos can be related to shares, but also to indexes, currencies, bonds or commodities.

For an investor, the different types of securities have obviously differing characteristics that relate to possible changes in market value and remunerations paid to the capital provider.
The market value of shares is mainly determined by the earning potential of the company concerned but also by the general stock exchange climate. The dividend payment on shares also depends on profit made by the company. The market value of bonds is mainly determined by the market interest rate (see chapter 8). Generally speaking, the market interest rate does not fluctuate very strongly during a particular period; as a result, the market value of bonds is fairly stable. The interest payment on bonds is usually a fixed amount, regardless of the company's profit.
The market value of options, futures and turbos is determined by the market value of the underlying assets. Holders of options, futures or turbos do not receive dividends as these are paid only to sharehlders at the time of dividend determination.

Return on investment

Risk

Investors are guided by two factors when faced with a choice between investment alternatives: *return on investment* and *risk*. The higher the expected return on investment, the more attractive the investment. The higher the risk of an investment in terms of potential loss or market value fluctuations, the less attractive the investment.

In table 10.1, the types of securities are compared, based upon return on investment and risk. For the sake of completeness, the possibility to deposit the capital on a savings account has been added.

TABLE 10.1 Comparison of investment instruments

Types of securities	Potential return on investment	Risk (exchange rate fluctuations)
Shares	High	High
Bonds	Reasonable	Limited
Equity options	Very high	Very high
Futures	Very high	Very high
Turbos	Very high	Very high
Savings	Low	Very low

TEST QUESTION 10.1
Which type of investment would an investor prefer if trying to avoid risks?

Actual return on investment, the yield

Of course, the yield, can only be determined once all outflows and inflows are known. The calculation of the actual return is similar to the calculation of the internal rate of return for an investment project (see paragraph 5.4).

EXAMPLE 10.1

An investor buys 1,000 shares on 1 April 2016, at a price of €7.50 per share.
On 31 March 2017, the investor receives a cash dividend of €0.05 per share.
On 31 March 2018, the investor sells the shares for €9 per piece.

The yield of this investment is equal to the discount rate at which the present value of the money received is equal to the invested amount.

The invested amount is 1,000 × €7.50 = €7,500.

The cash inflow is 1,000 × €0.05 = €50 after one year and 1,000 × €9 = €9,000 after two years.

The calculation of the yield is as follows:

$$€7,500 = \frac{€50}{(1 + i)} + \frac{€9,000}{(1 + i)^2}$$

The yield is approximately 10%.

TEST QUESTION 10.2

Verify that the yield in this example 10.1 is indeed approximately 10% by performing the required calculation using Excel.

10.2 Options

An *option* gives a holder the right to buy (*call options*) or sell (*put options*) a specific property, at a fixed price on or up to a fixed date. Share options therefore give the right to buy or sell shares.
Each option has a buyer and a seller, leaving an investor four possible options (see table 10.2).

Option
Call options
Put options

TABLE 10.2 Rights and obligations of buyers and sellers of options.

	Buyer	Seller
Call option	Right to buy shares at the exercise price	Obligation to sell the shares at the exercise price, if requested
Put option	Right to sell shares at the exercise price	Obligation to buy shares at the exercise price, if requested

Options listed on stock exchanges are standardized with regard to contract size, duration and exercise price. A share option always concerns 100 shares. The duration can vary from one month to several years. Exercising the option, which is to say buying or selling the shares through option rights, can be done over the entire duration.

Exercise price

The *exercise price* or *strike price* is the price at which the holder of an option can buy or sell shares. For each share and duration, different exercise prices are set: so-called option series, in which options are traded.

For example, a Call KPN Dec 2019 2.50 represents a call option on KPN shares with expiration date the third Friday of December 2019 with an exercise price of €2.50 per share.

Options do not have any significance for the financing of companies. It concerns a contract between buyer and seller; both investors who are attempting to generate profit through a contract. In exercising an option, one party sells already issued shares to the other party at a fixed exercise price. In practice, the right to exercise the option is rarely used. Buyers tend to sell most options before the end of their duration.

Value of an option

The market value of an option is determined by two factors: the market value of the underlying share and the length of the remaining duration of the option.

Intrinsic value

The difference between the market value of the share and the exercise price determines the *intrinsic value* of the option. The intrinsic value of an option is equal to the financial advantage that the option holder would obtain when exercising his option rights.

The intrinsic value of the option can be calculated as follows:

For a call option:
Intrinsic value of the option   = Number of shares of the option ×
                                       (Market value of share – Exercise price)
For a put option:
Intrinsic value of the option   = Number of shares of the option ×
                                       (Exercise price – Market value of share)

The intrinsic value of an option can obviously never be negative. If, for example, in the case of a call option, the share has a market value lower than the exercise price, exercising the call will not generate financial advantage and the intrinsic value of the option is zero.

EXAMPLE 10.2

On 12 May 2017, an investor holds one call option ING December 2017 15.00 and one put option ING December 2017 15.00. The market value of the ING share at that date is €15.32.

The intrinsic value of the call option is 100 × (€15.32 – €15.00) = €32. The option holder has a direct advantage of €32 by exercising the option. For 100 shares with a market value of €15.32 each, he pays only €15 per share.

The intrinsic value of the put option is €0 as the exercise price is lower than the market value of the share.

The *market value* of an option is higher than its intrinsic value because, in determining the value, an investor considers the changes in market value of a share during the remainder of its duration. If the market value of a share is expected to increase during the remaining period, the call option price rises because the financial advantage to be gained in future is higher. The difference between the market value and the intrinsic value of the option is called the *time value* as it reflects the expectations of investors of the market value during the remaining time.

Market value

Time value

Over time, the time value of an option lowers as the remaining duration of the option becomes shorter; this means there is less time for changes in market value of the underlying share.

The relationship between the market value of the share, the intrinsic value, the time value and the market value of the call and put option, is shown in figures 10.1 and 10.2.

FIGURE 10.1 The market value of a call option

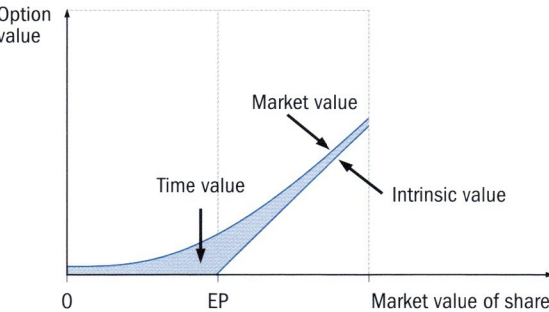

FIGURE 10.2 The market value of a put option

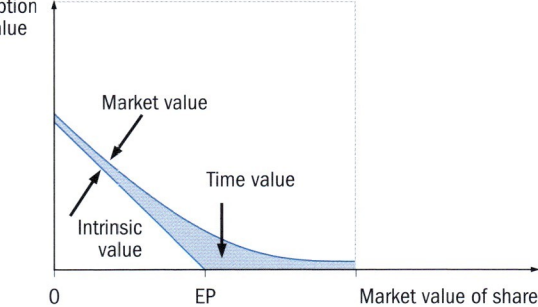

Since the buyer of the option does not pay the full share price but only invests in the difference between the exercise price and the share price, a *leverage effect* occurs; as a result, the change in value of the option in terms of percentage is greater than that of the underlying share.

Leverage effect

EXAMPLE 10.3

On 2 January 2017, an investor buys a call option Unilever December 2017 42 at a market value of €136. The market value of the Unilever share on 2 January 2017 is €39.25.

On 2 January 2017 the situation is as follows:

Market value option	€136
Intrinsic value option = 100 × (39.25 − 42)	€ 0
Time value option	€136

Five months later, on 12 May 2017, the market value of the Unilever share has risen to €49.15. The market value of the call option on that date is €742.
The situation is now as follows:

Market value option	€742
Intrinsic value option = 100 × (49.15 − 42)	−€715
Time value option	€ 27

The time value of the call option decreases as the originally expected increase in share value is partially achieved and the time left to generate share value increases has decreased.
The market value of the call option has increased by

€742 − €136 = €606. In percentage terms this is an increase of:

$$\frac{€606}{€136} \times 100\% = 445\%$$

whereas the market value of the underlying share has increased by €49.15 − €39.25 = €9.90, which in percentage terms is an increase of:

$$\frac{€9.90}{€39.25} \times 100\% = 25\%.$$

Example 10.3 shows one of the most appealing aspects of investing in options. Compared to a direct investment in shares, a smaller investment in options (€136 for one call option, compared to 100 × €39.25 = €3,925 for 100 shares) can generate a relatively large profit. The opposite, of course, also applies. If the market value of the share falls, the market value of the option falls by a larger degree. Investing in options is therefore very risky. A distinction should be made between buyers and sellers of options. For a buyer, the maximum loss is limited to the purchase price of the option. A seller can suffer even greater losses.

TEST QUESTION 10.3
Explain why the seller of an option can suffer greater losses than the buyer.

Objectives of the investor in options
Investors can have various motives for investing in options. Although an investment in options bears a relatively high risk due to market fluctuations, an investor can sometimes actually use this type of investment to reduce the total risk. The four objectives of investors in options are listed and discussed in greater detail below:
1   achieving (relatively high) profits
2   generating additional income
3   protecting from market fluctuations
4   fixing the purchase price of shares

Ad 1   Achieving (relatively high) profits
If an investor expects a market adjustment of a particular share, they can benefit by buying options. In the event of a rise in the share price, the purchase of a call option generates a high profit (see example 10.3). In the event of a decline of the share price, the same applies for the purchase of a put option.
When it comes to this objective, the speculative nature of an investment in options has high risks. The other three objectives always concern a combined investment of options and shares.

Ad 2   Generating additional income
If the investor holds shares, he can generate additional profit on his investment by selling call options. The sale of call options provides an immediate financiel advantage. The investor receives the purchase amount from the party who buys the option.
The advantage is that, should the price of the shares not rise by very much, the option will be worthless and the investor will therefore have generated additional income.
The disadvantage is that, should the price of the shares rise strongly or even above the exercise price, the investor has the risk of having to sell the shares at a lower price than the market value.

10

- -

EXAMPLE 10.4
An investor holds 1,000 shares ING on 12 May 2017, with a market value of €15.32 per share. The investor expects that this share will not rise very much in the next seven months, but still wishes to achieve a profit on the investment.
The investor therefore sells 10 call options ING December 2017 16 at €71 each. In return, he receives 10 × €71 = €710.

If the value of the ING share does not exceed €16 before the end of the term, the options will not be exercised and the investor will have made €710. If however, the value of ING shares rises to €16.50 at the end of the duration and the option is exercised, the investor will have to sell 100 shares ING at the exercise price of €16. The investor's loss compared to the sale of the shares on the stock exchange will be 1,000 × (€16.50 – €16) = €500.

- -

Ad 3 Protecting from market fluctuations

An investor holding shares can protect himself from strong decline of share value by buying put options. The put option entitles an investor to sell the shares at the exercise price, which reduces the investment risk. Of course, the purchase of the put options has to be paid.

EXAMPLE 10.5

An investor holds 1,000 shares ING on 12 May 2017, with a market value of €15.32 per share. The investor is uncertain with respect to the market development of the ING shares in the short term and invests in protection from major losses by buying 10 put options ING December 2017 15. The total costs are €1,110.

If the value of the ING share were to fall to €13.50 before December, then the investor would exercise the options and sell the shares for €15 which, compared to selling on the stock exchange, would result in an advantage of 1,000 × (€15 − €13.50) = €1,500.

Ad 4 Fixing the purchase price of shares

An investor who wishes to buy shares of a particular company in the future and does not wish to pay more than a certain amount for those shares, can achieve this by buying a call option. This fixes the maximum future price of the shares. In the event of a strong rise in the share price, the option is exercised and the investor pays the exercise price.

EXAMPLE 10.6

In May 2017, an investor is interested in purchasing ING shares because he anticipates a strong rise in the share value. The market value of the ING share at that time, however, is €15.32, and the investor does not wish to invest a large amount at that moment. He therefore buys 10 call options ING December 2017 16 and pays €700.

If an increase in the price of ING shares does indeed occur, with the market value rising to €17.50 per share in December 2017, the investor will be able to exercise their option and buy 1,000 shares ING for €16 per share, which would generate an immediate profit of 1,000 × (€17.50 − €16) = €1,500.

TEST QUESTION 10.4

In which of the four mentioned objectives does the investor use options to reduce the investment risk?

10.3 Investment Ratios

The best known investment is the investment in shares. To be able to make
a choice between the many equity funds listed on the stock exchange,
investors can compare investment ratios. Ratios that could be important
when making a selection between the various equity funds can be divided
into two categories:
1 Dividend-oriented ratios:
   • dividend yield
   • payout ratio
2 Price-oriented ratios:
   • price/earnings ratio
   • price/cash flow ratio
   • price/net asset value ratio

Dividend yield
Chapter 7 previously discussed dividend payments by corporations. The
dividend percentage discussed there is based on the par value of a share
and is therefore not important to investors.
After all, capital invested by an investor is not the par value of a share
but the market value. The investor should therefore not link the received
dividend to the par value but to the market value of the share. This ratio is
called the dividend yield.
The *dividend yield* is calculated by the ratio between the paid dividend and   **Dividend yield**
the market value per share at the end of the financial year.
The dividend yield is usually given as a percentage:

$$\text{Dividend yield} = \frac{\text{Dividend}}{\text{Market value end of financial year}} \times 100\%$$

The higher the dividend yield, the more appealing the fund.

Payout ratio
A corporation hardly ever chooses to pay out all its profit to the shareholders
in the form of dividend. Part of the profit is retained.
The *payout ratio* indicates which part of the profit is paid out as dividend.   **Payout ratio**

$$\text{Payout ratio} = \frac{\text{Dividend per share}}{\text{Profit per share}} \times 100\%$$

A high payout ratio is appealing in the short term, but deprives the company
of additional cheap capital, which hinders company growth, or requires the
company to attract additional autonomous capital.

Price/earnings ratio
To be able to assess whether a share fund is an attractive investment, an
assessment on the share's potential to value in the future should be made.
This is often linked to company profit. If the price is low when compared to
the profit, it is an interesting investment.

$$\text{Price/earnings ratio} = \frac{\text{Market value}}{\text{Profit per share}}$$

10

Price/cash flow ratio

Rather than profit, cash flow can also be used as an indicator for possible rise in share value.

Cash flow consists of profit and depreciation. Accordingly, cash flow indicates the net cash inflows a company can spend on activities.

$$\text{Profit/cash flow ratio} = \frac{\text{Market value}}{\text{Cash flow per share}}$$

Price/net asset value ratio

Profit and cash flow are important indicators, based on the concept of 'going concern'. If the net asset value of a company is high when compared to the market value, it can serve as an indication for the presence of valuable assets.

It can make a company appealing for a takeover or indicate the company's long-term profit potential.

$$\text{Profit/net asset value ratio} = \frac{\text{Market value}}{\text{Net asset value per share}}$$

EXAMPLE 10.7

In its 2016 annual report, DSM published the following financial data:

Balance sheet on 31 December 2016 (× €1 million)

Fixed assets	7,917	Equity	6,180
Current assets	5,041	Liabilities	6,778
	12,958		12,958

Income statement 2016 (× €1 million)

Net revenue	7,920
Depreciation	489
Net result	617

On 31 December 2016, a total of 175.1 million ordinary shares had been issued.

The market value of the shares was €56.96. For each share, a dividend of €1.75 was paid.

From these figures, the following calculations per share can be derived:
Profit per share: €617 million / 171.5 million = €3.52
Cash flow per share: (€617 million + €489 million) / 171.5 million = €6.32
Net asset value per share: €6,180 million / 171.5 million = €35.29

The investment ratios on 31 December 2016 were as follows:
Dividend yield: €1.75 / €56.96 × 100% = 3.1%
Payout ratio: €1.75 / €3.52 × 100% = 49.7%
Price/earnings ratio: €56.96 / €3.52 = 16.2
Price/cash flow ratio: €56.96 / €6.32 = 9.0
Price/net asset value ratio: €56.96 / €35.29 = 1.6

By comparing the outcome of the figures in example 10.7 to those of other companies, the attractiveness of an investment in DSM shares can be assessed.
Table 10.4 indicates the investment ratios for a several multinationals per the end of 2016.

TABLE 10.4 Investment ratios of four multinationals per end of 2016

Name	Dividend yield	Payout ratio	Price/earnings ratio
Akzo Nobel	2.8%	39.8%	14.3
DSM	3.1%	49.7%	16.2
ASML	1.13%	34.9%	31.0
Philips	2.8%	51.3%	18.6

TEST QUESTION 10.5
Based on the investment ratios of the equity funds mentioned in table 10.4, which multinational offers the most appealing investment?

10

Glossary

Derivative	A derived investment product whose value depends on an underlying value.
Dividend yield	The ratio between the paid dividend and the market value per share at the end of the financial year.
Exercise price/strike price	The price at which the holder of an option can buy or sell shares.
Future	An agreement between buyer and seller to buy a particular amount of the underlying asset at an agreed price, on a particular day in the future.
Near banking	Mutual granting of credit between companies.
Option	The right to buy or sell an asset at a fixed price during a particular period.
Payout ratio	Part of the profit that is paid out as dividend.
Price/cash flow ratio	The ratio between market value at the end of the financial year and cash flow per share.
Price/earnings ratio	The ratio between market value at the end of the financial year and profit per share.
Price/net asset value ratio	The ratio between market value and net asset value of a share at the end of the financial year.
Turbo	An investment in an underlying value, with a large part of the investment being financed by a bank.

Multiple-choice questions

10.1 Is the risk related to an investment in shares when compared to an investment in bonds, smaller, equal or larger?
a Smaller.
b Equal.
c Larger.

10.2 Which of the following securities would be preferable to a risk-avoiding investor?
a Shares.
b Bonds.
c Options.
d Futures.

10.3 On 1 January, an investor buys 100 shares at a purchase price of €40 per share. On 31 December, the investor sells the shares at €45 per share. What is the yield of this investment?
a 12.5%
b 15.2%
c 16.1%
d 20.3%

10.4 An investor expects a rise in the market value of a share. Which investment would probably generate the highest yield?
a The purchase of one call option, which entitles the buyer to purchase 100 shares.
b The purchase of 100 shares.
c The sale of one put option, which entitles the buyer to sell 100 shares.
d The sale of one call option, which entitles the buyer to purchase 100 shares.

10.5 An investor buys one Call Unilever December 48 and pays €280. The market value of the Unilever share is €49.15 at that moment. What is the intrinsic value of the option?
a €1.15
b €48
c €115
d €165

10

10.6   An investor buys one Call Unilever December 48 and pays €280. The market value of the Unilever share is €49.15 at that moment. What is the time value of the option?
   a €2
   b €115
   c €165
   d €211.50

10.7   What is a future?
   a An option on commodities.
   b An agreement between buyer and seller to buy or sell a particular amount of the underlying asset at an agreed price, on a particular day in the future.
   c An option with a duration of more than one year.
   d The value of a share after one year.

10.8   Which ratio can an investor use to estimate the profit potential of a stock exchange listed corporation?
   a The dividend yield.
   b The payout ratio.
   c The price/earnings ratio.
   d The net asset value ratio.

10.9   A low price/cash flow ratio can be an indication of what?
   a An expected bankruptcy in the near future.
   b A company that is overrated on the stock exchange.
   c An appealing investment opportunity.
   d A policy of dividend equalization.

10.10   How can the dividend yield of an investment in shares be calculated?
   a Payout ratio : price/earnings ratio
   b Payout ratio × market value per share.
   c Dividend per share/net asset value per share
   d Profit per share/market value per share.

PART 3
Management Accounting

11
Cost Structure

11.1   **Fixed and Variable Costs**
11.2   **Break-even Analysis**
11.3   **Operating Leverage**

In this chapter, the focus is on separating costs into fixed and variable. The
first paragraph discusses this separation, related to the behavior of costs
during an increase in production, in detail.
Paragraph 11.2 includes the role of revenue in these calculations; specifically,
the fact that this makes it possible to demonstrate the influence of cost
behavior on a company's profitability. The point at which a company's costs
and revenue are perfectly in balance is known as the break-even point.
Paragraph 11.3 addresses the consequences that differences in cost structure
have on profit. As the ratio of fixed costs becomes greater, changes in revenue
will result in greater profit fluctuations.

11.1 Fixed and Variable Costs

A company incurs costs to supply products or services to its customers. Costs are generated by the use of production factors. There is a relationship between cost level and production size.
Management should be well informed on the nature of this relationship. Examples of questions that might be posed, are:
- How do the costs of a hotel change if an additional room is rented for one night? And what if a room is rented for four nights?
- How do the costs of a real estate agent change if a house is accepted?
- How do the costs of a manufacturer of computer chips change if 10,000 extra chips are produced and sold?

These questions are usually not all that easy to answer. The costs of different production factors do not all change in the same manner.
The housing costs of a hotel (depreciation of the building) change barely, if at all, no matter how many more or fewer rooms are rented. The costs of raw materials for a computer chip manufacturer increases the more chips are manufactured.
Based on their relation to the output level, costs can be divided into two major groups: fixed costs and variable costs.

Fixed costs
Fixed costs remain constant, even if the output level increases or decreases. The rental costs of business premises are not related to the quantity of products manufactured in that building.

Variable costs
Variable costs change if production varies. The cost of raw materials for a computer chip manufacturer increase the more chips are produced.

EXAMPLE 11.1
A wine merchant delivers goods using a van.
The van was bought for €18,000 and is depreciated by equal amounts per year over four years. The residual value after four years is €2,000. The fuel costs of the van are €0.09 per kilometer.
The total depreciation of the van per year is (€18,000 − €2,000) / 4 = €4,000, regardless of the number of kilometers driven. These, therefore, are the fixed costs.
The fuel costs of the van are directly proportional to the number of driven kilometers. If, for example, 20,000 kilometers are driven this year, the fuel costs are 20,000 × €0.09 = €1,800. Therefore, the fuel costs are the variable costs.

Depreciation is a fixed cost if the wear and tear of a fixed asset is caused by the passing of time.
It is also possible for depreciation to be a variable cost, which is the case if the wear and tear of the fixed asset is mainly determined by use of the asset and not by time.

TEST QUESTION 11.1
Name a production factor for which depreciation is a variable cost.

Variable costs

Variable costs do not always increase in direct proportion to output level. Sometimes they increase more quickly, sometimes more slowly. Costs that vary in direct proportion to the output level are called *proportionally variable costs*. For each unit produced, the variable cost always remains equal. In practice, variable costs usually tend to increase or decrease proportionally, because, for each unit of product, the same amount of costs is incurred. *Degressively variable costs* are costs that increase relatively more slowly compared to production. This is generally the case if production levels are relatively low and are then increased. A consequence of degressively variable costs is that unit costs decline. This degression can result from cost savings made due to expansion of production, through improved efficiency (the learning effect) or through bulk discounts on large purchase orders of raw materials or parts.

Unlike degressively variable costs, the *progressive* development of variable costs is usually found at larger output levels. Total variable costs increase relatively more quickly than the produced quantity, which leads to an increase in unit costs. *Progressively variable costs* can, for example, be the result of extra costs from overtime or hiring a (more expensive) temporary workforce.

Table 11.1 shows the behavior of fixed and variable costs.

TABLE 11.1 Behavior of fixed and variable costs for increasing output level

	Total cost	**Unit costs**
Fixed costs	Remain equal	Reduce
Proportionally variable costs	Increase	Remain equal
Degressively variable costs	Increase	Reduce
Progressively variable costs	Increase	Increase

Figures 11.1 and 11.2 offer a graphic representation of the possible reactions of variable costs to a change in the output level over a certain period.

FIGURE 11.1 Behavior total variable costs

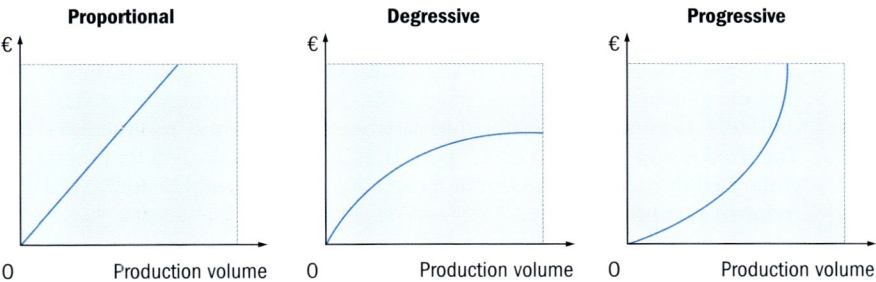

FIGURE 11.2 Behavior variable unit costs

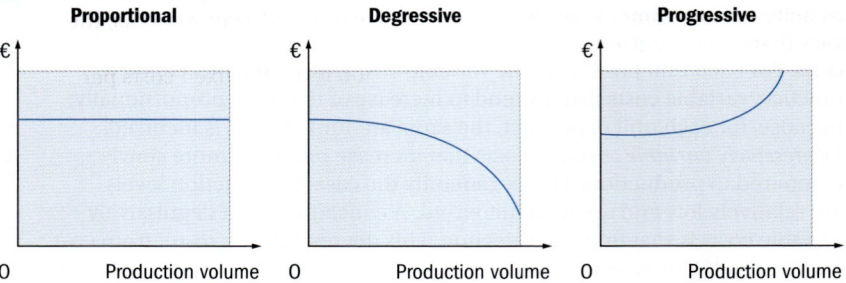

Table 11.2 for a numerical example clarifying this cost behavior.

TABLE 11.2 Numerical example of cost behavior

Output level (in units)	Total variable costs (in Euros)	Variable unit costs (in Euros)		
10,000	100,000	10.00		
11,000	107,250	9.75	}	Degressive
12,000	113,400	9.45		
13,000	117,000	9.00		
14,000	126,000	9.00	}	Proportional
15,000	135,000	9.00		
16,000	144,000	9.00		
17,000	154,700	9.10		
18,000	166,500	9.25		
19,000	180,500	9.50	}	Progressive
20,000	198,000	9.90		
21,000	220,500	10.50		

Fixed costs

Fixed costs are costs that do not change over a period if the output level changes. Of course, fixed costs can and do change for other reasons, e.g. an increase in the rental costs of the business premises halfway through the year causing an increase in fixed costs. The criterion for fixed costs, therefore, is purely the relationship between cost level and production size. The fixed nature of these costs (figure 11.3) is based on the fact that they are generated by the actual production capacity, which cannot be increased or reduced at short notice.

Since capacity volume determines the level of the fixed costs, these costs are also referred to as *capacity costs*. In the event of a decrease in production, **Capacity costs** capacity cannot immediately be adjusted to the reduced requirements; the costs therefore remain at the same level.

As the fixed costs are unrelated to the production level, the fixed costs per unit decrease following an increase in production.

FIGURE 11.3a Behavior total fixed costs

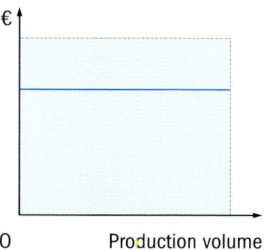

FIGURE 11.3b Behavior fixed costs per unit

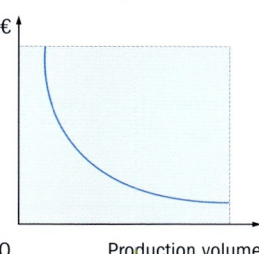

Fixed costs do not vary with output levels, as capacity over a certain period is considered fixed. If the period that is considered is sufficiently long, then the fixed costs can be influenced – since the long-term capacity can be adjusted.

Costs that cannot be influenced for the coming month might be influenced for the coming year. For example, a necessary capacity reduction may not, due to the legal notice period for employees, effect a reduction in fixed salary costs of the following month – but it may be possible to reduce these costs by the following year. Due to the long lead times of machines, it is possible that a short-term capacity expansion is not achievable.

This implies that costs are only really fixed if the output level is within the short-term capacity limits or *relevant production range* of the company.

FIGURE 11.4 Fixed costs in relation to capacity level and relevant production range

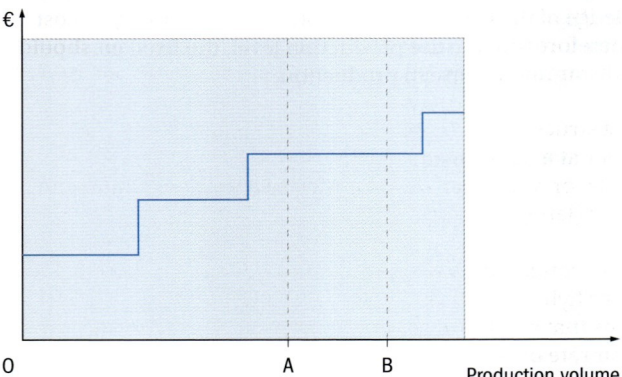

Step variable costs

Aside from the aforementioned types of cost behavior, there are also *step variable costs*. These occur if production factors are only partially dividable, but can be adjusted to the required volume in the short term. Costs are then fixed for a limited production range and rise to a new level above the interval, thus creating discontinuous development *within* the relevant production range.

EXAMPLE 11.2

For storage and transportation of 4,000 products, containers must be rented at €1,500 per unit. This creates a stepped increase of costs.

Step increase variable costs

Production (in units)	Number of containers	Rental costs (in Euros)
0–4,000	1	1,500
4,001–8,000	2	3,000
8,001–12,000	3	4,500
12,001–16,000	4	6,000
16,001–20,000	5	7,500

This is shown graphically in figure 11.5.

FIGURE 11.5 Step variable costs

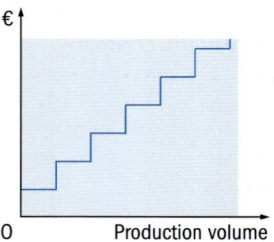

Total costs

A company can gain an advantage over its competitors by producing equal or better products and services at lower or equal costs. Doing so requires a thorough knowledge of the cost structure of one's own company. A cost analysis should therefore not be limited to manufacturing costs but should also relate to administration, sales, research, etc. These are, after all, part of the cost structure.

To analyze the cost structure as completely as possible, all costs should be assessed to see to what extent they are fixed or variable.

Consecutively, costs for raw materials are always of a variable nature and costs for fixed assets (land, buildings, machines, etc.) are always of a fixed nature.

Other cost types can contain both elements, making them partly fixed and partly variable – this hybrid type is known as *mixed costs*.   **Mixed costs**

An example of costs that are mixed are energy costs: a 'fixed fee' per year and a kilowatt-hour rate or rate per cubic meter. Although it could be important to know certain separate cost types, in practice companies are mainly interested in identifying the total costs of the production process. Research has proven that the cost structure (cost function) generally develops as shown in figure 11.6.

FIGURE 11.6 Behavior of total costs

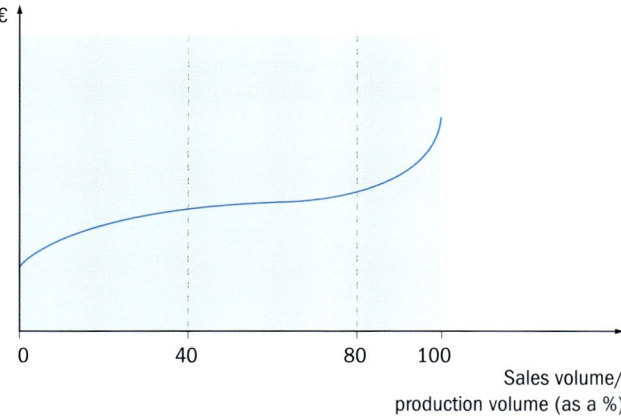

The total cost behavior in figure 11.6 is, of course, only a very global indication as the ratio between fixed and variable costs varies for each type of business. In production companies, the total costs consist mainly of variable costs, while the majority of total costs in a service-providing company is fixed, with variable costs being relatively unimportant.

In situations where variable costs are relatively important, costs concerned often involve a mainly proportional development (see figure 11.6, from 40% up to 80% capacity used). This linear relationship can sometimes be used to gain an insight into the cost structure, without necessarily determining whether each individual cost type is fixed or variable in nature.

11

EXAMPLE 11.3

For the first half year, the administration of a business shows the data as mentioned in the following table with respect to output level and total manufacturing costs:

Month	Production (in units)	Total costs (in Euros)
January	4,500	175,000
February	5,000	200,000
March	3,500	160,000
April	2,000	110,000
May	1,500	95,000
June	4,000	170,000

The total costs incurred for the production of a certain number of units comprise a monthly fixed amount and proportionally variable costs per product, resulting in the following cost function:

Total costs = Fixed costs + Number of units × Variable costs per unit

Using the data for the months with the highest (February) and lowest (May) output levels, the result is:

€200,000 = Fixed costs + 5,000 × Variable costs per unit
€95,000   = Fixed costs + 1,500 × Variable costs per unit

Subtracting one equation from the other gives:
€105,000 = 3,500 × Variable costs per unit

Therefore, variable costs per unit $= \dfrac{€105,000}{3,500} = €30$

Consecutively, the fixed costs per month can be calculated by entering this value for one of both months:

Fixed costs = Total costs – Variable costs
            = €200,000 – 5,000 × €30 = €50,000

or

Fixed costs = €95,000 – 1,500 × €30 = €50,000

The cost structure is therefore:

Total costs = €50,000 + €30 × Number of units

TEST QUESTION 11.2
What objection can be made to the method used in example 11.3?

Note that the high-low method provides only a global indication of the cost development. There are more accurate estimates, such as regression analysis, which do not fall within the scope of in this book.

High-low method

In aviation, which costs are fixed and which are variable? That is a matter of perspective. Whether or not a certain flight takes place does not influence wages of pilots working on a permanent contract. Those costs are fixed. If the cabin crew operates on an on-call basis, every flight that takes off comes with additional costs; those costs are variable. Fuel costs (following wages, the largest cost item in aviation industry) are also variable from a flight leg perspective, as are landing fees. From the perspective of the number of passengers transported per flight, nearly all costs are fixed. An aircraft that is nearly empty uses hardly any less fuel than one that is at full passenger capacity. Safety regulations dictate that there should be a fixed number of cabin crew aboard. Only the costs of meals and refreshments are reduced if there are less passengers. The financial ratio *Cost per Available Seat Mile (CASM)* is used to indicate the average costs of transporting a single seat over a distance of one mile. CASM is approximately €0.12.

11.2 Break-even Analysis

Company management is not only interested in the relationship between output level and costs, but also in the relationship between cost, sales and profit. This relationship can be visualized by adding sales in addition to costs as a function of the output level to a graph.

EXAMPLE 11.4
Wavekings manufactures and sells surfboards. It uses lightweight foam which is first poured into a mold, after which it has to set. Then, the board is cut in two and a wooden reinforcement is installed in the middle, after which both halves are glued back together.

The selling price is €625 per surfboard. The fixed costs comprise the rent of the business premises, depreciation on the production line and the salaries of employees; total fixed costs amount to €4,500,000 per year. The variable costs concern material and salaries of temporary staff and amount to €250 per surfboard.
Output level is equal to sales volume.

The development of total costs and sales as a function of production/sales is shown in figure 11.7.

FIGURE 11.7 Break-even chart

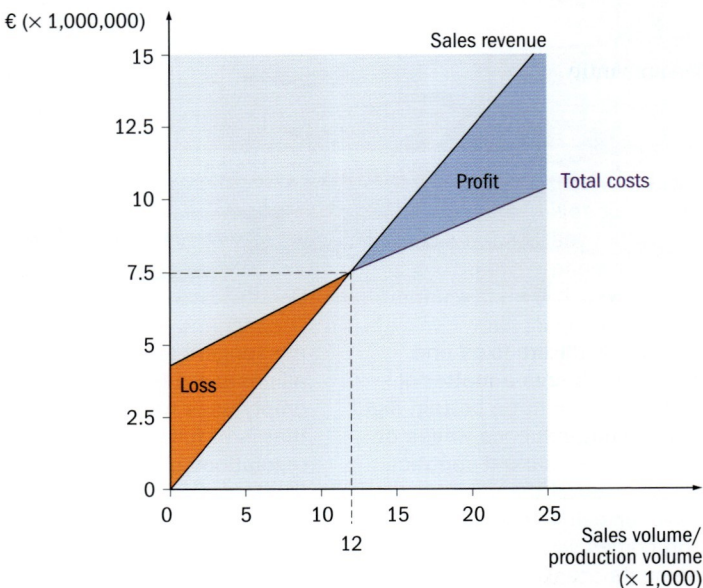

The chart shows that, for an output level and sales of 12,000 units, revenue is equal to total costs. For a number lower than 12,000 units, total costs are higher than the revenue, which indicates a loss. Past this point, the reverse is true: the revenue is higher than the costs, resulting in a profit.

For company management, it is very important to know what both sales volume and revenue should be in order to cover at least the costs to balance out the two, such as having to sell 12,000 units in example 11.4. This point is **Break-even point** called the *break-even point*, the point at which a company makes neither loss not profit. In such an event, total revenues are exactly equal to total costs.

The investigation into the relationship between sales, total costs and profit to the output level/sales volume and the determining of the break-even **Break-even** point is called the *break-even analysis*. Here, the distinction between vari- **analysis** able and fixed cost is of crucial importance.
At an output level and sales of 0 units, the loss is equal to the total fixed costs. Every produced and sold unit reduces the loss by the difference

between the selling price and the variable unit costs. This difference is known as the *contribution margin.*

Contribution margin

The break-even point is the number of units sold for which the contribution margin is exactly enough to cover the fixed costs

For the break-even quantity, the following applies:
Total revenue = Total costs
Break-even quantity × Selling price = Variable unit costs × Break-even quantity + Fixed costs
Break-even quantity × Selling price − Variable unit costs × Break-even quantity = Fixed costs
Break-even quantity × (Selling price − Variable unit costs) = Fixed costs

$$\text{Break–even quantity} = \frac{\text{Fixed costs}}{\text{Selling price} - \text{Variable unit costs}}$$

EXAMPLE 11.4 CONTINUED
Wavekings set their selling price at €625 per surfboard. Their fixed costs are €4,500,000 per year. Variable costs amount to €250 per unit.
Every manufactured and sold surfboard increases costs by €250 and adds €625 to revenue, which gives a contribution margin of €375.
The break-even quantity indicates how often this margin must be achieved in order to cover total fixed costs. This quantity can therefore be calculated by dividing these fixed costs by the contribution margin per unit:

$$\text{Break–even quantity} = \frac{\text{€4,500,000}}{\text{€625} - \text{€ 250}} = 12,000 \text{ units}$$

There is more to the break-even analysis than simply calculating the break-even point, which provides information to management on the minimum production and sales volume that must be achieved to break even. The analysis is particularly useful in determining the consequences of management decisions that are being considered. This requires an understanding of the relationship between revenue, costs and profit. With the aid of the break-even analysis, the following questions can usually be answered:
- What consequences will changing the selling price have?
- What is the influence of increasing fixed costs?
- What consequences do other production methods have?
- What sales volume is required to generate a particular profit?

EXAMPLE 11.4 CONTINUED
The objective of Wavekings is to achieve an annual profit of at least €150,000 (before tax).
In order to achieve this objective, sales need to be such that the total contribution margin is €150,000 more than total fixed costs. The number of units sold needed to achieve this is:

$$\frac{(\text{€4,500,000} + \text{€150,000})}{\text{€625} - \text{€250}} = \frac{\text{€4,650,000}}{\text{€375}} = 12,400 \text{ units}$$

The income statement can be drawn up to verify this calculation:

Sales revenue 12,400 × €625 = €7,750,000
Variable costs 12,400 × €250 = €3,100,000
                                ──────────

Total contribution   €4,650,000
Fixed costs   €4,500,000
                                ──────────

Profit before tax   €   150,000

TEST QUESTION 11.3
Using the information in example 11.4, how many surfboards need be sold if the company's objective is to achieve a profit of 10% of sales revenue?

The following is another example of the use of the break-even analysis for the purpose of decision-making:

EXAMPLE 11.5
At the introduction of a new investment fund, management states the following forecast figures for the first year to come:
- promotion costs: €1,950,000
- personnel costs: €800,000
- other expenses: €250,000
- number of transactions: 80,000
- average transaction size: €5,000

Commissions (a percentage over the transaction value) are the fund's only source of income. All costs are fixed costs. What is the commission percentage that must be achieved to break even?

The fixed costs are €1,950,000 + €800,000 + €250,000 = €3,000,000.
The contribution margin is the commission revenue as there are no variable costs.
The transaction value amounts to 80,000 × €5,000 = €400,000,000.

The break-even sales revenue is achieved if:
Commission % of €400,000,000 = €3,000,000
Commission % = €3,000,000 / €400,000,000 × 100 = 0.75%.

Assumptions at the basis of the break-even analysis
To be able to execute a break-even analysis in a simple way, three basic criteria need to be met.

1 Linearity of costs and revenues
In a break-even analysis, costs and revenues are assumed to progress along a linear pattern. As indicated in the previous paragraph, this usually only applies for costs within a particular production interval. Outside this interval, costs can have a degressive or progressive development. This also

applies to sales. To increase sales, it may be necessary to lower the price, which causes the sales revenue line too also become degressive.
In the event of non-linearity of costs and sales revenues, the graphic representation of these can appear as shown in figure 11.8.

FIGURE 11.8 Break-even points of non-linear costs and sales revenues

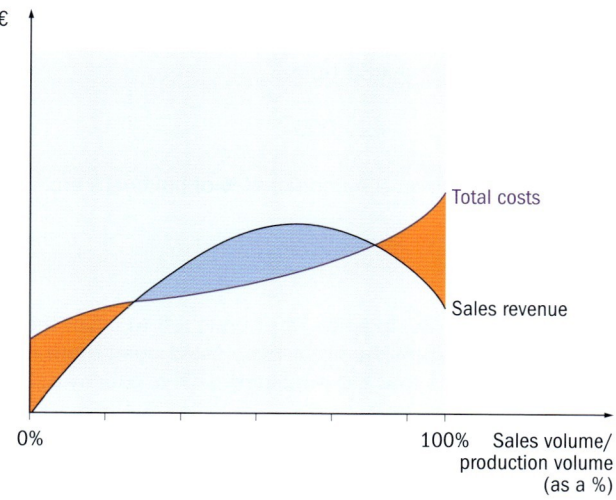

There are two break-even points here; the first at a fairly low sales volume, and the second at a high sales volume, with the necessary price concessions in combination with the progressiveness of variable costs turning a profit situation into a loss.

In a situation of non-linearity, mathematics must be used to calculate the break-even points.

2 One type of product
The next assumption at the basis of the break-even analysis is that a company manufactures only one type of product. If this is not the case, the contribution margin per product varies and the break-even point will also depend on the composition of production.
However, if the contribution margin as a percentage is always the same, it is possible to determine the break-even sales revenue. This is often the case for the retail industry.

- -

EXAMPLE 11.6
Tim Blackburn is the owner of a supermarket. He purchases the articles he sells from a number of wholesalers. Tim has set the selling price of these articles by adding 25% to the purchase price. This year, sales revenues are forecast at €400,000. Total additional costs over the purchase price of these products are estimated at €60,000, of which €44,000 are fixed costs; the remaining part of the additional costs is proportionally variable.

Tim is curious to know the forecast profit and the break-even sales revenue for this year.

On average, the purchase price is 80% $\left(\frac{100}{125}\right)$ of the sales revenue.

The gross margin of 20% $\left(\frac{25}{125}\right)$ must first be used to compensate for the additional costs. What remains of this margin is the profit. Therefore:

Gross margin 20% × €400,000 =	€80,000
Additional costs	− €60,000
The forecast profit	€20,000

As a percentage of the sales revenue, the additional variable costs are:

$$\frac{€60,000 - €44,000}{€400,000} \times 100\% = 4\%$$

Of the gross margin, 16% (20% − 4%) in sales revenue is left to cover the additional fixed costs and as profit. At the break-even sales point there is neither profit nor loss. This implies that the remaining 16% is exactly equal to the total fixed costs:

0.16 × break-even sales = €44,000

$$\text{Break–even sales revenue} = \frac{€44,000}{0.16} = €275,000$$

- -

3 Production = sales volume
Finally, the use of the break-even analysis assumes that production is equal to sales volume. In a service-providing organization, this assumption is normally true as there is no built-up inventory. If there is a difference between production and sales, the matter of when the profit is zero is up for debate. In the following chapter, the discussion on the use of direct costing explains how a break-even analysis can also be applied to a situation with inventory changes, since, in direct costing, profit only depends on sales levels (and not on production levels).

Safety margin
Obviously, a company's number one aim is to have sales volume, and therefore sales revenue, well above the break-even point. If sales start to fall, management needs to take timely measures.
The gap between actual sales and the break-even quantity is expressed by the safety margin. The *safety margin* is the maximum percentage by which sales can fall without reaching a point below break-even level. The safety margin indicates a leeway and has a signaling function.

Safety margin

The percentage is calculated as follows:

$$\text{Safety margin} = \frac{\text{Annual sales volume} - \text{Break–even sales}}{\text{Actual sales volume}}$$

EXAMPLE 11.4 CONTINUED
Wavekings achieved a sales volume of 20,000 items last year. Fixed costs
were €4,500,000 per year and variable costs were €250 per unit. The
previously calculated break-even quantity is 12,000 units.
The safety margin in this situation is:

$$\frac{20{,}000 - 12{,}000}{20{,}000} = 40\%$$

If sales volume drops by 40%, the break-even point is reached.

11.3 Operating Leverage

The link between profit and output level can be graphically presented at a
glance using the *profit-volume chart*, which shows no separate sales revenue
and cost lines, but only a profit line.

**Profit-volume
chart**

The profit line starts at a loss equal to the fixed costs. If there are no sales,
sales revenue and variable costs are zero – but there will still be fixed costs.
The slope of the profit line is determined by the contribution margin per
unit. Each increase in sales by one product results in a reduction of loss or
an increase of profit by the amount of the contribution margin.

EXAMPLE 11.4 CONTINUED
The fixed costs for Wavekings are €4,500,000 per year. The variable costs
are €250 per unit. The selling price is €625 per surfboard.

The profit-volume chart of Wavekings is shown in figure 11.9.

FIGURE 11.9 Profit volume chart of Wavekings

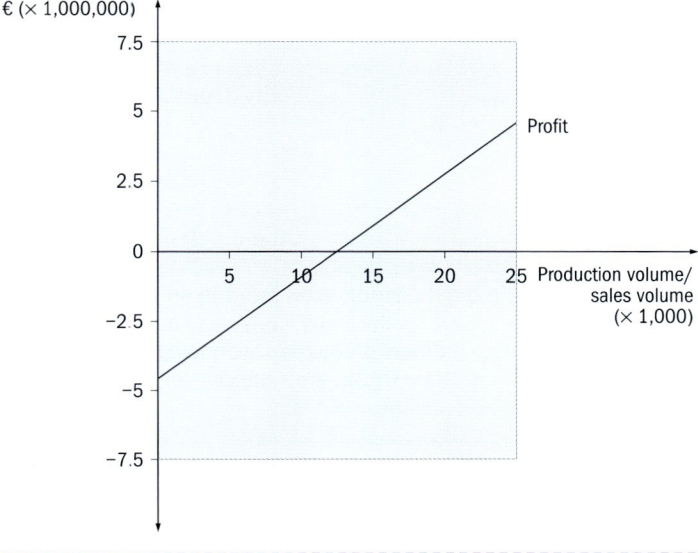

The slope of the profit line gives an indication of the *operating leverage*. The steeper the profit line, the larger the influence of any adjustments to sales volume on profit, and the higher the risk level of the business.

Due to ongoing automation, variable costs as part of the total costs reduce, and fixed costs increase. As a consequence, the contribution margin per unit increases. Changes in production and sales volumes therefore have greater impact on profit.

As the fixed part of the total costs increases, so does the operating leverage.

EXAMPLE 11.4 CONTINUED

Wavekings is considering an investment in new equipment which will cause annual fixed costs to rise by €3,000,000 to €7,500,000. The new equipment leads to a reduction in variable costs (less energy, less spoilage, less temporary staff, etc.), resulting in €100 in variable costs per surfboard.

Figure 11.10 shows the profit-volume chart for the new production technology.

FIGURE 11.10 Profit volume chart Wavekings with new versus old production technology

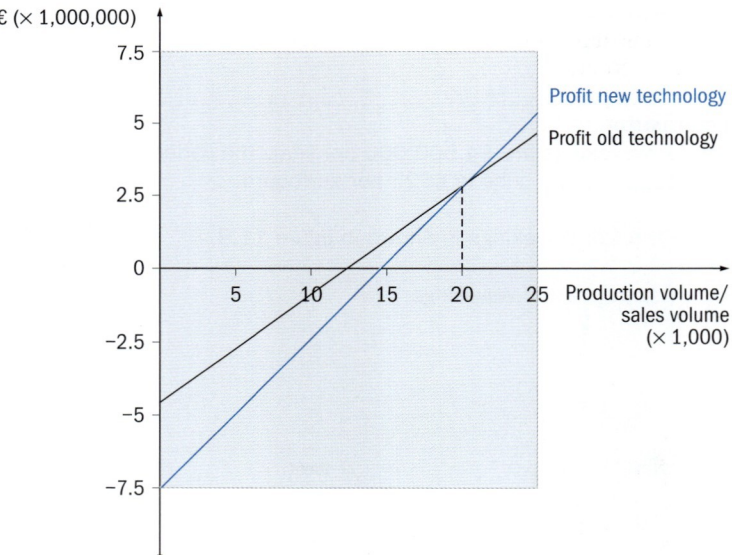

The profit line of the new production technology starts with large losses at sales equal to zero due to the higher fixed costs, but it is steeper than that of the current technology.

Every additional unit sold using the new production technology leads to an additional profit of €625 − €100 = €525. With the former production technology, that figure was €625 − €250 = €375.

If a company is presented with the possibility of switching to another production technology, it is important to know at what level the switch to the new technology becomes profitable. This indifference point is found at the output level at which the costs (and the profit) are equal for both production techniques.

11

EXAMPLE 11.4 CONTINUED
The indifference point with regard to the implementation of a new production method is at a production/sales volume of 20,000 items, and at sales of €12,500,000.
The point can be found by relating the increase of total fixed costs to the savings on the variable costs per product.

$$\frac{€3,000,000}{€250 - €100} = 20,000 \text{ units at } €625 = €12,500,000$$

TEST QUESTION 11.4
Calculate the break-even point for the new production technology.

Production companies deploying many machines in automated production lines deal with a cost structure that leads to high operating leverage. The same applies to service-providing companies, which deal with a large share of fixed salaries in their total costs.

Steel manufacturers are considered by investors to be cyclical funds, which is to say that their market value fluctuations are above average. There are two important reasons for this. Firstly, these companies operate in markets that are very sensitive to economic fluctuations and suffer the consequences of a recession before others do. Secondly, their share of fixed costs is very high as a consequence of the

11

capital-intensive nature of the business. Steel mills mainly incur fixed costs. If the capacity utilization degree is lowered, fixed costs continue – and the impact on profit is very large. Of course, as soon as the economy restores itself, the reverse effect occurs: extra orders generate more revenue, but the increase in costs is minimal due to the large share of fixed costs. Indian company Tata Steel has production sites in 26 countries, including the Netherlands. In the Dutch city of IJmuiden, steel has been produced since 1918. In 1999 *Hoogovens* was acquired by British company Corus Steel, which itself was the subject of a take-over by Tata Steel in 2007. Nowadays the European branch of Tata Steel is in a joint-venture with Germans ThyssenKrupp. IJmuiden will continue to be a production site.

A company can decide if these certain cost items are to be of a fixed or variable nature. A company which has orders delivered by its own expeditions department incurs greater fixed costs than a company that outsources this activity to a transport company, paying a fee per order. Through outsourcing, fixed costs are changed to variable costs.

TEST QUESTION 11.5
Which of the following companies has the greatest operating leverage?
1 A wholesaler in domestic appliances.
2 A tax consultancy.
3 A goldsmith.

Glossary

Break-even point	The sales volume or sales revenue at which the total revenues are exactly equal to total costs, which results in neither a profit nor a loss.
Contribution margin	Sales revenue minus variable costs; the amount that is available to cover the fixed costs.
Degressively variable costs	Costs that increase less steeply than those proportional to the output level, resulting in reduced unit costs.
Fixed costs	Costs that are independent of the output level in a particular period, but are connected to a certain capacity.
High-low method	Method that derives the cost function from the costs at the lowest and the highest output level over the past period.
Indifference point	The output level at which two different production methods generate the same total costs.
Mixed costs	Costs that are partially fixed and partially variable.
Operating leverage	The degree in which profit fluctuates as a consequence of changes in sales volume. The higher fixed costs in relation to total costs, the higher the leverage.
Profit-volume chart	Graph that shows the connection between sales volume and profit level over a period.
Progressively variable costs	Costs that increase more steeply than those proportional to the output level, resulting in increased unit costs.
Proportionally variable costs	Costs that increase in proportion to the output level, so that unit costs remain equal.
Relevant production range	The possible output level for the coming period, determined by short-term capacity limits.
Safety margin	The maximum percentage by which current sales volume or sales revenue can decrease without causing a loss.

| **Step variable costs** | Costs that vary discontinuously with the output level as a consequence of the limited possibilities to divide the production factors; these production factors can, however, be acquired or disposed of in the short term. |
| **Variable costs** | Costs that increase or decrease as a result of an increase or decrease in output level. |

11

Multiple-choice questions

11.1 What always occurs if the output level increases?
a The variable unit costs increase.
b The total variable costs increase.
c The variable unit costs decrease.
d The variable unit costs remain equal.

11.2 The following connection between output level and total variable costs of a production process is known:

Production (in units)	**Costs** (in Euros)
0	0
2,000	5,000
4,000	9,000
6,000	12,000

Which costs are generated in this case?
a Fixed costs.
b Degressively variable costs.
c Proportionally variable costs.
d Progressively variable costs.

11.3 Which of the following applies if the output level increases within the relevant production range?
a Total fixed costs remain equal and total variable costs increase.
b Total fixed costs remain equal and total variable costs decrease.
c Total fixed costs and total variable costs remain equal.
d Total fixed costs and total variable costs increase.

11.4 What is represented on the horizontal axis of the graph for the break-even analysis?
a Total sales revenue.
b Total costs.
c Production and sales volume.
d The number of periods.

11.5 A theater agency has contracted a well-known rock band for an exclusive performance for a fee of €12,500. The entrance tickets are €35 and are exclusively available at ticket presales addresses, which receive 5% per ticket sold. Rent for the theater is €2,000 plus €1.25 per visitor. The other fixed costs are €5,500.

11

How many tickets should be sold to break even?

a 563
b 593
c 602
d 625

11.6   A trading company imports an article for €2.50 per unit and sells it for €10. Fixed costs for this company are €25,000 per month. How much annual sales revenue has to be effected to generate €150,000 profit before tax per year?

a €500,000
b €600,000
c €750,000
d €800,000

11.7   A real estate agent receives a 1.8% average provision on total sales value. Fixed costs are €150,000 per year, variable costs are 0.2% of the sales value on average.
What is the break-even sales revenue (total sales value)?

a €7,500,000
b €8,333,333
c €9,375,000
d €10,000,000

11.8   A product is sold for €45. Fixed costs are €18 and variable costs are €4.50 per unit. What is the contribution margin for this product?

a 60%
b 50%
c €22.50
d 90%

11.9   This year, a company sells a product for €29 and expects a profit of €1 million, with a sales revenue of €7,250,000. Variable costs are estimated at €2,250,000 in total.
What is the break-even quantity?

a 112,500 units.
b 200,000 units.
c 312,500 units.
d 400,000 units.

11.10   Which event lowers break-even sales revenue?

a An increase in the quantity sold.
b An increase in the variable costs per piece.
c An increase in the contribution percentage.
d An increase in sales revenue.

11.11   The ABC company manufactures a product at €8 variable costs; fixed costs during a particular period amount to €24,000 and variable costs to €52,000 in total. The selling price is always €15 per unit and all 6,500 units manufactured are sold. What is the break-even quantity during this period?

a 3,000 units.
b 3,429 units.
c 6,000 units.
d 8,000 units.

11.12   Refer to question 11.11.
          What is the profit (before tax) during this period?
   a €19,500
   b €21,500
   c €23,500
   d €25,500

11.13   The Burminster hotel in Stalworthshire has 75 rooms. The price of
          one room is €150 per night (including breakfast buffet). Variable costs
          (cleaning, laundry, etc.) are €30 per night/per stay including breakfast. For
          the coming year, fixed costs are estimated at €1,150,000 personnel costs,
          €275,000 depreciation and €360,000 other expenses (excluding interest
          costs). Furthermore, interest costs for the coming year are €165,000 and a
          repayment of €180,000 has to be made. How many bookings are needed to
          achieve the break-even point for the coming year?
   a 14,875
   b 16,25
   c 16,958
   d 17,75

11.14   Refer to question 11.13.
          How many nights should be booked the coming year to achieve a profit after
          tax of 6.5% of the sales revenue (assuming a tax rate of 20%)?
   a 17,687
   b 18,087
   c 18,714
   d 20,286

11.15   A trading company expects annual sales of €8.2 million. Gross profit
          (contribution margin) is estimated at 39% of sales. All operating costs are
          fixed. Profit before tax is estimated at €148,000. What is the break-even sales
          revenue (rounded up to €1,000)?
   a €7,821,000
   b €7,957,000
   c €8,052,000
   d €8,443,000

12

Cost Calculations

12

12.1   **Absorption Costing and Normal Output Level**
12.2   **Direct Costing**
12.3   **Absorption Costing and Direct Costing as Instruments for Decision-making**
12.4   **Economic Life and Replacement of Fixed Assets**

This chapter focusses on cost calculations.
Paragraph 12.1 discusses the method known as absorption costing, which assigns all costs, both fixed and variable, to production.
Paragraph 12.2 covers direct costing. Using this method means that only the variable costs are considered to be product costs. These methods can lead to different results when calculating the profit over a period.
Paragraph 12.3 covers different types of decision-making as well as the usefulness of absorption and direct costing for arriving at a justified decision. Paragraph 12.4 deals with the issue of determining the economic life of fixed assets.

12.1 **Absorption Costing and Normal Output Level**

The unit cost of a product consists of the monetary value of all production factors sacrificed to manufacture that product. *Absorption costing* (or *full costing*) considers all costs to be *product costs*.

In principle, unit costs should be easy to calculate: divide the total costs for the actual output level by the number of products. If all costs are proportionally variable, this presents no problems as the unit costs are equal at every level.

Considering that costs can also be fixed, progressive, degressive or step variable, a unit cost based on this calculation method can vary.

The unit cost actually depends on the produced amount of goods and services: the activity level or output level.

If unit costs are calculated in this way, this could result for example in table 12.1.

TABLE 12.1 Average unit costs

Production (in units)	Total costs (in Euros)	Unit costs (in Euros)
1,000	15,000	15.00
2,000	26,000	13.00
3,000	36,000	12.00
4,000	46,400	11.60
5,000	58,750	11.75
6,000	72,000	12.00
7,000	87,500	12.50

The development of unit costs is shown in figure 12.1

FIGURE 12.1 Average costs per unit

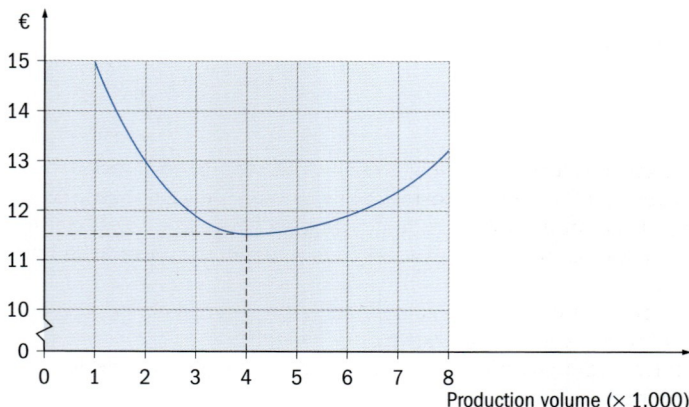

If it is assumed that total costs comprise fixed and proportionally variable costs only, situations like those presented in table 12.2 and figure 12.2, for example, could apply.

TABLE 12.2 Average unit costs for fixed and proportionally variable costs

Production (in units)	Total costs (in Euros)	Unit costs (in Euros)
1,000	15,000	15.00
2,000	26,000	13.00
3,000	37,000	12.33
4,000	48,000	12.00
5,000	59,000	11.80
6,000	70,000	11.67
7,000	81,000	11.57

FIGURE 12.2 Average unit costs for fixed and proportionally variable costs

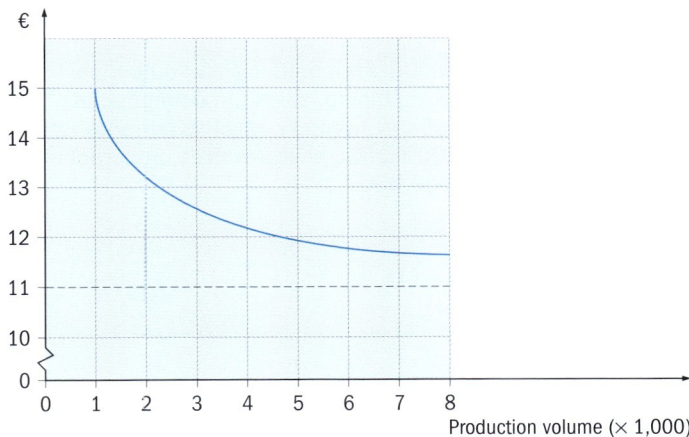

For certain decisions, it can be crucial to know the average costs per product. However, if the average costs are always considered as being unit costs, strong variations in unit costs, depending on the output level, are the result. In the case of an unusually low production level, unit costs are high, and vice versa.

In addition, unit costs can only be calculated at the end of a period when the number of units produced is known.

Unit costs that are known only in hindsight do not have much value for decision-making.

If, for example, unit costs are to be used for price setting, they need to be known before production starts. To that end, unit costs can be based on a previously determined output level *(production denominator level)*.

This output level can be established based on the production forecast for the following period. In this case, unit costs are available. However, the problem of different unit costs in different periods for the same product remains, depending on the coincidental output level during that period. It is therefore recommended to base the output level on the *normal output*: the average use of the capacity that is expected in the long term. The determination of unit cost then is as follows:

Normal output

$$\text{Unit cost} = \frac{\text{Total fixed costs} + \text{Total variable costs at normal output}}{\text{Normal output}}$$

If variable costs are entirely proportional, and variable unit costs are therefore a fixed amount regardless of the output level, this can be expressed as:

$$\text{Unit cost} = \frac{\text{Total fixed costs}}{\text{Normal output}} + \frac{\text{Total variable costs at forecast output}}{\text{Forecast output}}$$

TEST QUESTION 12.1
Is normal output usually above or below the break-even point?

EXAMPLE 12.1
Fixed costs for a company are €25,000 per month. Normal output per month is 50,000 units. For the coming month, sales are estimated at 55,000 products at €16. To build up the inventory, which is currently rather low, the production forecast is 60,000 units, which involves proportionally variable manufacturing costs of €360,000.
The unit cost for this product is:

$$\frac{€400,000}{50,000} + \frac{€360,000}{60,000} = €8 + €6 = €14$$

By dividing total fixed costs by the normal output level, an overhead rate to cover these fixed costs is included in the unit cost. If the estimation of the actual output level for the coming period deviates from the normal output level, a discrepancy will occur between actual fixed costs and the calculated fixed costs included in the unit cost of the products.

Output level variance

Transaction result

This potential discrepancy is called the *output level variance*, which is a correction of the *transaction result*, the profit calculation based on full unit cost.

The output level variance is determined as follows:

[(Expected) actual output – Normal output] × Applied fixed costs per unit

---

EXAMPLE 12.1 CONTINUED

The forecast result for this month can be determined as follows:

Transaction result: 55,000 × (€16 − €14) =	€110,000
Output level variance: (60,000 − 50,000) × €8 =	+ € 80,000
Profit	€190,000

The output level variance of €80,000 can be specified as follows:
The fixed costs are €400,000. For a forecast production of 60,000 units, and forecast sales of 55,000 units, the following cost figures are covered:

Costs of goods sold in the sales unit	55,000 × €8 =	€440,000
In the increase of the final inventory on the	5,000 × €8 = + €	40,000
balance sheet		€480,000

There is overcosting of €80,000.

If, at the end of a period, both sales and output level are below expectation (40,000 units and 45,000 units respectively), the following calculation of actual profit can be made:

Transaction result: 40,000 × (€16 − €14) =	€80,000
Output level variance: (45,000 − 50,000) × €8 =	€40,000 negative
Profit	€40,000

The relationship between actual costs, total unit cost and output level variance is shown in figure 12.3.

FIGURE 12.3 Actual costs, total unit cost and output level variance

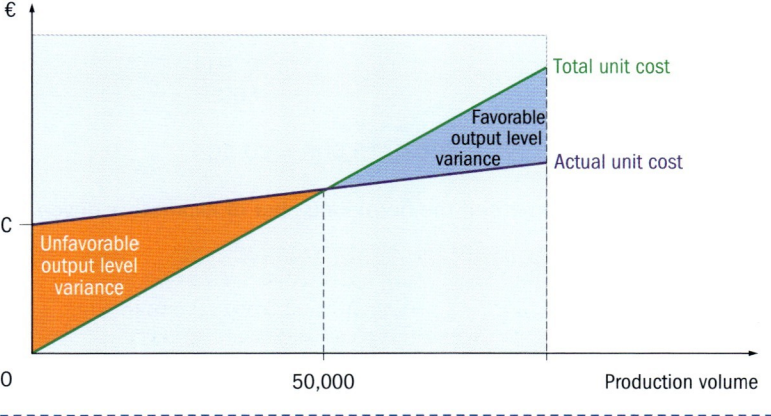

TEST QUESTION 12.2

What would be the maximum possible monthly negative output level variance in example 12.2?

Capacity utilization rate

If the utilized capacity (actual output level) is expressed as a percentage of the maximum available capacity, this is called the *capacity utilization rate.* The formula to calculate the capacity utilization rate is as follows:

$$\text{Capacity utilization rate} = \frac{\text{Actual volume}}{\text{Available capacity}} \times 100\%$$

Production companies express their available capacity in maximum units per year. In service companies, many different methods can be applied. For example, a hotel will use the number of available rooms per night.
The normal operating capacity is rarely equal to the available capacity. There should always be spare capacity, for example, with respect to maintenance, but also as a consequence of seasonal influences. The capacity utilization rate is therefore lower than 100%.

A specific problem in the service industry is that there can be no build-up of 'production'. The service industry cannot produce 'for inventory' during times when capacity is not used to the fullest. Unused hotel rooms, airline seats, theater seats, etc. cannot be transferred to a following period. This 'production', if not put to use, is therefore lost. This is in contrast to, for example, a car manufacturer who stores produced but unsold cars on its premises, awaiting a time when more clients will present themselves.

TEST QUESTION 12.3
The monthly costs of a mid-range car with an annual average use of 15,000 kilometers is:

Depreciation (based on time)	€156
Depreciation (based on distance in kilometres)	€ 56
Motor vehicle tax	€ 54
Maintenance (based on time)	€ 19
Maintenance (based on distance in kilometres)	€ 85
Fuel	€142
Insurance	€ 91
	€603

The price per kilometer is (12 × €603)/15,000 = €0.48.

What is the cost per kilometer if the normal number of kilometers driven per year is 21,000?

12.2 Direct Costing

Direct costing

Direct costing is a method that only allocates variable costs to products. Under this system, fixed costs are charged directly to the income statement. Fixed costs are considered *period costs* instead of product costs.
The name given to this method is rather unfortunate, considering that direct costing primarily differentiates between variable and fixed costs. *Direct costing*, however, suggests that a distinction is made between direct and indirect costs, which is not the case.

Table 12.3 shows the essential difference between absorption costing and direct costing.

TABLE 12.3 Absorption costing and direct costing

	Absorption costing	**Direct costing**
Variable costs	Product costs	Product costs
Fixed costs	Product costs	Period costs

To determine the profit for a particular period, the following basic procedure is applied in direct costing:

Sales revenue	€......
Variable costs of goods sold	− €......
Total contribution margin	€......
Total fixed costs (of period)	− €......
Profit	€......

EXAMPLE 12.2

A company produces an article sold at €10 per unit. Variable costs are €5 per unit, annual fixed costs are €300,000 and are evenly spread over the quarters of the year.
The normal output level is set at 25,000 units per quarter.
Production and sales during the past year were as follows (x 1,000 units):

	Quarter 1	**Quarter 2**	**Quarter 3**	**Quarter 4**	**Total**
Production	25	30	10	35	100
Sales volume	25	10	20	45	100

Firstly, unit cost must be calculated to be able to determine the results per period based on absorption costing. Unit costs are:

$$\frac{€300,000}{100,000} + €5 = €3 + €5 = €8$$

Consecutively, the following overview can be drawn up for absorption costing (x €1,000):

	Quarter 1	**Quarter 2**	**Quarter 3**	**Quarter 4**	**Total**
Sales revenue	250	100	200	450	1,000
Cost of goods sold	200	80	160	360	800
Transaction result	50	20	40	90	200
Output level variance	−	15	(45)	30	−
Profit (loss)	50	35	(5)	120	200

The income statement based on direct costing is as follows (× €1,000):

	Quarter 1	Quarter 2	Quarter 3	Quarter 4	Total
Sales revenue	250	100	200	450	1,000
Variable costs of goods sold	125	50	100	225	500
Transaction result	125	50	100	225	500
Output level fixed costs	75	75	75	75	300
Profit (loss)	50	(25)	25	150	200

The two overviews show that there are variances in the quarterly profits between both methods if there are *inventory changes*, i.e. if the quantity sold is not equal to the output level. These deviating profits are a consequence of assigning or not assigning part of the fixed costs that occur during a particular period to the following period via the book value of inventory. In the second quarter, profit in absorption costing is €35,000 and based on direct costing there is a loss of €25,000. The difference of €60,000 is caused by the built-up inventory of 20,000 units. In absorption costing, the inventory is valued on the balance sheet at a unit cost of €8. As a result, part of the fixed costs, namely 20,000 × €3 = €60,000, will not be charged to the second quarter. This is in contrast to direct costing, where the total fixed costs of €75,000 would be considered period costs. Since no inventory changes take place during the entire year, annual results are equal for both systems.

For the relationship between profit based on absorption costing and on direct costing, the following applies:
Output level > Sales volume → Profit absorption costing > Profit direct costing
Output level = Sales volume → Profit absorption costing = Profit direct costing
Output level < Sales volume → Profit absorption costing < Profit direct costing

The idea behind direct costing is that fixed costs are generated by the availability of production capacity (for example: machine capacity or labor capacity of employees). Even if this capacity is not fully used, supporters of the direct costing method state that the costs related to this capacity should be assigned to the period during which the capacity is available.

If a company were to decide to only produce in the first year and only sell in the second year, use of the direct costing would result in a loss for the first year by the amount of the fixed costs. It is debatable whether this is a realistic representation of the company's performance. In absorption costing, profit would be zero in the first year, on the assumption that the actual production is equal to normal production.
On the other hand, there is a strong argument that direct costing is fairer than absorption costing: in direct costing, profit can only increase where there is an increase in sales.
In absorption costing, additional profit can be generated by increasing the output level without actually selling the increased production. In this situation, the output level variance increases.

For seasonal companies in particular, direct costing leads to strong fluctuations in profit: the 'weak' months, during which there is production but few or no sales, show a loss equal to the fixed cost; the months in which sales take place, however, show very large profits.

For some companies, this does not only apply within a one-year period, but over several years. Ice skate manufacturers need a severe winter once every four years to be able to survive. In the meantime, production continues and the warehouses are filled up with hundreds of thousands of ice skates.

Application of direct costing would mean recording losses during years with warm winters.

In figure 12.4, the essential difference between absorption costing and direct costing is shown.

FIGURE 12.4 Processing of costs using absorption costing and direct costing

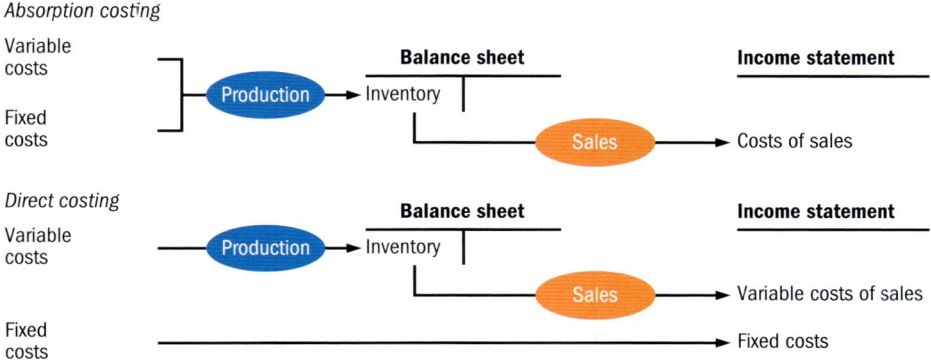

12

TEST QUESTION 12.4
Present a motivated argument discussing whether or not an output level variance may lead to a discrepancy in profit, based on direct or absorption costing.

Sales costs

One final remark regarding the comparison between absorption costing and direct costing: so far, it has been assumed that there are only manufacturing costs and no sales costs. If there are also sales and distribution costs, then these should not be included in the inventory valuation because the inventory has not yet been sold. For both absorption costing and direct costing, sales and distribution costs are considered period costs, which are charged to the profit of the period during which they were made.

12.3 Absorption Costing and Direct Costing as Instruments for Decision-making

The following paragraph discusses to what extent absorption costing or direct costing can be used in achieving the following three objectives:
1 Determining selling price.
2 Performing break-even analysis.
3 Performing bottleneck analysis.

Determining the optimum selling price is not easy. The higher the selling price, the lower the sales volume. In order to know whether a price increase has a positive effect on profit, knowledge of the price elasticity of the demand is necessary. For example, a price elasticity of 3 means that a price increase of 1% leads to a reduction in sales volumes of 3%.
If company management knows the price elasticity, it is possible to determine the optimal selling price, the selling price that leads to the highest profit. This is shown in Figure 2.5.

FIGURE 12.5 Profit maximization when price elasticity is known

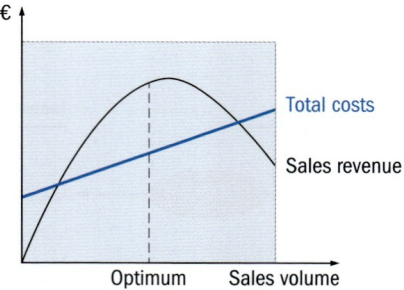

EXAMPLE 12.3
The Powertools company manufactures various types of industrial hardware, including power drills.

Fixed costs for the production line concerned are €1,500,000 per year and variable costs per drill are €20. The normal output level is 100,000 power drills per year.
The unit cost under absorption costing is:

$$\frac{€1,500,000}{100,000} + €20 = €15 + €20 = €35$$

The regular selling price must be set at no lower than €35.

A large foreign home improvement chain contacts Powertools and wants to order 10,000 drilling machines at €25 each.
Although this price is below the full unit cost, accepting the deal will generate an advantage for Powertools.
If a *differential calculation* is performed, which is to say if additional revenue and costs are compared, the result is as follows:

Additional sales revenue	10,000 × €25 =	€250,000
Additional costs	10,000 × €20 =	€200,000
Additional profit		€ 50,000

Since fixed costs are not related to output level, an increase in output level does not result in an increase in fixed costs. Of course, this only applies if the current production capacity offers sufficient space to execute the order. If a direct costing calculation is made for this situation, profitability becomes clear immediately: the contribution margin increases by €50,000 and fixed costs remain unchanged. Therefore, profit increases by €50,000. If absorption costing is applied, it could initially give a wrong impression, since the selling price is lower than the unit cost of €35. However, this is also a profitable order under absorption costing:

Additional sales revenue	10,000 × €25 =	€250,000
Additional costs	10,000 × €35 =	– €350,000
Less transaction profit		€100,000
Additional output level variance	10,000 × €15 =	€150,000
Additional profit		€ 50,000

If a company charges a lower price to certain customers compared to its regular customers, this is called *price discrimination.* Price discrimination has one obvious disadvantage: if regular customers were to discover that other buyers pay reduced prices, it could lead to price-cutting, as regular customers will also demand price reductions. This could have disastrous consequences for the company concerned.

Price discrimination is therefore only possible in strictly separated markets, where one group of costumers has no insight into the prices paid by the other group.
If a company applies lower prices for export than on the home market, this is called *dumping.* Under certain circumstances, dumping can be considered an unfair practice; the European Union has anti-dumping legislation, violation of which may result in fines for manufacturers outside the EU who dump their products in the EU.

In general, students have less purchasing power than other customers. Charging students regular selling prices may cause companies to lose out on this particular customer base. This is why hair dressers, for example, offer student discounts: students that bring their student ID-cards can get their hair cut at a reduced rate. As long as the salon is not yet operating at full capacity, such offers contribute to overall profit. This is an example of price discrimination.

Break-even analysis

The break-even analysis discussed in chapter 11 indicates the point at which the sales volume of the company reaches break-even. A direct costing approach is implicitly applied because fixed costs are considered period costs that need to be recouped by the contribution margin. If production = sales applies, then there is no difference in profit between absorption costing and direct costing and therefore the same break-even point is reached. If there is a difference between both methods, then profit in absorption costing could be zero for several sales volumes, depending on the resulting output level and output level variance.

Bottleneck analysis

If production cannot be expanded because capacity, for example, in the form of machine-hours, cannot be increased in the short term, then the machine is a *bottleneck factor*. A bottleneck determines output level. If the capacity concerned can be used to manufacture different types of products, an optimization problem arises: the machine must be used in such a way as to maximize profit. Thus, the direct costing approach is used. At a given capacity, fixed costs are not influenced. Therefore, they do not play a role in the question of how the available capacity should be best put to use. It is about maximizing contribution margins. This means that the product with the highest contribution margin per unit, related to the bottleneck factor, should be the primary production unit. The bottleneck analysis is an instrument that helps determine the most profitable production composition, the *optimal production plan*.

Optimal production plan

EXAMPLE 12.4
A company has a range of machines to manufacture products P and Q. For each production period, there are a total of 750 machine-hours available; fixed costs are €15,000. Each Product P requires 2 machine-hours, and each Product Q requires 1.5 machine-hours. A maximum of 400 units of P or Q each can be sold per period.
The following calculations were made for both products:

	Product P		**Product Q**	
Selling price		€280		€320
Variable costs	€120		€176	
Fixed costs	€ 40		€ 30	
Unit cost		€160		€206
Profit		€120		€114

At first, product P (with a profit of €120 per unit) appears more attractive than product Q (profit €114 per unit). However, basing the decision on the highest profit per product results in making the wrong choice. As previously noted, fixed costs incorporated into unit cost should not influence a short-term decision. These costs are the result of decisions made in the past (such as the purchase of a machine and the resulting depreciation); these decisions cannot be reversed and are therefore irrelevant for the future.

Choosing the P-product based on a higher contribution margin of (€280 − €120 = €160) per unit, compared to Q (€320 − €176 = €144) will not, by definition, result in the best solution.
The determining factor for optimal production is the bottleneck's contribution margin per unit. In this example, the bottleneck is the number of available machine-hours, which is insufficient to produce 400 units of both products. The contribution per machine-hour per product is:

$$\frac{€160}{2} = €80 \text{ for P and } \frac{€144}{1.5} = €96 \text{ for Q}$$

This implies that the Q-product is more profitable per machine-hour and therefore should be preferred over the P-product. The production of 400 Q-products (maximum output level) requires 600 machine-hours. This leaves 150 hours for P-products, resulting in 75 units of product P. Therefore, the optimal production plan is 400 Q and 75 P, with the profit being:

Contribution Q	400 × €144 =	€57,600
Contribution P	75 × €160 = +	€12,000
Total contribution margin		€69,600
Fixed costs		− €15,000
Profit		€54,600

The total contribution margin can also be calculated by multiplying the machine-hours required for the quantity of P and Q by the contribution margin per hour: 600 × €96 + 150 × €80 = €69,600

12

12.4 Economic Life and Replacement of Fixed Assets

Depreciation

Chapter 3 covered the depreciation costs of fixed assets. The application of annual *depreciation* is intended to distribute the costs of fixed assets over the years in which an asset is used. There are various methods for determining the depreciation per year. Apart from depreciation costs, capital investments in fixed assets also lead to other costs, namely *interest costs.*

Interest costs can be calculated as a percentage of the capital invested in the fixed asset.

Depreciation and interest costs derive from the *purchase* of a fixed asset. The *usage* of a fixed asset also results in costs. These costs include wage costs of a worker in charge of operating the machine, energy costs to power the machine, raw materials needed manufacture a product, maintenance costs to keep the machine in optimal working condition,

Complementary costs

etc. All these additional costs related to the use of the fixed asset are called *complementary costs.*

With the aging of the fixed asset, two effects can occur:
- The number of units of output the fixed asset is capable of producing decreases.
- The costs of usage of the fixed asset (the complementary costs) increases.

These effects are the result of technical wear and tear from the fixed asset being either in use or degrading over time, particularly in times when the asset is idle (e.g. corrosion). If technical wear and tear over time causes the fixed asset to no longer be suitable to deliver the output for which it was

Physical life

purchased, its *physical life* will have passed.

In many situations, fixed assets are mothballed before the end of their physical life.

The complementary costs will have become so high that the costs per unit of output are too high to deploy the fixed asset in a profitable manner. In such case, the 'economic life' of the fixed asset has passed.

Economic life

The *economic life* can be calculated as the period of use for which the fixed asset's average costs per unit of output are at their lowest. Past this period of use, the costs per unit of output increase, making it wiser to buy a new identical fixed asset to be able to produce at low cost again.

When determining the depreciation costs of cruise ships, it is generally assumed that the economic life will be 30 years, with a residual value of 15% of building costs. When determining economic life, both technical factors and expected long-term market-developments arte taken into account. Naturally, it is necessary to modernize the interior of a cruise ship over the course of its economic life.

The *Carnival Lines Shipping Company*, based in Miami, operates 25 cruise ships requiring an investment of approximately €600 million each. In 2018, the latest addition will be added to the fleet: the *Carnival Horizon*, with a capacity of 4,000 passengers.

EXAMPLE 12.5

Shakespeare Building Company LLC has bought cement trucks with a value of €100,000 and a lifespan of 5 years. The output of the cement trucks is measured in number of m^3 cement or concrete transported to the customer.

The residual value, complementary costs and output per truck per year are shown in the following table:

Year	Residual value at the end of the year (in Euros)	Complementary costs (in Euros)	Output in m^3 concrete
1	60,000	50,000	10,000
2	30,000	52,000	10,000
3	15,000	56,000	9,500
4	5,000	65,000	9,500
5	0	85,000	9,000

Average costs per unit of output are calculated for every possible period of use. All amounts are in Euros.

Period of use in years	Depreciation = purchasing value – residual value	Complementary costs	Total cost	Average costs per unit of output
1	40,000	50,000	90,000	9.00
2	70,000	102,000	172,000	8.60
3	85,000	158,000	243,000	8.24
4	95,000	223,000	318,000	8.15
5	100,000	308,000	408,000	8.50

Average costs per unit of output of the cement trucks are the lowest for a 4-year period of use. The economic life is therefore 4 years.

FIGURE 12.6 Average costs per unit of output for different periods of use

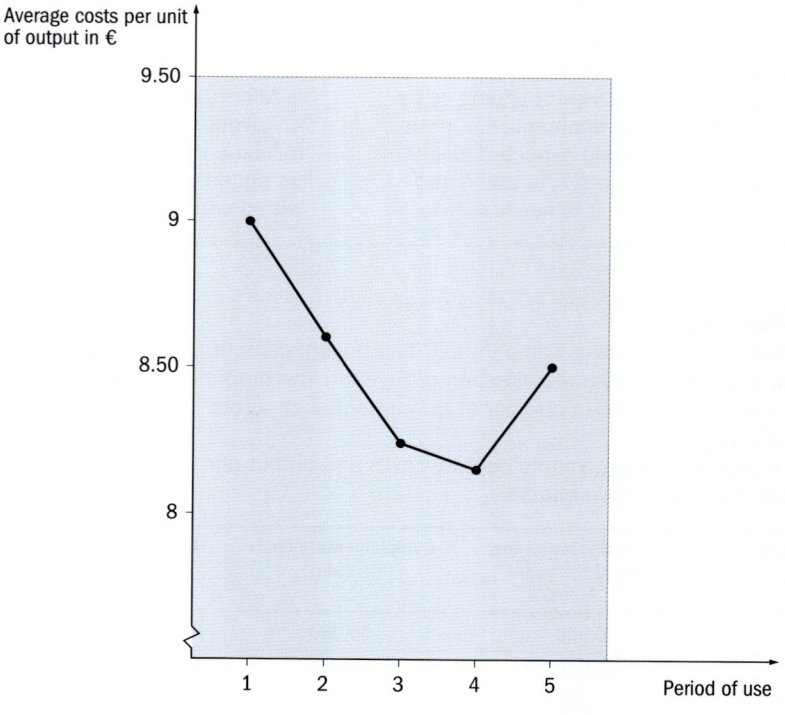

Unit cost should be equal, regardless of the year in which a unit is produced. To ensure equal unit cost throughout an asset's years of use, yearly depreciation costs are determined as a residual item: the difference between the total costs of outputs for the year and complementary costs in that year.

EXAMPLE 12.5 CONTINUED

The economic life is calculated at four years with appropriate annual depreciation, being the difference between total cost of output per year and complementary costs.

Year	Total costs of output (amount × €8.15)	Complementary costs	Depreciation (total costs of output – complementary costs – interest costs)
1	81,500	50,000	31,500
2	81,500	52,000	29,500
3	77,425	56,000	21,425
4	77,425	65,000	12,425

This calculation therefore determines annual depreciation in such a way that unit cost of the performance remains equal during the entire period during which the fixed asset is in use. This is not achieved using the depreciation methods described in chapter 3. Nevertheless, for the sake of convenience, the methods in chapter 3 are the ones that are most often used in practice. Note that the presented calculation method of depreciation works better in theory – but it is based on assumptions regarding performance development, complementary costs and residual value during the usage of the fixed asset. Whether these assumptions are correct is, of course, not known in advance.

TEST QUESTION 12.5

Which depreciation method in chapter 3 would need to be selected to mirror the optimal depreciation plan in example 12.5 as closely as possible?

In determining economic life, the current assumption has been that any replacement would take the form of an identical fixed asset. Due to technological developments, however, it is possible that a cheaper or more advanced fixed asset becomes available on the market during the period of use. This means that the unit cost for the same performance becomes lower for the new asset.

In such a case, the old asset is subject to economic aging or *obsolescence*.   **Obsolescence**
Whether immediate replacement by a new fixed asset is required can be determined by a differential calculation.

EXAMPLE 12.5 CONTINUED

Shakespeare Building Company LLC has had the cement trucks in use for two years. Meanwhile, a new type of cement truck has gone onto the market. It has equal capacity and a unit cost of €7.50 per m³ of concrete. When buying a new cement truck, the trade-in price for the currently owned model takes the form of a €25,000 discount on the purchasing price of the new cement truck.

The calculation of the differential costs for each of the two alternatives:
1 use the old cement trucks another year, or
2 replace the cement trucks now with a newer type.

The differential costs of alternative 1 are the complementary costs plus the opportunity costs of the currently owned cement trucks. Differential costs of the transport of 10,000 m^3 for this alternative are €56,000 + €25,000 = €81,000.

The differential cost of the transport of 9,500 m^3 after replacing the trucks by new ones consists of the absorption costs: 9,500 × €7.50 = €71,250.

Immediate replacement of the cement trucks by a new type generates a financial advantage of €9,750 per truck per year.

Glossary

Bottleneck factor	The production factor which determines the maximum output level, and whose capacity cannot be expanded in the short term.
Capacity utilization rate	The extent to which the maximum available capacity of a particular fixed asset is actually put to use.
Complementary costs	All costs, except depreciation, related to the use of a fixed asset, such as maintenance costs, wages of the operator, interest costs, etc.
Contribution margin	Selling price minus variable unit costs (i.e. sales revenue minus total variable costs).
Depreciation	Costs related to the decrease in value of a fixed asset.
Differential costs	Cost increase as a result of expansion of production.
Direct costing	Costing method that only allocates variable costs to production and charges fixed costs directly to the income statement.
Dumping	The strategy of selling at lower prices in the export market than in home markets; form of price discrimination.
Economic life	The period for which a fixed asset is economically useful.
Normal output	The average output level expected for the coming years.
Optimal production plan	The most profitable composition of production for a given capacity, and therefore given fixed costs.
Output level variances	The difference between total fixed costs during a period and fixed costs charged to production.
Physical life	The period for which a fixed asset is technically capable of delivering the performance for which it was acquired.
Price discrimination	Offering the same product or service at different prices.
Production level denominator	The output level used for unit cost calculation to determine the tariff for fixed unit costs.

Multiple-choice questions

12.1 A company set the production level denominator for 2016 at 8,000 units per year. In that year, production is 7,000 units.
What can be said with certainty?
  a It is a positive transaction result.
  b It is a negative transaction result.
  c It is a positive output level variance.
  b It is a negative output level variance.

12.2 Refer to question 12.1.
The production level denominator for 2017 was set at 7,500 units per year instead of 8,000 units per year. In 2017, production is 7,000 units.
What can be said with certainty?
  a Unit cost of the product is lower in 2017 than in 2016.
  b Profit in 2017 is higher than in 2016.
  c The negative output level variance is less in 2017 than in 2016.
  d The transaction result in 2017 is higher than in 2016.

12.3 For the coming period, a company has estimated production at 17,500 units. Fixed costs are €1.4 million and variable costs are forecast at €700,000 for this period. Normal output level is 20,000 units per period.
What are the full unit cost and the expected actual output, respectively?
  a €110 and €175,000 loss.
  b €110 and €200,000 loss.
  c €120 and €175,000 loss.
  d €110 and €200,000 loss.

12.4 In a production company, fixed manufacturing costs in the previous quarter were €1 million and the (proportionally) variable costs were €720,000. Normal production and sales are 160,000 units per year, evenly spread over the quarters. Actual production was 45,000 units during the past quarter, sales were 42,000 products at a selling price of €50. What is the profit over this quarter?
  a €378,000
  b €405,000
  c €503,000
  d €530,000

12.5 Which of the following costs is considered a product cost under direct costing?
  a Wages for permanent production personnel.
  b Depreciation of a machine which has depreciated based on careless use.
  c Sales provision of sales representatives.
  d Rent of business premises.

12.6 Over the previous month, a company achieved a profit of €50,000 based on direct costing. At the beginning of the month, there is an inventory of 13,000 units; the closing inventory was 18,000 units. Under absorption costing, the fixed production costs are €2 per product. What is the profit for that month based on absorption costing?
a €36,000
b €40,000
c €60,000
d €76,000

12.7 Excelsior PLC produced 50,000 X-products and sold 60,000 during the past year. At the beginning of the year, there was an inventory of 16,000 units. Which statement is correct for that year?
a Profit is higher and the value of the closing inventory is lower in absorption costing than in direct costing.
b Profit is higher and the value of the closing inventory is higher in absorption costing than in direct costing.
c Profit is lower and the value of the closing inventory is higher in absorption costing than in direct costing.
d Profit is lower and the value of the closing inventory is lower in absorption costing than in direct costing.

12.8 The unit cost of product X is as follows:

Raw material	€10
Depreciation machines	€ 5
Wages production personnel	€12
Salary sales personnel	€ 2
	€29

The machines have depreciated by a fixed amount per year; the wages and salary costs concern permanent employees.
What is the inventory appreciation per unit?
a €15 in direct costing and €29 in absorption costing.
b €10 in direct costing and €29 in absorption costing.
c €10 in direct costing and €27 in absorption costing.
d €12 in direct costing and €27 in absorption costing.

12.9 Refer to question 12.8.
The company takes on an incidental foreign order for the sale of 15,000 units at €14.
Which statement is correct?
a From the point of view of profit, it is not wise to accept this order.
b Based on absorption costing, this order gives a positive transaction result, but a negative output level variance. The total result on this order is positive.
c Based on absorption costing, this order gives a negative transaction result, but a positive output level variance. The total result on this order is positive.
d Profit on this order is larger with direct costing than with absorption costing.

12

12

12.10   What applies with respect to dumping?
 a It concerns different unit costs for the same product.
 b The export price of a product is higher than the price in the home market.
 c It is a form of price discrimination.
 d Larger customers pay less than smaller customers.

12.11   Why is direct costing better suited for a break-even analysis than absorption costing?
 a Because the non-linear sales revenues or cost lines do not provide a problem for direct costing.
 b Because the production of different products with different contribution margins, provide no problem for direct costing.
 c Because the cost functions in direct costing do not need to be known.
 d Because the difference between production and sales do not pose a problem for direct costing.

12.12   A company has a limited number of machine-hours available for the manufacturing of products A and B. Both products have the same selling price.
 The contribution margin of A is 40%, that of B is 60%. Four units of A require the same machine time as three units of B. The most profitable division of the remaining capacity is:
 a 100% for A.
 b 100% for B.
 c 40% for A and 60% for B.
 d 60% for A and 40% for B.

12.13   Refer to question 12.12.
 From the point of view of profit, when would it not matter which combination of A and B were manufactured?
 a If the contribution margin of A were 30% of the selling price.
 b If the contribution margin of A were 45% of the selling price.
 c If the contribution margin of A were 50% of the selling price.
 d If the contribution margin of A were 60% of the selling price.

12.14   Which of the following is not an example of technical wear and tear of an oil tanker?
 a Having to perform major maintenance over the years more frequently.
 b Increasing fuel usage over the years.
 c Increasing availability of underground pipelines for oil transport.
 b Being increasingly moored over the years due to malfunctioning.

12.15   For the production of an article, a company has to purchase a machine for €150,000, with which it produces 10,000 articles. Complementary costs during the first year are €20,000 and increase annually by €10,000. The residual value of the machine is €100,000 after one year, €70,000 after two years, €30,000 after three years and zero after four years. Based on this data, the economic life of the machine is:
 a 1 year.
 b 2 years.
 c 3 years.
 d 4 years.

13

Indirect Costs

As simple as cost calculation seems in theory, it often proves difficult in practice.
A company that manufactures several types of product will first need to establish which costs are caused by which products. Once that connection has been established, the costs can be charged to the various product types accordingly.
The allocation of (indirect) costs to calculation units is the focus of this chapter.
Paragraph 13.1 addresses the differences between direct and indirect costs, as well as the importance of correct cost allocation. Paragraph 13.2 discusses the relatively simple cost calculations in homogeneous mass production. Companies with diverse activities (heterogenic production) can apply different methods to allocate indirect costs. The methods used to assign indirect costs discussed in paragraph 13.3 are characterized by their simplicity – but also by their inaccuracy. Paragraphs 13.4 and 13.5 cover more complex allocation systems: the cost center and activity-based costing methods. Paragraph 13.6 approaches the problem from a different perspective, in which costs are not allocated to products but to customers. Knowledge of the level of customers' profitability is of great importance to a company.

13.1 **Consequences of Incorrect Cost Allocation**

To be able to calculate the unit cost of a product (order, project, service, etc.), the first step is to establish what the costs and the output level during a certain period will be. If only one type of a standard edition product is manufactured (*homogeneous production*), the calculation is simple and the unit cost can be calculated by using the process costing method (see paragraph 13.2).

Homogeneous production

The problem of cost allocation occurs at companies that produce different product types (*heterogenic production*). Here, the question becomes: how can total costs be allocated to the various products? Accordingly, the distinction between direct and indirect costs is important.

Heterogenic production

Direct costs are costs that are related to certain products in a causal and measurable way, in such a manner that they can be directly allocated to the products. Examples include the costs of raw material, materials and parts, labor for one type of product only.

Direct costs

For unit cost calculation, direct costs present little or no difficulty. *Indirect costs*, however, are a different matter. If more than one product type is manufactured, there will be costs that are generated for all products; a clear link between these costs and the respective product types is missing. Some examples are salary costs of the production head, maintenance costs, heating costs and depreciation of the production facilities. *Indirect costs*, therefore, are costs that cannot be directly allocated to products, as there is no obvious relationship.

Indirect costs

To calculate the correct unit cost, the indirect costs need to be incorporated. The *cost allocation methods* that could be applied are discussed in the following paragraphs.

Figure 13.1 shows the causal link between costs and products.

FIGURE 13.1 Causal link between costs and products

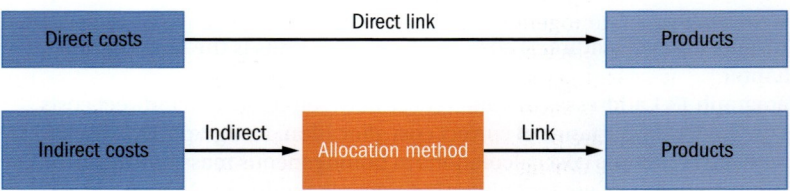

TEST QUESTION 13.1
A production company executes four different orders over a week. Orders A, B and C were carried out entirely during regular working hours.
Order D required overtime, which generated additional labor costs.
In which situations can these extra costs be directly allocated to order D?

Due to the lack of a clear link with production, there is a subjective aspect to the allocation of indirect costs to products when calculating unit cost. As discussed in the following paragraphs, different choices for allocation, lead to differences in unit cost.

Because the unit cost of a product is an important basis for establishing its selling price, cost allocation is very important.
If, based on inaccurately calculated unit costs, selling prices are set too high or too low, this can have a direct impact on a company's profitability.
There is also the risk of incorrect management decisions, as discussed in paragraph 12.3.
Management may, however, consciously choose to set a price below the full unit cost for certain products. This may be relevant for a company that has such a dominant market position for part of its product range that it is able to *increase* their selling price, meanwhile attempting to increase market share for other products by *decreasing* their selling price. Creating the possibility of low pricing of products in a competitive market through high prices in a non-competitive market is called *cross-subsidizing*. The company   **Cross-subsidizing** subsidizes, as it were, one or more products with the higher profits from other products.
The selling price is determined by various factors, including this type of competition consideration – but it does not influence unit cost, which must provide an objective benchmark for the financial value of the sacrificed production factors.

It is very important to determine the correct unit cost. However, selecting a cost allocation method should also be subject to a cost-benefit analysis. The following paragraphs will make clear that more complex cost allocation methods generate more accurate unit costs. These methods require more time (and thus more administration costs) than simple methods. Implementing a more complex method is only sensible if the benefits (i.e. of better decision-making as a result of accurate costing) outweigh the costs.

13.2 Process Costing and Equivalent Units Method

In general, calculating unit costs is easy in production processes characterized as homogeneous mass production. For each production period – for example, a week – the total costs and related output levels can be verified. By dividing these total costs by the number of products, the unit cost is obtained. This simple method is known as *process costing*. Given the fact that unit costs are preferably based on normal output levels, the period used should be one during which actual output is equal to the normal output.

EXAMPLE 13.1
The fixed costs of a cement producer are €60,000 per year. For the coming month, the production is estimated at 30,000 bags of cement (normal output) of 50 kg. The related costs are €47,500 for raw materials and €5,000 for packaging.
The unit cost is:

$$\frac{€112,500}{30,000} = €3.75$$

There is a minor complication in a production processes with an inventory of semi-finished product, or goods in progress, at the beginning and end of period. In this case, the actual production in a period consists of:
- the opening inventory of semi-finished products processed into a finished product
- products made during that period, from beginning to end
- the closing inventory of semi-finished products

The production in the period concerned is no longer a simple addition of these three numbers. After all, the opening inventory of semi-finished products was produced during the previous period; and the closing inventory is further processed in the next period. The three amounts should be aligned by expressing the opening and closing inventories of semi-finished products into a number of finished products produced during this period. This requires estimating how near to completion both inventories are.

EXAMPLE 13.2

A brick manufacturer produces one type of brick. In a particular week, 200,000 bricks were produced. At the beginning of the week, 10,000 bricks were unfinished; the closing inventory was 50,000. Total costs during this week were €33,000. Technically, both inventories can be considered 50% depleted. The weekly production is calculated as:
$200,000 - 50\% \times 10,000 + 50\% \times 50,000 = 220,000$ bricks.

Unit cost is:

$$\frac{€33,000}{220,000} = €0.15$$

In homogeneous mass production, it can also be the case that a production process has different phases, with a product passing through several departments. In this case, the cost calculation is focused on the departments. Although the calculation becomes slightly more complicated, with the addition of several possible variants, it still remains a type of process costing. However, the particulars of this specific type of costing system go beyond the scope of this book.

Equivalent units method

A variation on process costing which we will discuss here is the *equivalent units method*. In a situation where there is mass production that is not entirely homogeneous, ordinary process costing is not useful. The various products are similar but differ in, for example, size, contents or weight. With this method, the product types are aligned by expressing the total production as one product type, with the aid of equivalent units. This generates a mathematically homogeneous production, for which the unit cost can be calculated by use of process costing.

EXAMPLE 13.3

At a department of confectionery company Marsbury PLC, candy bars of 40, 75 and 200 grams are produced. These candy bars have the same composition and quality. Unit cost is assumed to depend on weight.

Normal production per period is 1,000,000 bars of 40 grams, 400,000 bars of 75 grams and 100,000 bars of 200 grams. The standard cost related to this production is €540,000.

The cost calculation is as follows:
A bar of 200 grams is equal to five bars of 40 grams and a bar of

75 grams is comparable to $\dfrac{75}{40}$ = 1.875 bar of 40 grams. With the aid of

equivalent units, the entire production is expressed in bars of 40 grams:
$5 \times 100,000 + 1.875 \times 400,000 + 1,000,000 = 2,250,000$ units of 40 grams.
Dividing the total costs of €540,000 by the equivalent production of 2,250,000 units results in a unit cost of €0.24 per bar of 40 grams. Thus, a bar of 75 grams has a unit cost of $1.875 \times €0.24 = €0.45$, and a bar of 200 grams $5 \times €0.24 = €1.20$.

TEST QUESTION 13.2

Calculate the unit costs used in example 13.3 by recalculating the entire production expressed in bars of 200 grams.

The use of equivalent units assumes a certain ratio between unit costs and products. Apart from using product weight or size, the required equivalent units can also be based on the ratio in which product types use certain production factors, such as number of man-hours or amount of raw materials.

13.3 Single Rate and Multiple Rate Mark-up Allocation Methods

As previously discussed, homogeneous production encounters hardly any allocation problems. All costs, including costs that are not directly related to the production process, must be included in the unit cost of the product and must be covered by the sales revenue of that product.

This is different for a company that produces a multiplicity of products. In such a case, separate calculations are required for each product type, project or order. This is known as *job costing*. Here, the distinction between direct and indirect costs becomes important. The distinction is determined by the nature of the production process. The costs of buildings, machines and equipment, management salaries, energy, etc. are often indirect costs. These costs are not specifically made for one type of product, but relate to the entire production process.
As a general rule, unit cost should comprise the sum of the direct costs and a fair part of the indirect costs.

Job costing

Allocation base

This gives rise to the question: what part is fair? In order to allocate indirect costs to product types, projects or orders, the first step is to determine an acceptable *allocation base* to achieve as realistic a distribution of indirect costs as possible. However, some degree randomness may be impossible to avoid.

Single rate markup

The simplest method of allocating indirect costs is the *single rate markup* method. Applying this method only requires a clear understanding of which costs are direct and which are indirect. Under the single rate method, indirect costs are linked to direct costs by expressing them as a percentage of direct costs.

For each product or each order, direct costs are calculated first, after which unit cost is determined by charging a markup on direct costs to cover indirect costs. This way, indirect costs charged to an order are made dependent on direct costs made for this order.

The calculation of the markup rate is based on estimated forecast amounts, preferably based on normal output for an accurate allocation of fixed costs to the products (see also chapter 12).

TEST QUESTION 13.3
Explain why it is vastly preferable to base the markup rate, covering indirect costs, on a normal output level.

In its simplest form, the single rate method links total indirect costs to direct costs.

EXAMPLE 13.4
Assuming a normal level of output, a building company has estimated the following costs for the coming year:

Direct material costs	€	750,000
Direct labor costs	€	500,000
Indirect costs	€	375,000
Total cost		€ 1,625,000

By linking total indirect costs to total direct costs, the following markup rate is established:

$$\frac{€375{,}000}{€1{,}250{,}000} \times 100\% = 30\%$$

Should a particular reconstruction order cost €3,400 in material, and direct labor costs for this assignment amount to €1,600, then unit cost becomes:

Direct costs €3,400 + €1,600	= € 5,000
Markup for indirect costs 30% × €5,000	= € 1,500
Total	€ 6,500

In a restaurant, the costs of a dish comprise only a very small part of direct costs, namely the costs of the ingredients. The costs of the kitchen staff, waiters, premises, energy, etc., are indirect. An average restaurant has the following cost structure:

Sales	100%
Purchase value sales	35%
Labor expenses	30%
Rent	16%
Depreciation	7%
Other expenses	10%
Profit	2%

In the restaurant business, the general rule is therefore: 'purchasing costs × 3'. In other words: to cover costs, the price of a dish needs to be at least three times the purchasing costs.

Using this method, the markup can also be based on direct material costs or direct labor costs. There are various options available. It is even possible to use quantities as a basis for the calculation, such as markup per labor hour.

EXAMPLE 13.4 CONTINUED
The building company can use a 50% markup on material costs (€375,000 / €750,000 × 100%) or 75% of labor costs (€375,000 / €500,000 × 100%) to cover its indirect costs.
The following unit costs can be calculated for this order:

With a markup on the material			With a markup on the direct labor costs		
Direct material costs	€	3,400	Direct material costs	€	3,400
Direct labor costs	€	1,600	Direct labor costs	€	1,600
50% × €3,400	€	1,700	75% × €1,600	€	1,200
Total	€	6,700	Total	€	6,200

TEST QUESTION 13.4
What advantage can a quantity-based allocation method offer when compared to a value-based allocation method?

The objection against a single rate method is that a causal relationship is assumed between the amount of direct costs of a product and the amount of indirect costs assigned to that product. This causal relationship is not at all certain, especially if only one cost rate basis is used, as in the single rate method. A wrongly chosen cost rate basis can have undesired consequences: by setting the unit cost too high, orders can be missed; by setting it too low, profitability can be jeopardized.

Multiple rate markup

The causal relationship can be increased by applying a *multiple rate markup* method. This method requires a global investigation into the nature of the indirect costs. They are split into groups, with each group having their own allocation basis.

EXAMPLE 13.4 CONTINUED
The indirect costs of a building company are divided as follows:

Warehouse costs	€ 60,000
Management salaries	€ 75,000
Equipment and tools	€ 150,000
Other indirect costs	€ 90,000
Total	€ 375,000

Warehouse costs are related to material usage, since the amount of material used is an important indicator of warehouse costs. The salary costs of the management and the costs of equipment and tools in this company are related to the direct labor costs. The other indirect costs are assumed to be proportional to the total costs.
The markup rates to be applied are:

$$\frac{€60,000}{€750,000} \times 100\% = 8\% \text{ markup on direct material}$$

$$\frac{€225,000}{€500,000} \times 100\% = 45\% \text{ markup on direct labor costs}$$

$$\frac{€90,000}{€1,250,000} \times 100\% = 7.2\% \text{ markup on total direct costs}$$

The order with €3,400 in material costs and €1,600 in direct labor costs therefore has a unit cost of:

Direct material costs	€ 3,400
Direct labor costs	€ 1,600
8% × €3,400 =	€ 272
45% × €1,600	€ 720
7.2% × €5,000 =	€ 360
Total	€ 6,352

Service-providing companies also use the markup method for costing purposes. Usually, an hourly rate is used as unit cost, with the direct labor cost per hour increased by a markup rate for indirect costs. When determining the rate, the number of productive hours per employee is used as a basis.

EXAMPLE 13.5

IT-companies that develop and install hardware and software, and/or maintain, advise and offer support in IT, are part of the IT-service industry. At one particular IT consultancy, 20 employees earn an average annual salary of €48,000.
Of course, the additional costs for the employer have to be included.
This results in the following salary costs per employee for the consultancy:

Salary	€48,000
Vacation pay	€ 3,840
Bonus	€ 2,000
For the account of the employer premiums employment insurances	€ 4,820
For the account of the employer premium health care act insurance	€ 3,619
	€62,279

The number of productive hours per employee is calculated by the consultancy as follows:

Number of working days in a year	260
National holidays	8
Vacation days	25
	227
Average sick leave 7%	16
	211

The number of workable hours on an annual basis is $211 \times 8 = 1,688$.
10% of the workable hours are assumed to be non-productive due to meetings, training, etc.
The number of productive hours on an annual basis therefore is 90% of $1,688 = 1,519$.

The hourly salary costs are €62,279 / 1,519 = €41.

The consultancy's costs, other than salaries, are of an indirect nature and amount to €498,000 per year. These costs are allocated by means of a markup on the salary costs.
The markup is:

$$\frac{€498,000}{€20 \times 62,279} = 40\%$$

To cover the costs, the minimum man-hour rate to be charged to the client therefore is $1.4 \times €41 = €57.40$

13

When it comes to lawyers, it is generally the case that the man is more important than the manor: customers only care about their lawyer's expertise. Lawyers normally work at an hourly rate in which they account for that expertise. This hourly rate comprises a lawyer's own remuneration plus a surcharge for indirect costs incurred (office, administrative support, etcetera). This surcharge amounts to around 10%. Hourly rates can vary from €100 to several thousands of Euros.

13.4 Cost Center Method

In complex business processes that produce a large assortment of goods or services, costs are mainly indirect. In such a case, applying the markup method is not sufficient.
In these situations, the cost center method can offer a solution. Compared to the markup method, this method requires much more knowledge of the cost structure and therefore results in more administrative costs.
Unit costs provided by this method are more accurate and offer a better decision-making basis.
Since indirect costs cannot be directly charged to the cost bearer, the cost center method initially allocates these to the business functions. The following classification is used:

1 *Service cost centers* are business activities that are not immediately 'productive' but support the main business process. Housing, management and warehouse are examples of service cost centers.
2 *Mission cost centers* are business activities that include the primary production and sales process.

Cost centers can coincide with actual departments in a company, but not necessarily. The division into cost centers is made to determine unit cost and is not related to the organizational structure.

Once the indirect costs have been allocated to business functions, they are charged to other cost centers based on the benefit that these other cost centers have enjoyed from the performance of the cost center that charges the costs. This requires the development of *distribution keys* to give a fair allocation of costs.

Costs gathered at service cost centers are charged to mission cost centers. Subsequently, costs gathered at the mission cost centers are allocated to products (cost bearers), again based on realistic distribution keys.

The entire allocation process is registered on a cost allocation sheet, shown schematically in figure 13.2.

FIGURE 13.2 Allocation of costs based on the cost center method

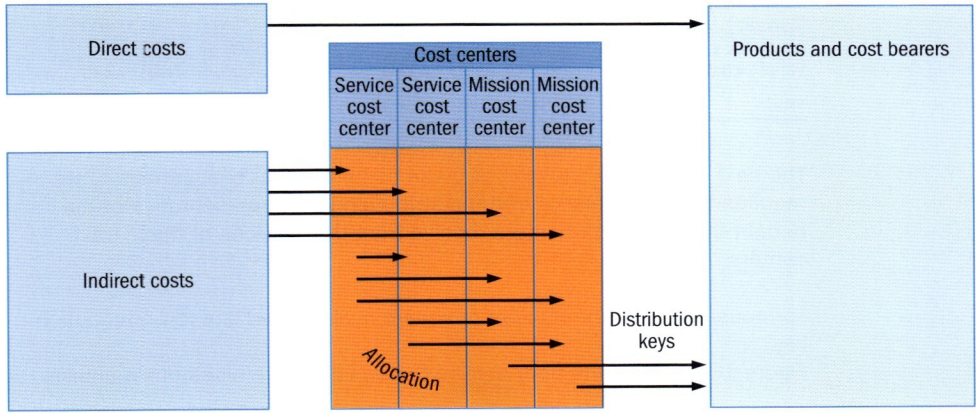

13

EXAMPLE 13.6
Urbanbike is a small bicycle manufacturer with two models in its range: the Basicbike, a bicycle without speeds and with coaster brakes; and the Superbike, with five speeds and handbrakes.
The frames, wheels and other parts are bought from suppliers in Taiwan and Korea. Urbanbike paints the frames in fashionable colors and assembles the bikes.
Direct costs comprise the costs of frames, wheels and other components. For each Basicbike, these costs are €215; for each Superbike, they are €340.
Indirect costs are estimated at €7,950,000 for the coming year, based on forecast production (equal to normal annual production) of 10,000 Basicbikes and 5,000 Superbikes.

Urbanbike indicates the following supporting functions (service cost centers): Housing, management, administration and warehouse (storage), with the primary functions (mission cost centers) of paint shop, assembly and sales.
Table 1 indicates how indirect costs are allocated to the cost centers.

TABLE 1 Indirect costs of Urbanbike (× €1,000)

	Housing	Management	Admin.	Storage	Paint	Assembly	Sales
Administration costs		350					
Depreciation buildings	370						
Depreciation machines				80	500	230	
Energy	30			40	100		
Paint					720		
Wages and social security	55	370	190	310	540	1,550	170
Marketing							300
Insurance	50			40	40	20	
Various costs	105	190	140	120	320	780	240
Total	610	560	680	590	2,220	2,580	710

The next step is the charging of these costs to other cost centers. This requires the development of the distribution keys representative of the benefit the other cost centers receive from the services of these cost centers.

For housing costs, the *number of square meters used* is a fair distribution key.
Figure 13.3 shows the floor plan of the business premises of Urbanbike.

FIGURE 13.3 Floor plan of the business premises of Urbanbike

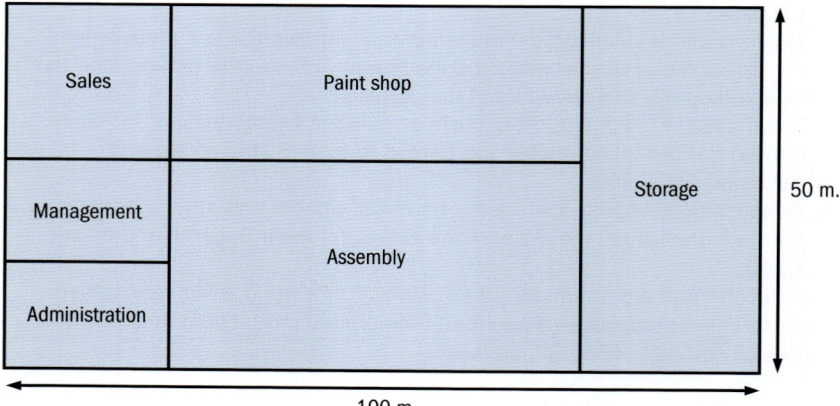

The surface area of the business premises is 5,000 m². Housing costs are charged at a rate of €610,000 / 5,000 = €122 per m².
This gives the following distribution:

Management	300 m²	€ 36,600
Administration	300 m²	€ 36,600
Warehouse (storage)	1,000 m²	€ 122,000
Paint shop	1,200 m²	€ 146,400
Assembly	1,800 m²	€ 219,600
Sales	400 m²	€ 48,800
		€ 610,000

After charging housing costs, the following costs are allocated to management:

Initial cost allocation	€ 560,000
Charged by housing	€ 36,600
	€ 596,600

Management performs a variety of tasks, and the choice of distribution key will therefore always be arbitrary. As managing people is an important part of the function, the chosen distribution key is *number of employees*. Management oversees 40 employees. The costs of management are charged at a rate of €596,600 / 40 = €14,915 per employee.

Administration	2 employees	€ 29,830
Warehouse	6 employees	€ 89,490
Paint shop	10 employees	€ 149,150
Assembly	20 employees	€ 298,300
Sales	2 employees	€ 29,830
		€ 596,600

After charging housing and management costs, the following costs are allocated to administration:

Initial cost allocation	€680,000
Charged by housing	€ 36,600
Charged by management	€ 29,830
	€746,430

The benefit which the next cost centers derive from administration could, for example, be determined by the number of invoices processed for these cost centers.
The annual number of invoices is 1,000. The costs of administration are charged at a rate of €746,430 / 1,000 = €746.43 per invoice.

Warehouse	20 invoices	€ 14,929
Paint shop	100 invoices	€ 74,643
Assembly	300 invoices	€ 223,929
Sales	580 invoices	€ 432,929
		€ 746,430

After charging housing, management costs and administration costs, the following costs are allocated to the warehouse:

Initial cost allocation	€ 590,000
Charged by housing	€ 122,000
Charged by management	€ 89,490
Charged by administration	€ 14,929
	€ 816,419

The warehouse provides services to the paint shop and assembly shop.

The frames and the paint are brought to the paint shop; the wheels and other parts are delivered to the assembly shop.

As an indication for the benefit that these two departments derive from the warehouse, the number of *goods movements* from the warehouse to the paint shop and assembly department is registered by a logistics student over a period of a week.

The number of goods movements in the related representative week were 850. The warehouse costs are charged at a rate of €816,419 / 850 = €960.50.

Paint shop	330 goods movements	€316,965
Paint shop	520 goods movements	€499,460
		€816,425 (rounded difference)

The performed cost allocations can be summarized on a cost allocation sheet as shown in table 2.

TABLE 2 Indirect costs of Urbanbike (x €1,000)

Service cost centers				Mission cost centers		
Housing	*Management*	*Admin.*	*Storage*	*Paint*	*Assembly*	*Sales*
610,000	560,000	680,000	590,000	2,220,000	2,580,000	710,000
	36,600	36,600	122,000	146,400	219,600	48,800
	596,600					
		29,830	89,490	149,150	298,300	29,830
		746,430				
			14,929	74,643	223,929	432,929
			816,419			
				316,965	499,460	
				2,907,158	3,821,289	1,221,559

The bicycle industry generates well over €50 billion in revenue the world over. China is the leading manufacturer, with an annual production of 60 million bikes. The e-bike is showing an upward trend, with a market share of 30% in Western Europe.

The last step to be made is to charge the costs gathered at the mission cost centers to the products in question: Basicbike and Superbike.

Painting is a capital-intensive process as the frames are powder-coated on an automated production line. Human input is fairly limited. The use of a rate per machine-hour seems obvious.
Annually, the production line is in use for 2,000 hours. The costs of the paint shop are charged to the cost bearers at a rate of €2,907,158 / 2,000 = €1,454 per machine-hour.
The assembly is mostly performed manually. For the allocation of the assembly, costs based on a man-hour rate are used.
Annually, 25,000 man-hours are spent in the assembly shop. The assembly costs are charged to the cost bearers at a rate of €3,821,289 / 25,000 = €152.85.
Determining a fair distribution key for charging costs to the sales department is more difficult, considering the number of activities the commercial department carries out. Assuming that a product with a higher unit cost also requires more sales effort (which is not necessarily always the case), sales and distribution costs could be charged as a *percentage of the manufacturing unit cost*.
The manufacturing unit cost is calculated first:

		Basicbike		**Superbike**
Direct costs				
Material costs		€215		€340
Indirect costs				
Paint shop	7 minutes	€169.63	10 minutes	€242.33
Assembly	1.5 hours	€229.28	2 hours	€305.70
Manufacturing costs		€613.91		€888.03

Sales and distribution costs are allocated to the bikes, based on the following markup on the manufacturing costs:

$$\frac{€1,221,559}{10,000 \times €613.91 + 5,000 \times €888.03} = 11.5\% \times 100$$

	Basicbike	**Superbike**
Manufacturing costs	€ 613.91	€ 888.03
Sales and distribution costs	€ 70.60	€ 102.12
Commercial unit cost	€ 684.51	€ 990.15

Multiplying the normal output level of Basicbike and Superbike with their unit costs, it becomes clear that all costs of Urbanbike are covered:

Direct costs	10,000 × €215 + 5,000 × €340 =	€ 3,850,000
Indirect costs		€ 7,950,000
		€11,800,000

Cost coverage: 10,000 × €684.51 + 5,000 × €990.15 = €11,795,850
(rounded difference)

Previously, costs were always assumed to be charged in one direction only, from left to right; this is known as the *step-down* method. This method, which is the most widely used in practice, assumes that a cost center supplies performances only to the next cost centers and not to the previous. In many situations, however, there is in fact a 'returning of services'. In the bicycle plant in example 13.6, management also has tasks concerning housing, e.g. if there are meetings with painters or maintenance services. This creates a problem of mutual dependency of the unit costs of those services or performances: costs from one cost center can only be determined if the costs of the other are known, and vice versa. This problem can be solved by describing this mutual dependency with the aid of a number of equations which, due to the specialized nature and complexity, is something that falls outside the scope of this book.

TEST QUESTION 13.5
Suppose that Urbanbike would have used the single rate markup method with total direct costs as a markup basis. What would the unit costs of these bikes have been then?

13.5 Activity-based Costing

Owing to continuously increasing automation, complexity and integration of production processes, the share of indirect costs in total costs has been increasing for many companies.

Activity-based costing

In response to the overall allocation of the indirect costs, the system of *activity-based costing* was introduced. Activity-based costing is a system which allocates costs to products based on the causal relationship between the products and necessary activities. To achieve this, the system requires a thorough investigation into these required activities to determine the

Cost drivers

most important *cost drivers* for each activity. A cost driver is the factor that determines the demand for an activity.

Since there are many activities in a company, activity-based costing groups

Cost pools

these into a limited number of *cost pools* based on their coherence. Activity-based costing is mainly a response to the shortcomings of the markup methods, but also to a lesser extent to that of the cost center method.

In practice, when using the cost center method, cost centers often coincide with existing departments. Insofar as these departments have a multitude of tasks, the distribution key for allocation is always arbitrary. As remarked in paragraph 13.4, the correct application of the cost center method implies that cost centers should be selected on the basis of performed activities and they should not be dependent on the organizational structure of the company.

What can be marked as a weakness in the cost center method is the fact that costs assigned to cost bearers are mainly determined by the output level. Costs gathered (directly or via the service cost centers) at the mission cost centers are normally charged to the products by means of volume-related distribution keys, such as machine-hours or man-hours.

However, quantity is not always related to costs.

FIGURE 13.4 Schematic of activity-based costing

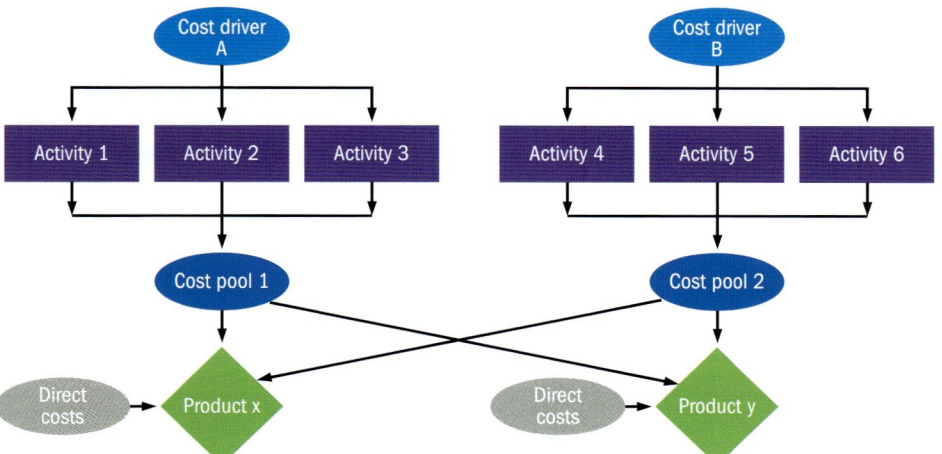

13

Activity-based costing therefore distinguishes between four types of costs:
1 *Unit-level costs* are costs related to the produced volume. These costs can
   therefore be charged by using volume-related bases.
2 *Batch-level costs* are costs that are related to a certain produced batch.
   Costs of switching the machine(s) for one batch have to be charged to the
   batch concerned and subsequently divided across the products of that
   batch.
3 *Product-sustaining costs* are costs that are related to a product but that are
   independent of the size of production. Development costs are an example
   of these types of costs. Ideally, these costs should be divided across the
   total forecast production over the years that the newly developed product
   is to be sold.
4 *Plant-level costs* are costs that are related to the company as a whole, such
   as housing and management. Activity-based costing also has problems
   in determining a distribution key for these types of costs, and allocation
   remains arbitrary.

Activity-based costing allocates costs directly to products; there is no
charging to cost centers.
As a result, the problem of allocating non-volume-related costs by means of
volume-related distribution keys does not occur – which it does under the
cost center method, as costs of service cost centers are first charged to the
mission cost centers and then to the products.

EXAMPLE 13.6 CONTINUED

In the bicycle plant, the paint shop processes batches of 100 Basicbikes, followed by 50 Superbikes. Switching the production line incurs an annual cost of €800,000.

A unit cost calculation based on activity-based costing would appear as follows:

Cost pool		Cost driver	Number	Rate
Housing	€ 610,000			
Management	€ 560,000			
Sales	€ 710,000			
	€1,880,000	Quantity of products	15,000	€125.33
Administration	€ 680,000	Number of invoices	1,000	€ 680
Warehouse	€ 590,000	Number of parts	180,000	€ 3.28
Paint shop,				
Switching	€ 800,000	Number of switches	100	€ 8,000
Other	€1,420,000	Number of machine-hours	2,000	€ 710
Assembly	€2,580,000	Number of man-hours	25,000	€103.20

The unit cost of the bicycles is:

	Basicbike	Superbike
Direct costs		
Direct material costs	€ 215	€ 340
Indirect costs		
Housing/management/sales	€ 125.33	€ 125.33
Administration		
For the Basicbike, 450 invoices were processed.		
To be included in unit cost: 450 × 680 / 10,000 =	€ 30.60	
For the Superbike, 550 invoices were processed.		
To be included in unit cost: 550 × 680 / 5,000 =		€ 74.80
Warehouse		
For the Basicbike, 100,000 parts were delivered.		
To be included in unit cost: 100,000 × €3.28 / 10,000 =	€ 32.80	
For the Superbike, 80,000 parts were delivered.		
To be included in unit cost: 80,000 × €3.28 / 5,000 =		€ 52.48
Switching costs paint shop		
Half of the switching costs should be charged to both bicycles.		
Basicbike 50 × €8,000 / 10,000 =	€ 40.00	
Superbike 50 × €8,000 / 50,000 =		€ 80.00
Other costs paint shop		
Basicbike 7 / 60 × €710	€ 82.83	
Superbike 10 / 60 × €710		€ 118.33
Assembly		
Basicbike 1.5 hours × €103.20	€ 154.80	
Superbike 2 hours × €103.20		€ 206.40
	€ 681.36	€ 997.34

TEST QUESTION 13.6
Why is the unit cost of a Superbike higher in activity-based costing than in the cost center method?

The activity-based costing method is very refined, but implementing and maintaining an administrative system that provides the required up-to-date information results in very high administrative costs. Over the years, many companies have found that the cost-benefit analysis can swing to the negative.

13.6 Costs and Customer Profitability Analysis

The previous paragraphs focused on determining a product's unit cost. In this case, allocating sales and distribution costs to products via a general distribution key (such as a percentage of the manufacturing costs) is justifiable. But this approach is not sufficient for determining the contribution of a particular customer to overall profit. This requires a *customer profitability analysis* instead: manufacturing costs (costs to *make*) can be used as previously calculated, but selling, distribution and service costs (costs to *serve*) are allocated to customers rather than products. In line with the activity-based costing philosophy, these costs must be split into cost pools; for each cost pool, a driver must be determined.

EXAMPLE 13.7
Ergocomfort supplies office furniture. Sales and distribution costs of €1,600,000 are charged to unit cost, based on a markup of 5% on the manufacturing costs.
Ergocomfort has among others, customers A and B, both LLC A and LLC B. Based on a general markup for sales and distribution costs, these two customers seem to have provided the following profit to Ergocomfort:

	Company A	Company B
Sales revenue	€200,000	€ 20,000
Manufacturing costs	€180,000	€ 18,000
Sales and distribution costs 5%	€ 9,000	€ 900
Profit	€ 11,000	€ 1,100

Using a customer profitability analysis, a trainee has separated sales and distribution costs into the following cost pools and selected a cost driver for each cost pool:

Cost pool	Costs	Cost driver		Rate
Representatives	€ 700,000	Number of customer visits	3,500	€200
Sales administration	€ 160,000	Number of invoices	2,000	€ 80
Transport	€ 900,000	Number of shipments	3,000	€300
Transport	€ 80,000	Number of consignments	500	€160
Helpdesk	€ 160,000	Number of calls	4,000	€ 40
	€2,000,000			

Based on this table, the following revised profit contributions can be
calculated for customers A and B, respectively:

		Company A			Company B	
Sales revenue		€200,000			€ 20,000	
Manufacturing costs		€180,000			€ 18,000	
Number of representative's visits	(4)	€	800	(4)	€	800
Number of invoices	(5)	€	400	(2)	€	160
Number of consignments	(10)	€	3,000	(3)	€	900
Number of return consignments	(5)	€	800	(2)	€	320
Number of calls to helpdesk	(7)	€	280	(3)	€	120
		€	14,270		€	300 negative

The customer profitability analysis shows that certain customers are
loss bearing, due to their relatively high demand for support by the sales
department. The analysis can be used to differentiate price setting by
customer (group), or to decide not to service certain customer groups
anymore.

Glossary

Activity-based costing	Costing method which allocates indirect costs to cost bearers via activities.
Batch-level costs	Costs that are related to a certain produced batch.
Charged costs	Costs that are charged from one cost center to another, or to cost bearers.
Cost allocation method	Method of allocating indirect costs to products.
Cost center	Business part (cost group) which provides a particular type of performance as a contribution to the production process.
Cost center method	Costing method which allocates indirect costs to cost bearers via cost centers and rates (production center method).
Cost driver	Activity responsible for generating costs.
Cross-subsidizing	Applying a larger profit margin to one product to be able to reduce the price of another product.
Customer profitability analysis	Research into profit, generated by a particular customer (rather than a particular product).
Direct costs	Costs that can be allocated directly to a calculation object.
Equivalent units method	Costing method which aligns production that is not entirely homogeneous by using ratios, after which process costing is applied.
Indirect costs	Costs that have no direct relationship to the calculation object.
Mission cost center	Business function that relates to a primary production or sales process.
Multiple rate markup method	Method which calculates cost price by increasing the direct costs by several surcharges to cover the indirect costs.
Plant-level costs	Costs related to the company as a whole (production location).
Process costing	Method which calculates unit cost by dividing total costs by total production.

13

Product-sustaining costs	Costs that are related to a product but do not depend on the output level.
Service cost center	Business function that offers support to the primary production or sales process.
Single rate markup method	Method that calculates cost price by increasing the direct costs by a surcharge to cover indirect costs.
Step-down method	Variant of the cost center method, which presents cost charging on the cost distribution sheet from left to right only.
Unit-level costs	Costs related to the produced volume.

13

Multiple-choice questions

13.1 What are indirect costs?
a Costs that are within certain limits, independent of the business activity level.
b Costs that cannot be differentiated in any way.
c Costs that are entirely dependent on the output level.
d Costs that cannot be directly allocated to the finished products.

13.2 Which of the following costs are indirect?
a Costs of business premises where one type of product is manufactured.
b Costs of raw materials.
c Fees paid to a tax consultant who keeps records of the time spent for each consultation.
d Catering costs made by a company that manufactures various household appliances.

13.3 Which statement is correct with regards to the unit cost?
a Unit cost is lower than the selling price.
b Unit cost is higher than the selling price.
c Unit cost is equal to the selling price.
d Unit cost is determined independently from the selling price.

13.4 Which costing method is particularly useful for a producer of household appliances?
a The equivalent units method.
b The cost center method.
c Dividing total costs by total production.
d Process costing.

13.5 What does costing using a markup method entail?
a Direct costs are increased by a markup for indirect costs.
b Direct costs are increased by a markup for fixed costs.
c Indirect costs are increased by a markup for variable costs.
d Variable costs are increased by a markup for fixed costs.

13.6 A company mass produces a certain product. The total production costs for the month of January were €120,000. In this month, 50,000 units were processed; 45,000 units of finished product were delivered. At the beginning of the month, there was no opening inventory for unfinished products; the inventory on 31 January can be considered 60% depleted.
What are the unit costs of production in January?
a €2.40
b €2.50
c €2.55
d €2.67

13.7   A metal plant produces 5,000 A-bolts, 4,000 B-bolts and 2,000 C-bolts.
Total material costs (steel) for this production are €6,000 per week.
The amount of steel per bolt, has a ratio of:
A : B : C = 2 : 3 : 5.
What are the material costs for a C-bolt?
  a €0.375
  b €0.5625
  c €0.9375
  d €1.0625

13.8   The following figures are a company's forecast for a certain production
period: €300,000 in raw materials, €200,000 in direct labor costs and
€225,000 in indirect costs.
The latter is made up of one-third indirect labor costs; the remainder is
from costs related to the use of raw materials.
For a particular order, €150 in direct labor costs and €350 in raw materials
costs are calculated.
What is the unit cost of the order?
  a €706.25
  b €731.25
  c €750
  d €775.50

13.9   A furniture manufacturer receives an order for the production of a number
of cupboards. The purchase price of the required wood and other direct
materials is €9,075 (including 21% VAT). Direct labor costs for this order are
estimated at €6,000.
The markup for indirect costs is 25% of the total direct costs.
What is the unit cost of the order?
  a €15,625
  b €16,462
  c €16,875
  d €18,844

13.10   During a particular period, a company has an actual production of 75%
of normal activity. Direct material costs are €60,000 and direct labor costs
€75,000 (60% fixed, the rest proportionally variable). Indirect costs are
€45,000 in total, 80% of which is fixed. For the coming period, material
prices are expected to increase by 5%, direct labor costs by 1% and indirect
costs by 3%.
What is the markup percentage for the coming period, based on the normal
output level and taking the price increases in consideration?
  a 27.5%
  b 29.1%
  c 29.3%
  d 33.3%

13.11 The Beach View hotel has two types of rooms: Standard and Deluxe. The hotel has its own laundry and maintenance service. For its cost allocation, Beach View uses a step-down variety of the cost center method. The following overview shows the costs that are initially allocated to the cost centers and the distribution keys used for charging.

	Maintenance	Laundry	Management	Standard rooms	Deluxe rooms
Costs	€570,000	€312,000	€231,000	€257,000	€480,000
Charging of maintenance		400 hrs	200 hrs	2,400 hrs	3,300 hrs
Charging of laundry				40,000 kg	60,000 kg
Charging of management				50%	50%

The standard rooms have an annual occupancy of 15,000 nights.
What is the unit cost of a night in a standard room?
a €38.40
b €49.20
c €53.70
d €57.50

13.12 Refer to question 13.11.
Which event does the step-down method not consider in terms of its financial consequences?
a The laundry washes management's clothing.
b There is maintenance at the management's office.
c The laundry washes maintenance staff clothing.
d There is maintenance at the laundry.

13.13 A soda company offers two flavors of soda; to fill bottles with a different flavor, the machines have to be switched.
How can the costs of switching the machines be qualified?
a Plant level costs.
b Unit-level costs.
c Batch-level costs.
d Product-sustaining costs.

13.14 A company produces wall racks and chests of drawers. A chest of drawers is more complex and requires more parts than a wall rack. The output level of the wall racks is twice the number of chests of drawers. So far, the company has been applying a markup method, but management is considering a switch to activity-based costing.
What consequences will this change have?
a The unit cost of the wall racks decreases less than the unit cost of the chest of drawers increases.
b The unit cost of the wall racks decreases more than the unit cost of the chest of drawers increases.
c The unit cost of the wall racks increases less than the unit cost of the chest of drawers decreases.
d The unit cost of the wall racks increases more than the unit cost of the chest of drawers decreases.

13

13.15 Which costs come under particular scrutiny in a customer profitability analysis?

a The manufacturing costs.
b The cost of raw materials.
c The cost to serve.
d The cost to make.

14

Budgeting and Variance Analysis

Planning and control are important management tasks.
Planning involves making decisions about activities and resources to achieve an organization's objectives.
Control is the process that verifies whether the execution of the planned activities is being carried out effectively and efficiently. In addition to planning, control requires measuring of actual results in comparison with planning; based on the results, additional management of activities could be required.
Budgeting is an essential instrument for planning and control. Through budgeting, management gathers insight into the expected results of future policy.
Paragraph 14.1 discussed budget functions. The total of all sub-budgets forms the master budget of a company, resulting in the forecast balance sheet and income statement. This subject is discussed in paragraph 14.2. Paragraph 14.3 focuses on which conclusions can be drawn based on the comparison of the budget and the actual results.

14.1 Budgeting as a Management tool

Chapter 4 covered the business plan. This overall plan comprises a marketing plan, a financial plan and a production plan, with the main focus being the relationship between the decisions made in the different fields. If such a plan has the nature of a prognosis, in other words a more long-term global forecast, the term *forecast* is usually used. In many organizations, for example, a forecast of the income statement is made for a number of years. This is usually known by the term 'multiannual forecast'.

Forecast

To make business objectives more tangible, short-term activities are incorporated into sub-plans or budgets.

Budget

A *budget* is a quantitative expression of a particular activity for the coming period, which usually has a task-oriented nature. In order to achieve the objectives, it is essential to establish an agreement between the various sub-plans and activities. Budgeting is therefore the ultimate tool for management to control increasingly complex processes.

Budgets are often drawn up for a one-year period, and can then be divided into quarterly, monthly or even weekly periods. The shorter the period, the more detailed the budget. The budget should also be linked to a company's organizational structure. This creates the possibility of using the budget as a benchmark for a department or budget holder and to measure actual performance.

Budgeting can serve several purposes as far as business management is concerned.

Budget functions

In general, a distinction is made between the following *budget functions*:
- planning
- communication and coordination
- task setting and authorization
- evaluation

Planning
By implementing a formal budgeting system, an organization can be coerced into planning. It is a tool for reflecting on future policies and to take into account the implications of activities derived from such policies. This can prevent too many 'ad hoc' decisions.

Communication and coordination
As there obviously exist relationships between the various business activities, budgets can never be drawn up independently. Production and sales, for example, must be coordinated and therefore require communication between the departments.

In this context, budgeting can be considered a business-communication-and-coordination tool.

Task setting and authorization
In general, a budget should be drawn up in consultation with the budget holder, the person for whom the budget is drawn up. If this participation results in budget approval by the budget holder, the budget becomes an objective for which they are responsible. In this case, the budget also acts as a policy transfer with delegation of power, which authorizes expenditures in line with the budget. The budget holders therefore know what is expected of them and what they are accountable for.

Evaluation

The budget is a tool that allows for the verification of the extent to which activities are executed according to planning at all levels of the organization. Deviations may be cause for corrective measures. The budget can also be used to assess the budget holder.

By its very nature, a plan is focused on the future. It gives direction to future activities. This is known as *feedforward*. Evaluation of the budget is an example of *feedback*. Comparison between planning and actual results can lead to corrective actions (see figure 14.1).

FIGURE 14.1 Feedforward and feedback

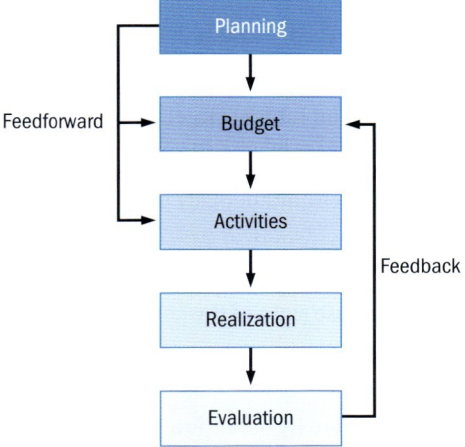

TEST QUESTION 14.1

What are the potential consequences of a deviation between budget and actual results for the following period?

Often, during a budget period, there is an increasing discrepancy between budgeted and actual figures. This could have a structural cause. A sales budget for the current year no longer provides a reliable forecast of the potential annual turnover if, for example, the competitive situation in the market suddenly changes.

In such an event, the budget loses its value as a benchmark to assess sales activities. This problem can largely be avoided by adjusting the budget periodically, in accordance with the changed circumstances. The nature of a budget should not be static; it should be dynamic. A budget is not a purpose in itself; it is a management tool. In practice, *rolling budgets* are used, such as four-quarterly or a twelve-monthly rolling budgets. Rather than working with a fixed annual budget, a realistic and achievable budget for the following four quarters (or twelve months) is drawn up every quarter (or month). By applying this procedure, business planning becomes much more realistic and continuous.

Top-down

The method of drawing up department budgets can differ for each organization. Due to the task-oriented nature of a budget, a top-down approach is sometimes preferred. Company management imposes a budget onto a department based on its own judgment. Such an approach can, however, result in a lack of support from the work floor, particularly if employees feel that the budget is unrealistic and therefore unachievable.

Bottom-up

A bottom-up approach, in which a budget is drawn up based on information provided by the department concerned, can usually count on more support – but does not always correspond with business objectives.

Budgeting also has certain disadvantages. It is not only time-consuming (and therefore expensive), but can also work counter-productively. Department managers will be tempted to follow the assigned budget and shift their focus to the department's (and their own) interest rather than the overall business interest. Cost center managers will attempt to obtain higher budgets than actually required, whereas their sales department

Budget slack

colleagues will wish for budgets that are more conservative. *Budget slacks* are incorporated.

Furthermore, management decisions based on budget targets can be damaging for the business. A sales manager who takes a relaxed approach to the rules when assessing the credit rating of a potential client could succeed in achieving the sales targets, while simultaneously putting the company's financial health at risk.

The weakness of budgeting is that managers are only assessed on their ability to achieve financial criteria. Therein lies the danger that those managers, in their strive for financial gain, lose sight of the company's long-term interests.

Balanced scorecard

Financial benchmarks, such as profitability, are by definition *lagging indicators,* which means they are performance indicators of activities executed in a previous period. To allow for a balanced assessment of managers, there should also be *leading indicators,* which are future-oriented indicators of how the currently applied policy will work out in the future. Nowadays, managers are assessed on more than merely financial benchmarks. An often-applied method is the *balanced scorecard.*

The balanced scorecard attempts to avoid the imbalance inherent in the budgeting process by assessing the manager from four perspectives: financial, customers, internal processes, innovation and learning.

By not merely focusing on the financial aspect, a more balanced assessment with respect to the functioning of the organizational unit concerned becomes possible.

The performance indicators for non-financial objectives should be defined in such a manner as to be both representative of and measurable for the perspectives concerned.

EXAMPLE 14.1

Retail fashion chain Fashion Gallery has developed the following balanced scorecard for assessing its store managers:

Perspective	Critical success factor	Key performance indicator
Financial	Profit	Gross profit
	Turnover	Turnover per m^2
		Inventory turnover ratio
Customer	Customer loyalty	Percentage of loyal customers
	Customer satisfaction	Number of complaints
		Survey results
	Awareness among public	Recognition ratio in holding location
Internal processes	Administrative processes	Audit result
	Safety	In conformity with fire regulations
	Inventory management	Number of 'no sales'
	General efficiency	Mystery shopper
Innovation and learning	Automation	Number of times ICT department's intervention required
	Development personnel	Percentage of employees who attended a company course this year
		Percentage of employees who made internal promotion this year
	Engagement	Number of suggestions made by personnel that were implemented

----

The order in which the four balanced scorecard perspectives are placed is not random.

The improvement of innovation and learning is a long-term procedure; if it pays off, the internal processes are improved. If the internal processes are improved, in the long run customers will be more satisfied. If customers are more satisfied, this eventually leads to a better financial performance. The key performance indicators of innovation and learning are therefore the most leading. Through the indicators of internal processes and customers, a company eventually arrives at the lagging indicators of the financial perspective.

14

FIGURE 14.2 Leading and lagging indicators

Financial

Customers

Internal processes

Innovation & learning

Lagging

Leading

14

In the hotel industry, non-financial benchmarks are very important. The success of a hotel business is mainly determined by the extent to which customer loyalty is successfully achieved through service and reputational image. In 1925, Conrad Hilton opened the first Hilton hotel in Dallas. Nowadays, the Hilton group owns 5,000 hotels worldwide. Its annual revenue is around €10 billion. In the 1990s, Hilton was one of the first multinationals to use the balanced scorecard methodology.

14.2 Master Budget

The overall company budget is referred to as the *master budget* (see figure 14.3). This master budget comprises the various sub-budgets and eventually results in an estimated income statement and balance sheet at the end of the budget period concerned. The compilation of the master budget, usually an annual plan, should of course be implemented in a logical sequence.

Depending on estimated sales and taking into considering available capacity, actual opening inventory and forecast closing inventory, a production plan is drawn up. Based on this planning, budgets for raw materials, other tools and materials, and required workforce can be drawn up. Following that, the purchasing budget and cash flow budget can be determined and the forecast balance sheet and income statement can be drawn up.

FIGURE 14.3 The master budget

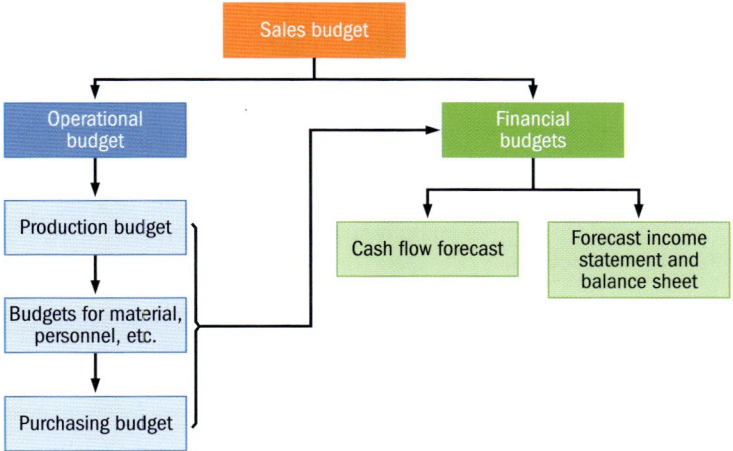

14

EXAMPLE 14.2

Sharp PLC is a manufacturing company that is part of a multinational corporation.

Sharp manufactures various products, including razor blades supplied in packs of five, which are sold worldwide to distributors at a fixed price of €2 per unit (each unit being one pack of five blades). The full cost, based on a normal output of 800,000 units per month, can be broken down as follows:

Material	€ 0.40
Direct labor costs	€ 0.30
Indirect variable costs	€ 0.15
Fixed manufacturing costs	€ 0.30
Manufacturing unit cost	€ 1.15

The variable sales and distribution costs amount to €0.10 per unit and the fixed sales costs to €40,000 per month. The financial controller at Sharp PLC draws up a monthly internal report, comprising a budgeted income statement (absorption costing) and a budgeted cash flow statement. Based on sales prognoses of the distribution companies, the following sales budget is drawn up for the second quarter of this year:

April	600,000 units
May	1,000,000 units
June	800,000 units

The following information must also be taken into account:
- 50% of the products supplied to the distribution companies are paid in the same month; the rest is to be received by Sharp in the following month.
- The inventory of finished goods at the end of the month must always be 30% of the estimated sales for the following month and the material inventory must always be sufficient to cover 20% of following month's production.
- 40% of the purchased material (€0.40 per pack) is paid during the month of purchase and 60% during the following month.
- The inventory at the end of March is not in accordance with the earlier mentioned inventory policy: the actual inventory of finished goods is 150,000 units and the material inventory is sufficient for 130,000 packs.
- 800,000 units were sold in March, and in that month, materials were bought for 900,000 packages (€0.40 per unit).
- €25,000 of the fixed monthly costs are depreciation costs. Unless specified otherwise, all other costs result in cash outflows during the month that they occurred.

First, the production budget is drawn up. This budget is the basis for the purchasing budget, after which the budgeted income statement and the budgeted cash flow statement can be determined.

Production budget (in Euros)

	April	May	June
Forecast sales	600,000	1,000,000	800,000
Forecast closing inventory	+ 300,000	+ 240,000	
	900,000	1,240,000	
Opening inventory	− 150,000	− 300,000	
Monthly production	750,000	940,000	

Purchasing budget materials April

Required for production of April: 750,000 at €0.40 per unit =	€	300,000
Forecast closing inventory: 20% × 940,000 at €0.40 per unit =	€	75,200
	+	
	€	375,200
Actual opening inventory: 130,000 at €0.40 per unit =	€	52,000
	−	
Materials purchased in April	€	323,200

Income statement April

Forecast turnover: 600,000 at €2.00 per unit =	€	1,200,000
Manufacturing costs: 600,000 at €1.15 per unit =	€	690,000
	−	
	€	510,000
Output level loss: 50,000 at €0.30 =	€	15,000
	−	
	€	495,000

Sales and distribution costs:	Variable € 60,000	
	Fixed + ————	
	€ 40,000	
		€ 100,000
		− € 395,000
Budgeted profit April		

Budgeted cash flow statement April
Incomes

From sales in March: 50% × 800,000 at €2 =	€ 800,000	
From sales in April: 50% × 600,000 at €2 =	€ 600,000	
	+ ————	
		€ 1,400,000

Expenses

Materials purchased in March: 60% × €360,000 =	€ 216,000	
Materials purchased in April: 40% × €323,200 =	€ 129,280	
Direct labor costs: 750,000 × €0.30 =	€ 225,000	
Indirect costs: 750,000 × €0.15 =	€ 112,500	
Fixed manufacturing costs: €240,000 – €25,000 =	€ 215,000	
Var. selling & distribution costs: 600,000 × €0.10 =	€ 60,000	
Fixed selling and distribution costs:	€ 40,000	
	+ ————	
		− € 997,780
Increase in cash and cash equivalents		€ 402,220

- -

TEST QUESTION 14.2
Draw up the budgeted balance sheet at the end of April using the
information in example 14.2.
Take into account that, at the end of March, the book value of the fixed
assets is €3.5 million and the available cash and cash equivalents are
€75,000.

14.3 Variance Analysis

Although the budgeting process is primarily focused on achieving business
objectives, it is also important with regard to cost control. If the emphasis
is on the efficient use of production factors, the term *cost budgeting* is   **Cost budgeting**
commonly used. A key factor in this respect is the ratio of each cost type
compared to the total production cost. If, for example, labor costs are
10% and material costs are 70% of the total costs, it is clear that the initial
emphasis should be on controlling material cost.
For this purpose, cost standards can be defined and translated into a cost
budget for each budget holder. When drawing up these cost budgets, it is
important to take into account how costs vary with the production size
(fixed costs versus variable costs).
Fixed costs are budgeted per period and variable costs are budgeted per
unit.

14

At the end of a budget period, the planning must be compared with the actual performance. If there are budget variances, their causes must be determined and the budget holders should be tasked with clarifying the discrepancies.

This procedure makes use of the budget as an accountability and assessment tool.

Responsibility accounting

From a cost control perspective, drawing up budgets for each organizational unit or budget holder is part of a system of *responsibility accounting*. Budget holders are only responsible for the costs they can influence: the controllable costs. The non-controllable costs should, in principle, not be included in the budget.

Sometimes, however, controllable costs are included in the budget, which provides a department manager with insight into the total costs related to their department. This can stimulate cost awareness.

Static budget

Flexible budget

Within the scope of cost control it is possible to distinguish between static and flexible budgets. A *static budget* is based on the forecast production level and is not adjusted if the actual production deviates from the forecast. Obviously, in that case a comparison of the budgeted and actual costs is not very meaningful. A *flexible budget* should therefore be used: a budget that is adjusted to reflect the actual production level.

EXAMPLE 14.3

A supplier of electronic devices has budgeted the costs of the complaints department at €700,000 in March. The budget is based on a forecast number of complaints of 8,000. In April, actual costs incurred were €730,000 and the actual number of complaints was 10,000.

It would be too simplistic to conclude that there is an unfavorable variance of €30,000 between budgeted and actual costs. Due to the higher output level, it is to be expected that the actual costs would exceed the budget.

Knowledge of a company's cost structure is required to draw up a flexible budget.

If the fixed costs of the complaints department are €500,000 per month and the variable cost €25 per complaint, then the flexible budget is €500,000 + 10,000 × €25 = €750,000. This means a favorable variance of €750,000 − €730,000 = €20,000.

It is important to determine the key factors correctly when establishing standards. Sometimes, information provided by a production equipment supplier can be an important resource. If this information is not available, extensive research should be conducted prior to establishing a standard. This includes analyzing historical data. In principle, the standard should not be set too strictly. Overly strict standards are demotivating because they can only be achieved under ideal circumstances.

It was previously mentioned that one of the objectives of the budgeting process is to evaluate the execution of various activities.

Possible variances between budgets and actual outcomes need to be
examined further to identify the cause. Any detected variance raises
questions that require answers and (potential) corrective measures to be
taken.

This *variance analysis* is applicable to sales activities as well as the
production process.

Variance analysis

A variance between budgeted and actual turnover can be caused by fewer
sales than expected, increased prices or differences in the product range
composition.

We shall focus on cost variances and therefore on the production side,
particularly price, efficiency and spoilage variances and the previously
discussed output level variances.

If a *standard costing system* is applied to a product or order, unit cost
must be based on a standard quantity and standard price. Based on these
parameters, budgeted costs (standard costs) per unit can be determined,
thus making the standards the actual 'building blocks' of a budget.

**Standard costing
system**

14

To assess efficiency in production, the concept of *actual costing* is used to
determine the actual quantities and the actual prices. The *budget variance*
is the difference between the total standard costs and the actual costs.

Actual costing
Budget variance

> Budget variance = (Standard quantity × Standard price) –
> (Actual quantity × Actual price)

- -

EXAMPLE 14.4

For a particular product, the standard quantity is set to 0.4 kg raw material,
at a standard price of €5 per kg. The estimated production for March is
10,000 units, which results in a cost budget of €20,000 for raw materials.

Standard quantity × Standard price = (10,000 × 0.4) × €5 =	€ 20,000
Actual costs at the end of March	€ 18,144
Variance	€ 1,856

Using only this information, we are not able to conclude that there is a
favorable variance of €1,856.

In a flexible budget system, the original budget must be adjusted to the
actual output level (actual budget).

If only 8,000 items were manufactured using 3,360 kg in raw materials, the
following calculation can be made:

Standard costs (budget) 8,000 × 0.4 × €5 =	€ 16,000
Actual costs	€ 18,144
Unfavorable budget variance	€ 2,144

Schematically:

FIGURE 14.4 Price and efficiency variance and standard costs

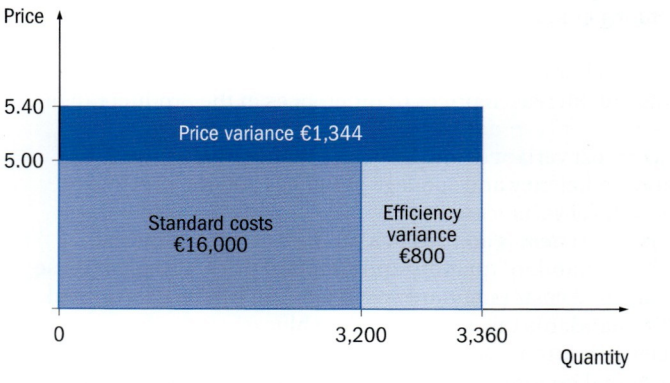

For each cost type, the budget variance can be divided into subsequent underlying causes. If the actual quantity deviates from the standard quantity, the company is experiencing an *efficiency variance*. The variance calculation is based on standard prices:

Efficiency variance

$$\text{Efficiency variance} = (\text{Standard quantity} - \text{Actual quantity}) \times \text{Standard price}$$

Price variance

If the actual price deviates from the standard price, there is a *price variance*, which is calculated on the basis of the actual quantity:

$$\text{Price variance} = (\text{Standard price} - \text{Actual price}) \times \text{Actual quantity}$$

EXAMPLE 14.4 CONTINUED
For the production of 8,000 units, 8,000 × 0.4 = 3,200 kg in raw materials is allowed. The efficiency variance is (3,200 − 3,360) × €5 = €800 unfavorable.
The actual raw material cost, are €18,144 / 3,360 = €5.40 per kg. The price variance is therefore (€5 − €5.40) × 3,360 = €1,344 unfavorable.

Chapter 12 discussed output level variances. An output level variance is caused by a discrepancy between the actual output level and the normal output level. The rate used in the unit cost to cover the fixed costs results in over- or under-costing of the fixed costs.

$$\text{Output level variance} = [(\text{Expected}) \text{ actual output} - \text{Normal output}] \times \text{Applied fixed costs per unit}$$

EXAMPLE 14.5

The standard unit cost of a product is

Direct labor costs at 0.3 hour at €25 =	€ 7.50
Raw materials 1.5 kg at €7.50 =	€ 11.25
Fixed manufacturing costs:	€ 30
Unit cost	€ 48.75

Fixed manufacturing costs are based on total fixed quarterly costs of €150,000. The production report from the previous quarter shows that 7,380 kg in raw materials and 1,500 hours direct labor were used to manufacture 4,600 products.

Costs of raw materials were €49,446 and costs of direct labor were €38,000.
Actual fixed costs corresponded with budgeted fixed costs. Based on this information, the following analysis becomes possible:

Actual costs: €49,446 + €38,000 + €150,000 =	€ 237,446
Standard costs: 4,600 items at €48.75 =	€ 224,250
Unfavorable budget variance	€ 13,196

This unfavorable result can be divided into:

Price variances

Raw materials: (€7.50 − €6.70*) × 7,380 =	€	5,904 favorable
Labor: (€25 − €25.3333**) × 1,500 =	€	500 unfavorable

* €49,446 / 7,380
** €38,000 / 1,500

Efficiency variances

Raw materials: (6,900* − 7,380) × €7.50 =	€	3,600 unfavorable
Labor: (1,380** − 1,500) × €25 =	€	3,000 unfavorable

* 4,600 × 1.5
** 4,600 × 0.3

Output level variance

Normal output = 300,000 / 60 = 5,000 units

(4,600 − 5,000) × €30 =	€	12,000 unfavorable
Budget variance	€	13,196 unfavorable

14

In the wood processing industry, efficiency variances play a crucial role.
If a tree is cut into planks for furniture or floors, obviously not all the wood can be used. Straight planks can only be cut from the core of the tree. An excellent sawing technique is indispensable for an optimal result. The remaining wood is used to make hardboard, pressed pallets or wood chips.

Relatively new is the use of residual wood for energy production. Combined with other plant residue and manure, this wood is used as 'bio-mass': raw material for energy plants. The most important wood-producing countries are the US, India and China.

In most business situations, the production manager is not responsible for purchasing activities. The responsibility for efficiency variances remains with the production manager, whereas it is the buyer who is responsible for price variances.
However, further analysis may prove that efficiency and price variances are interconnected. For example, there may be a favorable price variance due to the fact that a buyer purchased raw material of inferior quality at a lower price. This, in turn, could result in an unfavorable efficiency variance.

TEST QUESTION 14.3
What is a potential relationship between sales and an unfavorable price variance on labor costs?

Spoilage   A budget variance can also occur due to greater or lesser spoilage than budgeted. Finished or semi-finished products are considered *spoilage* if they do not meet the required quality standards. Based on spoilage ratio, the quality performance of the manufacturing process can be assessed. This provides important information for controlling business processes.

A high spoilage ratio can have numerous causes, such as improper work instructions or work ethics, inferior raw materials, incorrectly calibrated machinery or use of a machine near the end of its useful life.
Spoilage occurs not only at the end phase of the manufacturing process, but also during preceding phases. Therefore, intermediate quality control is necessary.
If, at the end of the production cycle the actual number of rejected products deviates from the standard spoilage, there is a spoilage variance.

EXAMPLE 14.6
An approved product has a unit cost of €25. Budgeted standard spoilage is 2%. During the production period, 14,000 units were manufactured, 340 of which were rejected. The rejected products have no value.
Spoilage variance for this period can be calculated as follows:

Budgeted spoilage: 2% × 14,000 units =	280 units
Actual spoilage	340 units
Unfavorable variance	60 units

Spoilage variance: 60 units at €25 = €1,500 (unfavorable)

TEST QUESTION 14.4
Verify the result from example 14.6 by comparing actual total spoilage costs against standard total spoilage costs.

These examples clearly indicate that the use of standard costs provides managers with vital information for cost control. Their usefulness, however, depends on the accuracy with which standards can be set.
The nature of the production process also plays a role. A standard costing system is easily applied to mass production. In the service sector, which mainly uses job production, determining reliable standards can be much more challenging – each service differs too much from the others as far as related costs are concerned.

EXAMPLE 14.7
At a tax consultancy, the number of hours for a consultation varies from 2 to 20 hours. This is caused by differences in complexity and difficulty level of individual dossiers on the one hand and by the speed and efficiency of the consultant on the other. It is virtually impossible to separate these two factors.

To conclude, a more detailed example of the variance between budgeted and actual profit is given, highlighting various causes.

EXAMPLE 14.8

Sensora PLC manufactures a product for which the following standard costing was drawn up:

Direct raw materials: 5 kg at €2.40 =	€ 12
Direct labor cost: ½ hour at €26.40 =	€ 13.20
Other variable manufacturing costs	€ 2.96
Fixed manufacturing costs	€ 16
Manufacturing unit cost	€ 44.16
Variable sales costs	€ 12
Fixed sales costs	€ 3.84
Profit surcharge	€ 20
Selling price	€ 80

All variable costs are proportionally variable. Normal production and sales are 20,000 units per year. Last year, however, actual production and sales amounted to 22,000 units. The average price of the raw materials was €2.50 per kg.

On average, hourly wages were 5% higher than budgeted. Due to quality deviations, some discounts were granted on the selling price. The income statement for the past year is as follows:

Income statement (in Euros)	
Sales revenue	1,742,400
Raw materials usage	286,250
Direct labor costs	290,136
Other variable manufacturing costs	65,200
Fixed manufacturing costs	320,000
Variable sales	263,500
Fixed sales costs	76,800
Profit	440,514

The difference between the actual profit and the budgeted profit is therefore: €440,514 − 20,000 × €20 = positive €40,514. The board has asked the controller to look into and explain this difference. The controller comes back with the following overview:

a   *Improved profit from improved sales:*
    (22,000 – 20,000) × €20 =   € 40,000   favorable

b   *Variance from discounts granted:*
    22,000 × €80 – €1,742,400 =   € 17,600   unfavorable

c   *Efficiency variance on raw materials:*
Actual usage: (€286,250 / €2.50) =	114,500 kg		
Standard usage: 22,000 × 5 =	110,000 kg		
Usage above standard	4,500 kg		
Variance: 4,500 kg × €2.40 =		€ 10,800	unfavorable

d   *Price variance on raw materials:*
114,500 kg × (€2.50 – €2.40) =   € 11,450   unfavorable

e   *Efficiency variance on labor:*
Actual labor: €290,136 / (1.05 × €26.40) = 10,466.67 hours

Normal labor: 22,000 × $\frac{1}{2}$ hours =   11,000 hours

Labor below standard   533.33 hours
Variance: 533.33 hours at €26.40 =   € 14,080   favorable

f   *Price variance on direct labor:*
10,466.67 hours × 5% × €26.40 =   € 13,816   unfavorable

g   *Variance on variable manufacturing costs:*
€65,200 – 22,000 × €2.96 =   €   80   unfavorable

h   *Variance on variable sales costs:*
22,000 × €12 – €263,500 =   €   500   favorable

i   *Output variance:*
Production: (22,000 – 20,000) × €16 =   € 32,000
Sales: (22,000 – 20,000) × €3,84 =   €   7,680

Output result above standard   € 39,680   favorable
     € 40,514   favorable

14

Glossary

Actual costing	Calculation of the actual cost amount based on real amounts and real costs.
Balanced scorecard	Planning and assessment system which determines targets with respect to four perspectives: finances, customers, internal processes, learning & growth.
Budget	Quantification of future activities for a defined period, often of a task-oriented nature.
Budget slack	A built-in safety margin in budgets to ensure they can be easily achieved.
Budget variance	The difference between actual costs and budgeted costs, based on actual output level.
Efficiency variance	The difference between standard quantity and actual quantity, calculated at standard price.
Flexible budget	A budget that is adjusted after the budgeting period based on reported deviations of the actual output level.
Lagging indicator	Assessment criterion which gives an indication of performances delivered in the past.
Leading indicator	Assessment criterion which gives an indication of the consequences of performances delivered for the future.
Master budget	A budget for the entire organization: a main budget comprising all sub-budgets.
Output variance	The difference between standard and actual production costs.
Price variance	The difference between the standard price and the actual price, multiplied by the actual quantity.
Rolling budget	A budget which always looks ahead using the same time intervals; once one such particular period has passed, the budget is extended for an equal period.

14

Spoilage variance	The difference between the actual rejected products and the budgeted standard spoilage.
Standard costing method	Calculating the permissible cost amount based on standard quantities and standard prices.
Variance analysis	Research into the size and causes of the differences between budget and actual.

14

Multiple-choice questions

14.1   Which function of budgeting is focused on feedback?
a Planning.
b Evaluation.
c Authorization.
d Coordination.

14.2   What is the disadvantage of a bottom-up approach when determining budgets?
a It uses knowledge of people on the work floor.
b It can lead to budget slack.
c It provides a commitment to achieving the budget.
d It allows employees to help think about the company's future.

14.3   The production budget for a given period is equal to the budgeted sales...
a Plus the planned increase in inventory.
b Plus the forecast closing inventory.
c Minus the forecast inventory increase.
d Minus the actual opening inventory.

14.4   An insurance company uses the balanced scorecard.
What would be a key performance indicator from the perspective of internal processes?
a Average damage claims per year.
b Increase in sales revenue.
c Number of employees who are holders of an insurance degree.
d Handling period of damage claims.

14.5   What is the most leading indicator?
a Profit per share.
b Number of employees who passed internal training.
c Number of wrongly completed forms.
d Score customer inquiry.

14.6   An importer of sports clothing supplies the retail trade at a 20% profit margin on purchase prices. The importer's balance sheet on 31 March shows an inventory of €150,000. For April, the estimated turnover is €240,000. In anticipation of the summer season, an inventory increase of 40% is planned for the end of April, relative to the inventory on 31 March. The purchasing budget for April is:
a €300,000
b €275,000
c €260,000
d €200,000

14.7   What is the difference between static and flexible budgeting?
  a In static budgeting, a top-down approach is used.
  b In static budgeting, actual business activities is not considered.
  c In static budgeting, estimated sales are used as a basis.
  d In static budgeting, there is no variance analysis.

14.8   A budget drawn up at the end of a period and based on the actual output level is known as:
  a A master budget.
  b A flexible budget.
  c A forecast budget.
  d A production budget.

14.9   Which variance is normally not the responsibility of the production manager?
  a The price per kilogram of raw materials used.
  b The amount of raw materials used.
  c The number of rejected products.
  d The number of direct production hours.

14

14.10   The standard budget for raw materials costs of a product is 5 kg at €10 = €50 for a given period. At the end of a budget period, the books show that 4,500 kg was purchased at €10.50 per kg. Only 4,000 kg of the purchased quantity was actually used; 750 products were manufactured. The unfavorable efficiency variance is:
  a €7,875
  b €7,500
  c €2,625
  d €2,500

14.11   The budgeted weekly production of an article is 300 items. The standard labor costs are 4 hours at €36 per hour. The actual production is 250 items, with an average of 3 hours at €39 per hour in labor costs. The unfavorable price variance on labor costs is:
  a €3,600
  b €3,000
  c €2,700
  d €2,250

14.12   The standard raw materials budget for 100 units of a mass product is 150 kg at €4 per kg. In week 12, 1,820 units were manufactured. The actual raw materials costs amount to €11,960, with a favorable price variance of €300. The actual quantity of raw materials used was:
  a 2,915 kg.
  b 2,990 kg.
  c 3,065 kg.
  d 3,075 kg.

14.13   The budget variance is equal to:
  a The variance between total sales revenue and total costs.
  b The variance between actual costs and standard costs.
  c The variance between actual fixed costs and charged fixed costs.
  d The variance between planned production and actual production.

14.14   Unit cost of an unchecked product is €69. Standard spoilage is 8%. Of the
total production in April, 1,050 units were approved and 75 units were
rejected.
What is the favorable spoilage variance for April?
a €621
b €675
c €1,035
d €1,125

14.15   Two hours of direct labor costs at €90 per hour are included in the unit cost
of a product.
In a given period, 200 units were manufactured. Staff worked 390 hours.
A total amount of €39,000 was paid.
In this period, the following applies for direct labor costs:

	Efficiency variance	Price variance
a	€900 favorable	€3,900 unfavorable
b	€900 favorable	€4,000 unfavorable
c	€1,000 favorable	€4,000 unfavorable
d	€1,000 favorable	€3,900 unfavorable

PART 4
Financial Accounting

15

Annual reporting

Various groups have an interest in information on the financial position of a company. Legislators have implemented disclosure requirements that obligate companies to make sure this information is provided. Paragraph 15.1 shows which companies are liable for disclosure requirements and which information they must provide in their annual report. The subsequent paragraphs discuss three components of a company's annual report: the financial statements, comprising the balance sheet and income statement, plus notes to the accounts (paragraph 15.2), the report by the managing board (paragraph 15.3) and the auditor's report (paragraph 15.4).

15.1 Stakeholders and Disclosure Requirements

A previous section of this book focused on the provision of information for management – but information regarding the financial ins and outs of a company also needs to be provided to others: in addition to *internal* reporting there should be *external* reporting.

There are various stakeholders when it comes to external reporting. Firstly, the *owners* of the company in such cases as these are other people than those in management. The management of a PLC or LLC, for example, has legal accountability towards its shareholders.

The *employees* also have a vested interest in the financial status of a company. Legislation on the employee council obligates management to provide this information.

The *tax authorities* that are entitled to a share of the company's profit can obtain the information required for taxation based on the tax law.

In general, *creditors* such as banks, are also in a position of entitlement to the necessary information on solvency and profitability prior to issuing a loan.

TEST QUESTION 15.1
Is it correct to classify the information provided to shareholders and employees as external reporting?

It should be noted that external reporting is subject to an additional dimension when compared to internal reporting, insofar that it is imaginable for company management to want to use the financial statements to reflect better on their company's position than reality would have it. Their reasons could be many and varied: securing bonuses, avoiding dissatisfied shareholders, retaining the possibility of borrowing capital at favorable conditions. 'Enhancing' the financial statements in this way is known as *creative accounting*. In this respect, the auditor serves as a watchdog.

Creative accounting

In most countries, governments have deemed it necessary to obligate legal entities to disclose information with regard to their financial performance, thus allowing all interested parties to access this information (even if they are not able to demand this access by specific legislation or by position). This is called a disclosure requirement.

The information that is the subject of the disclosure requirement to be published by means of the annual report comprises three components:
1 the financial statements
2 the report by the managing board
3 the auditor's report

The following paragraphs discuss the components of the annual report in detail.

In the European Union, countries can decide to impose stricter information obligations on large companies.

TEST QUESTION 15.2
Why would it be preferable to impose more information requirements on large companies than on small companies?

OVERVIEW DISCLOSURE REQUIREMENTS IN THE NETHERLANDS

Disclosure requirements are applicable for:
- public limited companies
- limited liability companies
- cooperatives
- mutual insurance companies
- associations and foundations, provided that commercial activities performed generate an annual revenue of at least €4,400,000

Size criteria	Large	Medium	Small	Micro
Value of assets	At least €20 million	Between €6 million and €20 million	Between €350,000 and €6 million	No more than €350,000
Net revenue	At least €40 million	Between €12 million and €40 million	Between €700,000 and €12 million	No more than €700,000
Average no. of employees	At least 250	Between 50 and 250	Between 10 and 50	No more than 10

Scope of disclosure requirements

Financial statements

Balance sheet	Extensive	Somewhat simplified	Highly simplified	Very concise
Income statement	Extensive	Somewhat simplified	None	None
Notes to fin. stat.	Extensive	Somewhat limited	Limited	None
Board report	Yes	Yes	No	No
Auditor's report	Yes	Yes	No	No

There are some side notes to be made with regard to the criteria applied in the division of these categories:
- A company is considered to be in a category if it meets two out of the three criteria in that particular category.
- Classification in a (new) category always occurs with a one-year delay; this principle prevents a company that operates on the boundary of a category criteria from being continuously confronted with different publication requirements.
- If a company has subsidiaries, the consolidated financial figures should be used: namely, the figures of the entire group (see paragraph 18.1).

In the Netherlands, disclosure requirements must be met by submitting a copy of the annual report to the Trade Register, which is maintained by the Chamber of Commerce in the area where the company is located.

15.2 Financial Statements

Financial statements comprise the balance sheet, the income statement and the notes to these accounts.
Within the European Union, two legislative sets apply with respect to financial statements.

15

IFRS
IASB

All companies listed on the stock exchange are obligated to apply the *International Financial Reporting Standards* (*IFRS*), compiled by the *International Accounting Standards Board* (*IASB*). The IASB is an organization whose purpose is to produce unambiguous rules on reporting that can be applied worldwide. The aim of the IFRS is to enable the comparison of profit figures between internationally operating companies. These standards are very detailed and offer little freedom of interpretation when compiling financial statements.

Owing to the mandatory application of IFRS for all stock exchange listed companies in the European Union, decision-making has become easier for the internationally oriented investor.

Those wishing to invest in a brewery are now able to compare the financial statements of Heineken (the Netherlands), AB Inbev (Belgium), and Carlsberg (Denmark) directly. The brands Heineken and Amstel are Europe's numbers 1 and 3 respectively where revenue is concerned. Globally speaking, Heineken's market share is over 9%. The AEX lists both Heineken Holding and Heineken nv shares. The Heineken family holds an interest in Heineken Holding of just over 50% – Heineken Holding, in turn, holds an interest in Heineken nv of just over 50%. Following the SAB Miller and AB Inbev fusion, the resulting company has become the world's largest beer producer by far.

Companies not listed on the stock exchange must adhere to the legislative rules of the country of its registered office. For these rules, EU standards indicate what minimum must be adhered to, but much has been left to the legislation of the member states. In the Netherlands, relevant legislation can be found in Book 2, Title 9, of the Civil Code. The rules are characterized by the relatively spacious amount of legroom they offer company management when it comes to drawing up financial statements. The foundation is that the accounting policies must be in accordance with socially acceptable standards in the business world.

In the Netherlands, companies not listed on the stock exchange have a choice of whether or not to adhere to the strict IFRS rules.

15

FIGURE 15.1 Scheme legislation

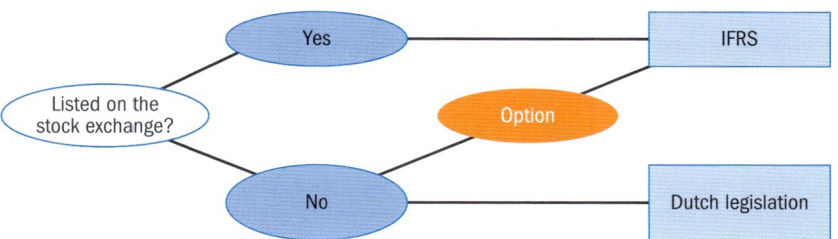

The obligations for stock exchange listed companies to adhere to IFRS only refer to the *consolidated financial statements*. These are the financial accounts that provide a picture of the financial position of the group as a total, namely the holding company and its subsidiaries. The *separate financial statements* of the holding (without its subsidiaries) may be drawn up in accordance with national legislation.

Consolidated financial statements

Separate financial statements

Financial reporting principles

Some fundamental principles must be adhered to when compiling financial statements. These basic principles, which are also laid down in legislation, have the purpose of drawing up the financial statements in a relevant and reliable manner.

'Relevant' is meant to imply that a reader should be able derive useful information from the financial statements. Specifically: they can obtain information that can be used in decision-making, such as that involved in selling shares or demanding a particular dividend payment, etc.

'Reliable' is meant to imply that the reader of the financial statements may assume the presented information to be a truthful representation of the company's financial position. Reliable also implies that the information should be verifiable: an external accountant should be able to pass judgment on the financial statements.

Unfortunately, it is impossible to implement both maximum relevance *and* maximum reliability: reliable financial statements are often less relevant (i.e. there is more information), and relevant financial statements are often less reliable (i.e. there is less information).

Accrual accounting

Chapter 3 discussed how financial statements are not based on a confrontation of cash inflows and cash outflows, but on revenues and costs. Cost and revenues should be assigned to the correct periods. This method of accrual accounting results in a certain amount of subjectivity with respect to the financial statements.

Company management has to make assumptions and estimates.

ESTIMATES

IFRS-compliant reporting requires management to make judgements, estimates and assumptions that affect the application of accounting policies and the reported value of assets, liabilities, income and costs. The estimates and underlying assumptions are based on past experience and various other factors which are considered fair under the circumstances. The results constitute the basis for judgements on the book value of assets and liabilities that cannot be simply derived from other sources. The actual results may differ from these estimates. The estimates and underlying assumptions are under constant review. Revisions to estimates are recognised in the period in which the estimate is revised if the revision only has consequences for that period, or in the revision period and future periods if the revision has consequences for both the reporting period and future periods. The most critical estimates relate primarily to measurement of tangible and intangible fixed assets, employee benefits and provisions. In the context of the reorganisation of the supply chain, estimates were also made in relation to the measurement of inventories and the restructuring provision.

Source: NEDAP, Annual report 2016

Rules for accrual accounting are determined by the realization principle on the revenue side and by the matching principle on the cost side.

Realization principle

A company earns its revenue from sales of goods and services. The realization principle determines that sales revenue must be recognized at the moment the company transfers the risks related to the delivered goods or services to the customer. At that point in time the company has fulfilled its side of the agreement. The realization moment is normally the moment when sale and delivery have taken place. It is therefore prohibited to delay recognition of profit registration until the customer has paid. Any risk of default can be taken into account by creating a provision for unrecoverable receivables.

Under certain circumstances the realization principle is not applied because it gives a distorted picture of the financial position of the company; paragraph 16.1 discusses how long-term projects (such as construction projects) can recognize interim profit.

Matching principle

The matching principle states that costs are assigned to the period from which the proceeds arise. If a company buys 1,000 units of a product in 2017 and consecutively sells these in 2018, this purchase cannot be documented as a cost in 2017; it has to be capitalized on the balance sheet (inventory) and recognized on the income statement (cost of sales) in 2018.

The purchase of a machine with an economic life of ten years in 2017 cannot be entirely charged to the profit of 2017. It must be capitalized, and in the coming ten years depreciation will be charged against proft. Ideally, annual depreciation is in proportion to the revenue the machine generates every year. As this is often difficult to determine, a system of linear depreciation is usually applied for the sake of simplicity.

The matching principle can be applied in two ways.
In *product matching,* costs are considered product costs: they are first allocated to the products whose manufacture was the source of these costs and subsequently charged to profit incurred in the period the products are sold. In *period matching,* costs are considered period costs: they are not included in the inventory valuation but are directly charged to profit in the period they relate to.

Product matching

Period matching

15

EXAMPLE 15.1

In a plant for semi-finished products, 10 million products are made for the computer industry in 2018. 8 million of those products are sold for a total amount of €55 million. The opening inventory was zero.
In 2018, the following costs were incurred:

Materials	€20 million
Wages of production staff	€25 million
Overhead costs	+ €15 million
	€60 million

Overhead costs comprise the costs of the business premises, management and supporting departments.

If product matching is applied, all costs are initially assigned to the inventory. The inventory valuation on the balance sheet per unit is €60 million/10 million units = €6.
Balance sheet valuation at the end of 2018 is 2 million × €6 = €12 million.
Profit over 2018 is:

Sales revenue	€55 million
Costs of goods sold 8 million × €6 =	– €48 million
Profit	€ 7 million

If, for example, period matching instead of product matching is applied for the overhead costs, the inventory valuation on the balance sheet per unit is:

€45 million/10 million units = €4.50.

At the end of 2018, the inventory is valued at:

2 million × €4.50 = €9 million.

Profit over 2018 is:

Sales revenue	€55 million
Cost of goods sold 8 million × €4.50 =	– €36 million
Overhead costs	– €15 million
Profit	€ 4 million

The difference in profit of 3 million Euros is caused by the fact that part of the overhead costs are not charged to profit in the first situation, but are capitalized as inventory on the balance sheet.

15

Prudence

In drawing up financial statements, it is necessary to make estimates: at balance sheet date, there are activities that have not yet been completed. Such estimates involve the remaining economic life of fixed assets, the number of unrecoverable receivables, pending lawsuits that could result in claims, etc.

If, on balance sheet date, a company expects losses resulting from one of the 'unfinished' activities, these losses are included in the financial accounts. Unlike profit, which has to be recognized when it is *realized*, losses are taken at the moment they are *identified*.

EXAMPLE 15.2

A transport company serves a damage claim to a vehicle import company in 2017. Their claim involves a belated delivery of an order of trucks. The delayed delivery has caused the transport company the loss of a major contract. The court is set to pass a verdict on the case in 2018.

The prudence principle states that the transport company cannot recognize the claim as a receivable on the balance sheet of 31 December 2017, as it is not yet certain that it will receive backing from the court. But if the court does rule in favor of the transport company in 2018, the claim is to be added to profit in 2018.

The vehicle import company, on the other hand, recognizes the claim on the balance sheet in 2017, as a liability in the form of a provision. Thus, the claim is charged to profit in 2017. If the court does not rule in favor of the transport company, the provision is to be reversed and added to profit in 2018.

Although prudence is a noble principle to which to adhere to , it should not be used to transfer profits to other years.

If the import company in example 15.2 is reasonably certain that – based on received legal advice – the claim will not be honored by the court, they could still be tempted to recognize a provision in 2017 if their profit in that year was very high, and they expect to incur less profit in 2018. By creating a provision, the importer can reduce his profit for 2017 and increase it for 2018 (since, in 2018, it becomes clear that he does not have to pay which allows the provision to be reversed and added to profit).

Paragraph 16.1 explains that this is the reason why, nowadays, there are strict requirements with respect to creating a provision to counteract the phenomenon of this type of profit steering as much as possible.

The going concern assumption

Financial statements are usually drawn up on the assumption that the company will continue to exist in the forseeable future. Going concern assumes that the company will earn back the capital invested in its resources. In this case, a valuation based on purchase prices is justifiable.

If it is likely that liquidation of the company (for example, due to bankruptcy) is imminent, the financial statements must be drawn up based on the *liquidation value*. This value is substantially lower than the going concern value: in cases of bankruptcy, there is a forced sale of the (separate) assets of the company. They are valued at a lower estimated realisable value.

Liquidation value

15

TEST QUESTION 15.3
No company aware of its pending bankruptcy is likely to draw up its financial statements based on the liquidity value. What could be a possible explanation?

Comparability
One thing that a reader of a financial statement is looking for is comparable figures.
Comparison can be made using previous financial statements by the same company (time comparison) and/or financial statements from the same year by other companies (business comparison).
To allow for a sensible comparison from year to year, the same accounting policies must be applied when drawing up the financial statements. Considering that legislation is frequently amended and that there is also a development of opinions on accurate reporting, it may be necessary to adjust basic assumptions. This is what is known as a *change in accounting policy*: replacing the principles used in drawing up financial statements. Such a change should therefore only be implemented if there are established reasons for doing so; and the effects of the change in accounting policy on equity and profit must be properly indicated.

Change in accounting policy

In view of business comparisons, it is important that companies compile their financial statements based on the same accounting policies. The implementation of IFRS for all stock exchange listed companies in Europe serves as an important stimulant for the possibility of comparing companies.

15.3 Report by the Managing Board

The *Report by the managing board* should contain at least two components. Firstly, there should be an explanation of the course of events during the past financial year and the financial situation of the company at balance sheet date. This part of the board of directors' Report by the managing board offers a 'verbal reflection' of figures in the financial statements. Secondly, attention should be paid to future expectations. The *forecast paragraph* is a very important part of the Report by the managing board. To an investor, for example, who considers buying shares of a particular company, it is obviously of interest to know how the company performed during the past year; but the question of how the company expects to perform in future years is even more important. An investor can consult the report by the managing board to identify the factors on which profit depends; this implies that information on the development of the 'market' should be included. Some companies express their views on profit expectations for the year following on the reporting year. Since that particular year has already started at the time of publication, all data to support the statement is available. Incidentally, if such a statement is provided, it is hardly ever quantified.

Forecast paragraph

15

OUTLOOK

Global milk production is expected to rise somewhat in 2017. A marginal increase in milk production is expected within the European Union. In the Netherlands, milk production is expected to decrease due to the introduction of the phosphate reduction measures. The demand for dairy products in Europe is expected to remain stable or stay on a slightly declining trend. In Africa, the Middle East and South America, a further decline in demand is foreseen. In Asia, particularly in China, a slight increase in the demand for dairy products is expected. As a consequence of the above-mentioned trends, it is expected that the prices for basic dairy products will continue to fluctuate around the year-end 2016/beginning of 2017 level.

Revenue is expected to increase due to the acquisition of the controlling interest in Engro Foods, the higher price levels of dairy products in 2017 in comparison to the price levels in the first half of 2016 and further volume growth in added-value products. Due consideration is provided to an increase in the purchase prices of most raw materials.

There are uncertainties due to the persistent stagnation of the economies in oil-exporting countries in the Middle East and Africa, geopolitical tensions in some regions and negative currency trends. In Europe there will be elections in Germany, France and the Netherlands, as well as elsewhere. Furthermore, negotiations between the EU and the United Kingdom concerning Brexit will commence.

In 2017, investments amounting to approximately 500 million euros are foreseen in quality improvements and the expansion of capacity. In 2017, investments in Research & Development will increase by approximately 10 percent in order to be able to further improve the competitive position over time. Focused spending on advertising and promotion, of which increasingly more is spent on digital communications, is to contribute to the growth of brands in the most important product-market combinations.

The acceleration and increase in the decisiveness, effectiveness, efficiency and cost reduction in production facilities worldwide as well as in offices in Europe (Fast Forward project) are essential in terms of making investments possible and increasing competitive strength.

FrieslandCampina's financial foundation is solid and provides an excellent starting position for the realisation of plans in the context of the route2020 strategy. It is expected that in 2017, FrieslandCampina will be able to comply with the financial ratios specified by its financiers.

FrieslandCampina does not make any pronouncements concerning the development of the result in 2017.

Source: FrieslandCampina, Annual report 2016

15.4 Auditor's Report

No outsider is able to assess whether the financial statements have been drawn up correctly. They do not have access to the financial data which form the basis for the balance sheet and income statement and, in general, are not able to assess whether legal requirements concerning the financial statements have been adhered to. Company management is therefore obligated to request an accountant to conduct an audit of the financial statements. In the Netherlands, this *compulsory auditing* applies only to large and medium size companies.

Compulsory auditing

15

Types of auditor's reports

The auditor's report can result in the following conclusions:

1 If the auditor is of the opinion that the financial statements meet the requirements, he issues *an unqualified opinion.*
2 If there are considerations or uncertainties which do not diminish the approved nature of the statement but are still so serious that they need to be expressed, the auditor will issue a *qualified opinion.*
3 A *disclaimer of opinion* is issued if the uncertainties are of such a nature and such magnitude that the auditor cannot pass judgment on the reliability of the financial statements.
4 An *adverse opinion* is issued if the auditor has come to the conclusion that the financial statements do not meet the requirements.

INDEPENDENT AUDITOR'S REPORT

To: the shareholders and supervisory board of Stern Groep N.V.

Report on the audit of the financial statements 2016 included in the annual report

Our opinion

We have audited the financial statements 2016 of Stern Groep N.V., based in Amsterdam. The financial statements include the consolidated financial statements and the company financial statements.

In our opinion:

- The accompanying consolidated financial statements give a true and fair view of the financial position of Stern Groep N.V. as at 31 December 2016, and of its result and its cash flows for 2016 in accordance with International Financial Reporting Standards as adopted by the European Union (EU- IFRS) and with Part 9 of Book 2 of the Dutch Civil Code.
- The accompanying company financial statements give a true and fair view of the financial position of Stern Groep N.V. as at 31 December 2016, and of its result for 2016 in accordance with Part 9 of Book 2 of the Dutch Civil Code.

The basis for our opinion

We conducted our audit in accordance with Dutch law, including the Dutch Standards on Auditing.

Our responsibilities under those standards are further described in the "Our responsibilities for the audit of the financial statements" section of our report.

We are independent of Stern Groep N.V. in accordance with the Verordening inzake de onafhankelijkheid van accountants bij assurance-opdrachten (ViO, Code of Ethics for Professional Accountants, a regulation with respect to independence) and other relevant independence regulations in the Netherlands. Furthermore we have complied with the Verordening gedrags- en beroepsregels accountants (VGBA, Dutch Code of Ethics).

We believe the audit evidence we have obtained is sufficient and appropriate to provide a basis for our opinion.

15

From the matters communicated with the supervisory board, we determine those matters that were of most significance in the audit of the financial statements of the current period and are therefore the key audit matters. We describe these matters in our auditor's report unless law or regulation precludes public disclosure about the matter or when, in extremely rare circumstances, not communicating the matter is in the public interest.

Amsterdam, 8 March 2017

Ernst & Young Accountants LLP

F. de Bruijn

Source: Stern, Annual report 2016

Note that a statement of unqualified opinion is not a solid guarantee that the financial statements meet the legal requirements. Legislative stipulations are often generally worded and are therefore open to interpretation. In the Netherlands, stakeholders (including shareholders and employee councils) who are of the opinion that the financial statements are not in agreement with the legal requirements may start **Ondernemings-** judicial proceedings at the *Ondernemingskamer* of the Amsterdam court, **kamer** a specialized supervisory court focusing on company law. If the Enterprise Division honors a claim, it instructs the company to organize the financial statements in agreement with the judicial ruling. For stock exchange listed companies, the Authority Financial Markets (AFM) monitors the quality of the financial statements and the quality of the audit. If necessary the AFM can bring a case to the Enterprise Division.

Food giant Unilever originated in 1930 from a merger between the Dutch Margarine Unie and the English Lever Brothers. There are still two parent companies (Unilever NV and Unilever PLC) and two head offices (in Rotterdam and in London). In 2018, Unilever decided to continue with one head office in Rotterdam. The board members of the NV are the same as those of the PLC. Each year, Unilever pays approximately €14 million to KPMG's auditors for activities related to the annual audit. €4 million of which is for the audit of the consolidated financial statements of the parent companies and €10 million for the annual audit of the hundreds of subsidiaries.

In additional to the financial statements, the *report by the managing board* is also part of the auditor's report. The assessment of this component of the annual report is only limited in scope, however, since auditors cannot sign off on a qualified or unqualified opinion of the future prospects paragraph that is a required part of the board report – it will not be possible to prove the board's expectations for the future to have been correct or false until the future becomes the present. The auditor may be *of the opinion* that the board's outlook for coming years is overly positive or negative, but that does not mean there is concrete proof to back up that opinion.

The auditor's responsibilities do extend to the section of the board report dealing with the reporting year. The auditor is required to check whether the figures mentioned in this section are in accordance with the financial statements.

Report by the managing board

Glossary

Accrual principle	Implies that cost and sales revenues are assigned to the correct period.
Annual report	The combined financial statements, report by the managing board and other information.
Auditor's report	Statement by the auditor on the accuracy of the financial statements.
Comparability	Implies that a company should apply the same principles for determining equity and results every year, unless special circumstances justify an adjustment.
Creative accounting	The use of optimistic estimates for the financial statements, to make the company appear healthier.
Financial statements	The balance sheet, income statement and notes on both.
Going concern assumption	Valuation principle that should be used if a company expects to continue to exist in the near future.
IFRS	International Financial Reporting Standards; the principles for external reporting as they have been determined by the International Accounting Standards Board.
Liquidation value	Valuation principle that should be used if a company expects to become disabled in the near future.
Matching principle	Implies that costs are assigned to the period from which the proceeds arise.
Period matching	Charging costs to the result of the period in which they were made.
Product matching	Allocating costs to the inventory and charging them to the result at the moment the inventory is sold.
Prudence principle	Implies that profits are only taken after realization, and losses as soon as they are acknowledged.
Realization principle	Implies that profits are based on sales, if sale and delivery has taken place.

Relevance	The extent to which a reader of the financial statements can use them to gather useful information.
Reliability	The extent to which a reader of the financial statements can rely on the correctness of the information presented.
Report by the managing board	Report made by the directors on the events during the financial year and the expectations for the future.

15

Multiple-choice questions

15

15.1 Which of these companies is *not* obligated to publish any financial statements?
a Trading company NOVA LLC.
b Cooperative Milk Factory Our Interest.
c Partnership Steptoe and Son.
d Water Company Dunes PLC.

15.2 Which of the following is *not* an example of creative accounting?
a Recognizing high provisions in a good year with the intent of reversing them in a poor year.
b Valuing fixed assets in a different way because the rules for external reporting have changed.
c Overestimating the possibilities of payments on accounts receivable.
d Extending the depreciation period in order to reduce depreciation costs.

15.3 Which part of the financial statements is a Dutch company in the 'small' category required to publish?
a Auditor's report.
b Income statement.
c Report by the managing board.
d Balance sheet.

15.4 On 31 December 2017, a company's expenses include those under a through d.
Which of these is a cost in 2017?
a The payment of an insurance premium for 2018.
b The purchase of a machine by means of cash payment.
c The payment of a supplier's account.
d Payment of salaries over December

15.5 In which event is there a cash inflow before the sales revenue can be registered?
a A buyer pays a bill due to an earlier delivery.
b An article is delivered to a buyer by means of cash payment.
c A buyer makes a down payment for an article that is to be delivered later.
d A buyer receives their money back due to delivery of a faulty product.

15.6 On 1 January 2017, the balance of a certain company is as follows:

Building	€400,000	Equity	€310,000
Office equipment	€100,000	5% Loan	€200,000
Current account	€ 10,000		
	€510,000		€510,000

The building has a remaining economic life of 20 years and other fixed assets a remaining economic life of two years. The residual value of the building and the other assets is zero. The company applies straight-line depreciation. The annual repayment of the loan is €20,000 on 31 December. On the same date, the interest for the current year is also paid. The company generates €600,000 sales in 2017; of those sales, €570,000 has been received by the end of the year. The remaining amount is to be received in 2018. The other operating costs were €460,000 in 2017 and were paid in 2017.
What is the profit over 2017?
a €30,000
b €40,000
c €50,000
d €60,000

15.7   Refer to question 15.6.
What is the balance sheet total on 31 December 2017?
a €520,000
b €550,000
c €580,000
d €610,000

15.8   A company closes a sales contract in October 2017. The goods are delivered in November 2017. In December 2017, the invoice is submitted; the amount is received in January 2018.
To which month is the profit assigned?
a October 2017.
b November 2017.
c December 2017.
d January 2018.

15.9   A bicycle manufacturer starts its activities in 2017; in that year, 20,000 bikes are produced. This number is considered to be the normal output. End of 2017, the inventory is 2,000 bicycles. The selling price of a bicycle is €500.
In 2017, the following costs were made:
Material   €2,000,000
Wages   €3,500,000
Other costs   €2,500,000
Product matching is applied to materials and wages; period matching is applied to the other costs.
What is the profit over 2017?
a €450,000
b €850,000
c €1,000,000
d €1,550,000

15.10 Refer to question 15.9.
20,000 bicycles are produced and 22,000 bicycles are sold in 2018. Cost and selling price remain the same as for 2017.
Which statement is correct for the total profit over the years 2017 and 2018?
a The costs to which product matching are applied is not a factor that impacts the total profit.
b Since product matching is applied to more products, the total profit increases.

c Since product matching is applied to more products, the total profit decreases.

d The valuation of the closing inventory on 31 December 2018 is higher since product matching is applied to more products.

15.11 A company's financial statements record the following statement:
'An amount, corresponding with the assumed unrecoverable amount, has been deducted from the nominal value of the accounts receivable.'
To which principle does this behavior refer?
a Continuity.
b Realization.
c Matching.
d Prudence.

15.12 Which of the following statements is correct?
a In general, a company's going concern value is lower than its liquidation value.
b Future expectations with regard to the company must be incorporated in the notes to the accounts in the financial statement.
c Creative accounting means using optimistic estimates for the financial statements, thus making the company's position appear healthier.
d The principle of comparability states that a change in accounting policies is prohibited.

15.13 Which of the following statements is correct?
a An opinion of disclaimer implies that the auditor has insufficient data to verify the correctness of the financial statements.
b The 'Ondernemingskamer' acts as judge and jury with respect to affairs concerning financial statements.
c Small companies are exempt from compulsory audit.
d The director's report is not part of the audit.

15.14 Which of the following statements is correct?
a An unqualified audit statement prevents the Enterprise Division from becoming involved in assessing the financial statements.
b Only large companies are obliged to publish a report by the managing board.
c The value of assets is one of the criteria that determines in which size category a company is classified.
d The auditor's report should be included in the notes on the financial statements.

15.15 Why would an auditor issue a qualified opinion?
a He does not have time to assess all information in the financial statements.
b He is of the opinion that the financial statements are not faithful to reality.
c He has not been able to assess important administrative information
d He is of the opinion that there is a number of uncertainties which, nevertheless, does not detract from an overall faithful report.

16

A Closer Look at Financial Statements

The balance sheet and the income statement together form the heart of the financial statements. Paragraph 16.1 discusses the classification of the income statement and considers the definition of an asset. Paragraphs 16.2 and 16.3 cover fixed and current assets, with special attention being paid to the questions of whether leased company resources may be considered assets and how the balance sheet should treat long-term projects. Paragraphs 16.4 and 16.5 discuss the credit side of the balance sheet, which documents a company's sources of capital. These sources can be subdivided into equity on the one hand and liabilities on the other. The income statement, being the other part of the financial account, are covered in paragraph 16.6, which also addresses the concept of added value; a concept particularly suited to indicate a company's economic significance.

16.1 Balance Sheet: Assets, Equity and Liabilities

Paragraph 3.1 introduced the balance sheet as the overview of a company's assets, equity and debts.
Figure 16.1 represents a model balance sheet such as might be used for external reporting.

16

FIGURE 16.1 Main layout of balance sheet

Balance sheet

Fixed assets	*Equity*
Intangible assets	*Share capital*
Fixed assets	Share premium
Financial fixed assets	Reserves
Current assets	
Inventories	*Provisions*
Current projects	
Accounts receivable	*Long-term liabilities*
Securities	
Cash and cash equivalents	*Current liabilities*

This is type of balance sheet is known as a T-form balance sheet. Another frequently used format is that of the vertical layout.

Asset

Before discussing the different balance entries, the concept of an *asset* should be explained first. There are two conditions that define an asset:
1 It must be controlled by the company.
2 It is expected to generate economic benefits for the company.

A truck owned by a transport company is an asset, since 1) the company can deploy it as they see fit (power of control) and 2) its deployment generates revenue (economic benefit).

On-balance sheet

Off-balance sheet

Later paragraphs will address situations where there is doubt as to whether both requirements of the definition are met. In those situations, the question remains whether the object concerned should be recognized on the balance sheet, (*on-balance sheet*) or kept off the balance sheet (*off-balance sheet*).

A company's liabilities consist of provisions and debts. When it comes to debts, there is an established requirement to pay. When it comes to provisions, there is a matter of uncertainty regarding the amount to pay or the requirement to pay.

The value of the assets minus the value of the liabilities is known as equity.

Paragraphs 16.2 through 16.5 cover the individual components of the balance sheet in detail.

CONSOLIDATED STATEMENT OF FINANCIAL POSITION

Per 31 December

In thousands of euros	2016	2015
ASSETS		
Non-current assets		
Intangible assets	181,969	237,432
Property, plant and equipment	26,767	49,726
Investments in associates	48,143	24
Deferred tax assets	44,636	38,397
Other receivables	719	1,077
Total non-current assets	302,234	326,656
Current assets		
Inventories	1,175	1,859
Tax assets	46	623
Trade and other receivables	58,256	73,811
Cash and cash equivalents	19,485	42,928
Assets classified as held for sale	15,848	62
Total current assets	94,810	119,283
Total assets	397,044	445,939
EQUITY AND LIABILITIES		
Equity		
Issued capital	11,588	11,588
Other reserves	215,797	223,592
Attributable to equity holders of Telegraaf Media Groep N.V.	227,385	235,180
Non-controlling interests	–	7,974
Total shareholder's equity	227,385	227,206
Liabilities		
Interest-bearing loans ans borrowings	–	472
Post-employment benefit liabilities	4,722	5,183
Provisions	–	216
Deferred tax liabilities	10,190	18,023
Total non-current liabilities	14,912	23,894
Interest-bearing loans and borrowings	6,200	25,546
Trade and other payables	131,593	131,943
Provisions	16,113	36,209
Tax payable	841	1,141
Total current liabilities	154,747	194,839
Total liabilities	169,659	218,733
Total equity and liabilities	397,044	445,939

Source: TMG, Annual account 2016

16.2 Fixed Assets

Fixed assets are durable means of production; they prove their worth to a company over several years and can be divided into intangible fixed assets, tangible fixed assets and financial fixed assets.

Intangible fixed assets

Intangible fixed assets are those means of a company that cannot be 'held'. The following categories of intangible assets are discussed below:
1 Research and development;
2 Purchased concessions, patents and brands.

Purchased goodwill is also part of the intangible fixed assets; this balance item is discussed in paragraph 18.1

Ad 1 Research and development

To many companies, research and development expenditures are of vital importance.

To be able to survive, such companies must release new products onto the market regularly. The costs incurred by the 'research lab' can be considered an investment intended to bear fruit at some later date.

A closer look at the definition of the concept of 'asset', however, makes it doubtful whether R&D actually meets the second criterion (expected economic benefit). Obviously, R&D expenditures are made with the intention of future economic benefit; however, at the time of the expenditure, there is no certainty of result. In pharmaceutical companies, for example, only an average of one in every ten research projects results in a new medicine. Accordingly, *research expenditures* should not be capitalized on the balance sheet according to IFRS rules as there is insufficient certainty of economic benefit. Research costs therefore have to be recognized as expenses in the period in which they are incurred. Expenditures made to bring a new product to the market (development costs), however, are to be capitalized and therefore recognized as an asset on the condition that their technical performance has been proven and that there is sufficient expectation of economic benefits. Such expenditures include costs of manufacturing prototypes and performing trial runs for the manufacturing process.

EXAMPLE 16.1

In 2017, a producer of consumer electronics invested €10 million in initial research into the possibilities of a new type of synthetic material which could reduce the weight of TVs, washing machines, etc. Technicians performed tests with different configurations of the synthetic material.
A further €15 million was spent on a prototype and a trial run for the production of a new model of vacuum cleaner. After a few test runs, the model was ready for production. The company is stock exchange listed and must therefore conform to IFRS rules. The amount of €10 million was spent on research and may therefore not be capitalized. This amount is recognized as an expense and deducted from profit in 2017.
The amount of €15 million is related to development expenditures which are considered an investment; it is capitalized on the balance sheet of 31 December 2017.

TEST QUESTION 16.1

Which accounting principle has priority with respect to research expenditures, and which principle with respect to development expenditures?

16

It takes an average of 12 years before a new medicine is made available for use. The process involves some 400 researchers performing around 6,000 experiments.

Roche, with its headquarters in Basel, Switzerland, is the world's number one pharmaceutical enterprise. In 2016, the company spend more than €10 billion on research into and development of new medicines. Roche charges both research and development costs to the profits of the year in which these costs are incurred. Until a particular new medicine has received proper approval from the proper authorities, Roche cannot assume any sufficient expectations of economic benefit. None of the costs incurred before a medicine is approved by medical authorities can be capitalized. Nearly all pharmaceutical companies apply this rule.

Ad 2 Purchased concessions, patents and brands

The category of 'purchased concessions, patents and brands' concerns 'hard', intangible assets, as they involve contractually agreed rights. An oil company which pays for a concession to drill in the North Sea can count on economic advantages (if test drilling proves that there is oil); therefore, the concession is recognized on the balance sheet as such. The same applies for the amount paid to an inventor to be allowed to commercially exploit their invention.

The value of a company is becoming less and less determined by its physical production possibilities and more and more by its capacity to distinguish itself to its customers. Therefore, the value of brands is becoming increasingly important; nearly everyone can produce laundry detergents, but positioning a brand is much harder. If a company buys a brand from another company, it has to capitalize the amount paid.

Brands

Tangible fixed assets

Tangible fixed assets include company premises, buildings, machines, cars, computers, etc. In this category, the probability that the assets can generate an economic benefit is usually taken for granted. There could, however, be doubts on the criterion of being controlled by the company, which demands that purchased production factors should be treated on-balance sheet and rented production factors should be treated off-balance sheet.
Of course, the rental costs are mentioned on the income statement.

16

Leasing

Paragraph 5.5 discussed the fact that production resources can also be obtained via leasing. It was also mentioned that there are two types of leasing:
- *An operational lease* is an agreement which can be terminated at short notice and which assigns maintenance costs to the lease company. This form of leasing can be compared to renting and is treated accordingly in the financial accounts: the leased object is not recognized on the balance sheet, and the lease instalments are recognized in the income statement as costs.
- *A financial lease* is an agreement that is made for the estimated economic life of an object. The agreement cannot be terminated. The maintenance costs are borne by the user in a financial lease. In this type of lease agreement, the user bears the risk of obsolescence (i.e. if newer, more efficient types become available on the market) and the risk of high maintenance costs.
These risks are comparable to the risks to which regular buyers are submitted. The user of the financial lease also resembles a buyer where the duration of the right to use the item is concerned. Both lease users and buyers have the item at their disposal throughout its entire economic life. The *risks and rewards* of financial leasing are equivalent to those suffered by an owner. Although the user of the financial lease contract is not legally its owner, there is no difference in terms of economics. This is the reason why financial leases are treated as on-balance sheet transactions.

FIGURE 16.2 Processing a lease in financial statements

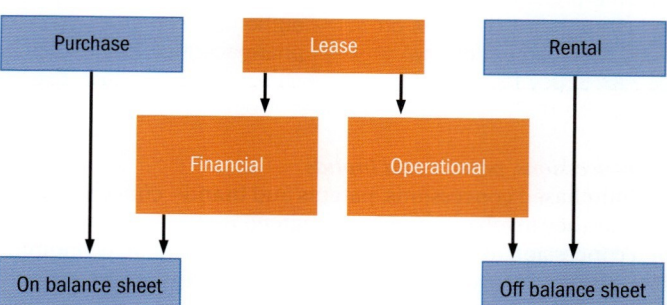

In a financial lease, the leased object is recognized on the balance sheet as a tangible asset. Annual depreciation is charged to profit.
However, financial leasing contains also a financing element; it is comparable to purchasing, combined with a loan to finance the purchase. This implies the credit side of the balance sheet should mention the obligations towards the lease company, and that the annual financing costs, which are included in the contract, should be charged to the profit.

FIGURE 16.3 Financial lease

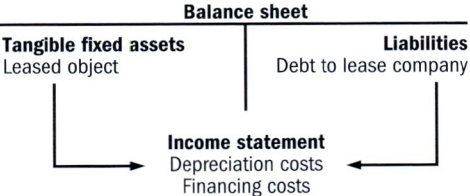

Balance sheet

| **Tangible fixed assets** | **Liabilities** |
| Leased object | Debt to lease company |

Income statement
Depreciation costs
Financing costs

EXAMPLE 16.2
A company enters into an irrevocable agreement with a lease company on
1 January 2017. The company acquires possession of a machine for four
years (equal to its estimated economic life). The machine has a value of
€100,000. The company is to pay €32,600 annually to the lease company
at the end of 2017, 2018, 2019 and 2020. The contractually agreed
financing costs are 11.5%. The residual value of the machine is set to zero.
The company applies linear depreciation on machines.

The consequences for the company's financial statements are as follows:
A machine is acquired at a value of €100,000 and is wholly financed with
debt.

The balance sheet of 1 January 2017 shows the following entries with
respect to the lease agreement:

Balance sheet on 1 January 2017 (in Euros)

Fixed assets		*Liabilities*	
Machine	100,000	Debt to lease company	100,000

In 2017, the machine depreciates by €25,000. The book value at the end
of 2017 is €75,000.
So far as the financing element is concerned, the company has borrowed
€100,000 and has to pay four instalments of €32,600 each. In fact, this
is an annuity loan; the €32,600 comprises both interest and redemption of
the principal sum.
The interest amounts to 11.5%; the interest part in the first year is
therefore 11.5% of €100,000 = €11,500. The redemption of the principal
sum is €32,600 – €11,500 = €21,100.
The debt to the lease company on 31 December 2017 is €78,900.

Income statement over 2017 (in Euros)

Machines	– 25,000	Debt to lease company	– 21,100
Cash and cash equivalents	– 32,600	Profit	– 36,500
	– 57,600		– 57,600

The contract means that €25,000 in depreciation costs and €11,500 in
interest costs are charged to the income statement over 2017.

Depreciation of fixed assets

Since fixed assets are in the service of a company for several years, they should also be depreciated over time.

Depreciation

The depreciation to be applied to the intangible and tangible fixed assets is determined based on the purchasing price, the estimated useful life and the estimated residual value. The distribution of an asset's total depreciation amount over the years should be based on the benefits its annual use will earn the company. This follows from the matching principle (see paragraph 15.2). Two different methods of depreciation can be distinguished: straight-line and degressive depreciation (previously addressed in paragraph 3.3).

Straight-line depreciation means that the asset depreciates by the same amount each year (thereby assuming that the fixed asset yields the same benefits for the company each year).

Degressive depreciation means that the depreciated amount decreases each year (thereby assuming that the benefits yielded by the fixed assets decrease each year). Degressive depreciation is applied, for example, when using the book value method: the book value of the asset decreases by a fixed percentage each year.

DEPRECIATION AND AMORTISATION

Intangible assets and assets used tor operating activities are amortised and depreciated on a straight-line basis according to the schedule below. Goodwill is not amortised or depreciated on investment property, assets under construction or land.

Intangible assets	
Contract-related assets	33 years
ICT development	3-5 years
Software licences	3-5 years
Assets used for operational activities	
Runways and taxiways	15-60 years
Aprons	30-60 years
Paved areas, roads etc.:	
- Car parks	30 years
- Roads	30 years
- Tunnels and viaducts	40 years
- Drainage systems	40 years
Buildings	20-60 years
Installations	5-30 years
Other assets	5-20 years

Source: Schiphol, Annual report 2016

If the book value of the fixed asset is not expected to be fully redeemed through future income, an impairment should be applied. If the asset is unlikely to redeem the amount invested in its acquisition, the prudence principle (see paragraph 15) requires that the resulting loss is taken directly. The size of the impairment is determined by comparing the book value of the asset to its realisable value. This is the amount the asset could be

expected to yield upon its sale (its net selling value) or on the amount the
asset would yield if it were to remain in operational use (the value in use).
If the net selling value is below the value in use, there is no financial reason
to sell the asset: it would yield a greater benefit if it were to remain in use in
business operations. If the net selling value is greater than the value in use,
the best option is to sell the asset straight away.
This means the realizable value is whichever of the two is higher: net selling
value or value in use.

16

EXAMPLE 16.3
A transport company's fleet numbers 50 trucks, all purchased at €200,000
each in early January 2013. The estimated lifespan of these trucks is 8
years; they are depreciated to zero using the straight-line method. Towards
the end of 2016, the situation on the transport market is far from ideal.
At that point in time, the book value of each truck amounts to $4/8 \times$
€200,000 – €100,000. It must now be determined whether the trucks will
be able to redeem their book value.
The truck dealer is prepared to take back the trucks at €50,000 each – the
net selling value.
The board assumes that, over the remaining 4 years of operational use,
each truck will be able to yield a turnover of €100,000. Driver wages are
€40,000 per year; additional costs (fuel, taxes, maintenance) also amount
to €40,000 per year.
The operational value is based on the trucks' earnings capacity for
continued operational activity: over the next 4 years, there is an expected
net inflow of €20,000. At first glance, this would make the value in use $4 \times$
€20,000 = €80,000. However, the cost of capital must also be considered:
the investment in the trucks resulted in financing costs. In order to reflect
those costs, the annual cash inflow should be discounted at the company's
weighted average cost of capital. Assuming the company's weighted
average cost of capital is 10%, the value in use of a truck is:

$$\frac{€20,000}{1.10} + \frac{€20,000}{1.10^2} + \frac{€20,000}{1.10^3} + \frac{€20,000}{1.10^4} = \text{appr. } €63,000$$

The realizable value is the higher of €63,000 and €50,000, i.e. €63,000.
This means an impairment of €37,000. The balance sheet on 31
December 2016 documents the trucks at €63,000 each. Per truck, standard
depreciation costs of €25,000, as well as a €37,000 impairment, are
recognized in the 2016 income statement.

If, following an impairment, it turns out that, on a later date, the net selling
value and/or value in use must be estimated at a higher figure due to a
change in circumstances, the book value of the asset should be raised
by means of a reversal of the earlier impairment. This value increase,
however, may never result in a book value that is higher than the book value
according to the original depreciation schedule.

16

EXAMPLE 16.3 CONTINUED

Assuming that, by 2018, the transport market will have returned to its former levels, the board estimates that, over the last two operational years, each truck could yield a turnover of €140,000 per year (if wages are €40,000 and other costs are €40,000). This would result in a value in use of:

$$\frac{€60,000}{1.10} + \frac{€60,000}{1.10^2} = \text{appr. } €104,000$$

The book value of the trucks at the end of 2018 is 2/4 × €63,000 = €31,500. If the original depreciation schedule had been used, the book value at the end of 2018 would have been: 2/8 × €200,000 = €50,000. The trucks will be valued on the 31 December 2018 balance sheet at €50,000 each. In 2018, normal depreciation costs are 1/4 × €63,000 = €15,750 and a reversal of impairment is recognized, amounting to (€50,000 − €31,500) = €18,500.

The changes in the book value of a truck are displayed in graph form in Figure 16.4

FIGURE 16.4 Graphic representation book value truck

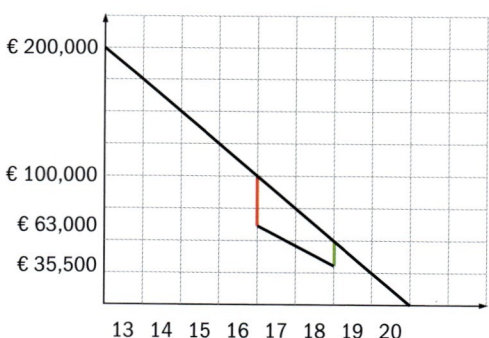

TEST QUESTION 16.2

Why should the trucks from example 16.3 not be valued at the value in use of €104,000 at the end of 2018?

IMPAIRMENTS AND REVERSALS

As a result of developments in the lease portfolio of a station complex in the Netherlands, a review has been performed of the recoverable amount of this complex. The recoverable amount is set at €78 million. This has resulted in an impairment loss of €24 million.

The calculations that give rise to the impairments and their reversals are based on a weighted average post-tax discount rate that is between 5.5% and 7% (2015: between 5.5% and 7%).

Source: Nederlandse Spoorwegen, Annual report 2016

Financial fixed assets
Financial fixed assets mainly concern a controlling interest in the share
capital of other companies. This is discussed in detail in paragraph 18.1.

16.3 Current Assets

Current assets are expected to be realized within a year; they can be divided
into inventories, current projects, claims, securities, and cash and cash
equivalents.

Inventories
For external reporting, the matching principle is of great importance; costs
are assigned to the period from which the proceeds arise. For inventory
valuation, this implies that purchasing costs (in a trading company) or
manufacturing costs (in a production company) have to be included in the
inventory valuation in such way as to be charged to profit as 'costs of goods
sold' during the period in which they are sold (and revenue is generated).
All costs related to bringing the inventory into its current position and
current state must be capitalized. In addition to costs *directly* related to
the inventory (direct costs), there are often indirect costs. These should be
assigned as best as possible. In practice, not all incurred costs are assigned
to inventory, i.e. product matching is not applied to all costs. Costs that are
not assigned to the inventoriy are subject to period matching. Interest costs
are often an instance of the latter (see paragraph 15.2).

Purchasing similar goods in different batches
If similar goods are purchased as part of separate processes, a company
needs to decide which purchased batch to draw from when it comes to a sale.
The following methods may be used to address this question:
- The *FIFO* method (first in, first out), which assumes that the first   **FIFO**
  purchased goods are the first to be sold.
- The *LIFO* method (last-in-first-out), which assumes that the last   **LIFO**
  purchased goods are the first to be sold.
- The *WAC* method (weighted average cost), which calculates the purchase   **WAC**
  price based on a weighted average. The average purchase price of the
  existing inventory is calculated following each new round of purchases,
  and sales costs of the following sale are based on the average purchase
  price per sold unit.

If purchase prices are subject to changes or fluctuations, the choice of an
inventory costing method has consequences for the level of profit.

- -

EXAMPLE 16.4
An entrepreneur has saved up €20,000 to be invested in his startup
enterprise, hedge clipper retail company Trimbush.
On 1 January, Trimbush purchases 500 hedge clippers at €16 each,
followed by 500 clippers at €24 each on 1 April (following a 50% price
increase by the supplier).
On 1 June, Trimbush sells 600 clippers at €40 each. For the sake of
simplicity, no operating costs are assumed.

The balance sheet and income statement for each of the mentioned methods would be constructed as follows:

Balance sheet 31 December (in Euros)

	FIFO	LIFO	WAG			FIFO	LIFO	WAG
Inventory					Starting equity	20,000	20,000	20,000
400 × €24	9,600				Profit	13,600	10,400	12,000
400 × €16		6,400						
400 × €20			8,000					
Cash	24,000	24,000	24,000					
	33,600	30,400	32,000			33,600	30,400	32,000

Income statement (in Euros)

		FIFO	LIFO	WAG
Sales revenue		24,000	24,000	24,000
Cost of goods sold	500 × €16 + 100 × €24	10,400		
	500 × €24 + 100 × €16		13,600	
	600 × €20			12,000
Profit		13,600	10,400	12,000

- -

Individual and collective LIFO

The LIFO method uses one of two variants:

1 *Individual* LIFO applies the LIFO principle on the existing inventory at each separate sales transaction.
2 *Collective* LIFO does not evaluate which goods are assumed to have been sold in each separate sales transaction. Instead, the inventory at the end of the period is compared to the inventory at the beginning of the period. If the closing inventory is smaller than the opening inventory, the closing inventory is understood to consist of the oldest batches of the opening inventory. If the closing inventory is greater than the opening inventory, then the closing is understood to consist of the opening inventory plus the first purchase batch(es) from this year. This means that, using collective LIFO, it is an administrative possibility for a purchase by a company that takes place after a sale to a customer to have supplied units that have been retroactively used in that sale.

The collective variant of the LIFO method can only be used to determine periodical profit. Transaction profits (from individual sales) cannot be calculated in this way. When applied to the Trimbush example, both variants lead to the same amount of profit.

IFRS does *not* allow the use of LIFO.

Cost or market, whichever lower

An impairment on the inventory is needed if the expected net selling value (being the sales price minus the costs to be incurred until the sale) of the good(s) concerned is lower than the asset's book value. This is also known as cost or market, whichever lowest.

EXAMPLE 16.4 CONTINUED

If, on 31 December, it were to appear that the net selling value of the hedge trimmers is €18 per unit, this would have the following consequences:
- In case of FIFO: the inventory is valued at 400 × €18 = €7,200. This sets profit at €11,200.
- In case of LIFO: none.
- In case of WAG: the inventory is valued at €7,200. This sets profit at €11,200.

16

INVENTORIES

Inventories are carried at the lower of cost, using the FIFO method, or market value, which is taken as being the estimated sales value in normal circumstances, less selling costs. The carrying amount includes allowances for internal distribution, whereas bonus discounts are deducted.

Source: Sligro, Annual report 2016

Work in progress

In case of *long-term projects,* such as a large housing construction project, the question arises whether the realization principle should be strictly adhered to.

This principle (see paragraph 15.2) determines that profit should only be recognized if the goods or services are sold and delivered; in long-term projects, profit is realized upon handing over the project.

If a company works on one project exclusively for three years, applying the realization principle results in zero profit during the first two years and (hopefully) a very large profit in the third year. This accounting method is known as the *completed contract method.*

Nowadays, it is a generally accepted notion that the completed contract method results in an inaccurate picture: at an equal activity level, the profit level is subject to major fluctuations. Therefore, preference is given to the *percentage of completion method*: profit is recognized gradually, corresponding with the progress of the work.

If it is possible to make a reliable estimate of the costs to be incurred during the different phases of construction, the percentage of completion method should be used. Completed contract should only be applied if such an estimate is not possible.

Long-term projects

Completed contract method

Percentage of completion method

CONSTRUCTION CONTRACTS FOR THIRD PARTIES

If the outcome of a construction contract for third parties can be reliably determined, then the revenue and costs are reported in proportion to completion at the balance sheet date. The stage of completion is calculated on the basis of the related costs incurred for services provided in comparison to the total expected project costs, unless this is not representative for the stage of completion. Variations in contract work, claims and incentive payments are included to the extent that the customer will approve this, they can be determined reliably and settlement is likely.

If the outcome of a construction contract cannot be measured reliably, revenue is accounted for the costs incurred if it is probable that the benefits will be realized. Contract costs are recognized as expenses in the period that they occur. If the expected project costs exceed the expected project revenue, then the expected loss is provided directly and deducted from the construction contracts.

Source: TKH, Annual report 2016

16

EXAMPLE 16.5

The balance sheet of a road construction company on 1 January 2016 is as follows:

Balance sheet on 1 January 2016 (× €1 million)

Cash and cash equivalents	15	Share capital	15

The company wins a tender for a project for €12 million at the beginning of 2016. Costs are estimated at €10 million, of which €6 million is incurred in 2016 and €4 million in 2017. For the sake of convenience, costs are assumed to also be cash outflows. The execution of the project occurs exactly according to schedule; in December 2017, the project is handed over and the contracted sum is received. Profits are entirely retained.
If it is not possible to make a reliable prior estimate of the costs to be incurred, the completed contract method is applied. This results in the following balance sheets:

Balance sheet on 31 December 2016 (× €1,000)

Work in progress	6,000	Share capital	15,000
Cash and cash equivalents			
15,000 − 6,000	9,000		
	——		——
	15,000		15,000

Balance sheet on 31 December 2017 (× €1,000)

Cash and cash equivalents		Share capital	15,000
9,000 − 4,000 + 12,000	17,000	Profit	2,000
	——		——
	17,000		15,000

However, if it is possible to make an estimate of the costs incurred during the various phases of construction beforehand, the percentage of completion method is applied.
This involves recognizing a profit on the balance sheet on 31 December 2016. This profit is a percentage of the total profit of €2 million. The percentage is determined by the stage of completion of the work. An

objective way to determine the stage of completion is to relate the costs made to the total expected costs, in this case:

$$\frac{\text{Actual cost in 2016}}{\text{Total forecast costs}} = \frac{\text{€6 million}}{\text{€10 million}} = 60\%$$

At the end of 2016, the company therefore recognizes a profit of 60% of €2 million = €1.2 million by valuing the work in progress at cost plus allocated profit.

Balance sheet on 31 December 2016 (× €1,000)

Work in progress		Share capital	15,000
6,000 + 1,200 =	7,200	Profit	1,200
Cash and cash equivalents	9,000		
	16,200		16,200

Applying the percentage of completion method therefore means the project is not valued at cost but at sales value. End of 2016, the work is 60% complete, which means it is valued at 60% of the contracted sum of €12 million = €7,200,000

Balance sheet on 31 December 2017 (× €1,000)

Cash and cash equivalents	17,000	Share capital	15,000
		Retained profit	1,200
		Profit	800
	17,000		17,000

If a loss is expected, the company should apply an impairment, with the project being valued at a lower realisable value.

EXAMPLE 16.5 CONTINUED
Assume that during the completion of the work in example 16.5 the company is met with adversity in 2016. The costs in that year come to €9 million; over 2017, the forecast costs still are €4 million. Thus:

Revenue	€12 million
Estimated costs €9 mln + €4 mln =	€13 million
Expected loss	€ 1 million

The prudence principle dictates that these losses should be recognized immediately; the balance sheet on 31 December 2016 documents this loss by valuing the project at its total costs so far (€9 million) minus the expected loss (€1 million) = €8 million. Another way to arrive at this amount is by taking the contracted amount of €12 million and subtracting the future costs of €4 million needed to complete the project.

In that case, the balance sheet would come to:

Balance sheet on 31 December 2016 (amounts × €1,000)

Current projects	9,000 – 1,000 = 8,000	Share capital	15,000
Cash and cash equivalents	15,000 – 9,000 = 6,000	Profit	– 1,000
	14,000		14,000

TEST QUESTION 16.3
Why are the losses not distributed across the project's runtime but instead recognized at once?

Financial assets
If a company temporarily has excess cash or cash equivalents and invests these resources in shares, then that package of shares is classified under the heading of 'financial assets'.
Financial assets can be valued at purchase price, in which case the package holder recognizes the incurred dividends as profit. Any increase in value of the package is only recognized as profit if the financial assets are sold.
A disadvantage of this method is that is does not offer a good insight into the management's investment achievements. Moreover, it gives company management the opportunity to compensate for dissappointing profits by boosting investment income, through selling shares that have increased in value.
It is therefore preferable to value shares at their sales value, with increases in value recognized in the income statement directly. This method disregards the realization principle.

EXAMPLE 16.6
In early 2017, a company acquires shares in a stock market listed company as a way of investing excess cash. The shares are purchased at a total of €100,000. Over the course of 2017, the company earns €5,000 in dividend on the shares. The market value of the shares per end of 2017 is €120,000.

The purchase of the share package leads to the following balance sheet entries:

Financial assets	+ € 100,000		
Cash and cash equivalents	+ € 100,000		

Income from dividend:

Cash and cash equivalents	+ €5,000	Profit	+ € 5,000

When valued at purchase price, the profit from the investment over 2017 is €5,000

When valued at sales price, the following entry is recorded at the end of 2017:

Financial assets	+ € 20,000	Profit	+ € 20,000

A total investment result of €25,000 is recognized.

If the shares are sold in early 2018, a valuation at purchase price would lead to a profit of €20,000; a valuation at sales price leads to zero profit as the shares had already been valued at their sales price and the increases in value has already been recognized in 2017.

TEST QUESTION 16.4
Assume that the market value of the shares in example 16.6 is €90,000 by end of 2017.
What is the investment income when the shares are valued at purchase price and what is it when shares are valued at selling price?

16.4 Equity

Equity is a residual item, since its amount is determined by the difference between assets and liabilities. There is no separate valuation basis for equity. The valuation method of assets (and liabilities) determines the amount of equity.
Chapter 7 discussed the different components into which the equity of a PLC or LLC can be divided: share capital, share premium and retained profits.
Profit from the past book year can be stated on the balance sheet as a separate entry (balance sheet before profit appropriation) or or stated in the entries 'Retained earnings' (equity) and 'Dividend payable' (liabilities) according to the proposed profit appropriation.
IFRS rules only allow a balance sheet before profit appropriation; Dutch legislation allows either alternative.

16.5 Liabilities

A company's liabilities can be divided between two types of obligations: provisions and debts.

Provisions
Provisions must be recognized if it is probable business activities during the past year will lead to an obligation or an expected loss in a later year, which cannot be exactly determined but can be globally estimated. Paragraph 3.3 already served to introduce the concept of provision, and paragraph 8.6 discussed provisions in detail.
If a company issues a warranty on produced and sold articles, it will be able to make a reasonable estimate on balance sheet date with respect to the warranty claims next year, based on sales during the current year. These claims should be taken into account both from a prudence point of view

16

(recognize losses when they are known) and a matching point of view (costs of goods to be repaired or returned find their origin in the year they were sold). Provisions should only be recognized if there are obligations or losses resulting from a specific risk at the balance sheet date. If a company wishes to create a buffer with respect to general business risks (worsening of the economic situation, for example), this can be done by retaining profit. Companies with strong fluctuations in their profit over the years can be tempted to reduce these fluctuations by recognizing an overly large amount in provisions in good years. In fact, this means that profit is retained under the pretense of provisions: profit appropriation dressed up as profit determination.
Consecutively, in less profitable years, the overly large provisions are (partially) reversed and added to profit. This is a form of creative accounting.

The obligation on which a provision is based is required to be of a legal or constructive nature. A legal obligation is enforceable in court by the counter party; a constructive obligation is not enforceable, but not meeting it will result in serious reputation damage since the company had already made its intent to honor its obligations known to third parties.

EXAMPLE 16.7
At the end of 2017, a company finds itself part of a lawsuit in which a client, as a result of inadequate delivery, has demanded remuneration of damages of €100,000. The company lawyer deems it likely that the claimant will win the case.
In addition, one of the company's ideas in 2017 has been to contribute an amount of €20,000 to the staff association in 2018, since the last few staff outings came in over budget. The staff association has not yet been informed of this idea.
IFRS state that a provision has to be recognized for the probable obligation that follows from the lawsuit. No provisions can be recognized for the staff association contribution, since no constructive obligation exists.

If there are probable losses at the balance sheet date which can be directly linked to a certain asset, the provision should be balanced against that asset. The provision therefore does not show up on the credit side of the balance sheet, but will have been subtracted from the debit side.

EXAMPLE 16.8
On 1 January 2017, a company is owed €250,000 from its buyers; the company estimates that 5% of that amount will be irrecoverable. Over 2017, sales on account amount to €2,400,000; an amount of €2,300,000 is obtained from the buyers. Over 2017, an amount of €15,000 proves to be definitively unclaimable as a result of the buyers concerned filing for bankruptcy. Per 31 December 2017, the estimate is that 7% of trade receivables will be irrecoverable.

The balance sheet on 1 January 2017 documents the Account receivables as:

Face value	€250,000
Provision irrecoverability 5%	€ 12,500
	€237,500

Per 31 December 2017, the Account receivables are valued as follows:

Face value €250,000 + €2,400,000 – €2,300,000 – €15,000 = €335,000

Provision 7%	€ 23,450
	€311,550

In 2017, an addition to the Provision irrecoverability of €25,950 is recognized in the income statement.

The running overview of the Provision irrecoverability over 2017:

Amount 1/1	€ 12,500
Write-off due to definitive irrecoverability	€ 15,000 –
Addition charged to income in 2017	€ 25,950 +
Amount 31/12	€ 23,450

In 2015, Volkswagen was proven to have installed software into its diesel-fueled cars that recognized when those cars were placed on a mechanic's dyno for a check-up. As soon as the software detected a garage check-up, it limited the car's damaging exhaust fumes, thus making it appear more environmentally friendly than it actually was. This tampering software led to many legal procedures against the Volkswagen concern. As of end of 2014 (prior to Dieselgate), Volkswagen's balance sheets recognized provisions for legal procedures for a total of €1.3 billion. At the end of 2015, this amount had increased to €8.4 billion; by end of 2016, it was €11.7 billion.

Debts

Debts should be split into long term and short term. The dividing line falls at the one-year mark: everything that has to be paid back within a year is considered a short-term debt and everything longer a long-term debt. If the debt is partly paid back every year, the amount to be paid back within a year is transferred to short-term; the remainder is long-term.

16

Capital base

Chapter 8 discussed subordinated loans: loans on which interest and principal sums are only paid after all other obligations to creditors are settled. Subordinated loans – together with equity – are a company's *capital base* because they serve as a buffer towards other creditors. On the balance sheet, however, they are recognized under liabilities.

16.6 Income Statement

The income statement can be presented using two different layouts, by nature of expenses or by function of expenses. The two differ from one another in how costs are grouped.

Nature of expenses income statement

The *nature of expenses income statement* provides information on different categories of expenses.

FIGURE 16.5 Nature of expenses income statement

Revenue	....	
Other operating income	....	+
Changes in inventories*	....	+/–
Raw materials and consumables used	....	–
Employee benefit expenses	....	–
Depreciation	....	–
Other expenses	....	–
	_____	
Operating profit	....	
Finance expense	....	–
Finance income	....	+
	_____	
Profit before tax	....	
Income tax	....	–
	_____	
Profit	....	

*On the nature of expenses income statement, the expenses are based on the number of units *produced* over the year. Since revenue is based on the number of units *sold*, the change in book value of inventory of finished goods (and work in progress) is used to make amends for this mismatch.

Function of expenses income statement

The *function of expenses income statement* provides insight to the costs of a number of functions within the company, the manufacturing, sales and the administrative functions.

FIGURE 16.6 Function of expenses income statement

Revenue	....	
Cost of goods sold	....	−
	_____	
Gross profit	....	
Other operating income	....	+
Distribution expenses	....	−
Administrative expenses	....	−
Other expenses	....	−
	_____	
Operating profit	....	
Finance expense	....	−
Finance income	....	+
	_____	
Profit before tax	....	
Income tax	....	−
	_____	
Profit	....	

Gains or losses can emerge which are not generated by business activities. Examples are damage from natural disasters, expropriation, or nationalization of a foreign subsidiary. The unusual nature of these items means they are recorded as *separate disclosure items* on the income statement.

Direct changes in equity
Revenues and costs lead to profit, and therefore cause a change in equity. However, not all changes in equity are caused by profits incurred or losses suffered.
Equity can also change as the result of a shift in capital between the company and its owners. In an LLC or PLC, for example, the equity may be increased by issuing shares and increased by paying dividend.
These events are, of course, not recognized in the income statement. They are *direct changes in equity*. Dividend paid to shareholders is not recognized on the income statement as a cost since there is no profit determination, only profit appropriation. Payments by shareholders for future shares are not recognized on the income statement as gains; they are recorded under the share capital and share premium.

Segmentation
A company active across different industries or in different countries benefits from a breakdown of information known as segmentation.
A breakdown of information by a company active across different industries or in different countries (segmentation), helps users of financial statements to gain an insight in the company's financial position; by indicating the percentile distribution of the total revenue across the different branches or regions, it becomes easier to draw a conclusion about which percentages of total revenue are from growing or shrinking markets, and which are from politically stable or unstable countries. The IFRS specifies a more detailed form of segmentation than Dutch legislation.

OPERATIONAL SEGMENTS

Information about reportable segments

	Bicycles		Parts & accessories	
	2016	**2015**	**2016**	**2015**
	× €1,000	× €1,000	× €1,000	× €1,000
External revenues	785,536	719,021	262,616	267,381
Inter-segment revenue	32,243	25,825	19,958	22,033
Segment revenue	**817,779**	**744,846**	**282,574**	**289,414**
Segment profit (loss) before interest and tax*	**56,385**	**60,537**	**17,493**	**15,622**
Depreciation and amortization	7,350	6,916	2,901	2,529
Share of profit (loss) of equity-accounted investees	571	282	–	–1,212
Segment assets*	**537,171**	**549,078**	**146,508**	**170,834**
Equity-accounted investees	6,947	4,981	–	–
Capital expenditure	9,876	6,883	1,639	5,036
Segment liabilities*	**187,126**	**165,314**	**33,865**	**35,070**

*The presentation of the comparative figures is adjusted in the comparative figures 2015 for presentation purposes. A reference is made to the significant accounting policies for a note on these changes.

Source: Accell, Annual account 2016

Added value

Net profit as a benchmark to assess a company's performance focuses on the owners of the company. It indicates the amount available to the shareholders. The concept of net profit implicitly assumes that the company is there for the benefit of the shareholders and is therefore a limited understanding of profit as a concept. Nowadays, a company is considered to be a cooperation of different groups of stakeholders. The employees, for example, are stakeholders in the company, as well as the shareholders. A concept that relates to this is that of added value, which is the broadest profit concept. It can be described as the total income generated for the benefit of all stakeholders in the company.

If the goods and services purchased from third parties are deducted from revenue, the result is the added value. This is subsequently divided among the various stakeholders: employees, shareholders, credit providers and the government.

FIGURE 16.7 Net profit compared to net added value

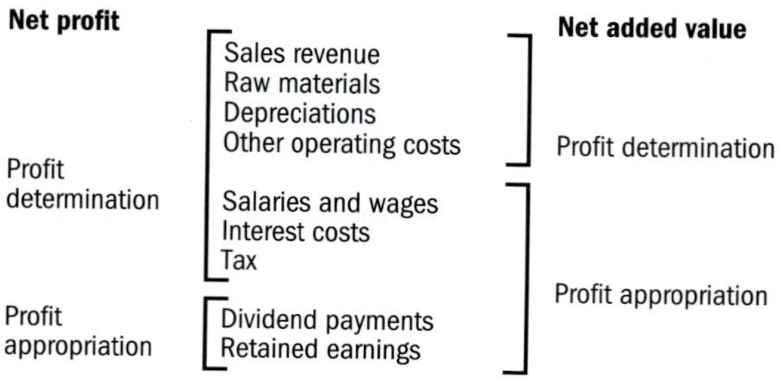

Therefore, if the concept of net profit treats employee benefits as an expense
and therefore as part of the determination of profit, the concept of added
value is part of the appropriation of profit.

There is a distinction between gross and net added value. The difference
between *net and gross added value* is caused by the treatment of
depreciation: in the calculation of net added value it is deducted, and in the
calculation of gross added value, it is not.

Net and gross added value

16

Publishing the added value on a financial account is not required. Some
larger companies publish the added value as a financial ratio as part of the
notes.

TEST QUESTION 16.4
Refer to the Agrifirm income statement below.
Calculate Agrifirm's net added value over 2016, and the distribution across
the different participants.

CONSOLIDATED PROFIT & LOSS ACCOUNT

(in thousands of euros)	2016		2015	
Net turnover	2,170,360		2,385,246	
Other operating income	13,481		8,480	
Total revenues		2,183,841		2,393,726
Cost of raw materials and consumables	−1,693,655		−1,892,076	
Personnel costs	−191,757		−185,554	
Depreciation and amortisation	−44,706		−37,950	
Other operating expenses	−222,065		−230,152	
Total operating expenses		−2,152,183		−2,345,732
Operating income		31,658		47,994
Financial income	1,949		2,043	
Financial expenses	−4,738		−9,392	
Net finance expenses		−2,789		−7,349
Profit before income tax		28,869		40,645
Income taxes		−11,560		−9,800
Result participating interests		13,834		46,465
Profit for the period		31,143		77,310
Non-controlling interest		−540		−1,080
NET INCOME		30,603		76,230

Source: Agrifirm, Annual account 2016

Glossary

Capital base	The combined total equity and subordinate loans.
Completed contract method	Method which recognizes profit on long-term projects upon handing over.
Cost or market, whichever lowest	Principle that determines that the book value should be revised downwards if the net selling value is lower than the book value.
Current assets	Asset providing services for the company for any period shorter than a year.
First in, first out method	Inventory costing method, which assumes that the oldest inventory is sold first.
Fixed assets	Asset providing services for the company for any period longer than a year.
Gross added value	The difference between revenue and costs of goods and services purchased from third parties.
Impairment	Write-off charged to profit if the book value of an asset is higher than the realisable value.
Income statement by function of expense	Income statement that gives an insight into the company's functions, such as manufacturing, sales and general management.
Last in, first out method	Inventory costing method which assumes that the most recent inventory is sold first.
Nature of expense income statement	Income statement that gives an insight to the different cost categories, such as employee benefits and depreciation.
Net added value	The difference between revenue on the one hand and costs of goods and services purchased from third parties, and depreciation on the other.
Percentage of completion method	Method which recognizes profit on long-term projects in proportion to work progress.

Realisable value	Whichever value is higher: net selling value or operational value.
Segmentation	The breakdown of information into product groups and geographical areas.
Separate disclosure items	Results whose nature is incidental or not characteristic of the company.
Weighted average cost method	Inventory costing method which calculates an average price.

16

Multiple-choice questions

16.1 A company has issued a loan to its director which must be repaid in ten years.
Under which balance item is this loan classified?
a Intangible assets.
b Financial fixed assets.
c Accounts receivable.
d Creditors.

16.2 Which principle is opposed to capitalizing research expenditures?
a The prudence principle.
b The matching principle.
c The permanence principle.
d The going concern principle.

16.3 On 1 January 2017, a company enters into a financial lease contract for a machine with a catalog value of €200,000. According to the contract, an amount of €50,000 should be paid over a period of five years, with the first payment on 31 December 2017. The contractually agreed financing costs are 8%. The machine is depreciated straight-line over four years. The residual value is zero.
Which amount related to the machine is charged as a cost to profit in 2017?
a €32,600
b €36,500
c €46,100
d €57,600

16.4 Refer to question 16.3.
What can be said with certainty if the company were to have entered into an operational lease contract for the machine?
a The profit over 2017 would be higher.
b The current ratio per 31 December 2017 would be higher.
c The debt ratio per 31 December 2017 would be lower.
d The equity per 31 December 2017 would be lower.

16.5 What is the difference between depreciations and impairments of fixed assets?
a Depreciations are charged to profit; impairments are not.
b Depreciations are determined when the asset is purchased; impairments are determined while the asset is in use.
c Depreciations are applied incidentally; impairments are applied systematically.
d Depreciations are based on the prudence principle; impairments are based on the matching principle.

16.6 A trade company began its activities in 2017. Over the course of that year, the following transactions took place:

1 Jan	Purchased	3,000 unit €5.00 each
9 May	Sold	900 units €7.50 each
12 Oct	Purchased	1,900 units €5.50 each
31 Dec	Sold	1,200 unit €8.50 each

What is the profit over 2017 when applying FIFO?
a €5,850
b €5,600
c €5,450
d €6,450

16.7 Refer to questions 16.6. What is the value of the inventory on 31 December 2017 when applying WAC?
a €14,665
b €14,875
c €15,925
d €16,225

16.8 The balance sheet on 31 December 2016 shows trade inventory with a total value of €10,000, consisting of 1,000 units, purchased at €10 each at the end of December 2016.
In 2017, the following transactions occur:

15 Feb	Sold	500 units €15.00 each
18 Jun	Purchased	900 units €8.00 each
3 Oct	Sold	300 units €14.00 each
30 Dec	Purchased	600 units €6.50 each

The estimated net return value of the inventory per 31 December 2017 is €6.00 per unit.
What is the profit over 2017 when applying FIFO?
a €800
b €2,200
c €3,700
d €3,950

16.9 A construction company has spent €2 million in 2016 on costs for a project; it is expected that this work will generate €4 million and €2 million in costs in 2017 and 2018 respectively. Upon the handover of the project in 2018, the contract sum of €9 million is to be received. The construction company applies the percentage of completion method.
Which amount is recognized on the balance sheet at the end of 2016 for the work in progress?
a €1,000,000
b €2,000,000
c €2,250,000
d €3,000,000

16.10   Refer to question 16.9.
The work progresses as scheduled.
Which statement is correct?
a In 2018, the profit based on the percentage of completion will be €250,000 lower than it would have been based on the completed contract method.
b In 2018, the profit based on the percentage of completion will be €750,000 lower than it would have been based on the completed contract method.
c In 2018, the profit based on the percentage of completion will be €250,000 higher than it would have been based on the completed contract method.
d In 2018, the profit based on the percentage of completion will be €750,000 higher than it would have been based on the completed contract method.

16.11   In April 2017, the *Allegro* PLC purchased 10,000 shares in the Indexmix investment fund at €11 per share. In June, €0.40 of dividend is distributed per share. At the end of 2017, the market value is €11.70. In February 2018, the PLC sells their shares at €12.20 each.
Allegro values their securities at market value.
What is the investment result on 2017 and on 2018?
a On 2017: €7,000; on 2018: zero.
b On 2017: €11,000; on 2018: €12,000
c On 2017: €11,000; on 2018 €5,000
d On 2017: zero; on 2018: €5,000

16.12   Which of the following is *not* recognized in the income statement?
a A flooding which causes a company to suffer €1,000,000 in damages.
b An issue of shares earns a company €2,000,000.
c A visit from the labor inspectorates results in a €100,000 fine for a company.
d A restructuring provision of €500,000 is recognized.

16.13   Which of the following provisions is *not* permitted?
a A provision for guarantees by a manufacturer of household electronics.
b A provision for damage claims issued by customers.
c A provision for pension obligations of the director/main shareholder of a company.
d A provision for the costs of the construction of an additional warehouse due to company expansions.

16.14   Which item is *not* found on a categorical income statement?
a Depreciation costs.
b Finance expense.
c Sales costs.
d Net revenue.

16.15   Which costs are not subtracted when calculating added value?
a Paid interest.
b Accountant fees.
c Office paper usage.
d Fuel costs for representatives.

17

Cash Flow Statement

17.1   **Function and Status**
17.2   **Deriving the Cash Flow Statement from the Financial Statements**

The cash flow statement provides an overview of the origin and spending of cash resources. Along with the balance sheet and income statement, it is the third basic overview of external reporting. Paragraph 17.1 discusses the legislation with respect to the cash flow statement and to the informative value of incorporating the cash flow statement into the financial statements. Paragraph 17.2 uses an example to show how the cash flow statement can be derived from balance sheet, income statement and the notes to both.

17.1 Function and Status

Chapter 15 discussed the financial statements, which comprise the balance sheet, the income statement and the notes to these statements.
Companies often add a third financial overview to these two statements in the annual report: the cash flow statement. This statement shows where the company received cash from, and how that cash was spent. Under the IFRS, incorporating the cash flow statement is obligatory. Dutch legislation does not have this obligation. If the cash flow statement is included, it is part of the audit.
Compared to the income statement, the cash flow statement has the advantage of using objective measurements which are not susceptible to manipulation: cash inflows and cash outflows. The outcome of the cash flow statement, the increase or decrease in cash and cash equivalents over a period, is a hard fact.
The income statement, however, consists of a confrontation of revenue and costs. Paragraphs 3.2 and 15.2 discussed the fact that revenues and costs must to be allocated to a certain period. For the allocation of revenues, the realization principle applies; for the allocation of costs the matching principle applies. In the allocation process, certain assumptions and estimates have to be made. This makes the outcome of the income statement, profit, a subjective measurement unit.

EXAMPLE 17.1
Early 2017, a company invests €10 million in a production line.
The resulting cash flow in 2017 is a cash outflow of €10 million.
The expenses allocated to the income statement in that year depend on the estimated economic life and residual value, and the choice for a particular depreciation method.
By estimating the economic life at 10 years, estimating the residual value at €2 million, choosing linear depreciation, the costs in 2017 are €800,000. Using a different estimate, the economic life and/or the residual value, and by applying another depreciation system, the costs would be different.

As mentioned elsewhere: 'Cash is fact, profit is an opinion.'
Of course, the cash flow statement does not replace the income statement. The success of the company cannot be simply derived from an increase in cash flow.

TEST QUESTION 17.1
In 2017, a company experiences a cash flow increase of €100,000; in 2018, it experiences a cash flow decrease of €50,000. Based on this information, can the company be concluded to have performed worse in 2018?

The cash flow statement can be divided in various ways.
A frequently used method of categorizing uses the following activities:
- *Operational activities*: includes cash consequences of daily production and sales processes.

- *Investing activities*: includes purchase and disposal of production factors.
- *Financing activities*: includes financing transactions, such as initial offering of shares, attracting or repaying loans.
  Financing, directly resulting from the business process, such as suppliers' credit, is taken into account in the cash flow of operational activities.

It should be noted that 'cash flow statement' and 'cash transaction' refer to cash and cash equivalents not only in the form of hard currency, but also in the forms of current accounts and short-term assets that can be converted to cash on short notice, such as bank deposits.
In principle, it is possible for the user of an annual report to compile a cash flow statement by using the information contained in the balance sheet and the income statement (including the notes). The cash flow statement does therefore not provide any new information; it merely organizes given information in a different manner.

The cash flow statement can be compiled in two ways, using either the direct or the indirect method. The difference between these methods is only related to cash flow from operating activities. The *direct method* shows which amounts are received from sales of goods and services and which are paid to suppliers, employees, etc. It is, in fact, a summary of the cash book. The *indirect method* takes company profit for the year as a starting point and then makes adjustments for the items that affect profit but not cash flow. Normally, the most important item is depreciation, which reduces profit but does not involve payments. It is for this reason that, under the indirect method, depreciation appears as a positive item on the cash flow statement. Changes in net working capital also generate discrepancies between profit and cash flow: an increase in, for example, the accounts receivable implies that there has been revenue (and therefore profit) without a resulting cash inflow. Companies are free to choose either method; the most frequently used is the indirect method.

Direct method

Indirect method

NOTES TO THE CONSOLIDATES STATEMENT OF CASH FLOWS
The net cash flow of 2016 is negative. The key developments with respect to cash flows in 2016 are:
- The cash flow from operating activities increases mainly due to a higher net result and the increase in operating capital following the acquisition of Palm N.V. The changes in working capital have been adjusted for the relevant items from the acquisition balance sheets of the acquired group companies.
- The cash flow from investment activities increased because of larger investments and acquisitions. This only concerns the portion of the purchasing price paid in 2016.
- On balance the cash flow from financing activities is negative. On balance, the dividend payments and repayments exceed the received financing and capital contributions. To increase transparency here, the long-term debt has been split into receipts and repayments.

In the preparation of the statement of cash flows, account was taken of changes that do not involve cash flows, including:
- The change in accounts payable to suppliers and trade creditors has been adjusted for the outstanding investment invoices at year-end.

- The change in working capital from other receivables and debts concerns the total changes in receivables and current liabilities category on the balance sheet, excluding trade receivables, creditors (shown separately) and credit institutions and the current portion of the long-term debts (shown in cash flow from financing activities).
- The investments have been adjusted for the outstanding investment invoices to provide insight into the cash flow from investing activities.

Source: Swinkels Family Breweries, Annual account 2016

17.2 Deriving the Cash Flow Statement from the Financial Statements

The compiling of the cash flow statement by using other data in the annual report is discussed in example 17.2.

EXAMPLE 17.2

Tradex PLC has included the following information in its financial statements over 2017:

Balance sheet 31 December (× €1 million)

	2017	2016		2017	2016
Buildings	202	183	Share capital	70	50
Equipment	78	66	Share premium	60	50
Inventory	120	80	Retained profit	45	40
Accounts receivable	23	41	Profit financial year	32	20
Cash and cash equivalents	32	60	Provisions lawsuit	10	–
			Mortgage loan	170	220
			Creditors	60	45
			Tax payable	8	5
	455	430		455	430

Income statement 2017 (× €1 million)

Revenue		698
Profit on inventory sold		2
		700
Cost of goods sold	500	
Depreciation on buildings	6	
Depreciation on equipment	14	
Employee benefits	80	
Other expenses	49	
		649
Operating result		51
Financial expenses		11
Profit before tax		40
Income tax		8
Profit		32

Statement of changes in fixed assets (× €1 million)

	Buildings	Equipment
Book value 1 Jan 2017	183	66
Investments	25 +	31 +
Divestments	0 –	5 –
Depreciation	6 –	14 –
Book value 31 Dec 2017	202	78

Statement of changes in equity (× €1 million)

	Share capital	Share premium	Retained profit	Profit financial year
Book value 1 Jan 2017	50	50	40	20
Profit distribution 2016			5 +	20 –
Shares issue	20 +	10 +		
Profit 2017				32 +
Book value 31 Dec 2017	70	60	45	32

Based on this data, the following cash flow statement can be drawn up using the *direct method:*

Cash flow statement 2017 based on direct method (× €1 million)

Received from customers	716 +	
Payments to suppliers	525 –	
Payments to employees	80 –	
Other costs paid	39 –	
Interest paid	11 –	
Corporate tax paid	5 –	
Cash flow from operational activities		56 +
Investments in fixed assets	56 –	
Divestment of fixed assets	7 +	
Cash flow from investing activities		49 –
Shares issue	30 +	
Repayment mortgage loan	50 –	
Dividend paid	15 –	
Cash flow from financing		35 –
Change in cash and cash equivalents		28 –

The items on the cash flow statement are derived as follows:

Received from customers
The sales revenue was €698 million; however, this amount, which is recognized on the income statement as revenue, is not equal to the amount of cash inflow through sales. Sales revenue is recognized on the income statement at the moment that sold goods are delivered; cash

17

inflows occur at the moment the customer pays. An amount of €23 million in sales had not yet been received by the end of 2017 (see accounts receivable on the balance sheet of 31 December 2018). On the other hand, an amount of €41 million was received for sales that took place in 2016 (see accounts receivable on the balance sheet of 31 December 2016). The amount received in 2017 is therefore:

Sales revenue	€ 698 million
Closing balance of accounts receivable	€ 23 million −
Opening balance accounts receivable	€ 41 million +
	€ 716 million

Payments to suppliers

The cost of goods sold was €500 million. This amount is used to calculate the purchase amount for 2017. At the end of 2017, there is an inventory of €120 million. At beginning of 2017, the inventory was at €80 million.

Cost of sales	€ 500 million
Closing inventory	€ 120 million +
Opening inventory	€ 80 million −
Purchases	€ 540 million

Consecutively, the balance sheet entry 'Creditors' is used to determine how much was paid to suppliers in 2017:

Purchases	€ 540 million
Closing balance creditors	€ 60 million −
Opening balance creditors	€ 45 million +
	€ 525 million

Payments to employees

The amount paid is equal to the amount registered on the income statement as labor costs.

Other costs paid

Other costs were €49 million. However, this amount includes an addition of €10 million to the provision for a lawsuit. This amount is included in the costs but has not yet been paid. Therefore, paid costs were €39 million.

Interest paid

The amount paid is equal to the amount registered on the income statement as expenses.

Income tax paid

In 2017, income tax over 2016 was paid.

Investments in fixed assets

These amounts are taken directly from the statement of changes in fixed assets.

Divestments of fixed assets
The statement of changes in fixed assets includes €5 million in divestments.
This amount is based on the book value of the assets sold. The income statement includes an amount of €2 million as the book profit of asset sales.
The divestment has therefore generated €7 million.

Shares issue
The amount paid by the shareholders consists of an increase in share capital and share premium as mentioned in the statement of changes in equity.

Repayment of mortgage loan
The reduction of the mortgage loan is equal to the repayment of the principal sum.

Dividend paid
Profit after tax over 2016 was €20 million. According to the statement of changes in equity, €5 million was added to retained earnings. The remainder of €15 million was paid out.

If, on 1 January, a transport company signs a financial lease contract for a truck with a catalog value of €150,000, the truck will appear on the balance sheet for €150,000. The debt to the leasing company, conversely, is also €150,000.
It would be imaginable for the category of *Cash flow from investment activities* on the cash flow statement to mention a cash outflow of €150,000 and for the category *Cash flow from financing activities* to mention a cash inflow of €150,000. However, this would not be correct: as the contract does not result in a payment, there cannot be an entry on the cash flow statement.

Suppose that the lease agreement is for eight years (estimated economic life of the truck) and that on 31 December the first term of the lease contract – an amount of €30,000 – is paid. The effective interest is approximately 12%. The interest portion during the term is therefore 12%

of 150,000 = €18,000, and redemption is €12,000. On the cash flow statement, a cash outflow of €18,000 is entered under *Cash flow from operational activities*; a cash outflow of €12,000 is entered under *Cash flow from financing activities*.

EXAMPLE 17.2 CONTINUED

The example continues with the cash flow from operational activities from example 17.2, but based on the indirect method. For cash flow from investment activities and financing activities, there is no difference between the direct and indirect method.

Cash flow from operational activities based on the indirect method (× €1 million)

Profit		30 +
Adjustments to profit to arrive at cash flow:		
Depreciation		20 +
Addition to provision		10 +
Transactions net working capital:		
Increase in inventory	40 –	
Decrease in accounts receivable	18 +	
Increase in accounts payable	15 +	
Increase in tax payable	3 +	
		4 –
		56 +

Explanation

The starting point is a *profit* of €30 million. Although the income statement shows a profit of €32 million, €2 million is a book profit on an asset sale. This amount had already been included in the cash flow from investment activities.

Depreciation is a cost charged to profit, but it does not generate cash outflows. To derive cash flow from profit, depreciation must be added to profit (see also paragraph 5.2). The same applies for the addition to provisions: a cost but not a cash outflow.

The changes in working capital also require an adjustment. Accounts receivable, for example, are included in sales revenue in the income statement, but there is no cash inflow. An increase of the accounts receivable therefore results in a negative adjustment of profit to arrive at a cash flow statement. For the creditors, the reverse applies.

TEST QUESTION 17.2

The following is a consolidated cash flow statement.
By which amount did the book value of the tangible and intangible fixed assets change in 2016, assuming that divestments took place at book value?

Consolidated cash flow statement

in thousand €	2016	2015
Cash flow from operating activities		
Operating profit	**26,035**	30,699
Interest paid	**(148)**	(51)
Income tax paid	**(7,838)**	(4,443)
Depreciation and amortization	**11,168**	9,825
Costs share-based compensation	**301**	192
Movements in:		
– Inventories	**(2,457)**	(4,445)
– Receivables	**(4,345)**	(1,104)
– Provisions	**(340)**	(713)
– Current liabilities	**11,800**	5,857
– Other	**(131)**	192
	34,045	36,009
Cash flow from investing activities		
Additions to (in)tangible assets	**(16,534)**	(15,496)
Acquisitions	**(3,287)**	–
Disposals of (in)tangible assets	**325**	591
Changes in long-term accounts receivable	**(265)**	(124)
	(19,761)	(15,496)
Cash flow from financing activities		
Share (re)issuance	**–**	803
Dividend paid	**(18,004)**	(16,687)
	(18,004)	(15,884)
Change in net cash and cash equivalents	**(3,720)**	4,629
Net cash and cash equivalents at the beginning of the financial year	**25,512**	20,883
Net cash and cash equivalents at the end of the financial year	**21,792**	25,512

Source: Beter Bed, annual account 2016

17

Glossary

17

Cash and cash equivalents	All resources that can be changed into currency in the short term, such as cash, positive balance on a current account, deposits and short-term investments.
Cash flow from financing activities	Cash flow deriving from financing transactions that are not the result of daily production and sales processes.
Cash flow from investment activities	Cash flow generated by the purchasing or disposal of production factors.
Cash flow from operating activities	Cash flow generated by daily production and sales processes.
Cash flow statement	Overview of all available cash and cash equivalents that became available during a period and the manner in which they have been used.
Direct method	Presentation of the cash flow statement from operational activities as a summary of the cashbook.
Indirect method	Presentation of the cash flow statement from operational activities derived from the income statement.

Multiple-choice questions

17.1   Which of the following statements is *not* correct?
  a The cash flow statement is subject to an accountant's audit.
  b Companies can determine whether they use the direct or indirect method for the cash flow statement.
  c A cash flow statement offers 'harder' information than the income statement.
  d Under Dutch legislation, it is obligatory to incorporate a cash flow statement in the financial statements.

17.2   Which of the following items can *never* be part of the cash resources in the cash flow statement?
  a Accounts receivable.
  b Securities.
  c Cash and cash equivalents.
  d Positive balance on current account.

17.3   Which statement is correct?
  a The cash flow statement based on the indirect method differs from that of the direct method only with respect to cash flow from operational activities.
  b The cash resources in a cash flow statement comprise the hard cash that is available in the company.
  c The income tax paid is a component of the cash flow statement from financing activities.
  d Divestments are considered as cash inflows at their book value.

17.4   Which event results in a cash flow from operational activities?
  a Payment of the interest on a bank loan.
  b Repayment of a bank loan.
  c Book profit from selling a machine.
  d Purchase of inventory on credit.

17.5   Which event results in a booking of a cash flow from financing activities?
  a Payment of income tax.
  b Payment of a creditor.
  c Payment of dividend.
  d Payment of an account receivable by a customer.

17.6   What is shown as a negative item in the cash flow statement from operational activities if the indirect method is applied?
  a An increase of the creditors over the period.
  b An increase of the accounts receivable over the period.
  c An increase of the fixed assets over the period.
  d A decrease of the inventories over the period.

17.7   In 2017, a company creates a provision of €5,000,000 intended for
reorganization.
Which consequences does this have for the *cash flow from operational
activities* category of the cash flow statement over 2018 when the indirect
method is used?
a None.
b *Profit* negative €5,000,000.
   Adjustments to come from profit to cash flow: positive €5,000,000.
c *Profit* positive €5,000,000.
   Adjustments to come from profit to cash flow: negative €5,000,000.
d *Profit* negative €5,000,000.
   Adjustments to come from profit to cash flow: negative €5,000,000.

17.8   Refer to question 17.7.
In 2019, the reorganization is executed. It requires a payment of €4,500,000.
Which consequences does this have for the category *cash flow from
operational activities* on the cash flow statement over 2019 according to the
indirect method?
a None.
b *Profit* positive €4,500,000.
   Adjustments to come from profit to cash flow: negative €500,000.
c *Profit* positive €5,000,000.
   Adjustments to come from profit to cash flow: negative €4,500,000.
d *Profit* positive €500,000.
   Adjustments to come from profit to cash flow: negative €5,000,000.

17.9   At the end of 2018, the balance sheet of Pecunia LLC is as follows (the
comparative figures at the end of 2017 in brackets; all amounts × €1,000):

Fixed assets	750	(600)	Share capital	100	(80)
Inventories	320	(400)	Share premium	300	(100)
Accounts receivable	245	(190)	Retained earnings	870	(840)
Cash and cash equivalents	100	(80)	Profit financial year	60	(40)
			Creditors	70	(200)
			Tax payable	15	(10)
	1,415	(1,270)		1,415	(1,270)

Income statement over 2018 (× €1,000)

Sales revenue	15,000
Cost of goods sold	7,945 –
Depreciation	100 –
Other expenses	6,880 –
Profit before tax	75
Income tax	15 –
Profit	60

Which amount should be included for *cash inflows from customers* on the cash flow statement over 2018 when using the direct method?

a €14,810,000
b €14,945,000
c €15,000,000
d €15,190,000

17.10 Refer to question 17.9.
Which amount should be included on the cash flow statement over 2018 according to the direct method for *payments to creditors and employees?*

a €7,865,000
b €7,945,000
c €7,975,000
d €7,995,000

17.11 Refer to question 17.9.
Which amount should be included as adjustment item *transactions net working capital* when applying the indirect method?

a €100,000 –
b €95,000 –
c €160,000 +
d €215,000 +

17.12 Refer to question 17.9.
What is the cash flow from operational activities?

a €60,000 +
b €75,000 +
c €135,000 +
d €140,000 +

17.13 Refer to question 17.9.
What is the cash flow from investment activities?

a €250,000 –
b €150,000 –
c €150,000 +
d €250,000 +

17.14 Refer to question 17.9.
What is included as *dividend paid* in the cash flow from financing activities?

a €0
b €10,000
c €30,000
d €40,000

17.15 Refer to question 17.9.
What is the cash flow from financing activities?

a €10,000 +
b €120,000 +
c €210,000 +
d €220,000 +

17

18

Group Accounting

18.1   Equity Investments
18.2   Consolidation

A company acquiring shares in another company results in two points of attention with respect to external reporting.
Firstly, the shares must be recognized on the buyer's balance sheet. They must be categorized and valued in the correct manner, taking into account the importance of whether the acquisition concerns an associate or a financial asset. This subject is discussed in paragraph 18.1. If there is 'controlling interest' as a consequence of the shareholding, a group is formed, consisting of the holding company and one or more subsidiaries. As such, the holding has to publish consolidated financial statements as well as its own financial statements.
The consolidated financial statements do not reflect on each separate LLC or PLC but on the total group. The technique of consolidation as well as legislation on the subject are discussed in paragraph 18.2.

18.1 Equity Investments

Companies often hold shares in other companies. There can be various reasons for holding this kind of capital interest. It is possible for shares to only be held in order to receive returns on excess cash. Accordingly, the activities of the company whose shares were bought are irrelevant so long as the expected dividend and/or capital gains are achieved. Only the *stand-alone* value of the company in which the capital interest is held is important. In this case the shares are known as a *financial asset*.

It is also possible for shares to be held because the buyer of the shares expects advantages for his own business activities. In such cases, companies endeavor to achieve a synergy effect by way of for a connection between their own business activities and those of the company in which they take a capital interest; that company then becomes an *associate* of the buyer of the shares.

EXAMPLE 18.1

The cash position of company A is good. Company A anticipates paying a substantial amount of corporate tax within three months. A decides to invest the cash available during that period in shares in stock exchange listed company B PLC.

Company C, a temporary employment agency, buys shares in D, which specializes in company training, to secure training for its temporary staff.

The shares in B held by A are a financial asset; the shares in D held by C are an associate.

In general, the share packages bought for mere dividend or capital gain are relatively small. On the other hand, companies buy a relatively large interest if they are looking for advantages for their own business activities since, without fairly large control, this is difficult to achieve.

Relevant legislation draws the line at 20% of shares owned. An interest of less than 20% is considered a *financial asset*. If the interest is 20% or more, it is considered an *associate*.

The valuation of financial assets was previously discussed in paragraph 16.3. Associates are valued in accordance with the equity method, which uses the net-asset value as valuation base: the value of the associate's underlying assets and liabilities. If, in the acquisition of the shares, the amount paid is greater than the balance value of those assets and liabilities, the difference is known as *goodwill*. Goodwill is a form of excess value that is not recorded on the balance sheet of an associate. This value consists of factors such as reputation, a beneficial location or an established customer base.

Goodwill

Goodwill is separately recognized by the participant (under intangible fixed assets) and depreciated according to its expected economic lifespan.

EXAMPLE 18.2

The balance sheet on 31 December 2017 of Retailer LLC, including comparative figures for 31 December 2016, is shown below:

Balance sheet Retailer LLC (× €1,000)

	2017	2016		2017	2016
Building	4,500	5,000	Share capital	1,000	1,000
Inventory	4,200	3,700	Retained profit	3,800	4,000
Cash and cash			Profit for the year	1,800	0
equivalents	1,300	300	Liabilities	3,400	4,000
	10,000	9,000		10,000	9,000

Early in January 2017, Wholesaler LLC buys 40% shares in Retailer in order to acquire a new distribution channel for its products. The purchase price of the shares is €2,500,000.

In the course of 2017, Retailer pays €200,000 interim dividend.

The net asset value is the intrinsic value of the participation, the value of equity.

At the beginning of 2017, Retailer's equity is €5,000,000. Based on 40% of shares owned by Wholesaler, the participation in Retailer is recognized for 40% of €5,000,000 = €2,000,000. Nevertheless, Wholesaler paid €2,500,000. Assuming that the balance sheet of Retailer is a fair representation of the value of the assets and liabilities, the amount of €500,000 – paid on top of the intrinsic value – is due to the existence of goodwill.

At the beginning of 2017, the changes on Wholesaler's balance sheet are as follows:

(× €1,000)

Intangible fixed assets	
Goodwill	500 +
Financial fixed assets	
Associate	2,000 +
Cash and cash equivalents	2,500 –

At the end of 2017, the net asset value of Retailer is €6,600,000; the valuation of the participation on the balance sheet of Wholesaler is 40% of €6,600,000 = €2,640,000.

Assuming that Wholesaler depreciates goodwill over a period of 20 years, the remaining book value at the end of 2017 is €475,000.

The changes on Wholesaler's balance sheet (compared to the situation immediately after the purchase) are:

(× €1,000)

Intangible fixed assets		Profit	695 +
Goodwill	25 –		
Financial fixed assets			
Associate	640 +		
Cash and cash equivalents	80 +		

The profit of €695,000 is recognized on Wholesaler's income statement as follows:

(× €1,000)	
Depreciation of goodwill	25 −
Share of profit from associate	720 +
	695

When using the equity method, the participant always shows an amount of profit due to its interest in the associate equal to a proportional share of the profit made by that associate. The proportional share is equal to the percentage of participation. When using the equity method, dividend payment by the associate does not affect the participant's profit. If dividend is paid by the associate, the cash and cash equivalents of the participant increases, but the book value of the associate decreases by an equal amount.

EXAMPLE 18.2 CONTINUED

The result from the associate is €720,000, which is 40% of the €1,800,000 in profit incurred by Retailer over 2017.

If Retailer distributes dividend of €1,000,000 in 2018, it would cause the following changes on Wholesaler's balance sheet:

(× €1,000)		
Participation	400 +	
Cash and cash equivalents	400 −	

The previous use of the equity method is in accordance with Dutch legislation. IFRS states that goodwill should not be documented on the balance sheet separately but should instead be combined with the valuation of the associate. According to IFRS, goodwill does not depreciate systematically, but is reviewed yearly – paying particular attention to the question of whether the realisable value is still at least equal to the book value. If this is not the case, the company should apply an impairment.

18.2 Consolidation

If participation exceeds 50%, the participant establishes control over the company in which it holds shares. Equity investments of more than 50% are called *subsidiaries*, and result in the forming of a group. The term *associate* is limited to equity investments between 20% and 50%. Group forming is not reserved for large companies; it also occurs on a smaller scale. Nowadays, for fiscal and legal reasons, several LLCs are founded when setting up a company: a parent company, controlling 100% subsidiaries such as an working company, a pension LLC and possibly a real estate LLC which owns the business premises. If there is a group relationship, the parent company has extensive disclosure obligations. In this situation, consolidated financial statements have to

Consolidated financial statements

be included in the annual report. These reflect the financial position of all companies that are part of the group as if they were all the same company. The parent company's annual report therefore includes two financial statements: separate financial statements of the parent company and consolidated financial statements of the group as a whole.

Sky PLC (with main offices in London, Munich and Milan) is a holding that heads dozens of subsidiaries established in various countries, including the UK, Germany, Italy, the USA, Austria and Australia. Sky offers pay-per-view, broadband and telephone connections. Approximately 10 million households make use of Sky's services. Sky's consolidated annual report over 2016 recognized a revenue of £12 billion, which comes to approximately €14 billion.
One of Sky's group member companies is Tour Racing Limited, which houses Sky's cycling team, headed by multiple Tour de France winner, Chris Froome.

If a consolidated financial statement is included, the subsidiaries are exempt from publishing their own (separate) financial statements. A condition for this exemption is that the parent company is to be held severally liable for the debts of the subsidiaries.

TEST QUESTION 18.1
Why would this condition have been incorporated in legislation?

The obligation to publish consolidated financial statements does not apply if the group remains within the limits of a 'small company' (see paragraph 15.1).

The starting point for compiling the consolidated financial statements are the separate financial statements of the group members.
In principle, consolidation takes place by compiling the balance sheet items of the *separate financial statements*. However, the entries of the separate financial statements that only concern the intra-group relationships must

Separate financial statements

be eliminated because the reporting entity of the consolidated financial statement is the entire group. Only the relationship between the group and the 'outside world' is shown in the consolidated financial statements.

EXAMPLE 18.3

On 31 December 2017, the separate balance sheets of Enter LLC and Shift LLC are as follows:

Balance sheet Enter LLC on 31 December 2017 (× €1,000)

Intangible fixed assets			Equity		
Goodwill		246	Share capital	300	
			Retained earnings	12,340	
Tangible fixed assets		12,004	Profit	1,280	
					13,920
Financial fixed assets					
Subsidiary		2,120	Current liabilities		3,300
7% loan		1,500			
Current assets					
Accounts receivable	1,090				
Cash and cash equivalents	260				
		1,350			
		17,220			17,220

Balance sheet Shift LLC on 31 December 2017 (× €1,000)

Fixed assets		3,080	Equity		
			Share capital	200	
Current assets			Retained earnings	1,620	
Accounts receivable	590		Profit	300	
Cash and cash equivalents	150				2,120
		740	Non-current liabilities		1,500
			Current liabilities		200
		3,820			3,820

The Enter Institute for Computer Training holds all shares in Shift (a provider of digital photography courses), and uses the equity method for the valuation of the participation.
Throughout 2017, Shift had an outstanding debt of €1.5 million in loans from Enter.

The consolidated balance sheet is drawn up by adding the separate balance sheets to one another. As such, a number of eliminations must be performed to delete the intra-group relationships.

- The balance sheet entry 'Subsidiary' only appears on the separate balance sheet of Enter and cannot appear on the consolidated balance sheet. The share capital and retained earnings of Shift also have to be eliminated. Third parties are not entitled to that equity as all shares are controlled by Enter.

- The loan issued by Enter to Shift is considered a clawback arrangement; the 7% debt therefore has to be removed from Enter's balance sheet and from Shift's long-term liabilities.

When the amounts on the separate balance sheets are totaled and the eliminations have taken place, the result is the following consolidated balance sheet of the Enter/Shift group:

Consolidated balance sheet on 31 December 2017 (× €1,000)

Intangible fixed assets			*Equity*	13,920
Goodwill		246		
			Current liabilities	3,500
Tangible fixed assets		15,084		
Current assets				
Accounts receivable	1,680			
Cash and cash equivalents	410			
		2,090		
		17,420		17,420

On the consolidated balance sheet, equity is not split into share capital and retained earnings. A group is not a legal entity; it has no share capital and cannot pay out retained earnings.
If the subsidiaries are valued in the balance sheet of the parent company by using the equity method, consolidated equity is equal to that of the parent company. Net asset value means that participation is valued on the basis of the underlying equity: the balance between assets and liabilities.
On the consolidated balance sheet, this balance is replaced by the separate assets and the liability entries of the subsidiary.
Consolidated profit must also be equal to the profit of the parent company: when applying the equity method, the participant in a 100% subsidiary assigns the profit of the subsidiary to itself.

Acomo (main office in Rotterdam, the Netherlands) is a trading company specializing in (what is known on local markets as) exotic foodstuffs. The group consists of 28 subsidiaries, each focusing on a different specialty: spices, coconuts, tropical fruits, sunflower seeds, nuts, tea.

With the exception of the main office, the subsidiaries are all located in the most important harvesting zones, such as the USA, Kenya, Sri Lanka and Indonesia. Its 2016 consolidated annual report recognized a revenue of €682 million.

EXAMPLE 18.3 CONTINUED

Next, the consolidated income statement for the Enter/Shift group is drawn up.

First, the separate income statements over 2017:

Income statement Enter LLC over 2017 (× €1,000)	
Sales revenue	31,550
Labor expenses	22,570
Depreciation	1,540
Other expenses	6,305
Operating result	1,135
Benefits	105+
Share of profit in associate	300+
Profit before tax	1,540
Tax	260
Profit	1,280

Income statement Shift LLC over 2017 (× €1,000)	
Sales revenue	12,780
Labor expenses	5,845
Depreciation	460
Other expenses	5,995
Operating result	480
Financial expenses	105
Profit before tax	375
Tax	75
Profit	300

In compiling the consolidated income statement, the following eliminations must be performed:
- 'Profit participation' should *not* appear on the consolidated income statement, as it concerns an intra-group relationship.
- In both 'Financial revenue' and 'Financial costs', the interest on the loan from Enter to Shift should be removed. The amount concerned is 7% of €1,500,000 = €105,000.

Consolidated income statement over 2017 (× €1,000)

Sales revenue		44,330
Labor expenses	28,415	
Depreciation	2,000	
Other expenses	12,300	
		42,715
Operating result		1,615
Tax		335
Profit		1,280

Complication: controlling interest below 100%

If there is a controlling interest of less than 100% (but, by definition, of more than 50%), there are two ways to draw up the consolidated balance sheet.

The first option is *proportional consolidation.* Using this method, the assets and liabilities of the subsidiary are registered as a percentage (corresponding with the interest of the parent company in that subsidiary) of the book value for the balance sheet entries concerned.

Proportional consolidation

EXAMPLE 18.4

On 31 December 2017, the balance sheet of High LLC is:

Balance sheet High LLC on 31 December 2017 (× €1,000)

Tangible fixed assets	10,000	Share capital	1,000
Financial fixed assets	3,000	Retained profit	5,000
Current assets	2,000	Liabilities	9,000
	15,000		15,000

The financial fixed assets consist of a 60% interest in Low LLC, whose balance sheet on 31 December 2017 is:

Balance sheet Low LLC on 31 December 2017 (× €1,000)

Tangible fixed assets	5,000	Share capital	1,000
Current assets	2,000	Retained profit	4,000
		Liabilities	2,000
	7,000		7,000

In proportional consolidation, the assets and liabilities of Low LLC are registered on the consolidated balance sheet at 60%.

Consolidated balance sheet High/Low group using proportional consolidation (× €1,000)

Tangible fixed assets (10,000 + 3,000)	13,000	Equity	6,000
Current assets (2,000 + 1,200)	3,200	Liabilities (9,000 + 1,200)	10,200
	16,200		16,200

Proportional consolidation does not accurately reflect the financial position of a group: it makes it appear as though 'external' shareholders claim a proportional share of the assets of the subsidiary and are obliged to pay a proportional part of its debts. That is not the case. In the case of an interest greater than 50%, the parent company maintains full control over the subsidiary. The non-group shareholders would only be able to claim 40% of the equity if Low LLC were to be discontinued.

Therefore, *full consolidation* should be applied, which provides a better representation of reality: the assets and debts of the subsidiary are recognized on the consolidated balance sheet at 100%. The entitlement of the minority shareholders with regard to equity is recognized on the consolidated balance sheet as a *noncontrolling interest.*

Full consolidation

Noncontrolling interest

Consolidated balance sheet High/Low group using full consolidation (× €1,000)

Tangible fixed assets		Equity	6,000
(10,000 + 5,000)	15,000	Noncontrolling interest	2,000
Current assets		Liabilities	
(2,000 + 2,000)	4,000	(9,000 + 2,000)	11,000
	19,000		19,000

Should Low be discontinued, the non-group shareholders would be entitled to 40% of the equity of Low LLC: 40% of €5,000,000 = €2,000,000.

TEST QUESTION 18.2
Should a minority interest be considered a debt?

CONSOLIDATION
The consolidated accounts comprise the financial information of TBI Holdings B.V., the group companies in which TBI Holdings B.V. holds more than 50% of the voting capital or in which TBI Holdings B.V., by virtue of supplementary rules, exercises power of control over the management and financial policy, and other legal entities over which TBI Holdings B.V. can exercise power of control or central management. In general, these are participating interests of more than 50%. The assets and liabilities and results of these companies are consolidated in full. Minority interests in group equity and group profit or loss are shown separately.

Source: TBI, Annual account 2016

A similar procedure is followed when drawing up the consolidated income statement. The sales revenue and the costs of the subsidiary are initially included at 100%. External shareholders can, however, claim part of the profit. This claim is recognized on the consolidated income statement as Profit attributable to noncontrolling interest.

Glossary

Associate	Capital interest (between 20% and 50%) that is held to benefit one's own business activities.
Consolidated financial statements	Financial statements, presenting the financial position of all companies that are part of a group as if they were one company.
Equity method	Valuation method for associates and subsidiaries that is based on asset value.
Full consolidation	Method in which assets and liabilities, revenues and costs are recognized in the consolidated financial statements for 100%.
Goodwill	The difference between purchase price and net asset value of an associate or subsidiary.
Group	Group of companies controlled by a parent company.
Noncontrolling interest	The claim of non-group shareholders on the equity of a subsidiary.
Parent company	Company that owns the majority of shares in one or more other companies.
Profit attributable to noncontrolling interest	The claim of non-group shareholders on the profit of a subsidiary.
Proportional consolidation	Method in which assets and liabilities, revenues and costs are recognized in the consolidated financial statements in proportion with the participation percentage of the parent company.
Separate financial statements	Separate financial statements of a company within a group.
Subsidiary	Company of which the majority of the shares are held by another company.

18

Multiple-choice questions

18.1 Building company Cavwall holds shares in a number of companies. Which capital interest is a financial asset?
a A 30% interest in the building materials wholesale trade.
b A 70% interest in a plumbing company.
c A 40% interest in a building advisory agency.
d A 5% interest in a publishing company.

18.2 The balance sheet of company A on 1 January 2017 is as follows:

Fixed assets	€1,000,000	Share capital	€ 200,000
Current assets	€ 500,000	Retained earnings	€ 700,000
		Liabilities	€ 600,000
	€1,500,000		€1,500,000

On 1 January 2017, 40% of the shares in A are acquired by B at €500,000.

What is the book value of this associate in B's balance sheet on 1 January 2017?
a €360,000
b €440,000
c €500,000
d €560,000

18.3 Refer to 18.2.
Company A incurs a profit of €400,000 over 2017.
What amount in profit does company B recognize on its income statement as profit from its associate in A (excluding depreciation on goodwill)?
a €70,000
b €100,000
c €160,000
d €170,000

18.4 Company H LLC has an interest of 45% in company J LLC. On company H's balance sheet on 1 January 2017, company J is valued at €14.7 million. Over 2017, company J earns a profit of €3.2 million, pays its shareholders €1.1 million in dividend.
What is the value of J on H's balance sheet on 31 December 2017?
a €15,645,000
b €16,800,000
c €17,100,000
d €17,900,000

18.5 What participation percentage generally implies a subsidiary?
a Over 10%
b Over 20%
c Over 50%
d 100%

18.6 Company C LLC acquires all shares in company D LLC on 1 April 2017. The acquisition price is €8 million. On 31 March 2017, the balance sheets are as follows:

Balance sheet C (× €1,000)

Fixed assets	2,860	Share capital	500
Loan D	3,200	Retained earnings	12,010
Inventory	1,600	Long-term liabilities	7,570
Cash and cash equivalents	12,420		
	20,080		20,080

Balance sheet D (× €1,000)

Fixed assets	12,540	Share capital	200
Inventory	3,220	Retained earnings	6,600
Cash and cash equivalents	1,230	Long-term liabilities	10,190
	16,990		16,990

What is the balance sheet total of the consolidated balance sheet on 1 April 2017?
a €12,080,000
b €27,070,000
c €29,070,000
d €37,070,000

18.7 Company R LLC holds 70% of the shares in company S.
Which statement is correct with respect to the consolidated balance sheet?
a Under proportional consolidation, the balance sheet total is higher than in full consolidation.
b Under proportional consolidation, there will be a balance sheet entry 'Non-controlling interest'.
c Under proportional consolidation, equity is equal to that of full consolidation.
d Under proportional consolidation, fixed assets are valued higher than in full consolidation.

18.8 Which equality applies if group member companies are valued in accordance with the equity method in the parent's separate financial statements?
a The balance sheet total in the parent's balance sheet is equal to that of the consolidated balance sheet?
b The liabilities in the parent's balance sheet are equal to those of the consolidated balance sheet.

18

   c The profit in the parent's balance sheet is equal to that of the consolidated balance sheet.

   d The item 'subsidiaries' in the parent's balance sheet is equal to that in the consolidated balance sheet.

18.9   Company E LLC buys 80% of shares in company F LLC on 1 May 2018. The acquisition price is €1.1 million.
The balance sheet of F on 1 May 2018, is as follows:

Balance sheet LLC F (× €1,000)

Tangible fixed assets	850	Share capital	300
Inventory	520	Retained earnings	700
Cash and cash equivalents	30	Long-term liabilities	400
	1,400		1,400

What is the balance sheet entry 'Non-controlling interest' on the consolidated balance sheet immediately following the takeover?

   a €200,000
   b €220,000
   c €280,000
   d €300,000

18.10   Company T LLC, holds 55% of the shares in Company Q LLC. Over 2017, company Q incurs a profit of €500,000 and pays out €100,000 in dividend. What is the deductible 'Profit attributable to noncontrolling interest' over 2017?

   a €0
   b €180,000
   c €225,000
   d €275,000

Answers to Test Questions

Chapter 1

1.1 Other participants:
- suppliers
- customer
- banks that lend money to the company
- the government, who creates the conditions for companies to operate, and receives a reward in the form of tax revenues

1.2 Total income: $305,208,089
Total expenses: $305,206,256
Positive result: $1,833
A positive result does not mean the WWF performed well. A better indicator for their performance is the percentage of obtained resources the WWF spent in the benefit of their associated charities, here 85%.

1.3 1 Unilever: Unilever has a strongly automated manufacturing process with relatively low personnel costs.
2 Ahold Delhaize: a supermarket which sells products at a low profit margin, due to which its majority of costs comprise the value of purchased goods.
3 ING: a bank is a service-providing company which does not incur any raw materials costs.

1.4

Profit		€ 40,000
Minus: Self-employed tax deduction		€ 7,280
		€ 32,720
Minus: Profit exemption (14%)		€ 4,581
Taxable profit		€ 28,139
Tax		
Bracket 1: 36.55%	€ 7,361	
Bracket 2/3: 40.85%	€ 3,266	
Bracket 4: 51.95%	€ 0	
Total		€ 10,627
Minus: Tax credits:		
General tax credit	€ 1,891	
Labor tax credit	€ 3,002	
		€ 4,893
Payable income tax		€ 5,734

1.5   The members of a cooperative have a strong business relationship with their cooperative; they are either suppliers or customers. Shareholders of a corporation are much less involved in the day-to-day business of their company.

1.6   If large investments need to be made on which value added tax can be reclaimed.

1.7   The gasoline market is an example of an oligopoly; a few large oil companies dominate the market. For washing detergents, the same applies. The pharmaceutical industry and banks also show oligopolistic characteristics.

Chapter 2

2.1   A lower level manager may provide his direct superior with information showing results for the department that are better than those that were actually achieved.

2.2   In marketing and sales it is not wise to obtain orders at all cost.
An order is only attractive if the selling price compensates at least the costs that were involved in the execution of the order. A commercial employee must have sufficient knowledge of the cost structure of the goods and services they are selling.

Chapter 3

3.1   A bank may only offer a loan depending on, for example, the commitment of company management to first consult the bank when making important investment decisions.

3.2   Equity is negative if liability exceed assets. This situation can arise as a consequence of losses. Unless additional equity is found, this leads to bankruptcy of the company.

3.3   Reasons for creative accounting:
• safeguarding bonuses for company management
• keeping shareholders satisfied
• maintaining possibilities for obtaining a new loan

Chapter 4

4.1   Apparently the owner has demanded the rent for the building one year ahead by means of an advance payment. This is why the amount is included in Francine's investment plan. She has to pay €50,000 in advance, which can only be earned back over the course of the year by making sales.

4.2   A repayment of the principal sum does not result in a reduction of equity: though cash and cash equivalents decrease, liabilities do the same. Therefore, a repayment of the principal sum does not worsen the equity position.

Chapter 5

5.1   Replacement investments are particularly important for continuity objectives and expansion investments for profit objectives.

5.2 The method of financing is not known at the time of assessing the investment projects. From cash flows, payments to equity providers have to be made.

5.3 Since the profit achieved through the investment project should be added to the 'regular' profit, the company is required to pay the rate applicable to that extra profit.

5.4 Pre-tax profit during the first year is €50,000 lower, corporate tax is therefore €12,500 lower and profit after tax is €37,500 lower. By re-adding depreciation, the free cash flow becomes €12,500 higher, totaling €337,500. The increase in the free cash flow is equal to the decrease of the corporate tax due result of higher depreciation.

5.5 In calculating period profit, the amounts are sometimes re-allocated in time due to the matching and realization principles.
The purchase of a fixed asset, for example, results in a one-off payment at the time of purchase, whereas depreciation takes place over several years. Over the entire duration of the investment project, this does not show a difference.

5.6 In the third year, €150,000 still has to be received. €400,000 has already been received.
In the third year, therefore:

$$\frac{150,000}{400,000} \times 12 \text{ months} = 4.5 \text{ months required to receive the entire invested amount back.}$$

The payback period is 2 years and 4.5 months.

5.7 A bank pays compound interest on a savings account.

5.8 $$\frac{150}{1.195} + \frac{200}{1.195^2} + \frac{400}{1.195^3} - 500 \approx 0$$

$$\frac{100}{1.211} + \frac{100}{1.211^2} + \frac{100}{1.211^3} + \frac{100}{1.211^4} - 300 \approx 0$$

5.9 Accounting rate of return = 213.33 / 100 × 100% = 175%
The profitability is very high due to the low investment.
Notably, there is no investment in fixed assets.

Chapter 6

6.1 A shortening of the actual term of the accounts receivable results in a shortening of the duration of the additional financing requirement by 15 days. The bank credit is required for 1.5 months. The average bank credit is 1.5 × €10,000 = €15,000.

6.2 None: if the delivery time is longer, the order only needs to be placed earlier.

6.3 No, the safety inventory is ordered once.

6.4 Average inventory/purchase value $\times 365 = 145{,}197 \,/\, 4{,}581{,}341 \times 365 = 11.6$ days.

6.5 In factoring, the invested capital is smaller if the amounts received from the factoring company are used to repay debts. In all other cases, the invested capital is barely influenced.

6.6 Depreciation is not part of cash outflows.

Chapter 7

7.1 Equity = Total assets – Liabilities = $120 - 45 = 75$.

7.2 In a sole proprietorship, there can be no confusion regarding who contributes equity.

7.3 Objective of priority shares: to limit the control of ordinary shareholders.
Objective of preference share: financing of business activities.

7.4 Net asset value is based on the book value of the assets and is of (limited) importance in case of discontinuation of the company.
Capitalized earnings value is based on expected profit of the company and is of interest when determining the market value of the shares.
Market value is based on demand and supply of the share, and is important when selling shares.

7.5 During the purchase of a share on the stock exchange, a corporation receives nothing. At the public offering, the company receives the issue price.

7.6 The company does not receive any payment for the subscription rights, so it does not matter.

7.7 In both options the investor (theoretically) suffers an equal loss.

Chapter 8

8.1 For an investment in bonds, a fixed interest and a fixed maturity date is determined with a pre-determined principal value.

8.2 Mortgage bond: high security.
Subordinated bond: slightly higher coupon interest rate.
Zero or discount bond: low investment amount.
Junk bond: high interest rate.
Convertible bond: option to convert into shares.

8.3 The credit size in the line of credit can be adjusted in line with changing financing requirements.

8.4 The amount of capital is smaller for a bank credit.

8.5 No, since there is no comparable measure, such as the discount for cash payment in the case of trade credit.

8.6 Provisions are a form of liability; retained earnings are a form of equity.

Chapter 9

9.1 The level of the general market interest rate influences the costs of liabilities, and therefore the size of the financial leverage.

9.2 Elasticity requires the use of liabilities which influences the solvency in a negative way.

9.3 Cash flow forecast.

9.4 The current ratio becomes smaller.

Chapter 10

10.1 Not counting savings, a risk averse investor will choose to invest in bonds.

10.2

	A	B
1	Investment	-7,500
2	Return after 1 year	50
3	Return after 2 years	9,000
4	Yield	9.88%

Formula in cell B4: = IR(B2:B4;0,1)

10.3 For a buyer, the maximum loss is limited to the purchase price of the option. In the event of an unfavorable price development in the underlying value, the seller of an option can be forced to deliver or purchase that underlying asset at exercise price.

10.4 The last two objectives concern limitation of risks. In one case, the risk of a sharp fall in the market value of shares results in a lower price for future share sales. In the other case, the risk of a rise in the market value of shares results in a higher price for future share purchases.

10.5 The price-profit ratio is highest for ASML, which also has the lowest interest from dividend and payout ratio. The relatively high share price seems to have been based on an already expected increase in profit. This makes ASML the least attractive.
The other three are grouped together relatively closely in terms of profitability, but with the lowest payout ratio and the lowest price-profit ratio, Akzo Nobel would seem to offer the greatest chances of share price improvements.
Note that this would make Akzo Nobel attractive to companies looking for a takeover – which was confirmed by PPG's 2017 attempt to do just that.

Chapter 11

11.1 Production factors containing natural resources, for example, goldmines, oil fields, quarries, etc.

11.2 Only two levels of output level and their related costs are used; as these production levels are the highest and lowest levels, it is possible that they are not representative due to progressively or degressively variable costs.

11.3 Sales revenue – costs = 0.1 × sales revenue
0.9 × sales revenue = costs
0.9 × (€625 × q) = €250 × q + €4,500,000
€562.5 × q = €250 × q + €4,500,000
€312.5 × q = €4,500,000
q = 14,400

11.4 €7,500,000 / €525 × q
q = 14,286

11.5 A wholesaler and a goldsmith have high variable purchase costs. A tax consultancy has mainly fixed costs as the salaries are an important cost factor. The tax consultancy therefore has the highest leverage effect.

Chapter 12

12.1 Normal output should be above the break-even point, otherwise, long-term expectations are that the company will only incur losses.

12.2 A maximum of €400,000, which is the case if production is at zero.

12.3 For a yearly traveled distance of 21,000 kilometers, the monthly variable costs should be multiplied by 21,000 / 15,000 = 1.4:

Depreciation (based on timeline)		€ 156
Depreciation (based on dist. traveled)	€ 56 × 1.4 =	€ 78.40
Vehicle tax		€ 54
Maintenance (based on timeline)		€ 19
Maintenance (based on dist. traveled)	€ 85 × 1.4 =	€ 119
Fuel	€ 142 × 1.4 =	€ 198.80
Insurance		€ 91
		€ 716.20

The price per kilometer traveled is (12 × €716.20) / 21,000 = €0.41

12.4 Under absorption costing, the volume variances are explicitly shown, which is not the case under direct costing. However, volume variance does not result in a profit difference, as the variance is allocated to the relevant period.

12.5 A degressive depreciation method, such as sum-of-the-year digits, or a fixed percentage of the book value.

Chapter 13

13.1 The allocation of extra costs depends on the cause of the overtime for order D. If all orders have to be completed that week, and D was manufactured during overtime by coincidence, then the additional costs should be allocated to all orders as indirect costs. If overtime only occurred for order D, for example, for a rush order, then extra costs should be allocated as direct costs.

13.2 Unit cost of a 200-gram bar:

$$\frac{€540,000}{(200,000 + 150,000 + 100,000)} = €1.20$$

Unit cost of a 40-gram bar: 40 / 200 × €1.20 = €0.24
Unit cost of a 75-gram bar: 75 / 200 × €1.20 = €0.45

13.3 The unit cost should not depend on exceptionally high or low occasional volumes.

13.4 A price change in the direct costs (for example, fuel costs) does not result in higher indirect costs; using the quantity to determine the markup means that the percentage does not need to be adjusted following price changes in direct costs.

13.5 Markup for indirect costs:

$$\frac{\text{Total indirect costs}}{\text{Total direct costs}} = \frac{€7,950,000}{10,000 \times €215 + 5,000 \times €340} = 206\%$$

	Basicbike	Superbike
Direct costs	€ 215	€ 340
Markup 206%	€422.30	€ 700.40
	€ 637.30	€1,040.40

13.6 This is mainly because Superbikes are produced in smaller batches than Basicbikes. The switching costs (batch-level costs) are relatively high for Superbikes.

Chapter 14

14.1 It is possible that the standard was not correct, in which case it needs to be adjusted. It is also possible that the standards were indeed correct but that the execution of the work left much to be desired, in which case the work procedures need to be adjusted.

14.2

Balance sheet (× €1,000)

Tangible fixed assets	3,475,000	Initial equity (residual)	4,383,500
Inventory finished product	345,000	Accounts payable	193,920
Inventory material	75,200	Profit	395,000
Account receivables	600,000		
Cash and cash equivalents	477,220		
	4,972,420		4,972,420

14.3 A sudden increase in demand or rush orders can result in additional labor costs from overtime or employment costs of (expensive) temporary staff.

14.4 Costs of 98 approved products = 98 × €25 = €2,450.
This amount is equal to the cost of 100 unapproved products.
The cost for each unapproved product = €2,450 / 100 = €24.50.

Actual spoilage costs 340 × €24.50 =	€8,330
Covered spoilage costs 13,660 × €0.50 =	€6,830
Unfavorable spoilage variance	€1,500

Chapter 15
15.1 Internal reporting is supplied to management only; management are the only ones able to access all information generated within the company. Other participants in the company have to settle for the information provided by management (possibly following legal obligations).

15.2 The social impact is larger. A multinational that declares bankruptcy has much more impact on society than an own-account worker doing the same.

15.3 If the financial statements are based on the liquidation value, company management acknowledges that the company is considered unsalvageable. The consequences are that suppliers will no longer offer credit, banks will cancel their line of credit and customers will not place any more orders – eventually resulting in a self-fulfilling prophecy.

Chapter 16
16.1 In research costs, the prudency principle; in development costs, the matching principle.

16.2 That would be opposed to the realization principle, since it would involve recognizing a profit from the investment in the trucks that actually belongs to later years.

16.3 Spreading the losses would mean that only part of the losses incurred in 2016 are recognized in 2017.

16.4

Net revenue	2,170,360
Other operating gains	13,481 +
Resource and raw materials costs	1,693,655 –
Depreciations	44,706 –
Other operating costs	222,065 –
Financial gains	1,949 +
Result from participations	13,834 +
	239,198
Distribution:	
Staff	191,757
Capital providers	4,738
Government	11,560
Equity providers*	31,143
	239,198

*Agrifirm is a cooperative and does not have shareholders. It has members instead. Those members may decide to have part of the profit distributed in the form of a *member discount*.

Chapter 17
17.1 No, because there may have been substantial investments or a large order in 2017 which will only be paid for by the customer in 2018.

17.2	Depreciation and impairment	11,168 –
	Investments in tangible and intangible fixed assets	16,534 +
	Divestments in tangible and intangible fixed assets	325 –
		5,041 +

This does not take the *Acquisitions* item into consideration. Due to the acquisitions, more group member companies are added to the consolidated annual report, which also causes the book value of tangible and intangible assets to increase. This issue of consolidation is addressed in greater detail in chapter 18.

Chapter 18

18.1 Creditors of a subsidiary have a vested interest in separate balance sheets because they can only claim assets of the respective subsidiary.
As the group member companies are exempt from publishing separate balance sheets, this disadvantage for creditors is compensated by the fact that they can claim from the parent company.

18.2 On a consolidated balance sheet, the following format is generally used:
Parent company equity ....
Minority interest .... +

Group equity ....

In fact, this concerns the company's equity, since it belongs to the shareholders.
The fact that these shareholders are not the parent company but are 'outsiders' does not change the nature of the capital that was made available.

Answers to Multiple-choice Questions

Chapter 1

1.1 b	1.4 a	1.7 a	1.10 d	1.13 b
1.2 d	1.5 d	1.8 a	1.11 a	1.14 d
1.3 c	1.6 c	1.9 a	1.12 b	1.15 b

Chapter 2

2.1 a	2.3 c	2.5 c	2.7 d	2.9 d
2.2 c	2.4 b	2.6 c	2.8 b	2.10 d

Chapter 3

3.1 b	3.4 c	3.7 d	3.10 b	3.13 b
3.2 b	3.5 a	3.8 c	3.11 d	3.14 d
3.3 a	3.6 a	3.9 b	3.12 b	3.15 d

Chapter 4

4.1 b	4.3 d	4.5 a	4.7 b	4.9 a
4.2 a	4.4 d	4.6 a	4.8 a	4.10 c

Chapter 5

5.1 c	5.4 a	5.7 b	5.10 b	5.13 d
5.2 b	5.5 b	5.8 b	5.11 a	5.14 d
5.3 c	5.6 b	5.9 c	5.12 a	5.15 a

Chapter 6

6.1 b	6.4 d	6.7 c	6.10 b	6.13 a
6.2 a	6.5 d	6.8 a	6.11 c	6.14 a
6.3 c	6.6 d	6.9 b	6.12 c	6.15 a

Chapter 7

7.1 b	7.3 b	7.5 a	7.7 d	7.9 b
7.2 b	7.4 c	7.6 d	7.8 c	7.10 c

Chapter 8

8.1 d	8.4 c	8.7 b	8.10 d	8.13 c
8.2 a	8.5 c	8.8 b	8.11 b	8.14 c
8.3 c	8.6 d	8.9 c	8.12 c	8.15 d

Chapter 9

9.1 c	9.4 b	9.7 a	9.10 b	9.13 b
9.2 b	9.5 c	9.8 b	9.11 b	9.14 a
9.3 b	9.6 c	9.9 a	9.12 a	9.15 c

Chapter 10
10.1 c	10.3 a	10.5 c	10.7 b	10.9 c
10.2 b	10.4 a	10.6 c	10.8 c	10.10 a

Chapter 11
11.1 b	11.4 c	11.7 c	11.10 c	11.13 b
11.2 b	11.5 d	11.8 a	11.11 b	11.14 b
11.3 a	11.6 b	11.9 b	11.12 b	11.15 a

Chapter 12
12.1 d	12.4 c	12.7 c	12.10 c	12.13 b
12.2 c	12.5 b	12.8 c	12.11 d	12.14 c
12.3 a	12.6 c	12.9 c	12.12 b	12.15 b

Chapter 13
13.1 d	13.4 b	13.7 c	13.10 b	13.13 c
13.2 d	13.5 a	13.8 b	13.11 b	13.14 a
13.3 d	13.6 b	13.9 c	13.12 c	13.15 c

Chapter 14
14.1 b	14.4 d	14.7 b	14.10 d	14.13 b
14.2 b	14.5 b	14.8 b	14.11 d	14.14 b
14.3 a	14.6 c	14.9 a	14.12 c	14.15 a

Chapter 15
15.1 c	15.4 d	15.7 b	15.10 a	15.13 d
15.2 b	15.5 c	15.8 b	15.11 d	15.14 c
15.3 d	15.6 d	15.9 d	15.12 c	15.15 d

Chapter 16
16.1 b	16.4 c	16.7 a	16.10 b	16.13 d
16.2 a	16.5 b	16.8 a	16.11 c	16.14 c
16.3 b	16.6 d	16.9 c	16.12 b	16.15 a

Chapter 17
17.1 d	17.4 a	17.7 b	17.10 d	17.13 a
17.2 a	17.5 c	17.8 d	17.11 a	17.14 b
17.3 c	17.6 b	17.9 b	17.12 a	17.15 c

Chapter 18
18.1 d	18.3 c	18.5 c	18.7 c	18.9 a
18.2 a	18.4 a	18.6 b	18.8 c	18.10 c

Credits

123RF: pp. 326, 350
alamy stock photo: pp. 253, 260, 269, 298, 312, 318, 377
dreamstime: p. 275
getty: pp. 358, 363, 402, 407, 409
Hollandfintech.com: pp. 100, 102
iStock: pp. 236, 245, 272, 388, 395
shutterstock: pp. 185, 284, 291, 294, 338, 342
www.nationalebeeldbank.nl: pp. 14, 25, 42, 48, 57, 62, 66, 82, 85, 92, 111, 128, 139, 141, 164, 170, 174, 196, 204, 206, 216, 218
www.westfriesarchief.nl: pp. 152, 156

Index

Venture capital 87
Venture capital companies 86
Vertical integration 40

W
WAC 369
Weighted average cost of capital 104
Wholesale trade 24
Wilson Formula 135
Working capital 130

Y
Yield (the yield) 220

Z
Zero bonds 177
Zero rate 39

About the Authors

 **Wim Koetzier** (1958) graduated in fiscal economics at the University of Groningen in 1982. He lectures business economics at the Windesheim University of Applied Sciences in Zwolle and at the Managerial Controller post-graduate educational program. Wim Koetzier is the author of *Management accounting, berekenen, beslissen, beheersen* and *Externe verslaggeving voor profit-en non-profitorganisaties*.

 **Rien Brouwers** (1956) graduated in econometrics at the Tilburg University of Applied Sciences in 1981. He lectured at the Avans University of Applied Sciences in Breda and now holds a management position at this institute. Rien Brouwers is the author of various publications in the field of business economics for the professional and adult education sector and co-author of various works including *Bedrijfseconomische thema's* and *Basis van bedrijfseconomie voor non-financials*.